A Comprehensive Guide to Attention Deficit Disorder in Adults

Research, Diagnosis, and Treatment

A Comprehensive Guide to Attention Deficit Disorder in Adults

Research, Diagnosis, and Treatment

EDITED BY KATHLEEN G. NADEAU, Ph.D.

Brunner/Mazel *Publishers* • New York

Library of Congress Cataloging-in-Publication Data

A comprehensive guide to attention deficit disorder in adults: Research, diagnosis, and treatment / edited by Kathleen G. Nadeau.
    p. cm.
Includes bibliographical references and indexes.
ISBN 0-87630-760-8
1. Attention-deficit disorder in adults. I. Nadeau, Kathleen G.
[DNLM: 1. Attention Deficit Disorder with Hyperactivity—in adulthood. 2. Attention Deficit Disorder with Hyperactivity—diagnosis. 3. Attention Deficit Disorder with Hyperactivity—therapy. WL 354 C738 1995]
RC394.A85C65 1995
616.85'89—dc20
DNLM/DLC
for Library of Congress   94-44015
                                                                          CIP

Published by
BRUNNER/MAZEL, INC.
19 Union Square West
New York, New York 10003

Manufactured in the United States of America
10 9 8 7 6 5 4 3 2

Contents

Contributors

Joseph Biederman, M.D. is Chief, Pediatric Psychopharmacotherapy, Consolidated Department of Psychiatry, and Associate Professor of Psychiatry, Harvard Medical School, Boston, Massachusetts.

Susan H. Biggs, Ed.D. is an Education Consultant, Chesapeake Psychological Services, Annandale, Virginia. She is a coauthor with Kathleen G. Nadeau, Ph.D., and Ellen Dixon, Ph.D., of *School Strategies for ADD Teens* (Chesapeake Psychological Publications, Annandale, Virginia, 1993).

Thomas E. Brown, Ph.D. is a clinical psychologist in private practice in Hamden, Connecticut, and a Clinical Supervisor in the Department of Psychology at Yale University, New Haven, Connecticut. He is the author of the *Brown Attention Deficit Disorder Scales* (The Psychological Corporation, San Antonio, 1995) and is editor of the forthcoming *Attention Deficit Disorders & Comorbidities in Children, Adolescents and Adults* (American Psychiatric Press).

Ellen B. Dixon, Ph.D. is a Clinical Psychologist and founder of Chesapeake Psychological Services, Annandale, Virginia. She is a coauthor with Kathleen G. Nadeau, Ph.D., and Susan H. Biggs, Ed.D., of *School Strategies for ADD Teens* (Chesapeake Psychological Publications, Annandale, Virginia, 1993), and coauthor with Kathleen G. Nadeau, Ph.D., of *Learning to Slow Down and Pay Attention* (Chesapeake Psychological Publications, Annandale, VA, 1992).

Edward M. Hallowell, M.D. is in private practice in Cambridge, Massachusetts, and is on the faculty of Harvard Medical School, Boston, Massachusetts. He is also the coauthor with John J. Ratey, M.D., of *Driven to Distraction* (Pantheon Books, New York, 1994).

Paul Jaffe is the editor of *ADDendum*, a quarterly newsletter for ADD adults.

Kathleen M. Kelly, MSN, RN, CS is in private practice leading psychoeducational groups for adults with ADD, and is a nationally recognized speaker on adult ADD issues. She is a Partner/Owner of Tyrell & Jerem Press, which specializes in publications for adults and children with learning disabilities. She is a coauthor with Peggy Ramundo, of *You Mean I'm Not Lazy, Stupid, or Crazy?* (Tyrell & Jerem Press, Cincinnati, 1993).

Patricia Horan Latham is a Partner in the Washington law firm Latham, a principal in JKL Communications, and a Founder of the National Center for Law and Learning Disabilities. She is on the National Adult Issues Committee of CH.A.DD. She has coauthored with Peter S. Latham *Attention Deficit Disorder and the Law* (JKL Communications, Washington, DC, 1992), *Learning Disabilities and the Law* (JKL Communications, Washington, DC, 1993), *Succeeding in the Workplace* (JKL Communications, Washington, DC, 1994), and *Higher Education Services for Students with Learning Disabilities and Attention Deficit Disorder: A Legal Guide* (National Center for Law and Learning Disabilities, Cabin John, MD, 1994). She is a frequent speaker at national conferences and a contributor to disability publications.

Peter S. Latham is a Partner in the Washington law firm Latham and Latham, a principal in JKL Communications, and a Founder of the National Center for Law and Learning Disabilities. He has coauthored with Patricia Horan Latham *Attention Deficit Disorder and the Law* (JKL Communications, Washington, DC, 1992), *Learning Disabilities and the Law* (JKL Communications, Washington, DC, 1993), *Succeeding in the Workplace* (JKL Communications, Washington, DC, 1994), and *Higher Education Services for Students with Learning Disabilities and Attention Deficit Disorder: A Legal Guide* (National Center for Law and Learing Disabilities, Cabin John, MD, 1994). He is the producer of the "ABC's of ADD" and "Succeeding in the Workplace" videos. He has written numerous articles and spoken extensively on disability issues.

Bennett Lavenstein, M.D. is Clinical Associate Professor, Pediatrics and Neurology, Georgetown University, Washington, DC; Director of Pediatric Neurology at Fairfax Hospital, Fairfax, Virginia, and is in private practice in Fairfax County, Virginia.

Andrea C. Miller, M.A. is Program Director, Research and Medical Services for the Metro South Area, Department of Mental Health, Medfield, Massachusetts. She has coauthored with John Ratey, M.D., numerous articles on attention deficit disorder in adults.

Kevin R. Murphy, Ph.D. is an Assistant Professor and Chief, Adult Attention Deficit Hyperactivity Disorder Clinic, University of Massachusetts Medical Center, Worcester, Massachusetts. He is also a member of the Professional Advisory Board of CH.A.DD.

Kathleen G. Nadeau, Ph.D. is Director, Chesapeake Psychological Services of Maryland, Bethesda, Maryland. She is on the National Adult Issues Committee of CH.A.D.D. and is a member of the Board of Directors of the National Center for Law and Learning Disabilities. She is a coauthor with Ellen Dixon, Ph.D., and Susan Biggs, Ed.D, of *School Strategies for ADD Teens* (Chesapeake Psychological Publications, Annandale, Virginia, 1993). She has also coauthored with Ellen Dixon, Ph.D., *Learning to Slow Down and Pay Attention* (Chesapeake Psychological Publications, Annandale, Virginia, 1991). She is also the author of *A College Survival Guide for Students with ADD and LD* (Brunner/Mazel, New York, 1994).

Patricia O. Quinn, M.D. is a member of the Board of Directors, National Center for Law and Learning Disabilities, Inc. She is a coauthor with Judith Stern of *Putting on the Brakes: A Young People's Guide to Understanding Attention Deficit Hyperactivity Disorder (ADHD)* (Magination Press, New York, 1991) and *Putting on the Brakes Activity Book* (Magination Press, New York, 1993). She is also the author of *ADD and the College Student: A Guide for High School and College Students with Attention Deficit Disorder* (Brunner/Mazel, New York, 1993).

John J. Ratey, M.D. is an Assistant Professor of Psychiatry, Harvard Medical School, and the Director of Research for the Metro South Area, Department of Mental Health, Medfield, Massachusetts. He is a coauthor with Edward Hallowell, M.D., of *Driven to Distraction* (Pantheon Books, New York, 1994).

Mary McDonald Richard is a member of the professional staff in the

Student Disability Services Office at the University of Iowa. She is also a member of the National Board of Directors, CH.A.D.D. and President-Elect of CH.A.D.D., as well as editor of the CH.A.D.D.ER Box newsletter.

Adrian D. Sandler, M.D. is Assistant Professor of Pediatrics, Department of Pediatrics, Clinical Center for the Study of Development of Learning, University of North Carolina at Chapel Hill, Chapel Hill, North Carolina. He is also the Director of the Center for Child Development and Rehabilitation, Thoms Rehabilitation Hospital, Asheville, North Carolina.

Howard Schubiner, M.D. is Associate Professor, Departments of Internal Medicine and Pediatrics, Divisions of General Internal Medicine and Ambulatory Pediatrics, Wayne State University School of Medicine, Detroit, Michigan.

Thomas J. Spencer, M.D. is an Assistant Director, Pediatric Psychopharmacotherapy Clinic, Massachusetts General Hospital, and an Assistant Professor of Psychiatry, Harvard Medical School, Boston, Massachusetts.

Angela Tzelepis, Ph.D. is an Assistant Professor, Department of Internal Medicine, Wayne State University School of Medicine, in Detroit, Michigan. She is also a Consulting Psychologist, Children's Center of Wayne County, Detroit, Michigan.

Lawrence H. Warbasse, III, M.D. is Assistant Professor, Department of Internal Medicine, Wayne State University School of Medicine, Detroit, Michigan. He is also Adjunct Assistant Professor, Pharmacy Practice, College of Pharmacy and Allied Health Professions, Wayne State University, Detroit, Michigan.

Timothy E. Wilens, M.D. is a staff member, Pediatric Psychopharmacotherapy Clinic, Massachusetts General Hospital, and an Assistant Professor of Psychiatry, Harvard Medical School, Boston, Massachusetts.

Preface

The recognition of attention deficit disorder (ADD) in adults is expanding rapidly, while our knowledge base about diagnosis and treatment of adults with ADD struggles to keep pace. The *Diagnostic and Statistical Manual* of the American Psychiatric Association has waffled about the legitimacy of a diagnostic category for adults with attention deficit hyperactivity disorder (ADHD). The recently published *Diagnostic and Statistical Manual of Mental Disorders - Fourth Edition* (DSM-IV) recognizes that ADD persists into adulthood and even recognizes that it may not be identified until adulthood, although DSM-IV requires that some symptoms must have been present in childhood.

Most research on ADD continues to focus on the concerns of children. Ironically, some of the most often cited research on adult ADHD, Zametkin's work on glucose metabolism in the brain, was conducted not out of a primary interest in adults, but rather because the possible radiation exposure from the positron-emission tomography PET scans was considered too risky for children. Since 1990, when Zametkin's study was published, there has developed a growing research interest in adult ADD. The addition of the word *adult* to the name of the largest national group focusing on attention deficit disorder, now called Children *and Adults* with Attention Deficit Disorder [emphasis mine] (CH.A.D.D.), did not take place until 1993. Although the prescription of Ritalin or Dexedrine has become routine for children with ADD, unfortunately many physicians hesitant to prescribe these drugs for adults remain.

No broadly accepted standard yet exists for the diagnosis of attention deficit disorder in adults; we have no good measure of the frequency of this adult disorder in the general population; there is no empirical measure of the effectiveness of treatment approaches that are being developed at clinics around the country. And yet, despite this lack of research validation, the number of adults who believe their lives have been profoundly affected by ADD has fueled an engine which is propelling the topic of adult ADD into high visibility.

There is a tremendous need for public education about ADD in adults. Many in the general public do not yet recognize ADD in adults as a legitimate disorder. Those adults who are more mildly affected, who have been able to complete their education, hold a job, and establish a family may be seen as having "normal" difficulties. Because all of us experience problems with distractibility, planning, memory, and organization from time to time, it can be difficult to understand that these more functional adults with ADD have a legitimate neurobiological disorder. The extraordinary efforts made by these individuals in order to sustain their lives and the chronic anxiety and self-doubts that plague them tend to go unrecognized. Those who are more deeply affected by ADD, who may have never completed their education, who are underemployed or intermittently employed, may be viewed by the general public, or even by their families, as being lazy, undisciplined, or unmotivated, rather than being in need of treatment for ADD. Finally, there are those who are most seriously affected, who may have engaged in criminal activity resulting from their impulsive, overreactive response style. Such individuals are likely to be classified as criminals, without recognition that they need treatment and are likely to continue to commit impulsive and aggressive acts without such treatment.

Until the public is informed enough to understand that all of these people are manifesting varying degrees and subtypes of a common, treatable disorder, there will be little public support for the funding needed to increase our understanding of ADD in adults. A strong national spokesperson has yet to emerge to undertake the task of educating the public about the hidden cost to our society from adult ADD that goes untreated. This cost is hidden in divorce statistics, unemployment, underemployment, inefficiency, bankruptcy, substance abuse treatment costs, and the extraordinarily high cost of incarceration, not to mention the medical expenses of countless misdiagnosed adults who spend frustrating months or years in ineffective treatment of misdiagnosed conditions.

Sadly, it is not only the general public that does not understand ADD in its various manifestations. Because little training is available, significant numbers of the helping professions unwittingly work with ADD adults every day whose ADD is camouflaged by other labels. Counselors who work with the chronically unemployed, employee assistance personnel working with "difficult" employees, counselors working with substance abusers, probation and correctional officers, and numerous psychotherapists work with adults with ADD every day without recognizing their underlying attention deficit disorder.

Progress in developing more effective treatment approaches for the complex spectrum disorder of ADD is thwarted by a variety of prejudices and misconceptions, both within and without the community of professionals who treat adults with ADD. Although research may document in the future that a large proportion of the prison population suffers from ADD, there is currently little awareness of ADD in the correctional system. Given the current social climate, it may be a long uphill battle to convince the taxpayer or the correctional officer of the need for diagnosis and treatment of prisoners with ADD. A second large ADD subtype is found among substance abusers. Research into the relationship between ADD and substance abuse has received some funding recently; however, there is a fundamental philosophical difference between some in the medical/mental health community and the majority in the substance abuse treatment community. The former is more likely to recognize ADD as a disorder that benefits from medication, while the latter strongly espouses a "chemical-free" approach to treatment. This seeming irreconcilable difference must be addressed before we can effectively treat adult ADD substance abusers.

A source of potential divisiveness within the field of adult ADD comes from a subgroup of professionals who tend to minimize the negative impact of ADD. Such a "feel good" message is a welcome one for many adults with ADD, but there is a risk attached to that good feeling. We cannot simultaneously justify the need for research funding and adequate treatment facilities for adults with ADD, while we optimistically underplay its impact. Also of concern within the field is a perceived conflict of interest between the needs of adults and children with ADD. Only very recently has CH.A.D.D. included adult issues on its agenda. CH.A.D.D. was founded to serve the needs of children, but children grow up, and as they grow up, they continue to have needs; additionally, many parents of children with ADD are affected by ADD but remain undiagnosed. Slowly, because ADD is a lifelong condition for many individuals, CH.A.D.D. recognizes the need to broaden its reach to individuals with ADD across the lifespan.

Recently, a number of forces have been set in motion. The media, driven by the rapid growth of interest in adult ADD issues, has suddenly increased coverage of the topic. This, in turn, has led to increased demand for services, which has led to an upsurge in demand for training seminars for mental health professionals on the diagnosis and treatment of adult ADD. CH.A.D.D. has mounted an effort to address the needs of adults by forming an Adult Issues Committee. And, in a very exciting development, in 1993, the Attention Deficit Disorder Association (ADDA) sponsored the first national conference on ADD in adults and plans to make this conference an annual event. Because ADDA is not associated with any single discipline, this initial conference served to bring together professionals from the medical, mental health, and educational communities, allowing active cross-disciplinary communication. This interaction is a very healthy process which is likely to encourage interdisciplinary research and bring cross-disciplinary influences to bear as we continue in our rapid learning curve on ADD in adults.

Although our research base is small, and despite the fact that there is much misunderstanding and lack of recognition of ADD in adults, there is a strong and growing need for trained professionals who can serve the needs of adults with ADD. This volume is designed to make that educational process as broad and complete as possible at this early point in the development of the field. Although we have far to go and much to learn, we will best serve the adult population by training professionals in the diagnosis and treatment of ADD in adults as we now understand it, and by continually updating such training as our knowledge base expands. It is with this goal in mind that the contributors to this book, most of whom are pioneers in this new field, came together to create this volume on ADD in adults, written specifically for the professional community.

Editor's Note

The reader will note that in some chapters the author refers to ADD, while others refer to ADHD. To add even more confusion, some authors refer to the very recently published DSM-IV categories of ADD, while others continue to use DSM-III-R categories. As a general rule, medical researchers must conform to the exact guidelines and terminology of the current Diagnostic and Statistical Manual and therefore use the term ADHD. Meanwhile, many in the general clinical community, which has long recognized that the DSM-III-R guidelines did not seem to include the wide variety of apparent subtypes of attention deficit disorder seen in the clinical setting, have begun to use the term ADD as a more generic term meant to broadly include attention deficit both with and without hyperactivity, as well as to include other subtypes that have not yet achieved official recognition in the Diagnostic and Statistical Manual. For the sake of simplicity, throughout most chapters in this book the term ADD is used as a generic, all-inclusive term. The reader will have to bear with us through these times of change.

Acknowledgments

First and foremost, I want to express my appreciation to my colleagues at Chesapeake Psychological Services, in Virginia. In our years together, we encouraged, stimulated, and challenged each other as we strove to understand and to treat attention deficit disorder, first in children, and later in adolescents and adults. As Ellen Dixon and I sat together to write our first book, *Learning to Slow Down and Pay Attention*, for elementary school aged children with ADD, and later as we coauthored *School Strategies for ADD Teens* with Susan Biggs, the seeds were sown, that developed into the idea for this volume on adults. I also want to thank Lucy Martin, a gifted educational specialist, and her equally talented successor at Chesapeake, Susan Biggs, for sharing with me their expertise regarding the intricacies of neurodevelopmental disabilities. Without the benefit of my years at Chesapeake, this book would never have come into being.

Many people have contributed to my knowledge of and interest in ADD. Paul Satz, a professor of neuropsychology at the University of Florida during my graduate school days, piqued my earliest interest in neurodevelopmental issues. Years later, my fascination grew during seminars with Mel Levine, the renowned developmental pediatrician who heads the Clinical Center for the Study of Development in Learning at the University of North Carolina at Chapel Hill. Wade Horn, former Executive Director of CH.A.D.D., and Robert Resnick, President of the American Psychological Association, and Director of the Attention Deficit Disorder Clinic at the Medical College of Virginia, offered an encouraging welcome as I made my early forays into a specialization in attention deficit disorder. I have also greatly benefited from my contact with developmental pediatricians Karen Miller and Patricia Quinn.

My education in a whole range of issues for adults with ADD has been immeasurably enriched through my contact with my adult ADD clients, as well as with the members of the Montgomery County and Fairfax County Adult ADD Support Groups. Members of these groups generously shared stories of their trials and triumphs, and have been especially generous by "going public" with their ADD, out of a desire to benefit others who struggle with this disorder.

Dr. Alan Zametkin, Director of the Clinical Brain Imaging Center at NIMH, has been kind to take time from his perpetually overloaded schedule to consult with me on occasion. I am especially grateful to his colleague, Monique Ernst, for her detailed criticisms and suggestions. With regard to my chapter on career consultation with adults with ADD, my thanks go to Dr. Rodney Lowman, noted author on the clinical practice of career assessment, for his suggestions, comments, and painstaking editing. Although any errors in the chapter are mine alone, his remarks were very helpful. I am grateful to Gloria Monick, of GSM Associates in Washington, D.C., for her thoughtful comments about career issues for adults with ADD.

The contributors to this volume, all of whom responded with interest and energy as the project was proposed to them, deserve appreciation as well. The contributors to this book are pioneers in a fascinating field of inquiry. We will be hearing more from them as their contagious enthusiasm draws them into new issues relating to ADD in adults.

Finally, I express my gratitude to my husband, Bonnard, for his patience and encouragement as I labored through weekends and late night hours to complete this book. Hugs and thanks go also to my daughter, Langdon. Her valiant struggles with ADD provided a major inspiration to write this book so that more young adults like herself can receive accurate diagnosis and proper treatment.

SECTION I

History and Current Understanding of ADD as a Neurobiological Disorder

Section I addresses the history of our recognition of attention deficit disorder (ADD) and outlines our current level of understanding of ADD as a neurobiological disorder. Paul Jaffe, editor of the highly regarded newsletter *ADDendum*, a quarterly publication covering adult ADD issues, writes about the evolution of our understanding of the disorder and describes the very recent recognition of its existence in adulthood. Jaffe has played an important role in that growing recognition. He took it upon himself, very early in the development of the national organization CH.A.DD., Children with Attention Deficit Disorder (recently renamed Children and Adults with Attention Deficit Disorder) to lobby for recognition of adult ADD. He soon became recognized as a spokesperson for adult issues, and furthered this recognition through the publication of *ADDendum*. Jaffe brings a personal ardor to his writing and is avidly focused on the wide range of adult ADD issues that need to be addressed.

Patricia Quinn, a widely known and respected developmental pediatrician, has been involved in the treatment of children with ADD for many

1

years. Like many other professionals, her knowledge of and interest in adult ADD grew from her work with children. Quinn's chapter on the neurobiology of ADD lays a groundwork for the clinician to develop a scientific understanding of ADD within the limits of our current knowledge, and prepares the clinician to better understand the complexities of the assessment of ADD covered in section II.

1

History and Overview of Adulthood ADD

PAUL JAFFE

The classic perception of attention deficit disorder has been derived from one core image: the 8-year-old boy who can't sit still in the classroom.

Recently, the image has been recast. The following information has begun to circulate: ADD does not stop at the school door; ADD also afflicts girls; and physical hyperactivity is not *necessarily* a feature of the disorder. One particular has now been widely publicized: that ADD can outlast childhood. Or, as one headline writer succinctly put it, it is "Not Just Kids" who have ADD (Schweiger, 1993).

OBSTACLES TO RECOGNITION

Why did the "Not Just Kids" headline appear in 1993 instead of 1973? What accounts for the delay in the public recognition of adulthood ADD? It is impossible, of course, to come up with precise answers to such questions. But here are a few suggestions:

1. The various sides of the disorder—whether it is called minimal brain damage/dysfunction (MBD), hyperkinetic reaction of childhood (HRC), attention deficit disorder (ADD), attention-deficit hyperactivity disorder (ADHD), or attention-deficit/hyperactivity disorder (AD/HD)—have not always been appreciated. For example, in its better-known variant, ADD was a conception that united a *cognitive* disorder (attention deficit), a *motor* disorder (hyperkinesis or hyperactivity), and a *behavioral* disorder (impulsivity). But the latter two aspects—perhaps sides of the same coin (Lahey et al., 1988)—have usually prevailed in the minds of observers.

The defining of MBD/HRC/ADD/ADHD in behavioral terms has also helped define it in age-related terms. What in a youngster might charitably be called a behavior problem, in an adult would likely be dismissed as immaturity or irresponsibility—a moral flaw outside the scope of medical concern.

2. The association of MBD/HRC/ADD/ADHD with a common motoric element—excessive, often purposeless, physical activity—has also played a role. If a child's hyperactivity diminishes over time, as it often does, has the disorder itself disappeared? Yes, some observers have concluded (Laufer & Denhoff, 1957).

3. When MBD/HRC/ADD/ADHD *has* been described in cognitive terms, it has often been associated with learning disabilities (LD). The term *learning disability* implies educational problem, which in turn implies school and also childhood. And yet, as the first generation of LD-identified children matured, many graduated from school with their problems intact. The concept of "LD adults" preceded "ADD adults" by about a decade, and probably helped pave the way for recognition of the latter.

4. Some of the early child observations (Still, 1902) were later replicated under a unique set of circumstances: the 1916–27 encephalitis epidemic. Caused by a virus that attacked the human brain, the illness produced a potpourri of neurological and quasi-psychiatric follow-up symptoms in those who succumbed. Two symptoms predominated: in adults, a Parkinsonian trance, which sometimes lasted for decades; and in children, an extended bout of behavioral disinhibition (Hohman, 1922; Strecker & Ebaugh, 1924). Such behavior harked back to the defiance and aggression described by Still; and prefigured the restlessness, impulsivity, and impersistence selected as defining traits of ADD and ADHD, especially when mixed with either conduct disorder or oppositional-defiant disorder.

In the minds of many observers this dual outcome reinforced the link between children and behavioral disorders. However, two Yale psychiatrists (Kahn & Cohen, 1934) took a longer view of what they termed *organic drivenness*. They suggested that "the syndrome described is not infrequent in the adult, not only because many of the children concerned survive to adulthood, but also because encephalitis epidemica and the other encephalitides *are not the only conditions which produce this syndrome* [emphasis added]. We believe that there are individuals who are possessed of *organic drivenness* from birth, either as the consequence of a prenatal encephalopathy or injury, or of birth injury, or as a constitutional variant" (p. 752). They described two hyperactive adults, the first case studies of the kind.

5. The introduction of racemic (*dl-*) amphetamine in pill form set the stage for the first pharmacological study (Bradley, 1937) of what would

now be considered ADD. The subjects, who ranged in age from 5 to 13, developed a goal-directedness which they had never shown before. The locus of treatment shifted to childhood and stayed there for decades.

6. While some of the children studied by Bradley appeared calmer and quieter under the influence of *dl-* (and later *d-*) amphetamine, adult amphetamine subjects often reported or displayed an opposite effect. This was also true of adults who began to abuse the various stimulant drugs. While abusers craved stimulants for their euphoric properties—to which they often grew tolerant—neither euphoria nor tolerance was widely noted in the child patient group.

Such comparisons helped launch the notion that stimulants had paradoxical effects in children. In its checkered career, paradoxical effects was used to defend clinicians against charges that they were doing children a disservice by exposing them to habit-forming drugs. But such a defense—at least in its original form—promoted the idea that adults would not respond therapeutically to stimulant treatment. (For two variations on the paradoxical theme, however, see Arnold, Strobl, & Weisenburg, 1972; DeVeaugh-Geiss & Joseph, 1980.) This in turn slowed the expansion of clinical knowledge, as practitioners (with a few exceptions) bypassed opportunities to learn about adult MBD by treating it.

The fact that the children were taking small amounts, in pill form, while the adult abusers were taking much larger amounts, often intravenously, seemed to go unnoticed. It was years before the idea of paradoxical effects was empirically challenged (Rapoport et al., 1980), and the belief is by no means spent.

7. The first amphetamine studies and the appearance of the term *minimal brain damage* coincided roughly with the emergence of child psychiatry (Chess, 1988). The task of identifying and treating MBD became a staple of this emerging specialization. The split between adult psychiatry and child psychiatry (with their separate organizations, meetings, and publications) has helped institutionalize a variety of perceptions, as well as misperceptions, such as the implied insignificance of childhood depression or adulthood ADD (APA Task Force on DSM-IV, 1991, pp. B:19–B:20).

8. The above has been true also of psychology and neurology, and between pediatricians and family practitioners.

9. Although it was never widely used, the DSM-II term Hyperkinetic Reaction of Childhood (American Psychiatric Association [APA], 1968) also implied that the problem was one for pediatric psychiatrists, pediatric neurologists, and general pediatricians. The disorder's placement, under a variety of names, in the childhood disorders sections of subsequent DSM editions (APA, 1980; APA, 1987; APA, 1994) has also contributed to this perception.

HYPERACTIVE ADULTS?

While MBD/HRC/ADD/ADHD had been observed and described at the turn of the century, it had neither a name nor a home until child psychiatry established itself in the late 1930s. Two decades later, the first follow-up surveys inspired a variety of comments and investigations. In these reports:

a. Those who reexamined mixed populations after long interludes found that many of the former patients had failed to outgrow childhood difficulties (Mellsop, 1972; Morris, Escoll, & Wexler, 1956; O'Neal & Robins, 1958).

b. Later populations were more narrowly defined. They included some labeled "MBD" or "hyperactive" or described in ways that now suggest ADD or ADHD. Childhood symptoms had not always disappeared in these groups either (Anderson & Plymate, 1962; Borland & Heckman, 1976; Menkes, Rowe, & Menkes, 1967; Milman, 1979; Morrison, 1979), although some symptoms may have been outwardly transformed. Were these cases exceptional? Two observers suggested not: "Although there are innumerable variations, salient characteristics at any age are immaturity, poor interpersonal relationships, impulsivity, difficulty with change or the unstructured, and low frustration or stress tolerance which is manifested in incongruous worries, temper tantrums, rages, panics, or major catastrophic reactions often indistinguishable from schizophrenic episodes" (Anderson & Plymate, 1962, p. 494). After three decades, all but the last of these statements ring true, although they do not tell the whole story.

c. At times, treatment-seeking adults presented with symptoms reminiscent of what clinicians had seen or perhaps heard about in child patients (Hartocollis, 1968; Quitkin & Klein, 1969; Shelley & Reister, 1972).

d. Clinicians treating children came into contact with the parents, many of whom clearly had problems of their own. A number of families were studied systematically (Cantwell, 1972; Morrison, 1980; Morrison & Stewart, 1971; Stewart, deBlois, & Cummings, 1980). In a minority of parents, retrospective childhood hyperactivity was documented and linked with ongoing life-adjustment issues.

e. Later, comparisons were made between adoptive and biological parents of different groups of hyperactive children (Cantwell, 1975; Morrison & Stewart, 1973). Psychiatric symptoms were more prevalent among the biological parents. Where then did the hyperactivity come from? From heredity rather than parenting was the interpretation favored by the researchers. A second question was, did the traits observed in the parents represent adulthood versions of those seen in the children?

They probably did, wrote Morrison and Stewart and Cantwell, who linked their results to a literature that stressed the relatedness of three sets of symptoms

(Woerner & Guze, 1968). These were alcoholism, sociopathy (what would now be called conduct disorder or antisocial personality disorder), and hysteria (a mixture of depression, anxiety, and somatization).

Today, these studies are hard to interpret. The relationship (or nonrelationship) between alcoholism and MBD/HRC/ADD/ADHD continues to be a topic of debate (Goodwin, Shulsinger, Hermansen, Guze, & Winokur, 1975; Mannuzza, Klein, Bessler, Malloy, & LaPadula, 1993; Morrison, 1980; Schuckit, Sweeney, & Huey, 1987; Tarter, McBride, Buonpane, & Schneider, 1977; Wood, Wender, & Reimherr, 1983). The term "sociopathy" probably defined an antisocial subtype of adult male ADHD. The term "hysteria" *may* have described adult female ADD or ADHD as it *looked* to observers trained in mid-20th-century psychiatry.

By way of contrast, a later study (Alberts-Corush, Firestone, & Goodman, 1986) linked adoptee hyperactivity to the inability of a biological parent to concentrate, a more recent consideration.

f. Next came a series of case studies of medication use (Arnold et al., 1972; Huessy, 1974; Mann & Greenspan, 1976; Morrison & Minkoff, 1975; Rybak, 1977). A majority of cases involved the use of antidepressant drugs.

g. Invoking an early British report (Hill, 1947), researchers at the University of Utah (Wood, Reimherr, Wender, & Johnson, 1976) ran a double-blind study using methylphenidate. (This stimulant had by then become the drug of choice in childhood MBD.) The results led the authors to suggest that "for some, MBD may persist well into adult life" before finally abating. They concluded: "The concept of MBD may tie together the group of adult impulse disorders and the pharmacological techniques useful in treating MBD in childhood may provide a rational basis for treating a poorly understood and generally treatment-unresponsive group of psychiatric patients" (p. 1460).

They followed this with a study of the recently introduced stimulant pemoline (Wender, Reimherr, & Wood, 1981), by a second study of methylphenidate (Wender, Reimherr, Wood, & Ward, 1985), and by studies of other pharmacological agents (Wender, Wood, & Reimherr, 1985). Some of these were controlled, others not. One controlled study, using methylphenidate, yielded negative results (Mattes, Boswell, & Oliver, 1984).

The Utah findings were augmented by a second round of medication-oriented case studies (Collis, 1978; Packer, 1978; Huey, Zetin, Janowsky, & Judd, 1978; DeVeaugh-Geiss & Joseph, 1980; Plotkin, Halaris, & DeMet, 1982; Yellin, Hopwood, & Greenberg, 1982). As in most published case studies, responses were positive.

Some of these data were pooled at a "Conference on MBD in Adults," held in Scottsdale, Arizona, on March 2–4, 1978. The 3-day meeting was chaired by New York psychoanalyst Leopold Bellak. Participants included

Drs. Arnold, Borland, Cantwell, Greenspan, Hartocollis, Huessy, Wender, and others. Conference papers were later collected (Bellak, 1979) in a volume that has since gone out of print.

PAYING MORE ATTENTION

During this decade the concepts of hyperactivity and minimal brain dysfunction were being transformed (Douglas, 1972; Douglas & Peters, 1979). The result was the revolutionary DSM-III category of Attention Deficit Disorder (APA, 1980). By its very name, ADD reframed the issue in a way it had never before been, as one of attention and inattention; and added impulsivity as another core feature. It made motoric hyperactivity optional; that is, it introduced two subtypes: ADD *with* and *without* hyperactivity.

In effect, the second subtype provided a scaffolding for a third, adult-specific subtype: Attention Deficit Disorder, Residual Type (ADD,RT). The literal definition of ADD,RT was ADD with hyperactivity that had evolved into ADD without hyperactivity: "Signs of hyperactivity are no longer present, but other signs of the illness have persisted into the present without periods of remission, as evidenced by signs of attentional deficits and impulsivity....[which] result in some impairment in social and occupational functioning" (p. 45). But that definition never caught on.

What did catch on were the hyperactivity-dependent Utah Criteria devised by Dr. Wender and his colleagues (Wender et al., 1981). These criteria—which specifically excluded a number of symptoms—were "stricter than those of DSM-III. First, the adult must have a history of ADD in childhood as defined by DSM-III. Second, the adult must have both attention and motor abnormalities plus two of the following five traits: poor impulse control, mood lability, short or excessive temper and/or irritability, poor organization with poor task completion, or low stress tolerance with overreactivity" (Wood, 1986, p. 23). More generically, ADD,RT was sometimes used to denote *any* extension of ADD into adulthood.

By the mid-1980s the first prospective (rather than retrospective) longitudinal studies appeared in print (Weiss, Hechtman, Perlman, Hopkins & Wehar, 1979; Gittelman, Mannuzza, Shenker, & Bonagura, 1985; Howell, Huessy, & Hassuk, 1985; Weiss, Hechtman, Milroy, & Perlman, 1985; Weiss & Hechtman, 1986). All showed that MBD/HRC/ADD extended beyond childhood in at least a minority of cases.

Elsewhere, a cross-sectional study of college men (Buchsbaum et al., 1985) linked retrospective and persistent hyperactivity with low scores on one version of the Continuous Performance Test, a measure of sustained attention. But a majority of those with low scores were not hyperactive, suggesting a persistence also of ADD *without* hyperactivity.

During this time, the first parent support groups were formed; they grew steadily if quietly through the decade.

ACTIVISTS ENTER THE FRAY

The year 1987 saw a lost opportunity to publicize adulthood ADD. DSM-III-R converted ADD,RT into ADHD,RS (Attention-deficit hyperactivity disorder, residual state). It did so in an appendix (APA, 1987, p. 411).

But two events heightened public awareness: a lay monograph (Wender, 1987) devoted a chapter to adults; and a first-person account (Wolkenberg, 1987) had, over the course of the next few years, a monumental impact.

In 1989 a clinic for ADD adults opened at Wayne State University in Detroit. In that year the parents' (predominantly mothers') movement crossed state lines, with a regional conference in Massachusetts and a national conference in Florida. At these meetings one could hear statements like "I have ADD" and "my husband has ADD." The notion that ADD runs in families continues to be popular among ADD activists, as well as professionals.

As the parents' meetings were publicized, they started to attract, and connect, stray ADD adults. The most active of these soon formed groups specifically for adults. By mid-1990 ADD adult support groups could be found in California, Illinois, Massachusetts, Ohio, and Wisconsin. On April 27 and 28 of that year, in Plymouth, Massachusetts, came two informal meetings of ADD adults drawn to the second annual conference of the Massachusetts-based Attention Deficit-Information Network. Two weeks later, on May 15, a panel entitled "Paying Attention to Attention Deficit in Adult Psychiatry"—led by Boston-area psychiatrist John Ratey—took place in New York at the annual meeting of the American Psychiatric Association (APA). He was joined by five others, including two veterans of the 1978 MBD conference. Dr. Ratey also organized a follow-up APA panel which convened in 1993.

These developments inspired the creation of newsletters aimed specifically at ADD adults. *ADDendum* and *ADDult News*—both of which are edited and published by ADD adults—premiered, respectively, in August and September 1990.

ADDendum, an independent publication, specializes in first-person accounts of ADD, digests of medical and scientific research, coverage of legal issues and legislative developments, support group listings, and opinion pieces. *ADDult News* focuses on personal stories, tips, coping skills, and reader feedback. It has been part of an ADDult Support Network set up by Ohio activist Mary Jane Johnson and affiliated with the Attention Deficit Disorder Association, one of two national ADD federations. Johnson's "pen pal" network has connected ADD adults, including some in prison. A few of their accounts have been collected (Johnson, 1993).

The fall of 1990 also saw the publication of an extensive set of guidelines (Kane, Mikalac, Benjamin, & Barkley, 1990) for assessing and treating ADHD adults. Later, on November 10, in Washington, a panel on adulthood ADD, featuring three ADD adults and four professionals, drew a large crowd. These proceedings were sponsored by Children with Attention Deficit Disorders, a parent-led national federation. The panel was followed by an informal networking session of ADD adults, the first of five such meetings and the first nationwide group to so assemble.

On November 15 came news of a landmark study (Zametkin et al., 1990) in which brain scans of ADHD and non-ADHD adults were compared. The differences suggested a physiological basis for ADHD. Adults were used because the procedure, positron-emission tomography, entailed a certain level of radiation exposure. The results of the study were broadcast worldwide, as was—for those willing to read the fine print—the existence of adulthood ADHD. One syndicated report (Bartlett, 1990) used the Zametkin study to peg a general discussion of ADD in adults.

By 1991 presentations on adult outcomes had become a regular feature at ADD conferences, and articles about adults began to appear in parent-oriented newsletters. In that year, adult support groups were formed in Colorado, Georgia, Maryland, Michigan, New Hampshire, New York, and Washington state. (The list grew longer in 1992, and longer still in 1993.) A second ADD adult clinic opened, this one at the University of Massachusetts Medical Center in Worcester. And the magazine racks provided a bit of summer reading (Perney, 1991a, 1991b).

In early 1992 the first popular work on adulthood ADD (Weiss, 1992) reached bookstores. In the spring and summer, two legal actions involving ADD adults became news. Under the new Americans with Disabilities Act, a law graduate sued for the right to take the bar exam with special accommodations; the matter was settled out of court but essentially in her favor (Jaffe, 1992a, 1992b, 1993a). In the other case, a major league pitcher was reinstated. It was ruled that the baseball commissioner, when making his decision to expel the pitcher for attempting to purchase cocaine, had failed to consider the implications of the pitcher's ADHD diagnosis (Jaffe, 1993b). Some of the underlying issues were discussed in a book on ADD-related disability law (Latham & Latham, 1992; see also chapter 17, this volume). Covered were such topics as workers' compensation, Social Security, the criminal justice system, military law, and the implications of the Americans with Disabilities Act.

In early 1993 a widely read article (Miller, 1993) focused on workplace and criminal justice issues. A second lay book became available (Kelly & Ramundo, 1993). The larger of the federations renamed itself Children *and Adults* with Attention Deficit Disorders [emphasis added], a move that attracted international interest.

In May of 1993, in Ann Arbor, Michigan, Mary Jane Johnson and local activist Jim Reisinger organized a conference on "The Changing World of Adults With ADD." It drew 364 participants from 30 states and two Canadian provinces. The keynote address was delivered by Boston-area psychiatrist Edward Hallowell, whose motivational speeches and writings had made him hugely popular.

Dr. Hallowell and other speakers raised issues ranging from self-concept and self-expectation, family conflicts, and interpersonal relationships, to stress handling, job defense, and substance abuse, to medication, neurobiology, and the postdiagnostic "grieving process." An old debate—whether to view ADD as a medically defined disorder or as a mismatch between personality and social environment—was renewed. A convocation of ADD adult support group leaders was the largest of its kind. A second conference was held May 20-22, 1994.

The summer of 1993 saw a spate of media coverage (Cowley, 1993; Dranov, 1993; Eisner, 1993; Richardson, 1993; Stich, 1993), including an August 30 segment on the *Today Show.* All of which have kept busy the existing hotlines and filled the schedules of professionals working in the field.

The sudden burst of recognition has also highlighted a risk: that ADD will be trivialized into a "diagnosis du jour," casually blamed for every modern ailment or malfunction. Partly in reaction to this perception, old criticisms of the MBD/HRC/ADD concept have resurfaced (Vatz, 1994). The field remains politicized and controversial, making life more difficult for those caught in the middle.

Will the positive publicity outweigh the negative and bring us closer to a full-fledged acceptance of adulthood ADD—and ADD in general—on the part of the medical profession, the insurance industry, the scientific community, and the pharmaceutical houses? Possibly; but much work—including research of the type described in this volume—remains to be done.

REFERENCES

Alberts-Corush, J., Firestone, P., & Goodman, J. T. (1986). Attention and impulsivity characteristics of the biological and adoptive parents of hyperactive and normal control children. *American Journal of Orthopsychiatry, 56,* 413-423.

American Psychiatric Association. (1968). *Diagnostic and statistical manual of mental disorders* (2nd ed.). Washington, DC: Author.

American Psychiatric Association. (1980). *Diagnostic and statistical manual of mental disorders* (3rd ed.). Washington, DC: Author.

American Psychiatric Association. (1987). *Diagnostic and statistical manual of mental disorders* (3rd ed., rev.). Washington, DC: Author.

American Psychiatric Association. (1994). *Diagnostic and Statistical manual of mental disorders* (4th ed.). Washington, DC: Author.

American Psychiatric Association Task Force on DSM-IV. (1991). *DSM-IV options book: Work in progress 9/1/91*. Washington, DC: American Psychiatric Association.

Anderson, C., & Plymate, H. B. (1962). Management of the brain-damaged adolescent. *American Journal of Orthopsychiatry, 32*, 492–500.

Arnold, E. L., Strobl, D., & Weisenburg, A. (1972). Hyperkinetic adult: A study of the "paradoxical" amphetamine response. *Journal of the American Medical Association, 222*, 693–694.

Bartlett, K. (1990, December 2). Attention deficit: Scientists move toward understanding of brain disorder once thought limited to children. *Houston Chronicle*, p. 6G.

Bellak, L. (Ed.) (1979). *Psychiatric aspects of minimal brain dysfunction in adults.* New York: Grune & Stratton.

Borland, B. L., & Heckman, H. K. (1976). Hyperactive boys and their brothers: A 25-year follow-up study. *Archives of General Psychiatry, 33*, 669–675.

Bradley, C. (1937). The behavior of children receiving benzedrine. *American Journal of Psychiatry, 94*, 577–585.

Buchsbaum, M. S., Haier, R. J., Sostek, A. J., Weingartner, H., Zahn, T. P., Siever, L. J., Murphy, D. L., & Brody, L. (1985). Attentional dysfunction and psychopathology in college men. *Archives of General Psychiatry, 42*, 354–360.

Cantwell, D. P. (1972). Psychiatric illness in the families of hyperactive children. *Archives of General Psychiatry, 27*, 414–417.

Cantwell, D. P. (1975). Genetic studies of hyperactive children: Psychiatric illness in biologic and adoptive parents. In R. R. Fieve, D. Rosenthal & H. Brill (Eds.), *Genetic research in psychiatry* (pp. 273–280). Baltimore: Johns Hopkins University Press.

Chess, S. (1988). Child and adolescent psychiatry comes of age: A fifty-year perspective. *Journal of the American Academy of Child and Adolescent Psychiatry, 25*, 151–157.

Collis, P. (1978). Does minimal brain dysfunction persist into adulthood? *South African Medical Journal, 53*, 477.

Cowley, G. (1993, July 26). The not-young and the restless. *Newsweek*, pp. 48–49.

DeVeaugh-Geiss, J., & Joseph, A. (1980). Paradoxical response to amphetamine in a hyperkinetic adult. *Psychosomatics, 21*, 247–252.

Douglas, V. I. (1972). Stop, look and listen: The problem of sustained attention and impulse control in hyperactive and normal children. *Canadian Journal of Behavioral Science, 4,* 259–282.

Douglas, V. I., & Peters, K. G. (1979). Toward a clearer definition of the attentional deficit of hyperactive children. In G. A. Hale & M. Lewis (Eds.), *Attention and cognitive development* (pp. 173–248). New York: Plenum Press.

Dranov, P. (1993, July). Feeling scattered, unfocused? You might have attention deficit disorder! *Cosmopolitan,* pp. 140–143.

Eisner, K. W. (1993). When you can't pay attention [broadcast segment]. *ABC News 20/20,* June 25.

Gittelman, R., Mannuzza, S., Shenker, R., & Bonagura, N. (1985). Hyperactive boys almost grown up: 1. Psychiatric status. *Archives of General Psychiatry, 42,* 937–947.

Goodwin, D. W., Shulsinger, F., Hermansen, L., Guze, S. B., & Winokur, G. (1975). Alcoholism and the hyperactive child syndrome. *Journal of Nervous and Mental Disease, 160,* 349–353.

Hartocollis, P. (1968). The syndrome of minimal brain dysfunction in young adult. *Bulletin of the Menninger Clinic, 32:* 102–114.

Hill, D. (1947). Amphetamine in psychopathic states. *British Journal of Addiction, 44,* 50–54.

Hohman, L. B. (1922). Post-encephalitic behavior disorders in children. *Johns Hopkins Hospital Bulletin, 33,* 372–375.

Howell, D. C., Huessy, H. R., & Hassuk, B. (1985). Fifteen-year follow-up of a behavioral history of attention deficit disorder. *Pediatrics, 76,* 185–190.

Huessy, H. R. (1974). The adult hyperkinetic. *American Journal of Psychiatry, 131,* 724–725.

Huey, L. Y., Zetin, M., Janowsky, D. S., & Judd, L. L. (1978). Adult minimal brain dysfunction and schizophrenia: A case report. *American Journal of Psychiatry, 135,* 1563–1565.

Jaffe, P. (1992a). Sue the gatekeepers–open the gates? *ADDendum,* 8, pp. 1–3.

Jaffe, P. (1992b). Settlement near in ADA case. *ADDendum,* 9, p. 6.

Jaffe, P. (1993a). Randi Rosenthal, J.D. *ADDendum,* 11, p. 14.

Jaffe, P. (1993b). Howe case stirs controversy. *ADDendum,* 11, pp. 6–9.

Johnson, M. J. (Ed.). (1993). *ADD–A lifetime disorder: Life stories of adults with attention deficit disorder.* Toledo: ADDult Support Network.

Kahn, R. L., & Cohen, L. H. (1934). Organic drivenness: A brain stem syndrome and an experience. *New England Journal of Medicine, 210,* 748–756.

Kane, R., Mikalac, C., Benjamin, S., & Barkley, R. A. (1990). Assessment and treatment of adults with ADHD. In R. A. Barkley, *Attention deficit hyperactivity disorder: A handbook for diagnosis and treatment.* New York: Guilford Press.

Kelly, K., & Ramundo, P. (1993). *You mean I'm not lazy, stupid or crazy?! A self-help book for adults with attention deficit disorder.* Cincinnati: Tyrell & Jerem Press.

Lahey, B. B., Pelham, W. E., Schaughency, E. A., Atkins, M. S., Murphy, H. A., Hynd, G., Russo, M., Hartdagen, S., & Lorys-Vernon, A. (1988). Dimensions and types of attention deficit disorder. *Journal of the American Academy of Child and Adolescent Psychiatry, 27,* 330–335.

Latham, P. S., & Latham, P. H. (1992). *Attention deficit disorder and the law: A guide for advocates.* Washington, DC: JKL Communications.

Laufer, M., & Denhoff, E. (1957). Hyperkinetic behavior syndrome in children. *Journal of Pediatrics, 50,* 463–474.

Mann, H. B., & Greenspan, S. I. (1976). The identification and treatment of adult brain dysfunction. *American Journal of Psychiatry, 133,* 1013–1017.

Mannuzza, S., Klein, R. G., Bessler, A., Malloy, P., & LaPadula, M. (1993). Adult outcome of hyperactive boys: Educational achievement, occupational rank, and psychiatric status. *Archives of General Psychiatry, 50,* 565–576.

Mattes, J. A., Boswell, L., & Oliver, H. (1984). Methylphenidate effects on symptoms of attention deficit disorder in adults. *Archives of General Psychiatry, 41,* 1059–1063.

Mellsop, G. W. (1972). Psychiatric patients seen as children and adults: Childhood predictors of adult illness. *Journal of Child Psychology and Psychiatry, 13,* 91–101.

Menkes, M. H., Rowe, J. S, & Menkes, J.H. (1967). A 25-year follow-up study on the hyperkinetic child with MBD. *Pediatrics, 39,* 393–399.

Miller, K. (1993, January 11). Attention-deficit disorder affects adults, but some doctors question how widely. *Wall Street Journal,* pp. B1, B5.

Milman, D. H. (1979). Minimal brain dysfunction in childhood: Outcome in late adolescence and early adult years. *Journal of Clinical Psychiatry, 40,* 371–380.

Morris, H. H., Escoll, M. D., & Wexler, R. (1956). Aggressive behavior disorders of childhood: A follow-up study. *American Journal of Psychiatry, 112,* 991–997.

Morrison, J. R. (1979). Diagnosis of adult psychiatric patients with childhood hyperactivity. *American Journal of Psychiatry, 136,* 955–958.

Morrison, J. R. (1980). Adult psychiatric disorders in parents of hyperactive children. *American Journal of Psychiatry, 137,* 825–827.

Morrison, J. R., & Minkoff, K. (1975). Explosive personality as a sequel to the hyperactive child syndrome. *Comprehensive Psychiatry, 16,* 343–348.

Morrison, J. R., & Stewart, M. A. (1971). A family study of the hyperactive child syndrome. *Biological Psychiatry, 3,* 189–195.

Morrison, J. R., & Stewart, M. A. (1973). The psychiatric status of legal families of adopted hyperactive children. *Archives of General Psychia-*

try, 27, 414–417.

O'Neal, P., & Robins, L. E. (1958). The relation of childhood behavior problems to adult psychiatric status: A 30-year follow-up study of 150 subjects. *American Journal of Psychiatry*, *114*, 961–969.

Packer, S. (1978). Treatment of minimal brain dysfunction in a young adult. *Canadian Psychiatric Association Journal*, 23, 501–502.

Perney, S. (1991a, July). The disorder that makes people hyper. *Good Housekeeping*, p. 175.

Perney, S. (1991b, August). Fatal distraction: The attention disease. *Mademoiselle*, p. 114.

Plotkin, D., Halaris, A., & DeMet, E. M. (1982). Biological studies in adult attention deficit disorder: Case report. *Journal of Clinical Psychiatry*, *43*, 501–502.

Quitkin, F., & Klein, D. F. (1969). Two behavioral syndromes in young adults related to possible minimal brain dysfunction. *Journal of Psychiatric Research*, *7*, 131–142.

Rapoport, J. L., Buchsbaum, M. S., Weingartner, H., Zahn, T. P., Ludlow, C., & Mikkelsen, E. J. (1980). Dextroamphetamine: Its cognitive and behavioral effects in normal and hyperactive boys and normal men. *Archives of General Psychiatry*, *37*, 933–943.

Richardson, D. (1993, August 20–26). A scientific explanation for a crazy-quilt career. *National Business Employment Weekly*, pp. 5–7.

Rybak, W. S. (1977). More adult brain dysfunction. *American Journal of Psychiatry*, *134*, 97–98.

Schuckit, M. A., Sweeney, S., & Huey, H. (1987). Hyperactivity and the risk for alcoholism. *Journal of Clinical Psychiatry*, *48*, 275–277.

Schweiger, A. B. (1993, July 14). Not just kids: Adults, too, diagnosed with attention deficit disorder. *Ann Arbor News*, pp. C1, C2.

Shelley, E. M., & Reister, F. D. (1972). Syndrome of MBD in young adults. *Diseases of the Nervous System*, *33*, 335–339.

Stewart, M. A., deBlois, S., & Cummings, C. (1980). Psychiatric disorder in the parents of hyperactive boys and those with conduct disorder. *Journal of Child Psychology and Psychiatry*, *21*, 283–292.

Stich, S. (1993, September). Why can't your husband sit still? *Ladies' Home Journal*, pp. 74, 77.

Still, G. F. (1902). Some abnormal psychical conditions in children. *Lancet*, *i*, 1008–1012, 1077–1082, 1163–1168.

Strecker, E., & Ebaugh, F. (1924). Neuropsychiatric sequelae of cerebral trauma in children. *Archives of Neurology and Psychiatry*, *12*, 443–453.

Tarter, R. E., McBride, H., Buonpane, N., & Schneider, D. U. (1977). Differentiation of alcoholics: Childhood history of minimal brain dysfunction, family history, and drinking pattern. *Archives of General Psychiatry*, *34*, 761–768.

Vatz, R. E. (1994, July 27). Attention deficit delirium. *Wall Street Journal*, p. A10

Weiss, G., & Hechtman, L. T. (1986). *Hyperactive children grown up*. New York: Guilford Press.

Weiss, G., Hechtman, L. T., Milroy, T., & Perlman, T. (1985). Psychiatric status of hyperactives as adults: A controlled prospective 15-year follow-up of 63 hyperactive children. *Journal of the American Academy of Child Psychiatry, 24*, 211–220.

Weiss, G., Hechtman, L. T., Perlman, T., Hopkins, J., & Wehar, T. (1979). Hyperactives as young adults: A controlled prospective 10-year follow-up of the psychiatric status of 75 children. *Archives of General Psychiatry, 36*, 675–681.

Weiss, L. (1992). *Attention deficit disorder in adults: Practical help for sufferers and their spouses*. Dallas: Taylor.

Wender, P. H. (1987). *The hyperactive child, adolescent and adult: Attention deficit disorder through the lifespan*. New York: Oxford University Press.

Wender, P. H., Reimherr, F. W., & Wood, D. R. (1981). Attention deficit disorder ("minimal brain dysfunction") in adults: A replication study of diagnosis and drug treatment. *Archives of General Psychiatry, 38*, 449–456.

Wender, P. H., Reimherr, F. W., Wood, D. R., & Ward, M. (1985). A controlled trial of methylphenidate in the treatment of attention deficit disorder, residual type, in adults. *American Journal of Psychiatry, 142*, 547–552.

Wender, P. H., Wood, D. R., & Reimherr, F. W. (1985). Pharmacological treatment of attention deficit disorder, residual type (ADD,RT, "minimal brain dysfunctional," "hyperactivity") in adults. *Psychopharmacology Bulletin, 21*, 222–231.

Woerner, P. I. & Guze, S. B. (1968). A family and marital study of hysteria. *British Journal of Psychiatry, 114*, 161–168.

Wolkenberg, F. (1987, October 11). Out of a darkness. *New York Times Magazine*, pp. 62, 66, 68, 70, 82–83.

Wood, D. R. (1986). The diagnosis and treatment of attention deficit disorder, residual type. *Psychiatric Annals, 16*, 23–24, 26–28.

Wood, D. R., Reimherr, F. W., Wender, P. H. & Johnson, G. E. (1976). Diagnosis and treatment of minimal brain dysfunction in adults. *Archives of General Psychiatry, 33*, 1453–1460.

Wood, D. R., Wender, P. H., & Reimherr, F. W. (1983). The prevalence of attention deficit disorder, residual type, or minimal brain dysfunction, in a population of male alcoholic patients. *American Journal of Psychiatry, 140*, 95–98.

Yellin, A. M., Hopwood, J. H., & Greenberg, L. M. (1982). Adults and adolescents with attention deficit disorder: Clinical and behavioral responses to psychostimulants. *Journal of Clinical Psychopharmacology*, 2, 133–136.

Zametkin, A. J., Nordahl, T. E., Gross, M., King, A. C., Semple, W. E., Rumsey, J., Hamburger, S., & Cohen, R. M. (1990). Cerebral glucose metabolism in adults with hyperactivity of childhood onset. *New England Journal of Medicine*, 323, 1361–1366.

2

Neurobiology of Attention Deficit Disorder

PATRICIA O. QUINN*

Over the past two decades, a great deal of scientific research has focused on various brain structures and processes, resulting in an increase in the knowledge and understanding of both normal and abnormal conditions. There now is a sufficient accumulation of neuroscientific data to document that disorders such as autism, depressive illnesses, learning disabilities, and attention deficit hyperactivity disorder (ADHD) are the result of neuroanatomical and/or neurochemical abnormalities. These, therefore, now may be described as *neurobiological disorders*, rather than being placed under the category of "mental illness." This term is being used to describe any severe, chronic "mental" illness that has a physical, neuroanatomical or neurochemical basis.

In this chapter we will look specifically at Attention Deficit Hyperactivity Disorder (variously referred to as ADHD, ADD, or ADHD-RT), its symptoms, and its qualifications as a neurobiological condition. To date, no single defect has been found to explain all of the symptoms of ADHD, which include motor restlessness, attention deficits, poor organizational skills, poor concentration, lack of task persistence, impulsivity, and emotional outbursts. But what has become evident is that ADHD symptoms are not always outgrown. In 1985 Paul Wender, observing that these symptoms exist in adults with a previous history of ADHD, referred to them as Attention Deficit Hyperactivity Disorder-Residual Type (ADHD-RT) (Wender et al. 1981, 1985). Other studies (e.g., Mannuzza, Klein, Bessler, Malloy &

*The author would like to acknowledge the assistance of Andrea Miller in the preparation of this chapter for publication.

18

LaPadula, 1993; Weiss & Hechtman, 1993) that followed ADHD children into adulthood also found a persistence of symptoms, with less stability and satisfaction in areas such as employment and marriage. Underachieving and impulsivity with emotional lability were also seen. In another study, only about one half of the group at follow-up were found to be functioning in the "normal" range (Barkley, 1986).

THE CATECHOLAMINE HYPOTHESIS

In order to look at the complex range of attentional, behavioral, and emotional manifestations of ADHD, we must look at both functional anatomy and the biochemistry of neurotransmission in the brain. The brain is composed of networks of individual cells, or neurons, which transmit nerve impulses. These neurons manufacture and release special chemical messengers known as neurotransmitters. The transmitter molecules are released into the synapse or space between cells and act on specific receptor sites in the postsynaptic cell membrane to excite that cell to discharge. There are over 30 known substances that act as neurotransmitters at this time, with many more postulated. These neurotransmitters include dopamine (DA), norepinephrine (NE), epinephrine (EPI), acetylcholine, serotonin, GABA, MAO, and many more. Such symptoms as depression, anxiety, sleep disorders, aggression, decreased attentiveness, and over- or underarousal have all been related to the actions of these neurotransmitters within the brain.

The transmitters are not randomly distributed within the brain, but are localized in areas or nuclei within certain regions of the brain. Progress in brain mapping in recent years has been very successful in localizing areas important for specific transmitter systems for specific functions within the brain. Likewise, advances in looking at the energy metabolism in brain cells as a function of their glucose utilization have allowed the visualization of cells or groups of cells that are activated during a certain task or procedure.

This regional glucose metabolism is studied with the use of radioactively labeled glucose in a technique called positron-emission tomography, or PET scan. Brain imaging is also possible using blood flow studies, which give a three-dimensional picture of cerebral blood flow and provide an indirect measure of brain metabolism. These studies, are referred to as single photon emission computerized tomography, or SPECT. Magnetic resonance imaging (MRI) and topographic mapping of the electroencephalogram (EEG), or BEAM studies, also are useful tools in the investigation of brain function.

All of this new noninvasive technology, coupled with neurochemical data from pharmacological and animal studies, has led to considerable speculation about the role of various brain areas and systems in relation to certain ADHD symptoms. Investigations of neurochemical and physiological functioning in the frontal lobe and subcortical structures, including the limbic system and the reticular activating system, have provided us with increasingly appropriate models to account for the various behavioral and cognitive symptoms seen in ADHD. For the most part, the models have been progressive, with major findings adding to what we already know about ADHD, rather than detracting from what we thought we knew.

One of the first models used to explain ADHD was the catecholamine hypothesis (Kornetsky, 1970). This refers to the suspected faulty functioning of the neurotransmitters dopamine (DA) and norepinephrine (NE) in brain structures, as indicated by the effectiveness of the stimulants to treat the ADHD symptoms of impulsivity, hyperactivity, and impaired cognitive performance. The stimulants—methylphenidate (Ritalin), d-amphetamine (Dexedrine), and pemoline (Cylert)—increase the amounts of DA and NE available for use in the brain. Some tricyclic antidepressants, which primarily affect NE but have a weak action in the serotonergic system, also have been shown to reduce symptoms of ADD (Biederman, Baldessarini, Wright, Knee, & Harmatz, 1989). Specific mechanisms underlying the efficacy of the stimulants have proven elusive, however, as the stimulants increase availability of DA and NE at the synapse while not exhibiting direct receptor-stimulating effects.

Since 1970 numerous animal and clinical studies have solidified the fact that impaired use of DA and NE is implicated in ADHD. For example, some animal studies have indicated that hyperactive and impulsive behavior results from impairments in the catecholamine system (Shaywitz, Yager, & Klopper, 1976); other animal studies have found decreased levels of DA and NE in limbic structures (Bloomingdale, Davies, & Gold, 1984; Sagvolden, Wultz, Moser, Moser, & Morkrid, 1989). In addition, it is believed that dopamine is involved in learning and motor hyperactivity in the ADD syndrome (Beninger, 1989), in the operant-reward mechanisms which seem deficient in ADHD (Oades, 1989), and in working memory (Goldman-Rakik, 1991), the latter apparently impaired in ADD, although little research has been undertaken to examine the phenomenon. Shaywitz, Cohen, and Bowes (1977) determined that the concentrations of the metabolite of dopamine in the cerebral spinal fluid (CSF) were significantly lower in ADD children compared to those of normal children, suggesting reduced turnover of brain DA in this group. Concentrations of the principal metabolite of serotonin were not found to differ significantly.

More recently, Welsh and Pennington's group (Welsh, Groisser, & Pennington, 1987; Welsh, Pennington, Ozonoff, Rouse, & McCabe, 1988) proposed that a neurochemical disruption of depressed dopamine functioning found in children with early-treated phenylketonuria (PKU) was responsible for the impaired executive (frontal lobe) functioning found on testing. Disturbance in dopamine metabolism related to the receptor sites on the neuron has also been postulated.

Norepinephrine and serotonin have been implicated in positive-reinforcement learning, motivation, and arousal states, all of which are compromised in the ADD syndrome (Barkley, 1990; Shenker, 1992). In *Minimal Brain Dysfunction in Children,* Paul Wender (1971) was one of the first to propose that MBD children had an abnormality in the metabolism of the monoamines serotonin, norepinephrine, or dopamine. The role of serotonin in ADHD, however, has not been established in biochemical studies. Newer serotonergic agents, such as fenfluramine and fluoxetine, can be useful in treating comorbid conditions such as depression, but do not appear to address the core symptoms of attention, impulsivity, and hyperactivity.

In conclusion, although we still can assume that serotonin, DA, and NE are involved in ADHD, biochemical studies have had little success in correlating measures of NE, DA, or their metabolites with the ADD syndrome (Zametkin & Rapoport, 1987); we therefore cannot know the exact nature of the neurochemical dysregulation. For example, studies that have looked at the presence of catecholamine metabolites in urine (an indirect measure of the amount of the neurotransmitters in the brain) have alternately indicated decreased levels of brain DA and NE, no difference in levels, and increased levels. Such inconsistent results seem to be the one predictable phenomenon regarding research into the causes of ADHD! From a neuropsychiatric perspective, what remains evident is that the manufacturing and transmission processes of the neurons and synapses in the ADHD brain are dysregulated—that is, the delicate neurochemical balance needed to assure optimal brain functioning is impaired.

THE THEORY OF FRONTAL LOBE DISINHIBITION

The diverse results of neurochemical studies, the technological advances and possibilities of noninvasive brain studies, and the refinements in neuropsychological testing have all inspired researchers to move beyond the catecholamine dysregulation hypothesis in ADHD. They have begun to look seriously at the functioning of the anatomical structures of the brain, and how possible impairments in the functioning of various structures could be related to ADHD symptoms. These efforts have been facilitated by neuroscientific research which has begun to articulate how the brain receives, processes, stores, and retrieves information in such a way as to influence emotion, cognition, and behavior. An overview of information-processing phenomena can allow us to better conceptualize the connection between the brain and behavior in ADHD.

Initially, information from our environment is registered by the sensory cortices–discrete areas that are involved in sight, touch, hearing, and so forth–and sent to areas of the limbic system in the midbrain. The limbic system receives the sensory information and simultaneously compares it to stored information, retrieving stored information that is most applicable to current experience. Along with being involved in memory processes, the limbic system is the "center of emotion," and thus integrates incoming information and stored information with an appropriate emotional response. Depending on the nature of this integrated bundle of information, the limbic system may activate lower brain structures (the reticular activating system) which are responsible for our "fight or flight" reactions. Regardless of whether the alarm system is activated, the limbic system sends the integrated information bundle to the prefrontal cortices of the frontal lobes. It is here that moment-to-moment experience is integrated with stored information and emotional responses.

The task of the frontal lobe is to handle sequentially received information, to integrate current experience with past experience, to monitor present behavior, to inhibit inappropriate responses, and to organize and plan for the attainment of future goals. This ability is usually referred to as the *executive function* role of the frontal lobes. Executive function is defined as the ability to devise and maintain an appropriate problem-solving set in order to attain a future goal. The basic elements of executive function include the ability to initiate, sustain, inhibit, and shift attention (ISIS, for short). Our ability to respond and behave appropriately and consistently, as well as our capacity to be deliberate, responsible, and flexible, is contingent upon the proper functioning of the frontal lobes. Dysfunction of the frontal lobes can therefore lead to dysfunction in the areas of attention, production, impulse control, and/or cognition.

One of the greatest confusions regarding the functioning of the frontal lobes is their role in cognition (Stuss & Benson, 1986). Many studies show that individuals can have severe executive function deficits despite normal-range IQs as measured by psychological tests (Welsh et al., 1988). It now is generally believed that ADHD is the result of a *disinhibition of the frontal lobes*, where the frontal lobes fail to inhibit emotional responses, inappropriate cognitive or psychological responses, and behavioral impulses. ADHD has been described as a disorder of disinhibition or dysregulation of the frontal cortex by Douglas (1984) and Gualtieri, Ondrusek, & Finley (1985), respectively. In 1986 Chelune and colleagues (Chelune, Ferguson, Koon, & Dickey, 1986) proposed the frontal lobe hypothesis of ADHD, defining hyperactivity as the result of a disturbed higher level of cortical inhibition, based on neuropsychological studies that localize the disinhibitory disorder in the frontal lobes. Since Chelune's report, many other neuropsychological studies have confirmed frontal lobe disinhibition in people with ADHD (see Barkley, Grodzinksy, & DuPaul, 1992, for review).

Chelune's group supported their conceptualization with observed similarities between ADHD symptoms and symptoms of individuals with frontal lobe damage, as well as with findings from Lou, Henriksen, & Bruhn (1984), who found decreased cerebral blood flow in the frontal lobes of ADHD children. Since the frontal lobe disinhibition model was proposed, other neuroimaging studies have noted frontal lobe and striatal deactivation. Significant prefrontal deactivation has been seen to occur in ADHD patients when asked to respond to an intellectual challenge, with some demonstrating decreased prefrontal activity even during rest (Amen, Poldi, & Thisted, 1993). Lou et al. found hypoperfusion in the striatal areas of ADHD children, and Lubar et al. (1985) found abnormal brain-wave activity in the frontal lobes of ADHD children as compared to controls.

Most exciting of all are the results from studies using new noninvasive techniques to study brain metabolism. Zametkin and colleagues at the National Institute of Mental Health first published their landmark findings in November 1990 in the *New England Journal of Medicine*. The study measured glucose metabolism in adults who had histories of hyperactivity in childhood and who continued to have symptoms in adulthood. Each adult was the biological parent of a hyperactive child. PET scanning was used to measure regional cerebral glucose metabolism while subjects performed an auditory attention task. Results indicated that glucose metabolism was lower in the adults with hyperactivity than in normal controls. Among the regions of the brain with the greatest reduction of metabolism were the premotor cortex and the superior prefrontal cortex, areas already thought to be responsible for the control of attention and motor activity.

Zametkin's study provided documentation that left little doubt that the frontal lobes make up a major part of the very complex attentional system, and most likely are a major contributor or mediator in the ADHD syndrome. It is important, however, when attempting to study ADHD in more depth, to consider the role of other neuroanatomical areas, with their unique characteristics and neurotransmitter systems. In Zametkin's PET study of 25 patients they demonstrated a decrease in metabolism in both cortical and subcortical areas. Additional research has looked at abnormalities in these subcortical structures. Hynd and colleagues (Hynd, Semund-Clikeman, Lorys, Novey, & Eliopulos, 1990), using MRI studies, have found differences in both the frontal areas as well as in the corpus callosum. This group found that children with ADHD differed significantly from controls in the right frontal width measurement. They suggested that subcortical structures might reflect deviations in neurodevelopment in these children, and that one such subcortical structure is the corpus callosum, which is easily seen on MRI scans.

The corpus callosum is that structure of the brain that connects the two hemispheres of the cortex–the visual, aggregative right side and the analytic, verbal left side–and is vital for transfer of information between them. Results of another study (Hynd, et al., 1991) provided preliminary evidence that potentially important differences existed in the morphology of the corpus callosum in children with ADHD. Certain areas of the corpus callosum–namely the genu, anterior to the splenium, and the splenium– were smaller in children with ADHD. It is known that it is the premotor, orbitofrontal, and prefrontal areas of the brain that are interconnected by fibers in the genu. This is of particular interest, because it is the frontal system that we have been discussing as deficient in individuals with ADHD. Findings indicating anomalies of the corpus callosum may therefore be related to abnormalities in the frontal structures, particularly on the right, as determined in these previous studies.

The role of the brain stem, specifically the reticular activating system (RAS) and the locus coeruleus, have been implicated in the etiology of ADHD. The RAS is the pacemaker for EEG rhythms and affects the sympathetic and parasympathetic functions of the autonomic nervous system, that is, the body's physiological alarm response and corrective, stabilizing response. Ascending pathways of the RAS reach into higher cortical areas and "awaken" the higher structures so that they can receive information from sensory cortices and the limbic system. In addition, descending pathways allow transmission of impulses from the motor cortex to muscles and limbs. Through excitatory and inhibitory pathways with limbic structures and higher brain structures, this system allows an organism to orient and habituate to stimuli (Voeller, 1991). In animal studies, behaviors apparently equivalent to distractibility result when the norepinephrine pathways of the RAS have been undermined.

The locus coeruleus (LC) is the primary site of NE production and firing, and recent research makes the compelling argument that increased firing activity of the LC may be involved in ADHD. In an exhaustive review of biochemical and pharmacological studies associated with ADHD, Shenker (1992) observes, "An interesting new model of attentional dysfunction has been proposed in which...the LC neurons of children with ADHD fire at an abnormally high rate because of a neurochemical defect in the brain stem systems that modulate LC activity" (p. 352). Shenker points out that drugs that have proven effective in the treatment of ADHD–including the stimulants, tricyclic antidepressants, and clonidine–decrease the firing rate of the LC. As the firing rate of the LC decreases, more NE becomes available for use at the synapses of other brain structures. On the other hand, drugs that exert effects on the DA and NE systems but do not decrease LC firing have not been as effective in treating the major symptoms of ADD.

AN INTEGRATED MODEL

We can begin to see how the catecholamine hypothesis and the theory of frontal lobe disinhibition may complement one anther. Dopamine and norepinephrine are believed to modulate information processing, enhance the response of target cells to inhibitory and excitatory inputs, and affect the ability to detect a "signal," or a relevant stimulus, when it is embedded in "noise" (Servan-Schreiber, Printz, & Cohen, 1990). Both are localized in mid- and lower brain structures, with extending pathways to the frontal cortex.

According to Zametkin and Rapoport, in their review of the neurobiology of ADHD (1987), DA is localized in limbic areas that are assumed to be involved in the expression of ADHD, including the nigrostriatal tract—which regulates and modulates motor movements—and the mesolimbic mesocortical tract, thought to have some role in modulating emotion and sensory input to the cortex. NE has vast projections throughout the brain and consists of the dorsal noradrenergic system, lateral tegmental system, and medulla and spinal cord system. The dorsal system seems to be most implicated in ADHD, as this system is widespread and influences both cortical and subcortical functioning.

The prefrontal cortex is abundant in catecholamines. The DA mesolimbic and nigrostriatal tracts form pathways between the motor center and the limbic center to the frontal structures, and the prefrontal cortex also receives NE input from lower brain structures. Consequently, the presence and regulation of DA and NE in the prefrontal areas may be crucial to the proper functioning of the frontal lobes. As previously mentioned, it is increasingly believed that behaviors, thoughts, and affective expressions are under cortical control—appropriately inhibited or expressed by the regulatory functioning of the frontal lobes, which receive, integrate, coordinate, and translate into action information received from mid- and lower brain structures. Thus, the inhibitory function of the frontal areas may be compromised by dysregulated AD and NE systems. Some research suggests that aged monkeys whose prefrontal cortices are deficient in dopamine and norepinephrine perform poorly in delayed response tests (Goldman-Rakik, 1991); other research has found that severe depletion of DA in the monkey prefrontal cortex impairs performance on complex behavioral tasks.

A simplified, integrated model of the neurochemical and neuroanatomical findings related to ADHD could be summarized as a dysregulation of certain neurotransmitters, perhaps originating in lower brain and limbic structures, which influences the adequate processing of internal and external stimuli. These neurotransmitters, particularly dopamine and norepinephrine, probably affect the production, use, and regulation of other neurotransmitters, as well as the maturation or functioning of some brain structures. The dysregulated system impairs the capacity of the frontal lobes to perform properly—that is, blood flow and glucose metabolism studies indicate that the activity of frontal areas is depressed, and clinical and neuropsychological studies suggest that frontal areas are unable to inhibit or control input from lower brain structures.

The result of such a phenomenon parallels the symptoms we see in ADHD: Distractibility and the inability to stay on task are the failure to "put the brakes" on attention and thought; emotional lability and hypersensitivity are the failure to modulate limbic input; behavioral impulsivity and motor hyperactivity are the failure to delay gratification and inhibit actions. These symptoms, in turn, frequently influence learning, memory, and information processing.

Stimulants and some tricyclic antidepressants appear to improve the symptoms of ADHD by allowing better use of the catecholamines. These medications may regulate and stabilize the neurochemical system, and improve the functioning of brain structures and pathways. The frontal lobes become "stimulated" and are able to increase their inhibitory capacity. The ability to deliberate, anticipate, plan, and learn is increased, while motor restlessness is decreased.

A GENETICALLY BASED NEUROBIOLOGICAL DISORDER

Needless to say, the true neurological cause of frontal area hypofunctioning is not entirely understood. Confounding the picture is the fact that the specific cause of frontal lobe dysfunction may vary from person to person. As Anastopoulos and Barkley (1988) have noted, multiple suspected causes of ADHD lead to an uneven distribution of symptoms. It becomes difficult to generalize about the symptoms of ADHD, and it may even be true that different symptom clusters represent different subtypes of ADHD, with each subtype the result of a different kind of neurobiological dysfunction. Some investigators are postulating as such, based on recent SPECT studies of ADHD children, which seemingly group children according to different neuroanatomical patterns of decreased cerebral blood flow and metabolism (Amen et al., 1993). The benefit of a sophisticated determination of ADHD-related neurological dysfunction rests in the subsequent ability to customize drug therapy according to the area of dysfunction. It may also allow us to determine whether neurobiological differences exist between ADHD and ADD without hyperactivity. It is important to note, however, that the use of SPECT scans has not been generally endorsed by the scientific community as appropriate for use with children.

Despite the varied clinical picture of ADHD, investigators are becoming more certain that ADHD, as a neurobiological disorder, has a genetic basis. Evidence for the heritability of ADHD is being found in family studies, twin studies, and molecular genetic studies. Studies of identical and fraternal twins (Gilles, Gilger, Pennington, & DeFries, 1992; Goodman & Stevenson, 1989) find a significantly higher incidence of ADHD in identical rather than fraternal twins, suggesting a genetic predisposition to the disorder.

Similarly, epidemiological and familial risk studies signify that the tendency toward ADHD is passed down from parent to child. Many parents of ADHD children eventually receive the ADHD diagnosis. Biederman's group (see Biederman, Faraone, Keenan, & Tsuang, 1991; Faraone, Biederman, & Chen, 1992) has discovered that the near relatives of ADHD children have a greater risk for the disorder than do relatives of control children; and, interestingly enough, immediate family members and near relatives of ADHD children have much higher rates of anxiety and depressive disorder than do controls, suggesting a fundamental genetic bias toward neurobiological dysfunction.

The heritability of ADHD is being supported by work in molecular biology. Research in this area includes genetic studies of the dopamine receptor gene. Although we do not yet understand the genetic basis of ADHD, recent findings (Comings et al., 1991) suggest that there may be a link between the dopamine D_2 receptor locus and several neuropsychiatric disorders, including ADHD. In addition, genetic transmission of the ADHD symptoms was postulated after research by Hauser and colleagues (1993) at the National Institutes of Health found ADHD linked in patients with a genetically inherited thyroid hormone disorder. In this study, 70% of the children and 50% of adults with generalized resistance to thyroid hormone (GRTH) also met the criteria for attention deficit disorder.

The gradual realization that ADHD is a genetically based neurobiological disorder has liberated many parents from the feeling that their ADHD child is inherently bad, lazy, and careless. As we recognize that ADHD symptoms persist into adulthood, affecting not only ADHD adults but their partners and children as well, it becomes just as important to liberate adults from their sense of failure. An understanding of the neurobiological consequences of ADHD, therefore, allows the clinician to educate and empower the adult. It also suggests appropriate courses of treatment. Knowledge of the specific neurotransmitter systems that control and regulate particular anatomical areas certainly can be useful in determining the best suited therapy for each patient. For example, individuals with the "classic" pattern of hypoprofused frontal lobe deactivation may be found to respond best to stimulants, while individuals with an overaroused activating system may be more responsive to alpha-2 noradrenergic agonist drugs such as clonidine.

The roles of various neurotransmitter, pathways, and brain structures must therefore be considered in understanding and treating the symptoms of ADHD in both children and adults. Future clinical research, noninvasive neuroanatomical and neurobiochemical studies, and molecular genetics will continue to elucidate the underlying neurobiological processes involved in ADHD, and hopefully provide us with more clues in our attempts to effectively treat the underlying neurobiological dysfunction and the symptomatic expression of this complex disorder.

REFERENCES

Amen, D. G., Poldi, J. H., & Thisted, R. A. (1983). *Evaluation of ADHD with brain SPECT imaging.* Paper presented at the annual meeting of the American Psychiatric Association, San Francisco, CA.

Anastopoulos, A., & Barkley, R. (1988). Biological factors in attention deficit hyperactivity disorder. *Behavioral Therapist, 11*(3), 47–53.

Barkley, R. A. (1986). Cited in G. Weiss & L.T. Hechtman, *Hyperactive children grown up.* New York: Guilford Press.

Barkley, R. A. (1990). *Attention deficit hyperactivity disorder: A handbook for diagnosis and treatment.* New York: Guilford Press.

Barkley, R. A., Grodzinsky, G., & DuPaul, G. J. (1992). Frontal lobe functions in attention deficit disorder with and without hyperactivity: A review and research report. *Journal of Abnormal Child Psychology, 20,* 163–188.

Beninger, R. J. (1989). Dopamine and learning: Implications for attention deficit disorder and hyperkinetic syndrome. In T. Sagvolden & T. Archer (Eds.), *Attention deficit disorder: Clinical and basic research* (pp. 323–338). Hillsdale, NJ: Lawrence Erlbaum Associates.

Biederman, J., Baldessarini, R. J., Wright, V., Knee, D., & Harmatz, J. S. (1989). A double-blind placebo controlled study of desipramine in the treatment of ADD: I. Efficacy. *Journal of the American Academy of Child and Adolescent Psychiatry, 28,* 777–784.

Biederman, J., Faraone, S. V., Keenan, K., & Tsuang, M. T. (1991). Evidence of familial association between attention deficit disorder and major affective disorder. *Archives of General Psychiatry, 48,* 633–642.

Bloomingdale, L. M., Davies, R. K., & Gold, M. S. (1984). Some possible neurological substrates in attention deficit disorder. In L. M. Bloomingdale (Ed.), *Attention deficit disorder: Diagnostic, cognitive, and therapeutic understanding* (pp. 37–66). New York: Spectrum Publications.

Chelune, G. J., Ferguson, W., Koon, R., & Dickey, T. O. (1986). Frontal lobe disinhibition in attention deficit disorder. *Child Psychiatry and Human Development, 16,* 221–235.

Comings, D. E., Comings, B. G., & Muhleman, M. S. (1991). The dopamine D_2 receptor locus as a modifying gene in neuropsychiatric disorders. *JAMA, 266*(13), 1793–1800.

Douglas, V. I. (1984). The psychological processes implicated in ADD. In L. M. Bloomingdale (Ed.), *Attention deficit disorder: Diagnostic, cognitive, and therapeutic understanding.* New York: Spectrum Publications.

Elia, J., Borcherding, B. G., Potter, W. Z., Meftord, I. N., Rapoport, J. L., & Keysor, C. S. (1990). Stimulant drug treatment of hyperactivity: Biochemical correlates. *Clinical Pharmacology Therapy, 48,* 57–66.

Faraone, S. V., Biederman, J., & Chen, W. J. (1992). Segregation analysis of attention deficit hyperactivity disorder. *Psychiatric Genetics, 2,* 257–275.

Faraone, S. V., Biederman, J., Lehman, B. K., & Keenan, K. (1993). Evidence for the independent familial transmission of attention deficit hyperactivity disorder and learning disabilities: Results from a family genetic study. *American Journal of Psychiatry, 150*(6), 891–895.

Gilles J. J., Gilger, J. W., Pennington, B. F., & DeFries, J. C. (1992). Attention deficit disorder in reading disabled twins: Evidence for a genetic etiology. *Journal of Abnormal Child Psychology, 20,* 303–315.

Gittelman, R., Mannuzza, S., Shenker, R., & Bonagura, N. (1985). Hyperactive boys almost grown up. *Archives of General Psychiatry, 42,* 937–947.

Goldman-Rakik, P. (1991). Working memory and the mind. *Scientific American, 267*(3), 110–117.

Goodman, R., & Stevenson, J. (1989). A twin study of hyperactivity: II. The etiological role of genes, family relationships and perinatal adversity. *Journal of Child Psychology and Psychiatry, 30,* 691–709.

Gualtieri, C. T., Ondrusek, M. G., & Finley, C. (1985). Attention deficit disorder in adults. *Clinical Neuropharmacology, 8*(4), 343–356.

Hauser, P., Zametkin, A. J., Martinez, P., Vitiello, B., Matochik, J., Mixson, J., & Wientraub, B. (1993). Attention deficit hyperactivity disorder in people with generalized resistance to thyroid hormone. *New England Journal of Medicine, 328,* 997–1001.

Heilman, K. M., Voeller, K. K., & Nadeau, D. E. (1991). A possible pathophysiologic substrate of attention deficit hyperactivity disorder. *Journal of Child Neurology, 6*(Suppl.), s76–s81.

Hynd, G., Semund-Clikeman, M., Lorys, A. R., Novey, D., & Eliopulos, D., (1990). Brain morphology in developmental dyslexia and attention deficit disorder hyperactivity. *Archives of Neurology, 47,* 919–926.

Hynd, G., Semund-Clikeman, M., Lorys, A. R., Novey, E., Eliopulos, D., & Lyytinen, H. (1991). Corpus callosum morphology in attention deficit hyperactivity disorder: Morphometric analysis of MRI. *Journal of Learning Disabilities, 24*(3), 141–146.

Kornetsky, C. (1970). Psychoactive drugs in the immature organism. *Psychopharmocologia, 17,* 105–136.

Lou, H. C., Henriksen, L., & Bruhn, P. (1984). Focal cerebral dysfunction in developmental learning disabilities. *Archives of Neurology, 41,* 825–829.

Lou, H. C., Henriksen, L., Bruhn, P., Borner, H., & Nielsen, J. B. (1989). Striatal dysfunction in attention deficit hyperkinetic disorder. *Archives of Neurology, 46,* 48–52.

Lubar, J., Bianchine, K. I., Calhoun, H., Lambert, E., Brody, Z., & Shabsin, H. (1985). Spectral analysis of EEG differences between children with and without learning disabilities. *Journal of Learning Disabilities, 18,* 403–408.

Mannuzza, S., Klein, R. G., Besller, A., Malloy, P., & La Padula, M. (1993). Adult outcome of hyperactive boys. *Archives of General Psychiatry, 50,* 565–576.

Oades, R. D. (1989). Attention deficit disorder and hyperkinetic syndrome: Biological perspectives. In T. Sagvolden & T. Archer (Eds.), *Attention deficit disorder: Clinical and basic research* (pp. 353–368). Hillsdale, NJ: Lawrence Erlbaum Associates.

Sagvolden, T., Wultz, B., Moser, E. I., Moser, M., & Morkrid, L. (1989). Results from a comparative neuropsychological research program indicate altered reinforcement mechanisms in children with ADD. In T. Sagvolden & T. Archer (Eds.), *Attention deficit disorder: Clinical and basic research* (pp. 261–286). Hillsdale, NJ: Lawrence Erlbaum Associates.

Servan-Schreiber, D., Printz, H., & Cohen, J. D. (1990). A network model of catecholamine effects: Gain, signal-to-noise ratio, and behavior. *Science, 249,* 892–895.

Shaywitz, B. A., Cohen, D. J., & Bowes, M. B. (1977). CSF monoamine metabolites in children with minimal brain dysfunction: Evidence for alteration of brain dopamine. *Journal of Pediatrics, 90,* 67–71.

Shaywitz, B. A., Yager, R. D., & Klopper, J. H. (1976). Selective brain dopamine depletion in developing rates: An experimental model of minimal brain dysfunction. *Science, 191,* 305–308.

Shenker, A. (1992). The mechanism of action of drugs used to treat attention-deficit hyperactivity disorder: Focus on catecholamine receptor pharmacology. *Advances in Pediatrics, 39,* 337–382.

Stuss, D., & Benson, F. (1986). *The frontal lobes.* New York: Raven Press.

Tannock, R., Schachar, R., Carr, R. P., Chajczyk, D., & Logan, G. (1989). Effects of methylphenidate on inhibitory control in hyperactive children. *Journal of Abnormal Child Psychology, 17*(5), 473–491.

Voeller, K. S. (1991). What can neurological models of attention, intention and arousal tell us about ADHD? *Journal of Neuropsychiatry, 3*(2), 209–216.

Weiss, G., & Hechtman, L. T. (1993). *Hyperactive children grown up* (2nd ed.). New York: Guilford Press.

Welsh, M. C., Groisser, D., & Pennington, B. F. (1987). Performance of preschool phenylketonuric children on prefrontal measures. *Journal of Clinical and Experimental Neuropsychology, 9,* 28.

Welsh, M. C., Pennington, B. F., Ozonoff, S., Rouse, B., & McCabe, E. (1988). *Neuropsychology of early treated PKU: Specific executive function deficits.* Unpublished manuscript.

Wender, P. H. (1971). *Minimal brain dysfunction in children.* New York: Wiley.

Wender, P. H. (1987). *The hyperactive child, adolescent, and adult.* New York: Oxford University Press.

Wender, P. H., Reimherr, F. W., Wood, D. R., et al. (1981). Attention deficit disorders (minimal brain dysfunction) in adults. *Archives of General Psychiatry, 38*, 449–456.

Wender, P. H., Reimherr, F. W., Wood, D. R., et al. (1985). A controlled study of methylphenidate in the treatment of attention deficit disorder, residual type, in adults. *American Journal of Psychiatry, 142*, 547–552.

Zametkin, A. J., Nordahl, T. E., & Gross, M. (1990). Cerebral glucose metabolism in adults with hyperactivity of childhood onset. *New England Journal of Medicine, 323*(20), 1413–1415.

Zametkin, A. J., & Rapoport, J. L. (1987). The neurobiology of attention deficit disorder: Where have we come in 50 years? *Journal of the American Academy of Child and Adolescent Psychiatry, 26*, 676–686.

SECTION II

Differential Diagnosis and Comorbidity Issues in Adult ADD

The chapters in this section look at the process of assessment and differential diagnosis from various perspectives. While some professionals in the field of adult ADD believe that only a clinical interview and the completion of a few screening questionnaires are adequate for diagnosis, the assessment process is often much more complex. Because ADD is a spectrum disorder manifested in a variety of subtypes, and is expressed in degrees from mild to severe, the adequacy of an interview and questionnaires seems to presuppose a high degree of expertise which would allow the clinician to accurately interpret the data as well as to adequately screen for comorbid conditions. There is a wide range of differential diagnosis issues and comorbid conditions that need to be considered in the assessment process. This section aims to educate the clinician about ADD subtypes, about ADD-like conditions that must be differentiated from ADD, and about the myriad comorbid conditions.

Angela Tzelepis, Howard Schubiner, and Lawrence Warbasse, from Wayne State University, explore the connections between ADD and a host of psychiatric conditions, some of which are comorbid with ADD and some of which may be mistaken for ADD. Adrian Sandler, from the Clinical Center for the Study of Development and Learning at Chapel Hill, North Carolina, explores the interrelationships between attention deficit disorder and other neurodevelopmental disabilities that may interact with ADD to affect cognitive functioning. Bennett Lavenstein, affiliated with Georgetown University, provides a similar discourse from a neurological perspective. Because the symptoms associated with attention deficit disorder can result from a range of other neurological conditions, his chapter discusses the process of differential diagnosis and guides the nonmedically trained clinician to better determine when a complete neurological evaluation seems warranted in the assessment process. Thomas Brown, of Yale University, addresses ADD with and without hyperactivity, finding that there are many more similarities than differences between these two subtypes. Finally, Susan Biggs, of Chesapeake Psychological Services in Virginia, describes a range of assessment tools, including psychological, psychoeducational, and neuropsychological tests, which can be very useful in developing a full diagnostic picture of the different conditions that must be addressed in treating the adult with ADD.

3

Differential Diagnosis and Psychiatric Comorbidity Patterns in Adult Attention Deficit Disorder

ANGELA TZELEPIS, HOWARD SCHUBINER,
AND LAWRENCE H. WARBASSE, III

The evaluation of Attention deficit hyperactivity disorder (ADHD) in adults can be a difficult task for multiple reasons. By definition, ADHD has its onset in early life, thereby necessitating a review of symptoms and behaviors during childhood. Corroborated information provided by someone who knew the adult well as a child is often essential. Detailed memories of childhood behavior, particularly in an older adult, can often be difficult to establish. Therefore, the clinician may have to rely on more global descriptions of childhood behavior to assess the presence of the three primary factors of ADHD: inattention, impulsivity, and hyperactivity. For example, a statement such as "He was a really bright child, but he struggled through school and couldn't get the work done" might be an indication of symptoms of inattentiveness.

The retrospective identification of ADHD, predominantly inattentive type, can be more elusive. Children who are neither hyperactive nor impulsive but who are inattentive and manifest many of the cognitive deficits associated with attention deficit are often overlooked in childhood. Such individuals do not report the typical childhood history of behavior problems. Establishing the childhood diagnosis is even more challenging in those individuals with high intelligence. Despite their attention problems, often they have functioned well academically, thereby concealing their inherent difficulties.

Finally, establishing the existence of ADHD symptoms in adulthood can be equally difficult. Many of the symptoms of ADHD are experienced on occasion by most people and reflect variations of normal behavior. The distinction is that with ADHD, more symptoms are consistently displayed.

The ADHD evaluation must also elucidate whether the symptom constellation reflects concomitant psychiatric conditions. An essential component of the ADHD evaluation is to establish both a differential diagnosis of other illnesses, which can mimic ADHD symptoms (i.e., is something else going on?), and the existence of comorbid conditions, which are often associated with ADHD (i.e., what else is going on?). A good differential diagnosis is important because the symptoms of ADHD are very nonspecific and can be symptomatic of other psychiatric illnesses. For example, inattentiveness is associated with mood disorders, anxiety disorders, and the spectrum of schizophrenic disorders. Additionally, individuals who have experienced chronic physical and sexual abuse as children may manifest symptoms of ADHD, thereby confusing the diagnostic picture. It is not enough to simply evaluate the behaviors as indicators of ADHD. If only an ADHD diagnosis is pursued, then only ADHD will be found. Therefore, a primary goal of the ADHD evaluation is to determine whether ADHD symptoms may by explained by other psychiatric phenomena.

Of equal importance is investigation of comorbid psychopathology. Individuals with ADHD are at risk for developing maladaptive lifestyles which can lead to a variety of psychiatric conditions, including mood disorders, substance abuse, and antisocial behavior (Biederman, Munir, & Knee, 1987; Biederman, Munir, Knee, Armentano, et al., 1987; Gomez, Janowsky, Zetin, Huey, & Clopton, 1981; Tartar, McBride, Buonpane, & Schneider, 1977). Data from our ADHD clinic show that in a sample of 114 adults who were diagnosed with ADHD, 41% met diagnostic criteria for a current comorbid disorder, as assessed by the Structured Clinical Interview for the DSM-III-R (SCID) (Spitzer, Williams, Gibbon, & First, 1990). The SCID yields Axis I diagnoses of mood disorders, anxiety disorders, substance abuse disorders, somatization disorders, and eating disorders. Furthermore, 61% had a lifetime prevalence of a comorbid condition, with 38% having two or more conditions. Thus, in a self-referred clinical population, over half of the adults with ADHD have an additional psychiatric disorder, which will influence the presenting picture and can make the diagnosis of ADHD more difficult. This does not include the assessment of personality disorders which would likely increase the incidence of comorbidity. These associated psychiatric problems can have a significant impact on the treatment of ADHD, and frequently require additional pharmacologic therapy and/or psychotherapy.

Another set of issues contributing to the difficulty in making an ADHD diagnosis in adults is related to the motivation involved in seeking the evaluation. Some patients are coerced by family members who believe a diagnosis of ADHD will explain their loved one's difficulties. Such families often hold unreasonable expectations for the diagnosis and possible treatment. Often, the individual is minimally motivated to cooperate with the evaluation, and likely minimizes or denies symptomatic behaviors. In such situations, it is difficult to make a definitive diagnosis of any psychiatric condition.

In our experience, though, more frequently the opposite situation occurs, wherein the patient has made a self-diagnosis and is convinced the diagnosis is ADHD. Many individuals seeking the evaluation have high hopes that there will be a biological explanation for the lifelong misery they have experienced. In such situations, there is concern that the individuals may have reconstructed their memories to confirm the belief that they have ADHD. Clinically, it may be difficult to determine if a person has distorted information in the direction of ADHD and away from another psychiatric explanation. In both of these situations, clinical judgment must carefully dictate conclusions and recommendations.

DEPRESSION

Differentiating between the diagnosis of depression and ADHD is sometimes difficult. The overlap in the symptoms of depression and ADHD can be significant, and many adult patients may meet criteria for both ADHD and depression. This issue is highlighted in the following case of a 45-year-old male evaluated at our center. As an adolescent, he was diagnosed with ADHD and placed on methylphenidate by a family doctor. He responded well and eventually graduated from college as an engineer. He subsequently stopped taking the medication. He worked but changed jobs frequently and saw several therapists. Each time, he was diagnosed with depression and was unsuccessfully treated with a variety of antidepressants. The ADHD evaluation revealed a classic presentation of the disorder. As a child and as an adult, he met 13 of the 14 DSM-III-R criteria. Additionally, he had a long history of depressive symptoms and met the criteria for dysthymia at the time of presentation. He was not performing adequately on his job and was worried about losing it. He was diagnosed as having ADHD and dysthymia. Initially, it was decided to treat the symptoms of ADHD, and to observe if his depression had resolved. After treatment with methylphenidate, his work performance improved and he was promoted. He is now much happier with his family and himself. The sense of hopelessness and sad affect have been resolved.

Clinicians who are not aware of ADHD usually ascribe the symptoms of inattention, susceptibility to frustration, and irritability to depression. In fact, Ratey, Greenburg, Bemporad, and Lindem (1992) reported that mood disorders were the most common diagnoses given in adults seen for treatment, prior to the diagnosis of ADHD. Difficulty concentrating is one of the criteria for major depression, as are depressed mood, decreased interest in most activities, change in weight and/or sleep patterns, loss of energy, feelings of worthlessness, and recurrent thoughts of death. Dysthymia, a more chronic condition, is depressed mood with at least two of the above symptoms for a 2-year period (American Psychiatric Association [APA], 1994).

Some distinctions between ADHD and depression can be made based on the symptomatology. The hyperactivity and restlessness of ADHD may be seen as an agitated depression, but ADHD is a lifelong condition. Individuals with ADHD are often unable to finish projects, which can easily be considered as part of a depressive syndrome. This is usually due, however, to being easily bored and shifting to other projects, rather than to the loss of energy seen in depression. In addition, patients with ADHD often have difficulty in getting to sleep and staying asleep, usually attributed to "racing thoughts." Conversely, the type of sleep disturbance reported in depression is generally early-morning awakening or excessive sleep. Finally, adults with ADHD often have feelings of worthlessness after years of underachievement.

The childhood history and the onset of symptomatology are key factors in confirming the diagnosis of ADHD. This is particularly important for the differentiation of dysthymia from ADHD, due to the chronicity of symptoms for both of these disorders. For those with periodic episodes of depression, a careful review of times when the individual is not depressed to see if the ADHD symptoms persist may help in making the distinction. In addition to the differences described above, impulsivity and impatience are symptoms of ADHD not usually seen in depression.

Although in certain cases it may be possible to diagnose either depression or ADHD, cross-sectional studies of adults find that depression is a common comorbid condition and its presence does not rule out the diagnosis of ADHD. Shekim diagnosed major depression in 10% and dysthymia in 25% of a sample of adults with ADHD (Shekim, Asarnow, Hess, Zaucha, & Wheeler, 1990). In our sample of 114 adults with ADHD, we found a lifetime prevalence for major depression (based on the SCID) in 29%; and in 19% for dysthymia. Additional evidence of the comorbidity is provided by Biederman and colleagues, who have found higher rates of affective disorders among children and their relatives with ADHD (Biederman, Faraone, Keenan, & Tsuang, 1991). Yet longitudinal studies of ADHD children have not documented an increase in depression in comparison to control groups (Mannuzza, Klein, Bessler, Malloy, & LaPadula, 1993; Weiss & Hechtman, 1993).

Explanations for the differences in depression in the longitudinal studies in children and the cross-sectional studies in adults are not clear. Despite the low levels of clinical depression seen in the longitudinal studies, these studies do show that individuals with ADHD are more likely to have a lower income, a lower educational achievement, and more psychiatric morbidity than do control groups (Weiss & Hechtman, 1993). A lower sense of self-esteem and the perception of personal failure may eventually lead to the clinical diagnoses of major depression or dysthymia. The adults with ADHD in the cross-sectional data are older than the individuals in the longitudinal samples which may account for some of the differences, as the incidence of depression increases with age (Regier et al., 1990). In addition, the sample of adults referred for ADHD evaluation may represent a more disabled subset of individuals with ADHD. It is clear, however, that a significant number of adults with ADHD will have comorbid depression.

As illustrated in the case report of the co-occurrence of ADHD and dysthymia, the authors usually initiate a trial of stimulants to treat ADHD, as we consider ADHD to be the primary diagnosis. We may add an anti-depressant at a later date if the depressive symptoms do not abate. In patients in whom ADHD is suspected but cannot be confirmed, the depression or dysthymia would typically be treated to determine if the patient improves and the symptoms that are common to both ADHD and depression abate.

BIPOLAR DISORDER

Manic depression or bipolar disorder is a severe type of mood disorder, consisting of recurrent episodes of mania and depression. Hypomania is a variant of bipolar disorder, in which the manic phases are mild, with little associated impairment of functioning. Symptoms of mania include

1. An expansive, elevated, or irritable mood
2. Grandiosity, which may be delusional
3. Reduction in sleep
4. More talkative than usual or pressured speech
5. Flight of ideas or racing thoughts
6. Distractibility
7. Increase in activity or physical restlessness
8. Excessive involvement in activities that have high potential for painful consequences (APA, 1994)

Clearly many of the symptoms of mania or hypomania are shared with ADHD, making the differentiation confusing. Conservative opinion at this conjuncture states that the presence of a bipolar disorder is primary and excludes the diagnosis of ADHD (Kane, Mikalac, Benjamin, & Barkley, 1990; Wender, Wood, & Reimherr, 1985). Yet the clinician is left with the need to make a distinction between the disorders. A mere history of the diagnosis is not sufficient, as some individuals presenting for an ADHD evaluation have been previously misdiagnosed with bipolar disorder or hypomania. A careful evaluation is necessary to determine the accuracy of previous diagnoses. A well-described history of manic episodes and a family history of bipolar illness can be very helpful. Having established the presence of childhood ADHD should not be exclusively relied on in making the differential diagnosis, as many children with bipolar disorder meet the criteria for ADHD (Akiskal & Weller, 1989; Barkley, 1990).

The main feature differentiating ADHD from mania or hypomania is that the latter diagnosis requires that mood be elevated, expansive, or irritable for at least 1 week. The mood shifts, excitability, and irritability displayed in ADHD are far less predictable, lasting from hours to days, rather than the weeks to months seen in bipolar disorder (Wender & Garfinkel, 1989). Additionally, the moodiness of an ADHD adult does not follow a cyclical pattern. Emotional lability and irritability are the result of inherent impulsivity and low frustration tolerance, which can occur frequently throughout the day. Family history may also be a crucial determinant of the differential diagnosis, as individuals with ADHD are not very likely to have relatives with bipolar illness, while those with mania often demonstrate such histories.

ANXIETY DISORDERS

As with depression, there is significant overlap between the symptoms of anxiety and ADHD, and the diagnostic goal is to establish whether the symptoms are reflective of comorbid conditions or representative of a primary diagnosis. A broad overview of the literature pertaining to the relationship between ADHD and anxiety disorders yields conflicting results. Longitudinal studies have not found significant co-occurrence between the two disorders (Mannuzza et al., 1993; Weiss & Hechtman, 1993). However, support for the relationship is provided by a variety of methodological designs. Epidemiologic and clinic samples of children with anxiety disorders and samples of children and adolescents with ADHD have shown significant comorbidity (Anderson, Williams, McGee, & Silva, 1987; Last, Strauss, & Francis, 1987). Further evidence for the association is provided by studies investigating the families of ADHD children, which demonstrate an increased prevalence of anxiety disorders in their nonreferred relatives (Biederman, Faraone, Keenan, Steingard, & Tsuang, 1991).

Although less direct, another source of support is suggested by longitudinal studies of conduct disordered youth, indicating adult outcomes with significant presence of depression and anxiety disorder (Zoccolillo, 1992). Given the high comorbidity between ADHD and conduct disorder, it is likely that ADHD also characterized this population. Finally, cross-sectional studies with ADHD adults have found significant rates of anxiety disorder (Ratey et al., 1992; Shekim et al., 1990).

Although the DSM-IV delineates 10 types of anxiety disorders, this discussion will organize the review in three groups: (1) panic and generalized anxiety disorders, (2) phobias, and (3) obsessive-compulsive disorder. Post-Traumatic Stress Disorder and Acute Stress Disorder will not be discussed as they are clearly possible comorbid conditions that bear no resemblance to ADHD, and there is no evidence to suggest that ADHD individuals are at increased risk to develop these disorders.

Panic and Generalized Anxiety Disorders

Panic disorder is characterized by the presence of recurrent panic attacks that are discrete, unexpected, and unprovoked. The DSM-IV lists a variety of physiologic and cognitive symptoms which accompany the disorder (APA, 1994). There is sufficient dissimilarity between the symptoms of panic disorder and ADHD, permitting clear recognition of either a differential diagnosis or comorbid presentation.

Generalized Anxiety Disorder (GAD) is experienced as chronic anxiety without the eruptions of panic attacks. It is defined as uncontrollable excessive anxiety and worry about a number of events or activities which is present the majority of the time over a period of at least 6 months. The symptoms of GAD include restlessness, fatigability, difficulty concentrating, irritability, muscle tension, and sleep disturbance.

Clearly, GAD and ADHD share a number of symptoms. The main feature differentiating the disorders is the excessive worrying found in GAD. When present, along with the characteristic impulsivity and childhood history of ADHD, both disorders should be diagnosed. Clinically, many ADHD patients describe chronic tension and anxiety resulting from frequent procrastination and the anticipation of disappointment and failure. Tasks of daily life that involve the ability to organize and execute plans are often met with failure by the ADHD adult. Yet one's own expectation and that of others is to accomplish these seemingly simple tasks. The repeated failure leads not only to depression, as described above, but also to significant levels of anxiety.

The treatment of patients with panic and generalized anxiety disorders and ADHD may be difficult. Tricyclic antidepressants may be useful for such patients, as stimulant medication may increase anxiety and/or provoke panic attacks. In patients placed on a trial of stimulants, anxiolytics may be added to attenuate some of the negative effects. Psychotherapy is usually indicated to manage these patients effectively.

Phobias

Phobic symptoms are clearly distinguishable from ADHD. They involve a persistent fear of a circumscribed stimulus, which upon exposure invariably provokes an anxiety response at which point the stimulus is either avoided or endured with intense anxiety. The fear or avoidant behavior significantly interferes with the person's normal routine and ability to function (APA, 1994).

Two categories of phobia are described by the DSM-IV: Specific Phobias and Social Phobia. Common specific phobias consist of fears of stimuli such as heights, flying, closed spaces, blood, and animals. Few adults with ADHD in our sample had specific phobias. On the other hand, individuals with ADHD appear to be at particular risk of developing Social Phobia. Social phobia is a persistent fear of behaving in a way that will be humiliating or embarrassing. The fear leads to avoidant behavior that interferes with occupational functioning or with social relationships and activities. Data from our ADHD sample show that 12% suffer from Social Phobia.

Phenomenologically, the experience described by ADHD patients with social anxiety can be traced to interpersonal relationships from childhood. Childhood memories involve intense feelings of embarrassment, humiliation, and rejection by peers and adults in response to the person's impulsive behaviors. Frequently, socially inappropriate behaviors, such as not waiting for one's turn, saying inappropriate things, and interrupting and intruding on others, are frequently not accepted by others, resulting in punishment, loss of friends, and seclusion. Recognition of the inappropriateness of this behavior often leads to the emergence of anxiety. When confronted with social situations, a person's fear of saying something impulsively leads to feeling awkward and extremely uncomfortable around others. Not having the behavioral repertoire to replace impulsive behavior with more socially acceptable behaviors, the ADHD individual begins to withdraw.

Obsessive-Compulsive Disorder

Obsessive-Compulsive Disorder (OCD) is defined by the presence of either obsessions or compulsions. Obsessions are intrusive or recurrent thoughts or impulses that are senseless or repugnant, which the person attempts to suppress. The most common obsessions are thoughts of violence, contamination, or self-doubt. Compulsions are repetitive, purposeful, and intentional behavior performed stereotypically or according to certain rules. The most common compulsions involve counting, checking, hand washing, and touching. The ritual is typically viewed as senseless and unpleasurable despite its tension-relieving properties (APA, 1994; Zetin, 1991). Given the definition of OCD, the differential diagnosis between OCD and ADHD is not difficult to establish.

In contrast to OCD, the Obsessive-Compulsive Personality Disorder (OCPD) is characterized by perfectionism and inflexibility. Such perfectionism interferes with task completion because the person focuses on details rather than on the main point of an activity. Additional traits include being rigid, indecisive, controlling, stingy, and hoarding, as well as being overly conscientious, restricted in emotional expression, and excessively devoted to work. Unlike OCD, the personality disorder does not elicit conflict or anxiety in the individual. Instead, there is annoyance that others do not share the same behaviors.

Contrary to Shekim et al. (1990), data from our ADHD sample do not show OCD to be a frequent comorbid condition (13% vs. 4%). Clinically, however, we have found that a number of our ADHD patients possess the traits of OCPD. The most salient trait involves a level of perfectionism and preoccupation with some details that interferes with successful task completion. This behavior appears to have developed early on as compensatory for the lack of organization and unstructuredness that typifies ADHD behavior. Many ADHD adults verbalize a need to be rigid and inflexible as a way to inhibit the underlying impulsive traits. Similarly, some become indecisive, expressing a fear of making decisions, which, when made, are impulsive and disastrous. On occasion, the indecisiveness is substantially deleterious, as the individual becomes immobilized, questioning the capacity to make any thoughtful decisions.

Finally, another point to consider is that during the evaluation, some individuals colloquially refer to behaviors as "compulsive." Behaviors such as overeating, gambling, alcohol use, and spending money are described in this manner. Most often the patient is referring to impulsive behavior, distinguishable from true compulsions which are accompanied by extreme anxiety.

SUBSTANCE ABUSE

Substance abuse is a frequent concern in the evaluation of adult patients for ADHD. The diagnosis may be complicated by symptoms caused by intoxication by or withdrawal from alcohol, stimulants, or other drugs. In addition, treatment issues are complicated by the use or abuse of alcohol or other drugs. Nevertheless, it is possible to make a diagnosis of ADHD in patients with a history of either active or prior substance abuse.

Some preliminary studies point to the higher than expected prevalence of ADHD in populations of individuals seeking treatment for alcoholism. Rounsaville and colleagues documented childhood histories of ADHD in

22% of 157 opiate addicts (Eyre, Rounsaville, & Kleber, 1982), and in 35% of cocaine abusers (Carroll & Rounsaville, 1993). Various studies have found that ADHD can be diagnosed in 14–33% of adults with active substance abuse (DeMilio, 1989; Milin, Halikas, Meller, & Morse, 1991; Wood, Wender, & Reimherr, 1983). However, prospective studies of adolescents and young adults with ADHD have found that the only children with an increased risk for developing substance abuse are those with coexistent conduct disorder (Barkley, Fischer, Edelbrock, & Smallish, 1990; Gittelman, Mannuzza, Shenker, & Bonagura, 1985; Halikas, Meller, Morse, & Lyttle, 1990; Hechtman & Weiss, 1986; Tartar, 1988). In this group, the conduct disorder preceded the development of substance abuse.

Among adults who are diagnosed with ADHD, the prevalence of substance abuse disorders is significant. Shekim found that 34% had histories of alcoholism and 34% had histories of drug abuse or dependence (Shekim et al., 1990). Our data on 114 adults with ADHD reveal that the lifetime prevalence of chemical abuse or dependency was 36% for alcohol, 21% for cannabis, 11% for cocaine and other stimulants, and 5% for polydrug dependence. At the time of their ADHD evaluation, 13% met DSM-III-R criteria for alcohol abuse or dependence in the previous month, with the corresponding figures being 3% for cannabis and 1% for cocaine.

Substance *dependence* is defined as drug or alcohol use in larger amounts over longer periods than intended, with a persistent desire or unsuccessful efforts to cut down on substance use. With substance dependence, significant time is spent in activities involving the substance, with disruption in important social, occupational or recreational activities. The individual continues using the substance despite any psychological or physical problem it creates, and there are associated symptoms of tolerance and withdrawal. Substance *abuse* is a less severe condition involving the continued use of drugs or alcohol despite knowledge of social, occupational, psychological, or physical problems caused or exacerbated by the use or recurrent use of drugs or alcohol in situations that may cause physical harm (e.g., drinking and driving) (APA, 1994).

The evaluation of patients for ADHD should always include a careful history of the use of prescription and nonprescription medication, caffeine, alcohol, and other drugs. Caffeine is often consumed in large quantities by individuals with ADHD, perhaps as a form of "self-medication." If such a patient is treated with stimulants, a dramatic decrease in consumption of caffeinated beverages is necessary to avoid the risk of sympathetic overactivity symptoms or cardiac arrthymias.

It often requires a detailed interview to explore the relationship between alcohol and other drugs and ADHD in the adult. For example, it is well known that alcohol causes a "disinhibition" in low doses, which can lead to impulsive acts as well as decreases in attention and short-term memory, all classic symptoms of ADHD. Driving accidents and citations are common in adults with ADHD, but they are also a sign of problem drinking (Barkley, Guevremont, Anastopoulos, DuPaul, & Shelton, 1993). Patients who drink regularly may have frequent episodes of "mild" alcohol withdrawal, which may mimic ADHD by the exhibition of such symptoms as anxiety, restlessness, trouble sleeping, jitteriness, irritability, and disorientation (Goodwin, 1989). Because ADHD is commonly treated with stimulants, it has been suggested that stimulants might often be the drug of choice for abuse in individuals with ADHD (Khantzian, 1985).

The symptoms of cocaine abuse may mimic those of ADHD because it causes sympathetic overactivity and acute symptoms of increased alertness, increased energy level, and excessive talking (Warner, 1993). In addition, poor judgment, agitation, and restlessness may occur. Some of the many complications of cocaine use are psychiatric and include dysphoria, anxiety, and depression, which commonly occur in association with ADHD.

It is crucial to identify the temporal relationship of alcohol and other drug use to these symptoms to determine if they are caused by ADHD or are due to the alcohol or drug abuse itself. The symptoms associated with drug and alcohol abuse are more directly related to drug use, change in dosage, or withdrawal, while those of ADHD are more consistent and should be documentable from childhood. A clear history of ADHD from childhood with persistent adult symptomatology allows the diagnosis of ADHD to be made in addition to the recognition of substance dependence or an abuse disorder.

To assist clinicians in determining which adult symptoms should be applied in making psychiatric diagnoses in patients with coexistent substance abuse, Rounsaville (1991) have developed the following criteria: "For individuals who use psychoactive substances regularly, psychiatric symptoms elicited are counted unless these symptoms took place only during a period of marked change (either a marked increase or a marked decrease) in amounts of substances taken" (Rounsaville, 1991, p. 44). They also suggest that if the individual is a current user of alcohol or other drugs, they should be interviewed at least 5 to 7 days after alcohol or drug use has occurred to minimize the impact of the effects of prior use of or withdrawal symptoms on the information provided (Rounsaville, 1991).

Another difficulty in making the ADHD diagnosis in patients with active substance abuse is that their reliability and insight regarding their behavior may be limited. In cases with active and severe drug use, the history given by the individual may be given less weight than that of a reliable collateral source.

When there is a clear history of ADHD symptoms in childhood, it is easier to validate the symptoms of ADHD in the adult and consider the substance abuse as a comorbid factor. In this situation, treatment for ADHD should be considered in addition to management appropriate for the level of the substance abuse disorder. When childhood history of ADHD is not available or not conclusive and/or the cause of the adult symptomatology is unclear, a reevaluation after a period of abstinence from drugs and alcohol (3 to 6 months, if possible) may be helpful to establish the diagnosis of ADHD. During this time, active treatment for substance abuse should be initiated.

Finally, it is important to address two concerns related to the potential for abuse of stimulant medications. Adults who think they have ADHD (on the basis of the symptoms and/or the diagnosis in a close relative) may have obtained methylphenidate from their ADHD children or from an adult with ADHD and they may have taken it several times. This is common, and we have not found it to be a sign of "drug-seeking behavior." In fact, we have not as yet seen adult ADHD patients who have abused stimulant medications, although this is an important area to monitor.

Another common concern is that children who are treated with stimulants are more likely to develop substance abuse. While there are documented case reports of abuse of methylphenidate in adolescents (Goyer, Davis, & Rapoport, 1979; Jaffe, 1991), the only study addressing this issue did not find an increased incidence of substance abuse problems among adolescents who were treated with stimulants in comparison to those who were not (Henker, Whalen, Bugental, & Barker, 1981).

ANTISOCIAL DISORDERS

Over the years, much attention has been given to the relationship between ADHD and antisocial, aggressive behavior in children and adolescents. Any discussion of Antisocial Personality Disorder (ASPD) needs to include a review of the childhood manifestations of Oppositional Defiant Disorder (ODD) and Conduct Disorder (CD). In fact, the DSM-IV definition of Antisocial Personality Disorder (ASPD) includes evidence of CD prior to age 18.

ODD is considered a childhood disorder. The essential feature of ODD is a recurring pattern of negativistic, hostile, and defiant behavior that does not diminish as the child matures, and is most evident in interactions with an individual known well to the child (APA, 1994). ODD is likely to be associated with low self-esteem and poor peer relationships; a significant subset (up to 60%) goes on to develop CD (Lahey, Loeber, Quay, Frick, & Grimm, 1992). Approximately 65% of children with ADHD develop ODD (Barkley, DuPaul, & McMurray, 1990; Barkley, Fischer, et al., 1990).

CD is defined as a persistent pattern of conduct in which the rights of others and societal norms are seriously violated (APA, 1994). CD differs from ODD in that physical aggression is far more common. By adolescence, 40 to 60% of ADHD individuals develop CD (Barkley et al., 1993).

The combination of ADHD and CD significantly increases the risk for substance abuse and ASPD in adulthood. Convincing evidence of this relationship is reported by Mannuzza and colleagues, who have followed a group of ADHD children into adulthood. Compared to the normal control group, the ADHD sample was 10 times more likely to have ASPD in adulthood (Mannuzza et al., 1993). Clearly this dictates that clinicians working with ADHD adults must evaluate each individual for the presence of ASPD or similar traits.

Several authors (Barkley, 1990; Hinshaw, Lahey, & Hart, 1993) have integrated the mulative knowledge of the mechanisms underlying the association between ADHD and antisocial behavior. In sum, a number of factors are proposed to be influential in the evolution of antisocial behavior. First, negative child-rearing practices (Patterson, DeBaryshe, & Ramsey, 1989) and parental psychopathology (Barkley, 1990; Frick et al., 1992; Lahey et al., 1988) have been shown to increase the risk of developing antisocial behavior. Second, the combination of ADHD and aggression frequently leads to academic failure, which may exacerbate frustration and increase the probability of acting-out behavior (Hinshaw, 1992a, 1992b; Hinshaw et al., 1993). Also, aggressive ADHD children experience significant peer rejection, which is known to predict further antisocial behaviors (Parker & Asher, 1987). Finally, the impulsivity of ADHD may be the essential contribution to the development of antisocial behavior (White et al., in press).

Research that has investigated the connection between ADHD and ASPD has relied on the definition provided by DSM-III and its subsequent revision. This definition has been criticized for placing primary emphasis on overt delinquent and criminal behaviors. In its attempt to objectify criteria and enhance reliability of the diagnosis, the DSM committee eliminated classic views of sociopathy, which is characterized by an aggressive interpersonal pattern with an absence of loyalty, anxiety, or guilt. Many individuals who are not criminals fit into mainstream society displaying these traits through socially acceptable means (Millon, 1981; Skodol, 1989).

Millon (1981) has outlined traits that more appropriately define the sociopathic personality. These include

1. Hostile affect, illustrated by an irascible temper that flares quickly into argument
2. Social rebelliousness evidenced by contemptuousness toward authority
3. Social vindictiveness displayed by satisfaction when denigrating or

humiliating others

4. Fearlessness evident in impulsive behavior and attraction to danger
5. An assertive self-image, proudly characterizing oneself as self-reliant and hardheaded
6. Projection of one's own mistrustful and hostile attitudes onto others

Interestingly, these traits include behaviors similar to the childhood diagnosis of ODD. ODD behaviors include

1. Frequent loss of temper
2. Argumentativeness
3. Active defiance of rules or requests of others
4. Intentionally provoking others
5. Blaming others for one's own mistakes
6. Easily annoyed by others
7. Frequent feelings of anger or resentment
8. Being spiteful or vindictive (APA, 1994)

Our clinical experience has shown that many ADHD adults continue to display the ODD behaviors that characterized their childhood and adolescence. Most do not meet the DSM-IV definition of ASPD, but they display many of the traits of Millon's sociopathic personality.

In addition to evaluating the presence of ASPD, we routinely probe for the extent of ODD behaviors and the subsequent impact on social, occupational, and interpersonal functioning. Often, patients who have the most difficulty with their ADHD symptoms are the ones who continue to display the same ODD behaviors first evidenced in their childhood.

SCHIZOPHRENIA

The diagnosis of ADHD is preempted by the presence of schizophrenia, and most often it is not difficult to distinguish the disorders. Despite the common feature of attentional deficits in both disorders, there are marked symptomatic differences. In an acute phase, schizophrenics display delusions, hallucinations, incoherent speech, catatonic behavior, and flat or inappropriate affect. Even in the residual phase, behaviors are clearly different from ADHD, as there is often marked impairment in functioning, peculiar behavior, circumstantial speech, and affective flattening (APA, 1994).

Nevertheless, there are several circumstances in which the differential diagnosis may be difficult to make. One such situation is an evaluation of an individual predisposed to schizophrenia, prior to the onset of a psychotic episode. Behavior of the preschizophrenic child or adolescent is characterized by attentional deficits, emotional lability, poor frustration tolerance, and disciplinary problems (Weintraub, 1987; Winters, Cornblatt, & Erlenmeyer-Kimling, 1991). Prospectively and retrospectively, such behaviors could readily be diagnosed as ADHD and Oppositional Defiant or Conduct Disorder. Complicating the evaluation, particularly when presenting to an ADHD specialty practice, is the either conscious or semiconscious tendency to distort information to sway the opinion in the direction of ADHD.

An example of such a situation occurred in our ADHD clinic. The patient was a 19-year-old female referred by another mental health professional who diagnosed her with ADHD. The patient was described as having significant difficulty with inattentiveness as a child. Symptoms of impulsivity and hyperactivity as well as ODD surfaced with the onset of puberty and continued as a young adult. There was significant impairment in educational and occupational functioning, as well as in interpersonal relationships. Her parents were very hopeful that a diagnosis of ADHD would explain the young woman's difficulties and offer subsequent successful treatment.

There were several distinguishing features in this situation that shed light on a possible differential diagnosis. Minimized by the family was the occurrence of a psychotic episode, seemingly initiated by treatment with fluoxetine. Evidence of bizarre behavior was noted during childhood. From an early age, the girl kept a running list of anyone who was "mean" to her: she reviewed the list frequently. Results from the patient's MMPI-2 (Butcher, Dahlstrom, Graham, Tellegen, & Kaemmer, 1989) responses were also helpful in ruling out ADHD. This test showed significant elevations on scales most sensitive to psychotic and paranoid behaviors. Finally, there was a positive family history for schizophrenia and bipolar illness. The literature regarding predictors of schizophrenia onset indicates that having first-degree relatives with schizophrenia is the best predictor of schizophrenia in the patient (Parnas & Mednick, 1990; Parnas, Schulsinger, Schulsinger, Teasdale, & Mednick, 1982).

A similar word of caution applies to the diagnosis of schizoaffective disorder. We have on occasion encountered patients with extensive psychiatric histories, including a diagnosis of schizoaffective disorder, who are convinced they are suffering from ADHD. The disorder is conceptualized as an illness consisting of a mood disorder, either major depression or mania, with concurrent symptoms of schizophrenia. As has been described for each of those disorders, the symptoms can mimic those seen in ADHD. The same guidelines recommended to distinguish ADHD from those disorders should be applied in making the differential diagnosis of schizoaffective disorder.

Another situation which may complicate the differential diagnosis of schizophrenia and ADHD has been advanced by Bellak and associates, who hypothesize that certain psychoses are misdiagnosed as schizophrenia, when in fact they result primarily from ADHD (Bellak, 1994; Bellak & Charles, 1979; Bellak, Kay, & Opler, 1987). "ADD psychosis" occurs when cognitive and social development has been severely impaired by ADHD symptoms. The resultant personality structure is disturbed to the point of producing serious disturbance in reality testing, judgment, and self-image. The key distinctions between ADD psychosis and schizophrenia are outlined in Bellak et al. (1987). Emphasis is given to the differing symptomatology: for example, in ADD psychosis, there is an absence of hallucinations, magical thinking, and loose associations; when delusions appear, they are not well systematized; and poor reality testing occurs due to impulsivity. Those with an ADD psychosis show a lack of response or worsening of symptoms when treated with neuroleptics. Conversely, schizophrenics frequently decompensate when treated with stimulant medications.

As alluded to by these authors, the phenomenon of ADD psychosis may actually be ADHD with severe character pathology, such as borderline personality disorder. The co-occurrence of these disorders will be discussed in more detail in a subsequent section. Suffice it to say that the notion of ADD psychosis seems to confound the diagnosis of ADHD with that of a personality disorder. The characteristics described by Bellak et al. (1987) are likely secondary effects of ADHD rather than primary symptoms, and should be diagnosed and treated as separate entities.

BORDERLINE PERSONALITY DISORDER

Borderline Personality Disorder is characterized by a pervasive pattern of unstable mood, behavior, relationships, and self-image beginning by early adulthood (APA, 1994). Symptoms of affective lability, irritability, and impulsivity overlap with other disorders, including ADHD. Currently, prevailing opinion asserts that these two disorders are exclusive of each other (Kane et al., 1990; Wender et al., 1985). Such advice is well heeded at this point, given our lack of understanding of the disorders.

Yet, there are several reports in the literature suggesting that ADHD may be a precursor to the emergence of the borderline personality in a subgroup of individuals with the disorder. This subgroup is described as having an early onset of emotional and functional difficulties, including academic problems, hyperactivity, aggressive and antisocial behavior, and substance abuse during adolescence (Andrulonis, Glueck, Stroebel, & Vogel,

1982; Andrulonis & Vogel, 1984). Effective treatment of ADHD symptoms in a borderline patient was reported by Hooberman and Stern (1984), raising the possibility of the comorbidity of the two disorders.

Our clinical experience has suggested that the coexistence of ADHD and borderline personality may be possible. When encountered, these patients are markedly disturbed, presenting with significant dysfunction in many areas of life and often with histories of mood disorder and substance abuse. Unquestionably, further study is needed to determine the possible comorbidity of these conditions, as well as the appropriateness of treatment with stimulant medication. Until more is known, such patients should be treated cautiously.

HISTRIONIC PERSONALITY DISORDER

Although there are not published reports to date, our clinical experience has shown that some ADHD patients also have features of histrionic personalities. In fact, the features of Histrionic Personality Disorder significantly overlap with ADHD. The histrionic personality is described in an individual who is persistently seeking attention, stimulation, and excitement. When there is delay of gratification, behavior is often impulsive and overreactive. Interpersonal relationships are characteristically shallow and fleeting. Affect is highly labile, and endeavors are initially approached enthusiastically, then followed by rapid boredom (Millon, 1981).

ADHD behaviors that overlap with a histrionic personality are behaviors such as constant attention seeking as seen by interrupting and intruding, self-centeredness and demanding that one's needs be met without delay, low tolerance for delay of gratification, and being self-absorbed and unaware of the impact of one's own behavior on others. This is also seen in conversations where there is a lack of perception of the appropriate social cues and a tendency to dominate the interaction.

It is speculated that ADHD leads to the development of histrionic characteristics in some individuals, particularly those who have a chronic history of impaired social functioning. Many ADHD individuals describe being easily distracted and inattentive when interacting with others. Often they are unaware of the details of conversations and report feeling that their only successful social interactions occur when the discussions are short and uninvolved.

Coupled with the impulsivity, reactivity, and difficulty sustaining effort with any one event, some ADHD individuals seem prone to developing a histrionic personality style. At this point, this hypothesis is conjectural and is in need of supportive empirical evidence. Nevertheless, clinicians should note that such a style of interpersonal functioning may accompany the ADHD patient, and presence of these behaviors can have an effect on therapeutic outcome.

INTERMITTENT EXPLOSIVE DISORDER

There has been some suggestion that the explosive personality or Intermittent Explosive Disorder is a sequela to ADHD (Morrison & Minkoff, 1975). Intermittent Explosive Disorder is defined as discrete episodes of loss of control of aggressive impulses resulting in serious assaultive acts or destruction of property. The diagnosis is controversial, and many doubt the existence of episodic dyscontrol that is not symptomatic of other diagnoses that must be ruled out before this diagnosis can be made. These include psychotic disorders, Organic Personality Syndrome, Antisocial or Borderline Personality Disorder, Conduct Disorder, or intoxication with psychoactive substance (APA, 1994).

A feature critically distinguishing the disorder from ADHD is that there are not signs of generalized impulsivity or aggressiveness between the episodes. Clearly, ADHD is characterized by pervasive impulsivity, thereby making the diagnosis of Intermittent Explosive Disorder noncompatible with ADHD. When aggressive and explosive temper are present in the ADHD individual, additional diagnoses, such as those listed above, should be considered.

CONCLUSION

This review has examined the interrelationships between ADHD and other psychiatric conditions. Clinical and empirical evidence indicates that depression, anxiety, substance abuse, and personality disorders such as antisocial, obsessive-compulsive, and histrionic personalities can either coexist with or mimic the presentation of ADHD. Bipolar disorder and schizophrenia are considered conditions that preempt the diagnosis of ADHD, while the issue remains controversial with borderline personality disorder.

Evaluation of ADHD in adults is a complicated endeavor, involving a longitudinal perspective not only of the individual's development of ADHD symptoms but also of the negative outcomes of the untreated disorder. In addition to the various psychiatric disorders discussed in this review, ADHD can lead to significant impairment in interpersonal, occupational, and educational functioning. Therefore, a comprehensive evaluation should assess functioning in these domains, as well as assess possible psychiatric disturbance. A comprehensive evaluation lends itself to multimodal treatment which is often necessary for effective management of this population.

Conversely, the time has come for ADHD to be considered a routine part of all psychiatric evaluations of adults. Empirical evidence has definitively established the persistence of the disorder beyond childhood. Most individuals with ADHD are seen in settings that do not specialize in the diagnosis, and typically the symptoms are attributed to other causes. Proper identification and treatment can spare the patient continued suffering.

Finally, it should be noted that this discussion has focused on the presentation of ADHD in a clinical setting. It is likely that there are many individuals with ADHD who have led highly productive and satisfactory lives and have not experienced the impairment described in this review. Such individuals appear to have been able to compensate and develop strategies to cope with their ADHD symptoms. It is our hope that the strengths of these individuals will be identified and their skills taught to the less fortunate sufferers.

REFERENCES

Akiskal, H. S., & Weller, E. B. (1989). Mood disorders and suicide in children and adolescents. In H. I. Kaplan, & B. J. Sadock (Eds.), *Comprehensive textbook of psychiatry* (V, Vol. 2) (pp. 1981–1994). Baltimore: Williams & Wilkins.

American Psychiatric Association. (1994). *Diagnostic and statistical manual of mental disorders* (4th ed.). Washington, DC: Author.

Anderson, J. C., Williams, S., McGee, R., Silva, P. A. (1987). DSM-III disorders in preadolescent children. *Archives of General Psychiatry, 44,* 69–76.

Andrulonis, P. A., Glueck, B. C., Stroebel, C. F., & Vogel, N. G. (1982). Borderline personality subcategories. *Journal of Nervous and Mental Disease, 170,* 670–679.

Andrulonis, P. A., & Vogel, N. G. (1984). Comparison of borderline personality subcategories to schizophrenic and affective disorders. *British Journal of Psychiatry, 144,* 358–363.

Barkley, R. A. (1990). *Attention deficit hyperactivity disorder: A handbook for diagnosis and treatment.* New York: Guilford Press.

Barkley, R. A., DuPaul, G. J., & McMurray, M. B. (1990). Comprehensive evaluation of attention deficit disorder with or without hyperactivity as defined by research criteria. *Journal of Consulting and Clinical Psychology, 58,* 775–789.

Barkley, R. A., Fischer, M., Edelbrock, C. S., & Smallish, L. (1990). The adolescent outcome of hyperactive children diagnosed by research criteria: I. An 8-year prospective follow-up study. *Journal of the American Academy of Child and Adolescent Psychiatry, 29,* 546–557.

Barkley, R. A., Guevremont, D. C., Anastopoulos, A. D., DuPaul, G. J., & Shelton, T. L. (1993). Driving-related risks and outcomes of attention deficit hyperactivity disorder in adolescents and young adults: A 3- to 5-year follow-up survey. *Pediatrics, 92,* 212–218.

Bellak, L. (1994). The schizophrenic syndrome and attention deficit disorder: Thesis, antithesis, and synthesis? *American Psychologist, 49,* 25–29.

Bellak, L., & Charles, E. (1979). Schizophrenic syndrome related to minimal brain dysfunction: A possible neurologic subgroup. *Schizophrenia Bulletin, 5,* 480–489.

Bellak, L., Kay, S. R., & Opler, L. A. (1987). Attention deficit disorder psychosis as a diagnostic category. *Psychiatric Developments, 3,* 239–263.

Biederman, J., Faraone, S. V., Keenan, K., Steingard, R., & Tsuang, M. T. (1991). Familial association between attention deficit disorder and anxiety disorders. *American Journal of Psychiatry, 148,* 251–256.

Biederman, J., Faraone, S. V., Keenan, K., Tsuang, M. T. (1991). Evidence of familial association between attention deficit disorder and major affective disorders. *Archives of General Psychiatry, 48,* 633–642.

Biederman, J., Munir, K., & Knee, D. (1987). Conduct and oppositional disorder in clinically referred children with attention deficit disorder: A controlled family study. *Journal of the American Academy of Child and Adolescent Psychiatry, 26,* 724–727.

Biederman, J., Munir, K., Knee, D., Armentano, M., Autor, S., Waternaux, C., & Tsuang, M. (1987). High rate of affective disorders in probands with attention deficit disorders and in their relatives: A controlled family study. *American Journal of Psychiatry, 144,* 330–333.

Butcher, J. N., Dahlstrom, W. G., Graham, J. R., Tellegen, A., & Kaemmer, B. (1989). *MMPI-2 (Minnesota Multiphasic Personality Inventory-2): Manual for administration and scoring.* Minneapolis: University of Minnesota Press.

Carroll, K. M., & Rounsaville, B. J. (1993). History and significance of childhood attention deficit disorder in treatment seeking cocaine abusers. *Comprehensive Psychiatry, 34,* 75–82.

DeMilio, L. (1989). Psychiatric syndromes in adolescent substance abusers. *American Journal of Psychiatry, 146,* 1212–1214.

Eyre, S. L., Rounsaville, B. J., & Kleber, H. D. (1982). History of childhood hyperactivity in a clinic population of opiate addicts. *Journal of Nervous and Mental Disease, 170,* 522–529.

Frick, P. J., Lahey, B. B., Loeber, R., Stouhamer-Loeber, M., Christ, M. G., & Hanson, K. (1992). Familial risk factors to oppositional defiant disorder and conduct disorder: Parental psychopathology and maternal parenting. *Journal of Consulting and Clinical Psychology, 60,* 49–55.

Gittelman, R., Mannuzza, S., Shenker, R., & Bonagura, N. (1985). Hyperactive boys almost grown up. *Archives of General Psychiatry, 42,* 937–947.

Gomez, R. L., Janowsky, D., Zetin, M., Huey, L., & Clopton, P. L. (1981). Adult psychiatric diagnosis and symptoms compatible with the hyperactive syndrome: A retrospective study. *Journal of Clinical Psychiatry, 42,* 389–394.

Goodwin, D. W. (1989). Alcoholism. In H. I. Kaplan & B. J. Sadock (Eds.), *Comprehensive textbook of psychiatry* (V, Vol. 1) (pp. 686–698). Baltimore: Williams & Wilkins.

Goyer, P. F., Davis, G. C., & Rapoport, J. L. (1979). Abuse of prescribed stimulant medication by a 13-year-old hyperactive boy. *Journal of the American Academy of Child and Adolescent Psychiatry, 18,* 170–175.

Halikas, J. A., Meller, J., Morse, C., & Lyttle, M. D. (1990). Predicting substance abuse in juvenile offender: Attention deficit disorder versus aggressivity. *Child Psychology and Human Development, 21,* 49–55.

Hechtman, L., & Weiss, G. (1986). Controlled prospective fifteen-year follow-up of hyperactives as adults: Non-medical drug and alcohol use and anti-social behavior. *Canadian Journal of Psychology, 31,* 557–567.

Henker, B., Whalen, C. K., Bugental, D. B., & Barker, C. (1981). Licit and illicit drug use patterns in stimulant-treated children and their peers. In K. D. Gadow & J. Loney (Eds.), *Psychosocial aspects of drug treatment for hyperactivity* (pp. 443–462). Boulder, CO: Westview Press.

Hinshaw, S. P. (1992a). Academic underachievement, attention deficits, and aggression: Comorbidity and implications for intervention. *Journal of Consulting and Clinical Psychology, 60,* 893–903.

Hinshaw, S.P. (1992b). Externalizing behavior problems and academic underachievement in childhood and adolescence: Causal relationships and underlying mechanisms. *Psychological Bulletin, 111,* 127-155.

Hinshaw, S. P., Lahey, B. B., & Hart, E. L. (1993). Issues of taxonomy and comorbidity in the development of conduct disorder. *Development and Psychopathology, 5,* 31–50.

Hooberman, D., & Stern, T. A. (1984). Treatment of attention deficit and borderline personality disorders with psychostimulants: Case report. *Journal of Clinical Psychiatry, 45*(10), 441–442.

Jaffe, S. L. (1991). Intranasal abuse of prescribed methylphenidate by an alcohol and drug abusing adolescent with ADHD. *Journal of the American Academy of Child and Adolescent Psychiatry, 30,* 773–775.

Kane, R., Mikalac, C., Benjamin, S., & Barkley, R. A. (1990). Assessment and treatment of adults with ADHD. In R. A. Barkley, *Attention deficit hyperactivity disorder: A handbook for diagnosis and treatment* (pp. 613–654). New York: Guilford Press.

Khantzian, E. J. (1985). The self-medication hypothesis of addictive disorders: focus on heroin and cocaine dependence. *American Journal of Psychiatry, 142,* 1259–1264.

Lahey, B. B., Loeber, R., Quay, H. C., Frick, P. J., & Grimm, J. (1992). Oppositional defiant and conduct disorders: Issues to be resolved for DSM-IV. *Journal of the American Academy of Child and Adolescent Psychiatry, 31,* 539–546.

Lahey, B. B., Piacentini, J. C., McBurnett, K., Stone, P., Hartdagen, S., &

Hynd, G. (1988). Psychopathology in the parents of children with conduct disorder and hyperactivity. *Journal of the American Academy of Child and Adolescent Psychiatry, 27,* 163–170.

Last, C. G., Strauss, C. C., Francis, G. (1987). Comorbidity among childhood anxiety disorders. *Journal of Nervous and Mental Disease, 175,* 726–730.

Mannuzza, S., Klein, R. G., Bessler, A., Malloy, P., & LaPadula, M. (1993). Adult outcome of hyperactive boys. *Archives of General Psychiatry, 50,* 565–576.

Milin, R., Halikas, J. A., Meller, J. E., & Morse, C. (1991). Psychopathology among substance abusing juvenile offenders. *Journal of the American Academy of Child and Adolescent Psychiatry, 30,* 569–574.

Millon, T. (1981). *Disorders of personality DSM-III: Axis II.* New York: Wiley.

Morrison, J. R., & Minkoff, K. (1975). Explosive personality as a sequel to the hyperactive-child syndrome. *Comprehensive Psychiatry, 16,* 343–348.

Parker, J. G., & Asher, S. R. (1987). Peer relations and later personal adjustment: Are low-accepted children at risk. *Psychological Bulletin, 102,* 357–389.

Parnas, J., & Mednick, S. A. (1990). Early predictors of onset and course of schizophrenia and schizophrenia spectrum. In H. Hafner & W. F. Gattaz (Eds.), *Search for the causes of schizophrenia* (pp. 34–47). Berlin: Springer-Verlag.

Parnas, J., Schulsinger, F., Schulsinger, H., Teasdale, T. W., & Mednick, S. A. (1982). Behavioral precursors of the schizophrenia spectrum. *Archives of General Psychiatry, 39,* 658–664.

Patterson, G. R., DeBaryshe, B. D., & Ramsey, E. (1989). A developmental perspective on antisocial behavior. *American Psychologist, 44,* 329–335.

Ratey, J. J., Greenberg, M. S., Bemporad, J. R., & Lindem, K. J. (1992). Unrecognized attention-deficit hyperactivity disorder in adults presenting for outpatient psychotherapy. *Journal of Child and Adolescent Psychopharmacology, 2,* 267–275.

Regier, D. A., Farmer, M. E., Rae, D. S., Locke, B. Z., Keith, S. J., Judd, L. L., & Goodwin, F. K. (1990). Comorbidity of mental disorders with alcohol and other drug abuse. *Journal of the American Medical Association, 264,* 2511–2518.

Rounsaville, B. J. (1991). Psychiatric diagnoses of treatment-seeking cocaine abusers. *Archives of General Psychiatry, 48,* 43–51.

Shekim, W. O., Asarnow, R. F., Hess, E., Zaucha, K., & Wheeler, N. (1990). A clinical and demographic profile of a sample of adults with attention deficit hyperactivity disorder, residual state. *Comprehensive Psychiatry, 31,* 416–425.

Skodol, A. E. (1989). *Problems in differential diagnosis: From DSM-III to DSM-III-R in clinical practice.* Washington, DC: American Psychiatric Press.

Spitzer, R. L., Williams, J. B. W., Gibbon, M., & First, M. B. (1990). *Structured Clinical Interview for DSM-III-R–Patient Edition (With Psychotic Screen), Version 1.0.* Washington, DC: American Psychiatric Press.

Tartar, R. E. (1988). Are there inherited behavioral traits that predispose to substance abuse? *Journal of Consulting and Clinical Psychology, 56,* 189–196.

Tartar, R. E., McBride, H., Buonpane, N., & Schneider, D. U. (1977). Differentiation of alcoholics: Childhood history of minimal brain dysfunction, family history, and drinking pattern. *Archives of General Psychiatry, 34,* 761–768.

Warner, E. A. (1993). Cocaine abuse. *Annals of Internal Medicine, 119,* 226–235.

Weintraub, S. (1987). Risk factors in schizophrenia. *Schizophrenia Bulletin, 13,* 439–450.

Weiss, G., & Hechtman, L. T. (1993). *Hyperactive children grown up: ADHD in children, adolescents, and adults.* New York: Guilford Press.

Wender, P. H., & Garfinkel, B. D. (1989). Attention-deficit hyperactivity disorder: Adult manifestations. In H. I. Kaplan & B. J. Sadock (Eds.), *Comprehensive textbook of psychiatry* (V, Vol. 5, pp. 1837–1842). Baltimore: Williams & Wilkins.

Wender, P. H., Wood, D. R., & Reimherr, F. W. (1985). Pharmacological treatment of attention deficit disorder, residual type (ADD, RT), "Minimal Brain Dysfunction," Hyperactivity in Adults. *Psychopharmacology Bulletin, 21,* 222–231.

White, J. L., Moffitt, T. E., Caspi, A., Jeglum, D., Needles, D., & Stouthamer-Loeber, M. (1994). Measuring impulsivity and examining its relationship to delinquency. *Journal of Abnormal Psychology, 103,* 192–205.

Winters, L., Cornblatt, B. A., Erlenmeyer-Kimling, L. (1991). The prediction of psychiatric disorders in late adolescence. In E. F. Walker (Ed.), *Schizophrenia: A life-course developmental perspective* (pp. 123–137). San Diego: Academic Press.

Wood, D., Wender, P. H., & Reimherr, F. W. (1983). The prevalence of attention deficit disorder, residual type, or minimal brain dysfunction, in a population of male alcoholic patients. *American Journal of Psychiatry, 140,* 95–98.

Zetin, M. (1991). Obsessive-compulsive disorder. *Stress Medicine, 6,* 311–321.

Zoccolillo, M. (1992). Co-occurrence of conduct disorder and its adult outcomes with depressive and anxiety disorders: A review. *Journal of the American Academy of Child and Adolescent Psychiatry, 31,* 547–556.

4

Attention Deficits and Neurodevelopmental Variation in Older Adolescents and Adults

ADRIAN D. SANDLER

Attention deficits rarely exist in isolation. The truth of this somewhat controversial statement is especially evident in adults whose long-standing attention deficits are embedded in a complex and interconnected array of neurocognitive and psychiatric vulnerabilities and complications. Among the most common of these are learning disorders, underachievement, depression, and substance abuse. Clinicians who evaluate adults with attention deficits face the considerable challenge of elucidating and teasing apart these diverse factors and the relationships among them in order to manage effectively these problems of day-to-day living. No longer is it sufficient for clinicians to address the relatively simple question, Does the person have attention deficits? without also asking, What else is going on? The purpose of this chapter is to examine some critical "what else" issues in the realm of learning and achievement.

At the outset, it is necessary to introduce a term that appears in the title of this chapter—namely, *neurodevelopmental variation*. The conceptual framework, or paradigm, in which the term is embedded is discussed in depth later in the chapter. There are three important points implied by the term. First, the prefix *neuro* implies that our discussion of learning and its disorders is confined to neurologically based phenomena that have an impact on learning and achievement. While recognizing the important roles of emotional, motivational, and environmental factors in the development, expression, and outcome of learning problems, our focus is on individual variations in cognition and information processing. In this context, attention deficits are discussed as one of many critical neurologically based learning problems affecting adults. Second, the "developmental" dimension implied by the term stresses the changing manifestations of attention deficits over the lifespan as well as the constantly evolving task demands and performance expectations. Third, the use of the term *variation* implies that the author is considering that these neurodevelopmental phenomena occur along a continuum rather than as discrete syndromes. Decisions regarding the presence or absence of "dysfunction" are based on considerations of severity and observed impact on achievement and productivity, rather than on rigid and arbitrary cut points. In this regard, the discussion of neurodevelopmental variations in older adolescents and adults has more in common with dimensional models (Shaywitz, Escobar, Shaywitz, Fletcher, & Makuch, 1992) than categorical models (Yule & Rutter, 1985) of learning disabilities.

The chapter begins with a review of historical and present perspectives of learning disabilities. The heterogeneity of learning disabilities is stressed, and some research evidence supporting the conceptualization of attention deficits as a learning disorder is presented. Next, there is a discussion of the interactive developmental paradigm of learning disabilities that the author finds to be most helpful in clinical work with adolescents and adults. Issues of continuity, discontinuity, and development of these disorders over the lifespan are stressed. This leads into a description of the key learning disorders evident in older adolescents. The pivotal role of attention in learning and productivity in postsecondary education and the workplace is discussed. The author's perspective is based on extensive clinical research experience with the development of structured interview techniques in this age group.

LEARNING DISABILITIES: HISTORICAL AND PRESENT PERSPECTIVES

Although the early case studies of learning disabilities (Kussmaul, 1877; Hinshelwood, 1895) represented diverse manifestations of learning problems, the first efforts to develop a conceptual model of learning disabilities, beginning with Orton's theory of delayed cerebral dominance (1928), were based on single-factor deficit conceptualizations (Hooper & Willis, 1989).

Unitary explanations of learning disabilities continued through the 1970s as represented by Bender's theory of perceptual deficit (1956) and Ayres's theory of sensory integration deficit (1978), among others. This single-factor conceptualization led to the mistaken belief that the learning disabled population is a homogeneous group. Increasingly, such models were questioned because they failed to account for the clinical heterogeneity of learning disabilities.

The trend since the 1970s has been toward conceptualizations that reflect multidimensional mechanisms and that account for the heterogeneity that clinicians encounter. This trend is reflected in more recent definitions of learning disability (LD). An interagency committee sponsored by the National Institute of Child Health and Human Development (Interagency Committee on Learning Disabilities [ICLD], 1987) defined LD as "a heterogeneous group of disorders of presumed neurological origin which selectively interferes with the acquisition and use of listening, reading, speaking, writing, mathematics and social skills." Other recently proposed formulations (Association for Children with Learning Disabilities, 1985; ICLD, 1987) further broadened the definition of learning disabilities by acknowledging their chronicity and potential impact on social and vocational skills. Despite the trends and research evidence reflected in these definitions, there continues to be a narrow and slavish adherence to outdated and discredited discrepancy criteria whereby significant discrepancy between IQ and achievement test scores is taken as the sole indicator of whether or not a learning disability exists.

Most experts agree that there are discernible learning disability subtypes, with varying characteristics and effects. It has been 20 years since Denckla (1972) published her paper advocating increased emphasis on "splitting" children into different syndromes or profiles that more accurately reflect their unique abilities and disabilities. Subsequent research has approached the subtyping issue in two ways. Initial efforts were based on a clinical-inferential approach. More recently, many investigators have used computer-analyzed empirical categorization strategies to group children on achievement, cognitive, and/or linguistic measures. Both methodologies have a role. There is a modicum of consensus on the existence of two broad subtypes—namely, verbal and nonverbal learning disabilities (Rourke, 1989). Other investigators have proposed a greater number of subtypes based on research evidence. Among these is the recent work of Pennington (1991), who proposed a model of five modular brain functions, linking functional neuropsychological deficits to neuroanatomical data and evidence from family studies. The five modular functions and their localizations proposed by Pennington are shown in Table 4-1.

TABLE 4-1
Modular Brain Functions and Learning Disorders

Function	Localization	Disorder
Phonological processing	Left perisylvian	Dyslexia
Executive functions	Prefrontal	Attention deficits
Spatial cognition	Posterior right hemisphere	Specific math/writing
Social cognition	Limbic, orbital, right hemisphere	Autism spectrum
Long-term memory	Hippocampus, amygdala	Amnesia

Reprinted with permission from *Diagnosing Learning Disorders: A Neurological Framework* by B. F. Pennington. Copyright 1991 Guilford Press.

It is noteworthy that the executive functions module, largely residing in the frontal lobes, is considered to be primarily responsible for attention regulation, organization, planning, and strategy use. Indeed, Denckla uses a schematic to illustrate the *central* role of executive functions in input, processing, and output cognitive functions (see Figure 4-1). It is not surprising that executive dysfunctions, such as attention deficits, have enormous impact on a host of other cognitive functions. It is also to be anticipated that clinical evaluations of children with attention deficits frequently uncover evidence of other learning disorders and neurodevelopmental dysfunctions (Levine, 1987). Estimates of concurrent learning disabilities among children with attention deficits vary from 10 to 90%. Although there are no reliable data concerning the co-occurrence of these conditions in adults, our impressions are that the frequency is comparably high. The converse is also true, so that individuals with specific learning disabilities frequently have significant attention deficits also. We shall return to the critical role of attention in learning and productivity later in the chapter. Suffice it to say that numerous lines of evidence point to a multidimensional model of learning disabilities, in which attention deficits are pivotal.

AN INTERACTIVE DEVELOPMENTAL PARADIGM
OF LEARNING DISABILITIES

In our clinical evaluations of adolescents and adults with learning and attentional problems, we make use of an interactive and developmental paradigm of learning disabilities (Levine, Hooper, et al., 1993). The paradigm emphasizes rich clinical description of strengths and weaknesses, thereby going beyond generic labels. The strengths and weaknesses to which I refer are in the fundamental neurocognitive operations that contribute ultimately to learning and productivity. We call these *elemental functions.* Elemental functions can be thought of as subconstructs grouped within well established interdependent neurodevelopmental constructs, which include attention, memory, language, visual-spatial ordering, temporal-sequential ordering, neuromotor/graphomotor function, social cognition, and higher order cognition.

Central to this paradigm is the notion that elemental functions interact to achieve developmentally specific *production components*, which operate in synchrony to yield certain outcomes that are important for learning and productivity. A deficient outcome at a specific time in development (such as difficulty with algebra in high school) entails one or more weak elemental functions (such as procedural recall or attention to detail) which precipitate the breakdown of a necessary production component (such as quadratic equations). It is important to remember that no academic outcomes entail single elemental functions operating in isolation. Successful completion of a task demands the selective recruitment and integration of multiple elemental functions. This process is supported by research in reading, for example (Stanovich, 1980). Implicit in this paradigm is the notion that delineation of the production components of a task and the requisite el-

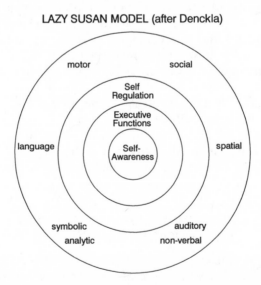

Figure 4-1. This schematic shows the "Lazy Susan" model of cognitive functions, with self-awareness, executive functions, and self-regulation occupying a central role in input and in processing and output functions. Reprinted with permission from Martha Bridge Denckla.

emental functions facilitates the diagnostic process and helps to generate specific management strategies to improve learning and productivity.

The unique contribution and relevance of such a model to a clinical understanding of adolescent and adult learning problems can best be illustrated with the example of reading. In the younger child, the emphasis is on decoding, and research has confirmed the critical role of phonological processing problems in the majority of children with specific reading disabilities. Many high school students, college students, and young people in the workforce also struggle with reading. For some, the problem is of long-standing, with significant decoding and reading comprehension problems having been evident in early elementary school. For many others, however, the increased reading demands in secondary school may have led to the emergence of reading problems for the first time. Whereas young children learn to read, adolescents must read to learn. In order to do so effectively, the two key production components of reading (decoding and comprehension) must be accomplished efficiently and in synchrony. These production components are highly dependent on critical elemental functions within the constructs of attention, memory, language, and higher order cognition (see Figure 4-2).

Attention to detail (*selective attention*) is essential for accurate decoding. If students are inattentive to the internal detail of words that are in their sight word vocabulary, and instead rely too heavily on first and last letters, they will make numerous impulsive errors, such as reading "station" for "stallion." Thus, an adolescent may continue to show evidence of decoding problems and dysfluency because of attention deficits. A tendency to be easily distracted or cognitively fatigued (weakly *sustained attention*) is likely to cause the "losing my place" or "tuning out" while reading phenomena. Such lapses in attention and mental effort maintenance are likely to have an impact on reading comprehension. This is especially the case in high school and beyond, where texts are packed with information that is dense and detailed, and momentary attentional lapses may lead to significant gaps in registration of information. Another critical attentional elemental function in reading is *self-monitoring*. Students with attention deficits are likely to get to the end of a page or even a chapter before realizing that they have tuned out and missed the entire text!

As discussed earlier, the executive functions are closely related to attentional function in modular concepts of learning and cognition. *Selective intention* is a necessary prerequisite for successful reading. That is to say, an adolescent must first determine what to read and how to read it. This poses a significant problem for many adolescents and adults with attention deficits who struggle to get started on a task because of multiple competing de-

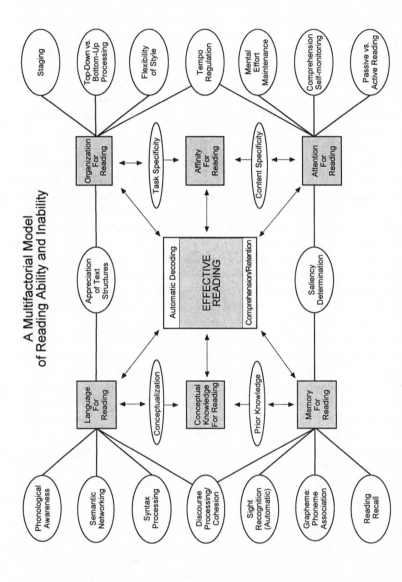

Figure 4-2. This schematic illustrates a multifactorial model of reading ability and inability, in which a range of elemental functions within the domains of attention, organization, memory, and language work in synchrony to accomplish the production components of decoding and comprehension. Reprinted with permission from M. D. Levine.

mands. *Task staging* and sequencing is also important, as large reading assignments may need to be broken down into more manageable chunks or stages. The reader continually has to make *determinations of saliency*, effectively prioritizing the information in the text. Reading styles need to be well suited to the purpose at hand and employed with *efficiency* and *flexibility*. For example, an adult who is reading the sports section of the newspaper to find a game score needs to scan the text to find specific information, rather than read the entire text. Conversely, a biology text that is laden with new vocabulary and concepts needs to be read slowly and with attention to detail. A mathematics textbook may demand "bottom-up" reading, whereas Walt Whitman's poems may be more suited to a "top-down" approach that allows more interaction with the reader's own ideas, experience, and interpretation. The reader needs to maintain an active dialogue with the text, engaging in comprehension self-monitoring. Clearly, these strategic and organizational elemental functions are essential for successful reading in adulthood.

Memory functions repeatedly have been shown to be of great importance in reading. Readers in high school and beyond are expected to master more complex vocabulary and to show highly automatized *sight word recognition*. These skills are highly dependent on *recall* of specific orthographic forms of written language. Adults whose recall is deficient are likely to struggle with decoding; their reading is slow and labored. Also, mature readers are required to process large chunks of written information and to suspend details from the text in *active working memory* while they are reading. In this way, details from the text are spliced together, allowing the student to engage in cohesive *discourse processing*. Students with active working memory deficits are likely to forget the beginning of a paragraph by the time they get to the end of it.

Language processing elements are also crucial for success in reading. *Phonological awareness* continues to play an important role in reading beyond elementary school, but many children develop compensatory strategies and show improvement in their reading problems in secondary school. Appreciation of language *morphology, grammar,* and *syntax* becomes increasingly important in secondary school. Mature readers need to master increasingly complex and specialized technical vocabulary. In addition, development of *semantics* in older adolescence entails the understanding and appreciation of ambiguity and figurative language. Thus, subtle language impairments in older adolescents and adults may present de novo with reading comprehension difficulties.

Reading comprehension in high school and beyond is also highly dependent on critical elemental functions in the domain of higher order cognition. Students need to develop *metalinguistic awareness* and an *apprecia-*

tion of text structures. They are increasingly required to draw *inferences* and to derive *verbal concepts* from their reading. Critical thinking and problem solving are also key functions. Students who lack these abilities have difficulty going beyond the printed word, developing abstract concepts, and applying what they know in other contexts.

IMPLICATIONS OF THE PARADIGM

The above discussion illustrates the interaction of discrete elemental functions in the accomplishment of the production components of reading. Similarly, when we consider tasks that adults face in college, in the workplace, and in their social lives, it is essential to examine a range of neurodevelopmental functions. Clinicians should not restrict their assessments to a catalogue of the typical symptoms of attention deficit disorder, but should consider instead the extent to which specific learning disabilities are contributing to the presenting symptomatology. Only by so doing can we move beyond global labels and into the area of descriptive phenomenology, where we can discern discrete areas of weakness that have specific prescriptive implications.

Another important implication of the paradigm is that adult outcomes are determined as much by strengths as by weaknesses. Clinicians who employ categorical models of attention deficits and learning disabilities tend to emphasize the presence of a specific syndrome or deficit, disregarding the coexistence of specific talents, interests, and affinities. In the school-age child, it is common for such strengths to be underutilized in a setting that rewards conformity and well-roundedness. Our work with the Schools Attuned project in middle schools around the United States has demonstrated that the utilization of preexisting strengths and affinities can enhance skills and improve self-esteem (Levine, Swartz, Reed, Wasileski, & Brown, 1993).

Children with attention deficits are better able to sustain attention in their areas of interest. In adulthood, there is far greater tolerance of nonconformity and opportunity for individuals with "specialized brains" to find vocations that are well suited to their strengths and interests. Indeed, a recent longitudinal study that followed children with attention deficits into adulthood showed generally favorable outcomes (Mannuzza, Klein, Bessler, Malloy, & LaPadula, 1993). Ninety percent of the adults were gainfully employed, many of them as entrepreneurial operators of small businesses, and only a small minority (11%) had significant ADHD symptoms. Adults with attention deficits that are having a major impact on college work may be taking the wrong courses, and those who are struggling in the workplace may be in the wrong jobs. Therefore, the potential for improving the outcomes of young adults with attention deficits by assisting them to develop their strengths is enormous. (For further discussion, see chapter 16 this volume.)

THE STRANDS PROJECT: PERSPECTIVES
FROM INTERVIEWS WITH YOUNG ADULTS

Since 1990 my colleagues and I have been engaged in the development and applications of a new assessment tool for older adolescents and young adults. The Survey of Teenage Readiness and Neuro-Developmental Status (STRANDS) comprises a questionnaire and structured interview, the primary goal of which is the generation of a profile of abilities as reported directly by the respondent. The STRANDS is predicated upon the premise that older adolescents and young adults are able to talk about their learning style and/or learning problem in such a way as to reveal important information about underlying cognitive, metacognitive, and motivational factors. Preliminary findings pertaining to the reliability and construct validity of the STRANDS have been encouraging (Sandler, Levine, Hooper, Watson, & Scarborough, 1993; Hooper, Sandler, Scarborough, Watson, & Levine, in press). During the course of the project, the STRANDS was administered to 228 high school students of ages 14 through 19 years, about one third of whom had learning disabilities by independent discrepancy criteria. We have also administered the STRANDS to approximately 50 college students and young adults who were no longer in school at the time of administration.

Data from this project have been helpful in several ways. The results have supported the potential utility of the structured interview approach in the assessment of adolescents with learning problems. They have also provided insights into the school-related concerns of older adolescents and young adults, and the nature of the specific learning disabilities that these learners commonly encounter.

The Academic Concerns of Adolescents

The concerns most commonly expressed by older adolescents were in the domain of attention and organization. Note taking, planning, and revision are critical for academic success in high school and college. The majority of the normal sample (only a small proportion of whom met clinical criteria for ADHD) endorsed moderate difficulties meeting these attentional and organizational challenges. The problems that they expressed were often situational, so that their difficulties were very evident in some classes but not in others. These findings have management implications for potentially large numbers of struggling students who might benefit from more appropriate course selection and training in cognitive strategies and organizational skills.

Adolescents with learning disabilities were more likely to express concerns in the areas of retrieval memory, efficiency, and rapid processing. For example, they reported that it is hard to memorize for a test, that they had trouble remembering things quickly when called upon in class, or that it was hard for them to get their ideas down on paper. These cognitive functions related to rate and automatization allow adolescents to engage in more efficient, sophisticated, and flexible problem solving. Traditional achievement tests generally do not assess these functions adequately. Therefore, the clinician who is evaluating an older adolescent or young adult with learning difficulties should consider these factors carefully before concluding that a learning disability is not present.

The Key Learning Disorders of Older Adolescents

A few patterns of neurodevelopmental dysfunction commonly encountered in clinical evaluations of older adolescents are described briefly below. These prototypes are intended to illustrate the heterogeneity of learning disorders in this age group, and some of the important entities in the differential diagnosis of attention deficits.

Phonologic Processing Disorder

There is considerable evidence that a disorder of phonologic processing underlies most cases of specific reading disability (dyslexia) in childhood (Stanovich, 1988). Human speech consists of sequences of language sounds or phonemes. During the elementary school years, normal readers master the process of linking alphabet symbols to phonemes. Delayed readers have impaired phonological awareness and processing. This may persist into adolescence and adulthood. For some, the problem is obvious and immediately apparent as they struggle to decode words. For many others, the problem manifests itself in more subtle ways. They may read reasonably well, using a whole word (lexical) route. Spelling is characteristically poor, however, with frequent dysphonetic errors (errors that indicate an inability to "sound out" a word). Some, through hard work and strong visual memory, may essentially overcome their reading and spelling difficulties. Usually, they will still report that reading is tiring, effortful, and slow.

Unfamiliar words and specialized technical vocabulary may be especially troubling. Learning a foreign language, with its unfamiliar and unique phonological system, may be especially difficult for these students, sometimes necessitating an exemption from such course requirements. Many adults, although relatively successful in their chosen careers, repeatedly encounter cycles of frustration and underachievement when required to take courses or continue their education. Bypass strategies, such as the use of a tape recorder and word processor, can be immensely helpful at these times.

Language Disorders

A broad spectrum of developmental language disorders may lead to underachievement in a number of academic areas, including reading, writing, word problems in mathematics, and content areas. Many older adolescents struggle to understand relationships among words, such as antonyms and synonyms. Words with ambiguous meanings, conjunctions, and transitional words may be elusive. Figurative language and metaphors are often poorly understood. Many language-impaired adults have adequate word knowledge, but their processing of discourse, either oral or written, may be impaired, so that passage comprehension is weak. They may have difficulty drawing inferences from text. Such adults may appear to be highly distractible in situations requiring sustained listening.

Expressive language problems may be evident in association with these receptive language disorders or in isolation. Some students report constant difficulties with word finding, both in oral and written expression. There may be a striking disparity between their receptive and expressive vocabularies. Others may have greater difficulty with narrative organization and summarization. Many such adults are painfully aware of their expressive language problems, and they may isolate themselves to avoid situations in which their difficulties might show. The slowness, imprecision, and hesitancy with which they express themselves cause frustration, both academically and socially.

Memory Disorders

Memory problems have a powerful impact on achievement in high school reading, writing, spelling, and mathematics. Short-term memory impairment may have been evident in earlier years, with parents reporting that a child had great difficulty following instructions. Many adolescents acknowledge that they have difficulty holding information in short-term memory. Some of them spontaneously develop and employ strategies to assist them in meeting memory demands. Subvocalization, association, rehearsal, and other metacognitive strategies are key to the effective management of short-term memory problems.

During the adolescent years, learners are expected to become increasingly adept at using active working memory and to acquire and/or enhance the ability to maintain in working memory multiple task components while actively processing information. Active working memory is essential in writing and mathematics. For example, many students report that they have trouble maintaining their ideas while struggling with spelling and writing mechanics, or that they forget what they were trying to solve while carrying out part of a multistep math problem. Further evidence of such active working memory problems may be found during psychoeducational testing.

Long-term memory problems are frequently encountered in older students. It is commonly assumed that as students mature, many of the skills attained earlier in their education have become automatic, permitting greater speed of processing and the completion of more complex problem solving. Students whose acquisition of these skills and capabilities is delayed may demonstrate an overly mechanical approach to tasks. Academic production may be slow and laborious, ultimately resulting in difficulties with incentive and motivation.

Adults are also required to automatically recall facts and procedures as they gain expertise in their work. Retrieval memory problems in the workplace may be associated with slow work output and overreliance on guidelines, instructions, and other memory aids. In the differential diagnosis of an adolescent or adult with memory problems, it is also important to consider whether alcohol, marijuana, or other drug use may be a contributing factor (Schwartz, Gruenewald, & Klitzner, 1989).

Metacognitive Deficits

One of the most salient developmental acquisitions in adolescence is the ability to reflect on one's own cognitive processes. This ability–metacognition–becomes a vital facilitator of learning (Brown & DeLoache, 1978). Metacognitive development continues among college students, particularly as specific areas of expertise evolve. Many adolescents with learning disorders have striking metacognitive deficits, so that they lack knowledge and insight regarding learning, strategy use, and problem solving. Their basic reading skills may be intact, but they do not have the capacity to think about what they are reading for, or to modify reading strategies for different purposes. They may not be cognizant of the most salient aspects of a chapter, and summarization skills may elude them. They may fail to pick up inconsistencies. Often, they fail to understand that they have not adequately understood a text. Such students' problems are worsened by the fact that they seldom reread, consult a dictionary, use contextual cues, or ask for help.

The volume and complexity of academic demands make the acquisition and use of efficient and facilitative strategies exceedingly helpful to students. This is the domain of executive function. Torgesen (1982) has described certain students as "inactive learners," underachievers who fail to engage in the strategies needed for effective learning. Students with poor memory strategies may have difficulty knowing what to study for an examination, which techniques to use for the active learning of new material, and how to test themselves.

Highly proficient students not only have facilitative strategies but also tend to have multiple alternative strategies, so that if one technique fails, other options remain. Many underachieving students have only one method available and apply this rigidly. When this isolated approach fails, they become discouraged, tune out, and lose interest. Similarly, many adults with metacognitive deficits fail to strategize and are seldom innovative. Their overly mechanical approach may result in loss of a promotion in their jobs and may lead to dissatisfaction and frustration.

CONCLUSION

It should be clear from the above discussion that a broad range of neurodevelopmental dysfunctions have the potential to impair learning and productivity in older adolescents and young adults. Many of these may mimic or be associated with attention deficits, thereby presenting multifaceted diagnostic challenges to clinicians. An adult who is struggling academically, socially, or at work may benefit from a thorough evaluation that is interactive and empathic, and that addresses neurodevelopmental dysfunctions and their effective management. It should also be evident that attention deficits need not be a disability, and that many adults with attention deficits can utilize their strengths, talents, and affinities to become scintillating, creative, and productive citizens.

REFERENCES

Association for Children with Learning Disabilities. (1985). ACLD offers new definition. *Special Education Today*, 2, 19.

Ayres, A. (1978). Learning disabilities and the vestibular system. *Journal of Learning Disabilities, 11*, 18–29.

Bender, L. A. (1956). *Psychology of children with organic brain disorders.* Springfield, IL: Charles C. Thomas.

Brown, A. L., & DeLoache, J. S. (1978). Skills, plans and self-regulation. In R. Seigler (Ed.), *Children's thinking: What develops?* Hillsdale, NJ: Lawrence Erlbaum.

Denckla, M. B. (1972). Clinical syndromes in learning disabilities: The case for "splitting" versus "lumping." *Journal of Learning Disabilities, 5*, 401–413.

Hinshelwood, J. (1895). Word-blindness and visual memory. *Lancet, 1,* 1506–1508.

Hooper, S. R., Sandler, A. D., Scarborough, A., Watson, T. E. & Levine, M. D. (in press). Discriminant validity of a new assessment tool for adolescents with learning problems: Preliminary findings on the Survey of Teenage Readiness and Neurodevelopmental Status. *Learning Disabilities Research and Practice.*

Hooper, S. R., & Willis, W. G. (1989). *Learning disability subtyping: Neuropsychological foundations, conceptual models, and issues in clinical differentiation.* New York: Springer-Verlag.

Interagency Committee on Learning Disabilities. (1987). *Learning disabilities: A report to the U.S. Congress.* Washington, D. C: National Institute of Child Health and Human Development.

Kussmaul, A. (1877). Disturbance of speech. *Cyclopedia of Practical Medicine, 14,* 581.

Levine, M. D. (1987). *Developmental variation and learning disorders.* Cambridge, MA: Educators Publishing Service.

Levine, M. D., Hooper, S. R., Montgomery, J., Reed, M., Sandler, A. D., Swartz, C., & Watson, T. E. (1993). Learning disabilities: An interactive developmental paradigm. In G. R. Lyon, D. B. Gray, J. F. Kavanaugh, & N. A. Krasnegor (Eds.), *Better understanding learning disabilities* (pp. 229–250). Baltimore: Paul H. Brookes.

Levine, M. D., Swartz, C. W., Reed, M. S., Wasileski, T. J., & Brown, T. T. (1993) [Schools Attuned to developmental variation: Evaluation of a project in sixteen sites]. Unpublished data.

Mannuzza, S., Klein, R. G., Bessler, A., Malloy, P., & LaPadula, M. (1993). Adult outcome of hyperactive boys: Educational achievement, occupational rank, and psychiatric status. *Archives of General Psychiatry, 50,* 565–576.

Orton, S. T. (1928). Specific reading disability-strephosymbolia. *Journal of the American Medical Association, 90,* 1095–2009.

Pennington, B. F. (1991). *Diagnosing learning disorders.* New York: Guilford Press.

Rourke, B. P. (1989). *Nonverbal learning disabilities: The syndrome and the model.* New York: Guilford Press.

Sandler, A. D., Levine, M. D., Hooper, S. R., Watson, T. E., & Scarborough, A. (1993). Adolescents with and without learning problems: Concurrent and discriminant validity of the STRANDS. [Abstract]. *Journal of Adolescent Health, 14,* 53.

Schwartz, R. H., Gruenewald, P. J., & Klitzner, M. (1989). Short-term memory impairment in cannabis-dependent adolescents. *American Journal of Diseases in Children, 143,* 1214–1219.

Shaywitz , S. E., Escobar, M. D., Shaywitz, B. A., Fletcher, J. M., & Makuch, R. (1992). Evidence that dyslexia may represent the lower tail of a normal distribution of reading disability. *New England Journal of Medicine*, *326*, 145–152.

Stanovich, K. E. (1980). Toward an interactive-compensatory model of individual differences in the development of reading fluency. *Reading Research Quarterly*, *16*, 32–71.

Stanovich, K. E. (1988). Explaining the differences between the dyslexic and the garden-variety poor reader: The phonological core variable difference model. *Journal of Learning Disabilities*, *21*, 590–604.

Torgesen, J.K.(1982). The learning-disabled child as an inactive learner: Educational implications. *Topics in Learning and Learning Disabilities*, *2*, 45–52.

Yule, W., & Rutter, M. (1985). Reading and other learning difficulties. In M. Rutter, & L. Hersov (Eds.), *Child and adolescent psychiatry: Modern approaches* (pp. 444–464). Oxford: Blackwell.

5

Neurological Comorbidity Patterns/Differential Diagnosis in Adult Attention Deficit Disorder

BENNETT LAVENSTEIN

The manifestations of Attention Deficit Hyperactivity Disorder (ADHD), including distractibility, motor restlessness, hyperactivity, impulsivity, difficulty sustaining attention, and difficulty with task completion, are also found in a variety of other neurological conditions. It is essential for the professional involved in the assessment of an adult with attentional difficulties to understand the parameters of differential diagnosis between the lifelong condition of ADHD and acquired attention deficit syndrome, which may result from toxicity, anoxia, lesions, head trauma, stroke, tumors, or degenerative diseases. It is also important for the mental health professional to be aware of neurological conditions that may be comorbid with ADHD in adults, and to be knowledgeable about the signs and symptoms that indicate the need for a neurological consultation as a part of the diagnostic process (Shaywitz & Shaywitz, 1988).

A careful clinical history is always essential to begin the assessment process. There are very strong indications that ADHD is a genetically transmitted disorder (Zametkin, Nordahl, & Gross, 1990). The presence of attention deficit symptomatology in the relatives of the adult in question is one strong indication that the attentional deficit in question is inherited rather than acquired (Biederman, Faraone, Keenan, & Tsuang, 1989). Because the recognition of ADHD in adults is relatively new, the adult in question is more likely to have a child diagnosed with ADHD than to have a relative of his or her own generation or previous generations with a clear ADHD diagnosis. Even though the formal diagnosis of ADHD in relatives of the same or previous generations is unlikely, it can be valuable in the assessment process to query the adult about patterns suggestive of ADHD in older generations.

A second criterion for the diagnosis of ADHD is the presence of attentional difficulties in the childhood history. It is important for the clinician to realize, however, that ADHD is manifested a varying degree and that, particularly in individuals of high intelligence and in individuals without hyperactivity, a history of academic difficulty and behavioral problems commonly associated with ADHD in children may not be reported.

When reviewing childhood history, the mental health practitioner needs to keep in mind that the presence of ADHD symptoms in childhood does not necessarily indicate the presence of ADHD; it can also be indicative of either prenatal or postnatal trauma that resulted in attention deficit syndrome. To explore such possibilities the clinician should carefully review gestation history, including drug, alcohol, or cigarette use on the mother's part; circumstances surrounding the individual's birth (prolonged labor, anoxia at birth, forceps delivery, prematurity, etc.); early developmental history; history of accidents, head injuries, and falls; possible exposure to toxins; and general medical history. One potential toxin often overlooked in taking a clinical history is the presence of lead-base paint. Exposure to lead-base paint, even in small quantities, has been associated with the development of neurological symptoms (Jenkins & Mellins, 1957). Such exposure can be a risk not only for children growing up in inner city housing but also for children in more affluent families who have purchased older homes.

It is also important for the clinician to recognize that the presence of ADHD does not rule out other neurological conditions which may contribute to attentional difficulties (Lou, Henriksen, & Bruhn, 1984). In fact, children who are impulsive and hyperactive are probably more accident-prone than other children and may, as a result, experience head injuries that further complicate their neurological picture. A careful review of possible head injuries during childhood is, therefore, an essential part of the assessment process.

A neurological screening is always in order as a part of the diagnostic process, even when the individual and family histories strongly indicate a diagnosis of adult ADHD. For the mental health professional without a medical background it may be helpful to use a structured questionnaire to assist in this screening process. One such questionnaire in frequent use is the Neurological Symptom Questionnaire (NSQ) developed by John A. Shinka. This questionnaire was developed by the consensus of numerous neurologists and neuropsychologists to assist the nonmedical clinician in conducting a brief, but comprehensive review of symptoms suggestive of the need for a neurological consultation. If the adult indicates symptoms of possible neurological conditions other than ADHD, then a referral for a neurological consultation is in order (Ferro, Matins, & Tavora, 1984; Joseph, 1987).

THE NEUROBIOLOGY OF ADD

As yet no single defect has been identified that can explain all of the symptoms of ADHD, including motor restlessness, impulsivity, distractibility, poor organization, impersistence, and emotional outbursts. There is widespread agreement at this point in our understanding of Attention Deficit Disorder that it is primarily a disinhibitory disorder of the frontal lobes (Douglas, 1984; Gualtieri, Ondrusek, & Finley, 1985; Chelune, Ferguson, Koon, & Dickey, 1986). Chelune noted marked similarities between the symptoms of individuals with frontal lobe damage and ADHD symptoms. Lou et al. (1984) found decreased blood flow in the frontal lobes of children diagnosed with ADHD. Zametkin et al. (1990) found decreased glucose metabolism in adults with histories of hyperactivity in childhood.

Although the frontal lobes are considered to be the primary contributor to ADHD symptoms, other areas have been implicated as well, including the reticular activating system (Voeller, 1991) and the corpus callosum (Hynd, Semund-Clikeman, Lorys, Novey, & Eliopolous, 1990). Shenker (1992) has recently proposed that the locus coeruleus (LC), the primary site of norepinephrine production and firing, may be involved in ADHD. A simplified model of ADHD could be described as a dysregulation of certain neurotransmitters, primarily dopamine and norepinephrine, perhaps originating in the lower brain and limbic structures, which impairs adequate functioning in the frontal lobes of the brain. (See chapter 2, this volume, for a more detailed discussion of the neurobiology of ADHD.)

DIFFERENTIAL DIAGNOSIS ISSUES

Differential diagnosis of Attention Deficit Disorder should include consideration of many disorders that by symptomatology may present as Attention Deficit or Attention Deficit Hyperactivity Disorder, but which are the result of different etiologies. Specifically, neurological disorders that may present as ADHD may include narcolepsy, learning disabilities, acquired attention deficits as a result of use of certain pharmocologic agents including barbiturates and benzodiazapines, and previous neurologic insults including prior trauma, infection, and structural disease of the nervous system. These will be addressed in the following paragraphs.

Trauma

Head trauma in the region of the frontal lobes is a common cause of acquired executive dysfunction, manifested by deficiencies in planning, organization, motivation, initiation, mental flexibility, and impulse inhibition. Benson (1991) described the human frontal lobes in terms of "executive control functions." In 1987, in his discussion of executive function of the brain, he specifically referred to the dorsal lateral prefrontal lobe as the site of executive action of the brain. Denckla (1989) and others have utilized the term executive function as an umbrella term to encompass the abilities to initiate action, sustain activity appropriately, inhibit impulses, and fluidly shift effort and attention from one task to the next as called for. Executive functions, in addition to prefrontal cortex involvement, may relate to subcortical structures (Butter, Rapcsak, Watson, & Heilman, 1988; Lou et al., 1989). The ability to stay alert and awake, to perform continuous mental tasks, and to remain task oriented is impaired in many individuals who have disruption of prefrontal and subcortical connections. Symptoms similar to those found in individuals who have experienced head trauma in the frontal region are, of course, seen in adults with attention deficit disorder. Zametkin et al. (1990) reported reduced glucose metabolism in the frontal areas of the brain in adults with attention deficit disorder. Thus, executive dysfunctions such as problems with attention, organization, and impulsivity can be suggestive either of attention deficit hyperactivity disorder or of an acquired neurological deficit.

Disease

Inflammatory disease of the nervous system may be associated with subsequent damage to cortical structures. In addition, subcortical abnormalities may be seen in patients who have had features of prior inflammatory disease of the nervous system. Of historical interest is the 1916–27 epidemic of encephalitis lethargica, which produced symptoms in children of restlessness, impulsivity, and impersistence. While these symptoms are also seen in children with ADHD, the features were noted secondary to a worldwide epidemic of influenza which resulted in a wide spectrum of neurologic symptoms including the late onset of postencephalitic Parkinsonism.

Also of historical interest was a report by Kahn and Cohen (1934) of the concept of "organic drivenness." Kahn and Cohen wrote that encephalitis epidemica and other encephalitides were not the only conditions that produced such behavior, which represented one of the early recognitions of ADHD as a separate entity. In their paper, which focused primarily on children, the authors also noted two patients who were hyperactive adults, possibly the first mention of this phenomenon in the literature.

More recent concerns regarding disease processes that may produce ADD-like symptoms include viral meningitis, viral encephalitis, or bacterial meningitis with neurological sequelae. The incidence of neurologic deficits including cognitive impairment in bacterial meningitides of childhood as a sequel may vary between 10 and 60% depending on the organism. With regard to viral encephalitides, such as herpes, the incidence of neurologic sequelae including impaired cognitive function in survivors may be as high as 60% in some series.

While rigorous diagnosis and treatment have markedly improved the morbidity of the outcome cognitively in these groups of patients, many are still left with features of cortical dysfunction with organically based attention deficit–related symptomatology. A careful history is necessary in order to identify the etiology of attention deficit symptoms.

Tumors

Tumors generally do not present with symptoms similar to those of Attention Deficit Disorder. However, structural disease of the nervous system with invasion of cortical pathways–including frontal, parietal, and temporal lobe regions–by tumor can certainly be associated with various forms of behavioral abnormalities. Hemispheric neglect syndromes, parietal neglect syndromes, apraxia, inattention, and behavioral outbursts with decreased inhibition, including diminished social inhibition, have all been described. Also of concern are the residual of postoperative, postradiation, and postchemotherapeutic changes. These essential modalities in the treatment of patients with brain tumors can result in a very high incidence of diffuse white matter changes, as evidenced on MRI scanning, in addition to cognitive and behavioral changes that include such features as depression, impaired cognition, impaired calculation, and changes in social attentiveness and awareness. All of this is dependent on the location of the underlying structural damage.

Stroke

Location of cerebral vascular insults may be associated with a wide spectrum of deficits from pure motor deficit without any cognitive involvement, as is seen in small vessel capsular or lacunar infarct with focal deficits, to features of diffuse involvement due to global infarction. Strokelike syndromes with infarction and subsequent encephalomalacia involving frontal lobe and/or temporal lobe may be associated not only with specific motor deficits related to those areas, but also with cognitive impairment and behavioral changes secondary to structural damage. Multi-infarct dementia, and multiple small vessel disease associated with multiple episodes of microinfarction, including asymptomatic multiple infarcts, are frequently associated with inattention and dementia-like symptomatology. In most cases, this can be readily differentiated by neurologists on the basis of history or imaging studies, and by ruling out other conditions that may mimic these findings.

Epilepsy

Certain forms of epilepsy—namely seizures that interfere with general alerting responses, as is well documented in childhood absence or primary generalized epilepsy, with characteristic 3 Hz spike and wave discharges—may well be responsible for impairment in attention and cognitive functioning. This pattern is particularly uncommon in adults, normally presenting in middle childhood, with a high likelihood of resolution by adulthood. However, paroxysmal episodic electrical events of a partial complex type, with electrographic correlates, may be associated with impaired cognitive performance (Williamson, Spencer, & Spencer, 1985). This may follow previous structural disease of the nervous system, as noted above, and can be responsible for a decline in performance.

Hypometabolic activity in the frontal cortex is noted by Zametkin et al. (1990) in adults with ADHD. Similar hypometabolism is noted in the interictal component of the clinical course of epilepsy (Devinsky & Vasquez, 1993; Wylie, 1993). These findings are correlated with abnormal cognitive performance (Terzano, Parino, & Mazzucchi, 1986). While not all symptoms associated with ADHD are found in individuals with this type of epilepsy (expertial complex figures), there is overlap between this type of epilepsy and ADHD in the area of impaired executive functions. Appropriate diagnosis with EEG monitoring and appropriate treatment with anticonvulsant medication may, in fact, improve these impaired cognitive functions.

Partial complex seizures in the temporal lobe region may be associated with emotional dysregulation which can be manifested in symptoms ranging from irritability to intense emotional overreactivity and episodic angry outbursts far out of proportion to the event triggering the anger reaction. Emotional dyscontrol has also been described in certain individuals with ADD (Barkley et al., 1990), as manifested by poor frustration tolerance and emotional overreaction. The conditions of ADD and partial complex seizures in the temporal lobe region may be comorbid conditions, and this possibility should be considered in individuals with ADD who show a more extreme emotional lability.

Neuro Disorders of Vigilance

A primary disorder of vigilance represents a condition described as an abnormality of the arousal state. The degree of arousal in any individual is dependent not only on the psychological state but also on the arousal network, which has its genesis in the brainstem and reticular activating system, with significant input from the right cerebral hemisphere and right posterior parietal cortex (Weinberg & Brumback, 1990). Disorders of vigilance may cause symptoms of attention deficit disorder without hyperactivity and may well represent a disorder of the right posterior parietal cortex. Patients with this disorder have been described as manifesting sleepiness, stretching, fidgeting, and motor restlessness (Weinberg & Brumback, 1992). Such conditions are not infrequent in the population and may be responsible for impaired cognitive performance due to underarousal.

Disordered functioning of the reticular activating system has also been described in ADD (Voeller, 1991). The treatment for such a disorder of vigilance is typically a stimulant medication. The symptoms of restlessness and fidgetiness found in individuals with disordered arousal systems are also typical of individuals with ADHD. Other symptoms of ADHD including impulsivity, poor organizational skills, and emotional outbursts, however, generally are not found in individuals with a disordered arousal state. A review of the full pattern of symptoms may allow the clinician to make a differential diagnosis.

Drug Side Effects

The clinician should always be aware that attention may be impaired in patients who are on specific drugs prescribed for a variety of reasons. Beta-blockers, antihistamines, benzodiazepines, and some anticonvulsants are among those that may cause such symptoms. Well known are the depressant effects of multiple mood-altering drugs. Major neuroleptic agents cause cognitive impairment that is associated with blunting of affect in addition to slowness of task completion and subjective drowsiness. The use of anticonvulsants can also be associated with some impairment in cognitive function.

While it was believed that perhaps some agents might be free of the side effect of impaired cognitive function, all of these have the potential to produce impairment in performance. Most notable among all medications that may produce ADHD-like symptoms, however, are the barbiturates, with phenobarbital primarily responsible for a well-described hyperactivity syndrome in 40% of children on this particular agent. To assist in determining whether ADHD-like symptoms may be a result of such substances, the clinician should routinely inquire about all medications, both prescribed drugs and those drugs taken as part of a pattern of substance abuse or recreational drug use.

Multiple Sclerosis

Multiple sclerosis (MS) has also been associated with cognitive and emotional difficulty. Extensive tests have been carried out evaluating intelligence, language, attention, memory, problem solving, and visual-processing tasks in patients with MS. Specifically, MS, a disorder that affects the myelin, may be associated with impairment in the rapid processing of information. The largest deficits that have been reported are those that require substitution of digits for symbols according to a novel rule (Beatty, 1993); in other words, the ability to shift set is impaired in MS patients. More severe impairments occur when written response is required. MS patients have also displayed impairment on the paced auditory serial addition task. Evidence from a variety of different tests indicate that MS patients generally process this information more slowly than do controls. Disturbances of memory are the most frequently reported form of cognitive impairment in MS patients. Memory impairment seems to involve deficits in both recent and remote memory. In addition, MS patients are found to be impaired in several different problem-solving tests and mildly impaired in visual processing tasks. Area of involvement is quite variable from patient to patient. Numerous authors have written extensively on this topic, a bibliography of which is readily available in Beatty (1993).

While some of the cognitive impairments from MS bear a similarity to those associated with ADD, restlessness and impulsivity are not included among typical MS symptoms. As in many other differential diagnosis cases, a careful history is important in distinguishing between cognitive impairments that may result from MS and those that may result from ADD. A lifelong history of ADD does not, of course, rule out MS.

Tourette's Syndrome

Tourette's Syndrome is a genetically transmitted neurobiological condition characterized by multiple muscle tics, vocal noises, and compulsive swearing, which was first described by Gilles de la Tourette in 1885. Tourette's is possibly the most common comorbid condition, with approximately half of all Tourette's patients showing ADHD symptoms (Comings, D., 1990). The typical age at onset of these symptoms is between two and fifteen years of age, and the most common symptom at onset is rapid eyeblinking (Comings, D., 1990) Studies of children with a history of both ADHD and TS show that symptoms of ADHD typically have an onset prior to TS symptoms (Comings, D. & Comings, B., 1988). Because ADHD is typically treated with stimulant medication, some physicians incorrectly concluded that stimulant medication prescribed for ADHD caused TS symptoms that emerged later, when this order of symptom emergence is typical of the development of the two related disorders. The primary treatment for tics involves the use of medications including haloperidol, pimozide, and fluphenazine, which serve to block the action of dopamine at the postsynaptic receptor. (Other medications are used as well, to treat both tics and the range of associated symptoms.) Comings writes that both ADHD and TS appear to be due to dopamine imbalance in different parts of the brain. The frontal lobe syndrome of ADHD symptoms are apparently due to too little dopamine in the frontal lobes, whereas the TS tics appear to result from a hypersensitivity to dopamine in the neostriatum (Comings, D., 1990).

COMORBID NEUROLOGICAL CONDITIONS

Neurological Problems Secondary to Substance Abuse

One of the very difficult aspects of the differential diagnosis of ADHD is the possibility of abnormal neurotransmitter function secondary to chronic substance abuse. Adolescents with an ADHD pattern of hyperactivity and poor impulse control are very prone to the use of recreational drugs. Impaired cognitive functioning later in adulthood may be a result of both the underlying ADHD and the chronic substance abuse throughout adolescence and young adulthood. An in-depth clinical interview regarding drug and alcohol abuse is essential to making such a determination.

The clinician should bear in mind the likelihood of underreporting or inaccurate reporting on the variety of drugs used and the extent to which they were used. The clinician should also be aware that useful clinical information can be gathered by discussing with the patient his or her reactions to various drugs that were used recreationally or were abused. Often this information can assist the clinician in understanding which classes of prescription drugs may be most effective in treating the patient. Drug abuse, in some cases, is an attempt at self-medication. (See chapter 4, this volume, for more discussion of ADHD and substance abuse.)

Sleep Disorders

Excessive daytime sleepiness, sleep, and sleep disorders are now well-known conditions in the general population. Excessive daytime sleepiness was previously thought to be related to narcolepsy, encephalitis lethargica, and hypersomnia secondary to organic brain disease. Further evaluation of patients with hypersomnolence—that is, excessive daytime sleepiness and problems with vigilance—has led to evaluation of these patients in sleep laboratories (Dement, 1976; Heilman, Schwartz, & Watson, 1978). We now know that the most frequent diagnosis responsible for daytime symptoms in adults is the obstructive sleep apnea syndrome. This has been demonstrated by nocturnal monitoring of sleep. The ability to detect these abnormalities has come about with the development of polysomnography, 24-hour electroencephalography, multiple sleep latency tests, and computerized electroencephalography (Duane & Epcar-Ziglar, 1991; Herman, Roffwarge, & Becker, 1989).

Anecdotal clinical reports suggest that many such adults experience a chronic pattern of feeling energized or restless late at night, of going to bed at erratic times, usually too late for an adequate amount of sleep, of racing thoughts which prevent falling asleep, of restless and disrupted sleep, and of resultant chronic daytime sleepiness. Such a pattern may continue throughout adulthood, and may significantly affect the daily performance of these adults. Sometimes the pattern of late-night arousal can be resolved by prescribing antidepressants to be taken in a single dose prior to bedtime, thereby inducing mild drowsiness.

For some adults with ADD, their sleep pattern is so disrupted that a full-scale sleep study seems warranted. A differential diagnosis between sleep apnea and a reported ADD pattern of late-night arousal, erratic sleep habits, and difficulty awakening should be made. The presence of ADD in adults does not rule out the possibility of sleep apnea.

Neurodevelopmental Disorders

Individuals with learning disabilities frequently manifest poor attention, distractibility, restlessness, and limited capacity to perform tasks. Like attentional difficulties, learning disabilities can be inherited or acquired. The famous neurophysiologist Charles Sherrington, as long ago as 1906, linked impairment of cortical (cognitive) functioning to an epileptic focus (Weintraub & Mesulam, 1983); Voeller (1986) links other types of neurological problems to learning disabilities or cognitive impairment.

Learning disabilities may be associated with specific structural abnormalities and may not respond to medication. Because the specific structural abnormality and/or neurotransmitter abnormality for learning disabilities have not been clearly identified, and are the subject of intense research at this time, speculation is not offered as to specific mechanisms. While educational tools in the formative years may be helpful to remediate some of these defects, many such neurodevelopmentally impaired individuals enter adulthood with continued significant impairment in performance.

Some types of learning disabilities may have a particularly strong linkage to attention deficit disorder, including memory deficits and verbal learning disorders (Levine & Oberklaid, 1980). The likelihood of some type of comorbid learning disability is strong. Learning disabilities may be found in 30–70% of young patients with attention deficit disorder and, in retrospect, may be seen in 15–50% of adults with attention deficit disorder (Gittelman, Mannuzza, Shenker, & Bonaquana, 1985) (See chapter 4, this volume, for a more complete discussion of neurodevelopmental functions as they relate to attention deficit disorder).

COMORBIDITY OR DIFFERENTIAL DIAGNOSIS PROCEDURE

Neurological Clinical Examination

In general the concept of "minimal brain dysfunction," a popular term in the 1950s and 1960s, has been discarded as more selective terminology and classification reflect our more sophisticated understanding of the phenomena encompassed by the term *minimal brain dysfunction.* Previously, neurologists, child neurologists, and pediatricians commented on the presence of soft signs. Such soft signs as slight clumsiness, maladroitness, and impaired facility in tandem walking, finger-to-nose testing, and rapid alternating movement have always intrigued examiners who have seen both adults and children with ADD. The presence of soft signs, however, provides little to further qualify, quantify, or classify patients with ADD as opposed to other neurological disorders.

Much more significant are the formal neuropsychological tests that can be used to evaluate and substantiate the diagnosis. In general, the neurologic examination of adults with ADD in the absence of structural disease of the nervous system does not reveal any specific focal deficit when these patients are evaluated in the examination room.

Neuropsychological Testing

Neuropsychological testing is of paramount importance in the evaluation and classification of patients who present with features suggesting an ADD syndrome. Neuropsychological testing can assist in answering the following key questions:

1. Does the patient on standard psychological tests demonstrate features of an organic brain syndrome?
2. Does the patient's performance on a specific battery of neuropsychological tests suggest the presence or absence of brain dysfunction?
3. Are there impairments of executive functions (organization, planning)?
4. Does the psychological testing demonstrate qualitative or quantitative findings suggesting the location of a lesion?
5. Is there impaired cerebral higher cortical function?

6. Will the results of a test help plan either educational or rehabilitation approaches?

Neuropsychological testing is complementary to other examination modalities such as clinical examination, neuroimaging, and electroencephalography, all of which have been discussed previously. Neuropsychological testing can be viewed as providing essential aid in the diagnosis as well as in the identification of specific syndromes. It is also particularly useful in monitoring changes, for example, the improvement or deterioration of cerebral function over time. The ability to detect and describe specific, suspected, or known abnormalities of brain function in terms of higher cortical function is also noted to be an advantage of neuropsychological testing. It is estimated that the ability to detect brain dysfunction when using neuropsychological testing is between 80 and 90%.

It is essential to establish correlations between neuropsychological testing and clinical history to determine the validity of test results. Because of the complex nature of the differential diagnosis of ADD in adults, the utility of neuropsychological testing cannot be underestimated and should, in fact, be emphasized.

Genetic Testing

In the process of the differential diagnosis procedure, it is important for the clinician to be aware of the possibility of genetic disorders that may be responsible for the presence of ADD syndrome. This may give the appearance of ADHD, due to both the manifestation of symptoms and early childhood presentation.

GRTH

One of the genetic conditions, reported by Hauser et al. (1993), is generalized resistance to thyroid hormone (GRTH), which is correlated with a mutation of the human thyroid receptor-beta gene. Among the subjects of Hauser's study, males with GRTH were approximately 3 times as likely to have a coexisting ADHD. Children with GRTH, tend to be of short stature and show difficulty gaining weight. In adults with an undiagnosed GRTH, the individual may experience chest pains, heart palpitations, and rapid pulse.

To test for GRTH, tests are performed to measure levels of T_3 (triiodothyronine) and T_4 (thyroxine), which are elevated when GRTH is present, and TSH (thyrotropin, a thyroid stimulating hormone), which may be of normal or elevated levels when GRTH is present. Research is planned to investigate the use of replacement T_3 as an effective medication for the treatment of GRTH-ADHD children.

The likelihood of GRTH among the general ADHD population is small. The non-medically trained clinician should be aware that GRTH is a different condition from other more common thyroid conditions such as hyper- or hypothyroidism.

Fragile X Syndrome

A second genetic condition that should be considered for in the differential diagnosis of ADHD is the Fragile X Syndrome. Research on Fragile X is limited but growing. A broad review of the research on Fragile X can be found in *The Fragile X Syndrome* (Davies, 1989).

Fragile X is an X-linked genetic condition in which males are affected and females are unaffected, or much less affected. In boys, Fragile X typically causes mental retardation or learning disabilities (LD), anxiety, and hyperactivity. In girls, much more subtle symptoms are common, including anxiety, social withdrawal, learning disabilities, and attentional difficulties (Freund & Reiss, 1991).

Fragile X is most commonly discovered when parents seek their physician's assistance to determine the cause of problem behavior. These children often present with hyperactivity, ADD syndrome, and social difficulties. Females, who may transmit the disorder to their offspring, may present with attentional and cognitive difficulties that mimic ADD and types of LD. A family history of retardation should always be screened for, and may suggest that genetic testing for Fragile X is indicated.

Laboratory Tests

The determination of the location of a lesion or lesions utilizing appropriate neurodiagnostic procedures is very helpful in correlating abnormal performance with neuropsychological findings and documenting specific focal deficits. The following are current techniques that have proven effective in the determination of the localization of lesions.

Computerized Axial Tomography (CAT Scanning)

CAT scanning uses x-ray techniques to image the contents and bones of the skull. Despite the use of contrast material, subtle differentiation of abnormalities involving the gray matter and white matter may be less well defined than with MRI scanning.

Magnetic Resonance Imaging (MRI Scanning)

MRI scanning has become a particularly sensitive tool in evaluating subtle abnormalities involving gray matter and white matter. In addition to demonstrating more fully the anatomy of the posterior portion of the brain and those areas adjacent to the brain stem, including the upper cervical cord, MRI scanning can be very sensitive in picking up small abnormalities which may be posttraumatic or developmental, and which could be suggestive of a latent seizure disorder. When not well visualized by CAT scanning, small tumors, small vascular malformations, and small congenital abnormalities are particularly well seen by MRI scanning. In addition, MRI scanning has the particular advantage of not involving radiation. Injection of a substance known as gadolinium can be particularly effective in helping to image any abnormalities suggested in MRI scanning.

MRI scanning also has special application in the evaluation of patients with progressive degenerative neurological diseases and may reveal subtle findings of inherited metabolic disorders that could account for intellectual decline and/or dementia, disorders not readily seen by CAT scanning. MRI scanning is more sensitive to the appearance of small vascular lesions reflecting small vessel disease, with small infarcts in the cortex, very frequently accounting for a multiple infarct dementia picture. In addition, MRI scanning is exquisitely sensitive in detecting the demyelinating lesions of multiple sclerosis in patients who have a course characterized by remissions and relapses.

Positron-Emission Tomography (PET Scanning)

PET scanning is a technique that utilizes the injection of an isotope tagged to a substance, frequently glucose in the form of fluorinated deoxyglucose. This material is absorbed by the brain and lodges within the cells. The degree of uptake of the isotopic-labeled material correlates proportionately with the metabolic activity of that area of the brain. This provides a helpful marker in detecting functional impairment. Through the use of PET scanning, specific studies of disorders ranging from schizophrenia to dementia, and certainly including adult ADD, have been well described in the literature (Zametkin et al., 1990).

Positron-emission tomography scanning is not available in general clinical settings. At present, it is confined to several research centers, due to its high cost and investigative nature.

Single Photon Emission Computerized Tomography (SPECT Scanning)

SPECT scanning is more readily available in many hospitals and medical centers throughout the United States. SPECT scanning is helpful in measuring the functional activity of the brain and may be particularly helpful in evaluating areas of hyper- or hypometabolism, that is, increased or decreased function. SPECT scanning generally does not offer the same spatial resolution as positron-emission tomography, but is in wider use because of its greater availability.

Computerized Electroencephalography

Sometimes in combination with MRI scanning (Knight, 1991; Ulrich & Frick, 1986), computerized electroencephalography has allowed for mapping of brain activity, embracing both structure and electrical function. This technique is currently being developed, and in the future should provide additional information to evaluate functional abnormalities related to specific associated structural abnormalities.

ANALYSIS OF DIAGNOSTIC TECHNIQUES IN PATIENTS WITH ATTENTION DEFICIT DISORDER

Neurologists are frequently asked to evaluate the patient with ADD. The essential part of that evaluation includes the history and the illumination of other conditions that may mimic ADD symptoms. Because the manifestations are rather protean, awareness of the neuroanatomical, neurophysiological, neurobehavioral, and neuropharmacological aspects of ADHD resides within the realm of the neurologist who is called upon to contribute and consult with the referring clinician. It is the neurologist's responsibility to determine whether there is readily discernible evidence of a neuroanatomical abnormality. It is also the neurologist's responsibility to determine whether the features can be ascribed to a specific neurologic disorder other than ADHD, such as those previously described in this chapter. The ability to detect prior insults to the nervous system is greatly enhanced by the following techniques: magnetic resonance imaging, electroencephalography, polysomnography including special sleep studies, multimodality-evoked potentials including cognitive-evoked potentials, CAT scanning, blood chemistries, and the application of neuropsycholgical test results.

At this time, neurologists may, as part of a team, play a major role in the assessment of adults who may have ADD, by combining information to establish a differential diagnosis and to rule out those neurological conditions that can be described as the great mimickers. Many neurologists are receiving special training in behavioral neurology, and there has been significant growth in this field. To serve as a member of a diagnostic team with adults who may have ADD, a neurologist needs to have special expertise in the following general categories: Neurologists must be particularly sensitive to the differential diagnosis and comorbid diagnosis concepts as outlined in this chapter. Neurologists also need to be familiar with the developing neurological specialty of brain-behavior relationships including aspects of nonverbal behavior, language disorders, disorders of vigilance, depression, the relationship between epilepsy and dysfunctional behavior, and the well-described neuroanatomic basis of developmental dyslexia and other learning disorders. The neurologist should be familiar with the burgeoning array of drugs that may be utilized in the treatment of adults with ADD, ranging from the initial use of amphetamines 40 years ago to the very recent exploration of the newest effective serotonin reuptake inhibitors. Expertise in these areas will provide a significant foundation for the neurologist addressing the issue of Attention Deficit Disorder. The scope of neurology extends to both an appreciation of the integration of neuropsychological test results in behavioral neurology contacts, and a clear understanding of pharmacotherapeutic approaches to the management of patients with ADD.

REFERENCES

Anderson, S. W., Damasio, H., Jones, D. R., & Tranel, D. (1991). Wisconsin Card Sorting Test performance as a measure of frontal lobe damage. *Journal of Clinical Experimental Neuropsychology, 13,* 909–922.

Barkley, R. A., Fisher, M., & Edelbrock, C. S. (1990). Outcome of adolescent hyperactive children diagnosed by research criteria: An 8-year prospective follow up-study. *Journal of the American Academy of Child and Adolescent Psychiatry, 29,* 546–557.

Beatty, W. (1993). Cognitive and emotional disturbances in multiple sclerosis. *Behavioral Neurology, Neurologic Clinics, 11*(1), 189–204.

Benson, D. F. (1991). Role of frontal dysfunction in attention deficit hyperactivity disorder. *Journal of Child Neurology, 6* (Suppl.), s9–s13.

Benton, A. L., & Howell, I. L. (1941). Use of psychological tests in the evaluation of intellectual functioning following head injury reported a case of post-traumatic personality disorder. *Psychosomatic Medicine, 3,* 138–151.

Biederman, J., Faraone, A., Keenan, K., & Tsuang, M. (1989). Family genetic and psychosocial risk factors in attention deficit disorder. [Abstract]. *Biological Psychiatry, 25* (Suppl.), 145A.

Butter, C. M., Rapcsak, S. Z., Watson, R. T., & Heilman, K.M. (1988). Changes in sensory inattention, directional hypokinesia and the release of the fixation reflex following a unilateral frontal lesion. *Neuropsychologia, 26,* 533–545.

Chelune, G. J., Ferguson, W., Koon, R., & Dickey, T. O. (1986). Frontal lobe disinhibition in attention deficit disorder. *Child Psychiatry and Human Development, 16,* 221–235.

Comings, D., & Comings, B. (1988). Tourette's syndrome and attention deficit disorder. In D. J. Cohen, R. D. Bruun, and J. F. Leckman (Eds.), *Tourette's Syndrome and Tic Disorders: Clinical Understanding and Treatment.* John Wiley & Sons, New York, pp. 119–135.

Comings, D. (1990). *Tourette Syndrome and Human Behavior.* Duarte, CA: Hope Press.

Davies, K. (Ed.). (1989). *The fragile x syndrome.* New York: Oxford University Press.

Dement, W. C. (1976). Daytime sleepiness and sleep attacks. In W.C. Dement, P. Passouant, C. Guilleminault. *Narcolepsy* (pp. 17-42). New York: Spectrum.

Denckla, M. B. (1989). Executive dysfunction. *International Pediatrics, 4,* 155–160.

Devinsky, G., & Vasquez, B. (1993). Behavioral changes associated with epilepsy. *Behavioral Neurology, Neurologic Clinics, 11*(1), 127–143.

Douglas, V. I. (1984). The psychological processes implicated in ADD. In L. Bloomingdale (Ed.), *Attention deficit disorder: Diagnostic, cognitive, and therapeutic understanding.* New York: Spectrum Publications.

Duane, D., & Epcar-Zigler, L. (1991). Pupilometry, sleepiness and vigilance in developmental disorders. *Neurology, 41,* 236.

Emslie, G. J., Roffwarg, H. P., & Rush, A. J. (1987). Sleep EEG findings in depressed children and adolescents. *American Journal of Psychiatry, 144,* 668–670.

Eslinger, P., & Damasio, A. (1985). Severe disturbance of higher cognition after bilateral frontal lobe ablation: Patient EVR. *Neurology, 35,* 1069–1071.

Ferro, J. M., Matins, I. P., & Tavora, L. (1984). Neglect in children. *Annals of Neurology, 15,* 281–284.

Freund, L. S. & Reiss, A. L. (1991). Cognitive profiles associated with the fra(X) syndrome in males and females. *American Journal of Medical Genetics, 38,* 32–39.

Galaburda, A. M., Sherman, G. F., & Rosen, G. D. (1985). Developmental dyslexia. *Annals of Neurology, 18,* 222–223.

Garfinkel, B., Wender, P. H., & Sloman, L. (1983). Tricyclic antidepressants and methylphenidate treatment of attention deficit disorder. *Journal of the American Academy of Child Psychiatry, 22,* 343–348.

Gittelman, R., Mannuzza, S., Shenker, R., & Bonaquana, N. (1985). Hyperactive boys almost grown up. *Archives of General Psychiatry, 42,* 937–947.

Gualtieri, C. T., Ondrusek, M. G., & Finley C. (1985). Attention deficit disorder in adults. *Clinical Neuropharmacology, 8*(4), 343–56.

Hauser, P., Zametkin, A.J., Martinez, P., Vitello, B., Motochik,J. A., Mixson, A. J., & Weintraub, B. J. (1993). Attention deficit hyperactivity disorder in people with generalized resistance to thyroid hormone. *New England Journal of Medicine, 328,* 997–1001.

Heilman, K. M., Schwartz, H. D., & Watson, R. T. (1978). Hypoarousal in patients with a neglect syndrome and emotional indifference. *Neurology, 28,* 229–232.

Herman, J. H., Roffwarge, H. P., & Becker, P. M. (1989). The evaluation of daytime vigilance: A new function for sleep disorders centers. *Journal of Sleep Research, 18,* 120.

Honda, Y., & Hishkawa, Y. A. (1980). Long term treatment of narcolepsy and excessive daytime sleepiness with pemoline. *Current Therapeutic Research, 27,* 429–441.

Hynd, G., Semund-Clikeman, M., Lorys, A. R., Novey, E., & Eliopolus, D. (1990). Brain morphology in developmental dyslexia and attention deficit disorder/hyperactivity. *Archives of Neurology, 47,* 919–926.

Hunt, R. D., Cohen, D. J., Anderson, G., & Mindera, R. (1988). Noradrenergic mechanisms in ADDH. In L.M. Bloomingdale (Ed.), *Attention deficit disorder: New Research in attention treatment and psychopharmacology.* New York: Pergamon Press.

Jenkins, C. D., & Mellins, R. B. (1957). Lead poisoning in children. *Archives of Neurology and Psychiatry, 77,* 70.

Joseph, J. (1987). Learning disability due to a primary deficiency of planning, organization, and motivation. *Neurology, 37* (Suppl.), 221.

Kahn, R. L., & Cohen, L. H. (1934). Organic drivenness: A brain stem syndrome and an experience. *New England Journal of Medicine, 210,* 748–756.

Knight, R. T. (1991). Evoked potential studies of attention capacity in human frontal lobes. In H. S. Levin, H. M. Eisenberg, & A. Benton, (Eds.) *Frontal lobe function-dysfunction* (pp. 139–153). New York: Oxford University Press.

Leckman, J. F., Anderson, G. M., & Cohen, O. S. (1992). Whole blood serotonin and tryptophan levels in Tourette's disorder, effects of acute and chronic clonidine treatment. *Life Science, 35,* 2497–2503.

Lenn, J. (1986). Childhood narcolepsy. *Pediatric Neurology, 2,* 314–315.

Levine, M. D., & Oberklaid, F. (1980). Hyperactivity–Symptom complex or complex symptom? *American Journal of Diseases of Children, 134,* 409.

Lou, H. C., Henriksen, L., & Bruhn P. (1984). Focal cerebral dysfunction in developmental learning disabilities. *Archives of Neurology, 41,* 825–829.

Lou, H. C., Henrickson, L., & Bruhn, P. (1989). Striatal dysfunction in attention deficit hyperkinetic disorder. *Archives of Neurology, 465,* 48–52.

Lowenthal, D. T., Matzek, L. M., & Macgregor, T. R. (1988). Clinical pharmacokinetic of clonidine. *Clinical Pharmacokinet, 14,* 287–310.

McGee, R., Feehan, M., & Williams, S. (1990). DSM-II disorders in a large sample of adolescents. *Journal of the American Academy of Child and Adolescent Psychiatry, 29,* 611–619.

Mesulam, M. (1981). A cortical network for directed attention and unilateral neglect. *Annals of Neurology, 10,* 309–325.

Poznanski, E. O., Mokros, H. B., & Grossman, J. (1985). Diagnostic criteria in childhood depression. *American Journal of Psychiatry, 142,* 1168–1173.

Prigatano, G. P. (1986a). Higher cerebral deficits: The history of methods of assessment and approaches to rehabilitation, Part I. *Barrow Neurological Institute Quarterly, 2,* 15–26.

Prigatano, G. P. (1986b). Higher cerebral deficits: The history of methods of assessment and approaches to rehabilitation, Part II. *Barrow Neurological Institute Quarterly, 2,* 9–17.

Puig, A., Goetz, J., & Davis, M. (1989). A controlled family history of pre-pubertal major depressive disorder. *Archives of General Psychiatry, 46*, 406–418.

Shaywitz, S. E., & Shaywitz, B. A. (1988). *Attention deficit disorder: Learning disabilities, Proceedings of the national conference.* Parkton, MD: York Press.

Shenker, A. (1992). The mechanism of action of drugs used to treat attention-deficit hyperactivity disorder: Focus on catecholamine receptor pharmacology. *Advances in Pediatrics, 39*, 337–382.

Shinka, John A. *Neurological Symptom Questionnaire.* Odessa, FL: Psychological Assessment Resources (PAR).

Terzano, M., Parino, L., & Mazzucchi, A., (1986). Confusional states with periodic lateralized epileptiform discharges (PLEDS): A peculiar epileptic syndrome. *Epilepsia, 27*, 446–457.

Ulrich, G., & Frick, K. (1986). A new quantitative approach to the assessment of stages of vigilance as defined by spatio-temporal EEG patterning. *Perceptual Motor Skills, 62*, 567–576.

Voeller, K. S. (1986). Right hemisphere deficit syndrome in children. *American Journal of Psychiatry, 143*, 1004–1009.

Voeller, K. S. (1991). Towards a neurobiologic nosology of attention deficit hyperactivity disorder. *Journal of Child Neurology, 6* (Suppl.), 52–58.

Weinberg, W. A., & Brumback, R. (1976). Mania in childhood: Case studies and literature review. *American Journal of Disorders of Childhood, 130*, 380–385.

Weinberg, W. A., & Brumback, R. A. (1990). Primary disorder of vigilance: A novel explanation of inattentiveness, daydreaming, boredom, restlessness and sleepiness. *General Pediatrics, 116*, 720–725.

Weinberg, W. A., & Brumback, R. A. (1992). The myth of attention deficit hyperactivity disorder: Symptoms resulting from multiple etiology. *General Child Neurology, 7*, 431–445.

Weinberg, W. A., & McLean, A. (1986). A diagnostic approach to developmental specific learning disabilities. *Journal of Child Neurology, 1*, 158–172.

Weintraub, S., & Mesulam, M. M. (1983). Developmental learning disabilities of the right hemisphere. *Archives of Neurology, 40*, 463–468.

Williamson, P. D., Spencer, D. D., & Spencer, S. S. (1985). Episodic aphemia and epileptic focus in nondominant hemisphere: Relieved by section of corpus callosum. *Neurology, 35*, 1069–1071.

Wylie, E. (1993). *The Treatment of epilepsy: Principles and practice.* Philadelphia: Lea & Febiger.

Zametkin, A., Nordahl, T., & Gross, M. (1990). Cerebral glucose metabolism in adults with hyperactivity of childhood onset. *New England Journal of Medicine, 323*, 1361–1366.

Zametkin, A. J., & Rapoport, J. L. (1987). Neurobiology of attention disorder with hyperactivity: Where have we come in 50 years? *Journal of the American Academy of Child and Adolescent Psychiatry, 26*, 676–686.

6

Differential Diagnosis of ADD Versus ADHD in Adults

THOMAS E. BROWN

When asked to think about someone who has attention deficit disorder, most people picture a young child, usually a boy, who is wildly hyperactive and does not pay attention because he is just not able to settle his body or mind long enough to focus attention on anything. Physical restlessness, constant chatter, intrusive interruptions, and disruptive behaviors are the most striking features of such "Dennis the Menace" children.

A BRIEF HISTORY OF DIAGNOSES FOR THE TWO TYPES

Most of the early diagnostic descriptions of what is now called attention deficit disorder focused on the hyperactive behavior of these disruptive children. Terms like hyperkinetic reaction of childhood disorder (American Psychiatric Association [APA], 1968) were used as diagnostic labels for a child who "carries out activities at a higher than normal rate of speed than the average child, or who is constantly in motion, or both" (Chess, 1940). Hyperactivity was assumed to be the core of the disorder.

As "hyper" children were studied more fully, it was noted that most of them had in common some problems other than just hyperactivity. They usually appeared to be both impulsive and inattentive. For many years three characteristics—inattention, impulsivity, and hyperactivity—have been considered the "holy trinity" of symptoms characterizing the core of what we now call ADDs (Note: In this chapter the plural term ADDs is used to refer to attention deficit disorders; it is intended to highlight the fact that there is not just one type of ADD). Even today, many parents, teachers, doctors, and others consider ADD as a possible diagnosis only if they see obvious signs of all three symptoms, particularly hyperactivity.

The first official recognition that inattention might be particularly important in this disorder was in DSM-III, published in 1980. That manual introduced the term attention deficit disorder to label a cluster of symptoms appearing sometimes with hyperactivity and sometimes without hyperactivity. Under DSM-III, children could be diagnosed as having ADD if from age 7 they demonstrated significant and chronic problems in sustaining attention, listening, avoiding distractions, organizing work, finishing tasks, and so forth. DSM-III recognized that some children having such problems were chronically hyperactive, while others were not; if the specified number of symptoms were present, the ADD diagnosis could be applied as either with hyperactivity (ADHD) or without hyperactivity (ADD W/O) (APA, 1980). Yet, at that time there was not much research to support the concept that ADDs occur in these two types.

When a revision of DSM-III was published in 1987, there was still not much published evidence to support the notion that ADDs occur without hyperactivity. Lacking such evidence, the diagnosis was renamed Attention-deficit Hyperactivity Disorder (ADHD). A list of 14 symptoms was specified, including items from each aspect of the trinity, any 8 of which, if chronically present since 7 years old, could be sufficient for the diagnosis of ADHD. DSM-III-R relegated the diagnosis of ADD W/O to a single paragraph as "Undifferentiated ADD," which gave no diagnostic criteria and explicitly questioned the validity of the diagnosis (APA, 1987).

From 1987 to 1994, while the official nomenclature of the American Psychiatric Association had no diagnostic criteria specified for ADD W/O, many research studies documented that ADD does, in fact, appear both with and without hyperactivity. Lahey and Carlson (1991) have reviewed research that established the validity of the ADD W/O diagnosis and provided the basis for a return to the two basic types of ADDs in DSM-IV. In the interim, many have continued to use the term ADD to refer to ADD W/O while reserving the term ADHD for the type with hyperactivity.

THE TWO TYPES OF ADDS IN DSM-IV

In 1994 the American Psychiatric Association published DSM-IV, which provides new diagnostic criteria for ADDs. These new criteria retain the old ADHD label, but a slash has been inserted between the two terms to indicate that the disorder may include either or both of the basic symptom types. The new terms for the basic types are Attention-Deficit/Hyperactivity Disorder, Predominantly Inattentive Type; and Attention-Deficit/Hyperactivity Disorder, Combined Type. A third category, AD/HD, Predominantly Hyperactive-Impulsive Type, has been added for cases in which hyperactive-impulsive symptoms occur without significant inattention symptoms. This third category is most likely to be useful for diagnosis of preschool children who manifest significant problems of hyperactivity and impulsivity at an age where children are not expected to demonstrate much sustained attention.

The new language of "Predominantly...Type" is clumsy, but it emphasizes that these basic types are not mutually exclusive categories. An individual with six or more DSM-IV symptoms of inattention may show some symptoms of impulsivity and/or hyperactivity and thus not truly be "without hyperactivity." Yet, if that person does not manifest at least six symptoms from the Hyperactivity-Impulsivity symptoms list, the appropriate diagnosis would be AD/HD, Predominantly Inattentive Type, not Combined Type. This departure from the either/or distinctions of DSM-III, with *or* without hyperactivity, reflects the reality that persons with AD/HD often do not fit neatly or exclusively into either of those diagnostic pigeon-holes, though they may not meet criteria for the combined type.

DSM-IV lists diagnostic criteria for ADDs in a chapter entitled: "Disorders Usually First Diagnosed in Infancy, Childhood or Adolescence." Yet the first paragraph of that chapter notes that some individuals with disorders listed in that chapter may not actually be recognized and diagnosed until adulthood (DSM-IV, p. 37). One point emphasized by this placement is that ADDs are defined as disorders with early onset. DSM-IV criteria require that some symptoms causing ADD impairments, whether recognized at the time or not, must have been present before age seven; if ADD symptoms appear in later life without any early childhood antecedents, an ADD diagnosis is not appropriate.

DSM-IV Inattention Criteria

Listed below are the DSM-IV criteria for symptoms of inattention; those who meet these criteria may be diagnosed as AD/HD (Predominantly Inattentive Type) without meeting any of the Hyperactivity-Impulsivity criteria. Although these criteria are labeled "inattention," five of nine items relate not to attention but to other domains of mental functioning, such as task organization, task completion, sustaining effort, and forgetfulness. This recognizes that ADDs involve impairments in a broader range of cognitive activities than simply paying attention.

1. *Inattention*: six (or more) of the following symptoms of inattention have persisted for at least six months to a degree that is maladaptive and inconsistent with developmental level:
    (a) often fails to give close attention to details or makes careless mistakes in schoolwork, work, or other activities
    (b) often has difficulty sustaining attention in tasks or play activities

(c) often does not seem to listen when spoken to directly
(d) often does not follow through on instructions and fails to fin-
     ish schoolwork, chores, or duties in the workplace (not due to
     oppositional behavior or failure to understand instructions
(e) often has difficulty organizing tasks and activities
(f) often avoids, dislikes, or is reluctant to engage in tasks that
     require sustained mental effort (such as schoolwork or
     homework)
(g) often loses things necessary for tasks or activities, e.g., toys,
     school assignments, pencils, books or tools
(h) is often easily distracted by extraneous stimuli
(i) is often forgetful in daily activities

(American Psychiatric Association, 1994, p. 83–84, reprinted with permission)

DSM-IV Hyperactivity-Impulsivity Criteria

Individuals meeting the DSM-IV criteria listed below may be diagnosed as AD/HD (Predominantly Hyperactive-Impulsive Type) if the above inattention criteria are not met; if both sets of criteria are met, the diagnosis would be AD/HD (Combined Type). Five of these nine hyperactivity-impulsivity symptoms describe observable behaviors, but four refer to reported or inferred patterns of internal experience, for example, feelings of restlessness, difficulty doing things quietly, always "on the go," difficulty waiting in lines or awaiting one's turn. These latter four suggest chronic feelings of urgency, stimulation-seeking, impatience, and inability to relax, which may be present even in persons who do not show a chronically high level of overt physical activity.

2. *Hyperactivity-Impulsivity*: six or more of the following symptoms of
    hyperactivity-impulsivity have persisted for at least 6 months to a
    degree that is maladaptive and inconsistent with developmental
    level:

Hyperactivity
(a) often fidgets with hands or feet or squirms in seat
(b) often leaves seat in classroom or in other situations in which
     remaining seated is expected
(c) often runs about or climbs excessively in situations where it is
     inappropriate (in adolescents or adults, may be limited to sub-
     jective feelings of restlessness)
(d) often has difficulty playing or engaging in leisure activities
     quietly

(e) is often "on the go" or often acts as if "driven by a motor"
(f) often talks excessively

Impulsivity
(g) often blurts out answers before questions
have been completed
(h) often has difficulty awaiting turn
(i) often interrupts or intrudes on others (e.g., butts into conversations or games)

(American Psychiatric Association, 1994, p. 84, reprinted with permission)

IMPAIRMENT REQUIRED FOR ADD DIAGNOSIS

To qualify for the diagnosis of AD/HD under DSM-IV criteria, an individual needs to not only manifest the symptoms listed above, but also be impaired by at least some of those symptoms in two or more settings, for example, at school, at work, or at home. This DSM-IV requirement for two "settings" in which impairment is found does not mention the two personal domains in which ADDs tend to be the most impaired: cognitive functions and self-esteem. Yet, this stipulation does raise the question of what clinically significant suffering, burdens or constraints are imposed on the individual by AD/HD symptoms. Impairment might refer to chronic unhappiness in a marriage where an ADD partner is experienced by the spouse as inattentive, or to a student's chronic underachievement, or to a worker's mediocre performance on a job. When such impairments are linked to a chronic pattern of AD/HD symptoms that occur in at least two domains of experience, the AD/HD diagnosis may be appropriate.

Impairment is often significant in ADDs. A recent study by Biederman and colleagues (Biederman, et al., 1993) demonstrated that referred and nonreferred adults diagnosed with ADDs were similar to each other and tended to be more disturbed and impaired than an adult comparison group. Overall, ADD adults demonstrated poorer school performance, greater cognitive impairments on a variety of objective measures, and lower global assessment of functioning scores than the non-ADD adult comparison group. Recognition of multiple, sometimes subtle ways in which ADD symptoms may be impairing an individual's functioning is an important element of making this diagnosis.

Context Variability in ADD Symptoms

Assessing impairment in ADDs is complicated by the fact that some ADD symptoms vary considerably depending on task and context. Clinical observations and self-reports indicate that most ADD patients are able to sustain concentration quite well during some tasks or in certain situations. A young child may have chronically poor concentration in school classrooms, yet demonstrate consistently good sustained attention while playing Nintendo for hours at a time. A student may be able to read science fiction stories with rapt attention, yet become drowsy and need to reread repeatedly when doing assigned academic readings. Often patients describe this situational variability as "I can pay attention very well sometimes, but only if the task is something that really interests me."

On the surface, such reports appear as simple variants of common experience; that is, most people are better able to sustain attention when doing something they enjoy. What seems different for ADD patients is their relative inability to "make themselves do it" when they need to get organized or sustain attention for relatively uninteresting tasks. Though they may recognize doing a certain task as necessary and, in that sense, "want" to do it, they are simply unable to force themselves to perform. In some ways their plight is similar to that of a situationally impotent male.

The problem of ADD patients is not so much a lack of the ability to organize or pay attention, but an inability to activate, mobilize, and sustain those functions when the task itself does not "turn them on." Denckla (1991, 1993) and Pennington (1991) have suggested that impairment of such "metaregulatory" or "executive" functions of the brain may be the primary dysfunction in ADDs and the underlying reason for situational variability of ADD symptoms.

"Invisibility" of ADD W/O Symptoms

Although both inattention and hyperactive-impulsive symptoms seem to vary situationally, the more overt, often disruptive behavioral symptoms of ADDs with hyperactivity make that syndrome much easier to recognize and diagnose. Obvious and persistent behavior-management problems with ADHD children in school, home, and neighborhood can put great pressure on parents and teachers to seek evaluations and referrals for treatment of ADHD children at an early age. But individuals whose ADDs do not include significant impulsive-hyperactive behaviors can easily be overlooked throughout childhood and adolescence and into adulthood; their chronic difficulties with inattention, disorganization, memory, and so forth may be attributed to laziness, stupidity, depression, or lack of motivation. ADD symptoms of inattention are "silent" relative to the "noisy" symptoms of hyperactivity.

Lack of established diagnostic criteria for ADD W/O during the past 7 years has certainly not helped clinicians learn to recognize the more subtle forms of ADDs that do not include hyperactivity. Epstein and colleagues

(Epstein, Shaywitz, Shaywitz, & Woolston, 1991) reported that experienced clinicians correctly identified 80% of a sample of children comprehensively diagnosed as having ADD with hyperactivity, but recognized only 50% of the children comprehensively diagnosed as having ADD W/O hyperactivity. The percentage of children, adolescents, and adults whose ADD W/O is not recognized, diagnosed, and treated is, of course, not known, but it seems likely that at present unrecognized cases of ADD W/O greatly outnumber those diagnosed and treated. In many ways, ADDs W/O tend to remain invisible, even to many clinicians.

Masking of ADDs by Comorbidities

One factor that reduces recognition of ADDs, especially without hyperactivity, is the problem of comorbidity. Reports by Biederman (Biederman, Newcorn, & Sprich, 1991), Jensen (Jensen, Shervette, Xenakis, & Richters, 1993), and Brown (in press) have highlighted high rates of comorbidity between ADDs and other psychiatric disorders. Under present diagnostic criteria it appears that more than 50% of those diagnosed with ADDs also meet diagnostic criteria for at least one other psychiatric diagnosis, for example, mood disorders, anxiety disorders, learning disorders, disruptive behavior disorders, and substance abuse disorders. (See chapters 3 and 4, this volume, for a more complete discussion of these issues.)

Since these other disorders, especially in adults, are more familiar to most physicians, psychologists, psychiatrists, and other clinicians than are ADDs, it is likely that a person with ADD and another comorbid disorder may be diagnosed and treated for the comorbid disorder and not for ADD. In this way, the ADD may remain hidden behind the comorbidity (e.g., depression), unresponsive to the treatment provided for the other disorder (e.g., tricyclics or SSRIs), while remaining persistent in sustaining impairment (poor concentration and slow information processing) which may be inaccurately attributed to the comorbid diagnosis (depression). This would not be a problem if the treatments were identical for the two disorders, but there is some evidence (e.g., Gammon & Brown, 1993) to suggest that antidepressants alone do not improve concentration and other ADD cognitive symptoms as effectively as stimulants alone or in combination with antidepressants. Similar problems of comorbidities masking ADDs may occur with a variety of other comorbid disorders in combination with ADDs with and without hyperactivity.

"Crossovers" from ADHD to ADD W/O

Another factor that may complicate diagnosis of ADDs is the phenomenon of crossovers from ADHD to ADD W/O. "Crossovers" is used here to refer to those who meet diagnostic criteria for ADD with hyperactivity during childhood and then, as they get older, gradually lose so much of their hyperactivity that they no longer qualify for an ADHD diagnosis. This pattern was described by Wender (1987) and was documented as typical of many maturing hyperactive children in longitudinal studies by Weiss & Hechtman (1986, 1993).

Currently available epidemiological studies do not provide adequate data to estimate how many individuals suffer from ADDs W/O, nor do they indicate how many of those with ADD W/O are crossovers from ADHD versus those ADD W/O patients who never met diagnostic criteria for ADHD.

HYPERACTIVITY AS PREREQUISITE FOR ADULT ADD

One of the widely used diagnostic criteria sets for adult ADD is the Utah Criteria proposed by Wender (1978; Wender, Wood, & Reimherr, 1991). These require retrospective evidence that the individual met criteria for ADHD (with hyperactivity) during childhood, with such evidence usually obtained directly from the individual's parent or older sibling, not simply by self-report. To meet the Utah Criteria for ADHD in adults, the individual must also manifest in current adult experience both persistent motor hyperactivity and attention deficits. In addition, the adult must currently manifest two of the following five symptoms—affective lability, inability to complete tasks, hot temper, impulsivity, stress intolerance—and not have antisocial personality disorder, major affective disorder, schizophrenia, schizoaffective disorder, or schizotypal or borderline personality disorder (Wender et al., 1991).

The Utah Criteria have no status in the DSM system and remain controversial in many ways. One fundamental problem with them is the stipulation that the diagnosis of ADD in adulthood requires evidence of hyperactivity, both retrospectively in childhood and currently in adulthood. By Utah standards, only those adults whose ADD included chronic hyperactivity in childhood that has persisted into adulthood would be eligible for diagnosis. No crossover would be eligible for diagnosis of adult ADD, nor would any adult whose ADD has always been of the "predominantly inattentive type." The Utah Criteria have enshrined hyperactivity as the core characteristic of ADDs, relegating attentional problems to subordinate status in a way not supported either by established diagnostic standards or by most research on ADD over the past decade. They certify for diagnosis only the most severe of one subtype of ADD.

AN "EXPANDED" CONSTRUCT OF ADDS

Building on the DSM-III notion that attentional problems constitute the core of ADDs, and following the DSM-IV premise that an ADD diagnosis can be appropriately made in the absence of impulsivity-hyperactivity, Brown (1995) has proposed an "expanded" construct for core symptoms of ADDs. This proposal expands the construct of inattention, while relegating hyperactivity-impulsivity to the status of an ADD subtype. Brown's construct includes some cognitive and affective symptoms often seen in ADD patients but not explicitly noted in the DSM-IV list.

As noted above, five of nine symptoms on the DSM-IV Inattention list relate to domains other than attention. Brown proposes conceptualizing the core of ADDs as five clusters, each of which taps a different domain of ADD symptoms that may be central to ADDs. Items in these clusters were derived from pilot testing of expanded lists of symptoms elicited from ADD patients; the clusters were derived conceptually from the resulting items.

Clusters of this proposed expanded model of ADDs include problems in

1. *Activating and organizing to work*: difficulties in getting organized and started on work tasks, as well as problems self-activating for daily routines, for example, "excessive difficulty getting started on paperwork or contacting people"

2. *Sustaining attention*: problems in sustaining attention to work tasks, excessive daydreaming or distractibility when listening or doing required reading, for example, "when reading, repeatedly loses track and needs to reread"

3. *Sustaining energy and effort*: problems in keeping up consistent energy and effort for work tasks, daytime drowsiness, for example, "very inconsistent work production, slacks off unless pressure is on"

4. *Moodiness and sensitivity to criticism*: difficulties with irritability, apparent lack of motivation, for example, "especially sensitive to criticism, feels it for a long time"

5. *Memory recall*: problems with forgetfulness and recall of learned material, for example, "difficulty memorizing names, dates, or information at work"

A self-report instrument, the Brown Attention Deficit Disorder Scale has been developed to measure symptoms of this expanded model. Available in one version for older children and adolescents and another for adults, in preliminary studies this instrument appears to discriminate ADD patients from nonpsychiatric controls (Brown, 1995). Especially when used with a recommended scoring system for subtests of the WISC-R/WISC III or WAIS-R IQ tests (see below), this instrument may be helpful in diagnosis of ADDs. One particularly striking finding from preliminary testing was a lack of difference between ADD subjects with and without hyperactivity

(Brown, 1995). This suggests that the proposed expanded core of ADD symptoms may be common to both basic types of ADD.

Although further testing of Brown's expanded concept of ADDs and related measures is needed before any strong inferences can be derived, his theory can be contrasted to Barkley's recent proposal that "poor response inhibition or inability to delay response is the major hallmark of ADHD" (Barkley, 1993, p. 1). While Barkley emphasizes impairment of inhibition as central to ADD, Brown highlights inconsistency in initiating and sustaining arousal of brain functions that metaregulate not only self-control but also organization, planning, energy, alertness, mood, and memory. Difference in arousal between the brains of adults with ADHD and normal controls was strikingly demonstrated in Zametkin's (Zametkin et al., 1990) PET study of cerebral glucose metabolism. Differences in thresholds of arousal of the brain in ADD may play a critical role in activation and motivation of a wide variety of functions subsumed under the neurologists' concept of impaired executive function (e.g., Denckla, 1991, 1993). Further research is needed to ascertain whether either of these models proposed by Barkley or Brown can be helpful for understanding complexities of ADD impairments.

DIAGNOSTIC SPECIFICITY FOR ADDS

At present, there is no single instrument or procedure that can adequately diagnosis ADDs. Unlike a twisted ankle, which can usually be definitively diagnosed by X ray as either broken or not broken, presently ADDs can be diagnosed only by convergence of several different measures that allow an experienced clinician to determine how well the individual's symptoms fit the profile of ADD, relative to other possible diagnoses.

Because most ADD symptoms are experienced at some time by virtually everyone, the evaluating clinician has the task of ascertaining whether the individual being assessed is impaired by these symptoms substantially more than most persons of the same age or developmental level. The question is not whether an individual has ADD symptoms that most people never have, but whether that person suffers substantially more intense, more frequent, and more sustained impairment from such symptoms than most others of the same age. It is one thing if a person occasionally, when very fatigued, becomes drowsy and repeatedly distracted while reading. It is quite another matter if an individual chronically experiences drowsiness and frequent distractions almost every time he tries to read, regardless of how well rested.

Because many ADD symptoms can also appear in other psychiatric disorders, the evaluator must consider whether some of the ADD symptoms reported have chronically impaired the person since early childhood, thus indicating the "built-in" pattern of ADDs, or whether the person was previously unimpaired in domains of ADD symptoms and is now impaired in those functions as a result of depression, anxiety, substance abuse, or some other psychiatric disorder.

DSM-IV criteria do not require all of the specified ADD symptoms to have been present since early childhood, but they do stipulate that "some symptoms that caused impairment were present since age seven." This requirement can help to discriminate ADDs with comorbid disorders, for example, depression, from depression without ADD, where symptoms of impaired concentration mimic ADD but are secondary to the depression itself. If a person complaining of drowsiness and frequent distractions while reading reports that this problem rarely occurred prior to 6 months ago when she or he began to feel depressed, that symptom is unlikely to indicate ADD. If the person reports that such symptoms have plagued her or him chronically since early childhood, long before the recent bout of depression, the possibility of ADD is more likely.

Ascertainment of premorbid functioning in domains of ADD symptoms is the key to this differential, which is often complicated by the fact that symptoms now recognizable retrospectively as ADD-related may not have been recognized as such by school, family, clinicians, or the patient in earlier years. An individual may report long-standing difficulties with sustaining attention in conversations, completing homework, staying on task for work, keeping track of belongings, and so forth, all explained by himself and others as due to laziness, lack of motivation, or characterological "spaciness." Such reports of lifelong persistence of ADD symptoms strongly argue for possible ADD diagnosis, whether or not such a diagnosis was ever considered in earlier years.

ASSESSMENT OF POSSIBLE ADDS

The most sensitive and useful instrument for assessment and differential diagnosis of ADDs is a well-conducted clinical interview. Protocols and techniques for clinical interviews to evaluate possible ADDs are discussed in other chapters of this volume.

After the clinical interview has established a context in which to understand the patient's complaints, the clinician evaluating for ADD should systematically ask about the wider range of ADD symptoms. A broad ADD symptom rating scale such as BADDS (Brown, 1995) may be useful in canvassing for difficulties in a variety of cognitive, affective, and behavioral domains that may be related to ADDs; such a survey may yield important data, which the person being interviewed might not even recognize as relevant. Self-report of such symptoms can be quantified in simple terms, for example, 0 to 3 responses indicating frequency of occurrence and/or degree of impairment for each symptom. In eliciting such scoring, however, the clinician should be sensitive to "incidental" comments, examples, or behavioral cues by the respondent that might help to elaborate or counterpoint the numerical response. Even these relatively structured and quantified interchanges with the client should be considered aspects of the ongoing conversation of the clinical interview.

After a broad screen for ADD symptoms has been done, the clinician should systematically query the individual regarding each item on the DSM-IV AD/HD symptom list. This should include enough follow-up questions to ascertain the degree to which, in the person's experience, each specific symptom has been present and impairing over the past 6 months and in earlier years. Both the inattention and the impulsive-hyperactive symptom lists should be utilized regardless of the clinician's initial impression of what type of ADD the individual might have.

A competent clinical interview to assess for ADDs should not conclude after assessing just for ADD symptoms and their context. Adequate differential diagnosis requires at least a screening for symptoms of other possible disorders which might be causing, contributing to, or comorbid with ADD. This does not require interrogating the person for every symptom of every possible disorder, but it does involve querying for categories of possible symptoms—for example, problems with excessive worries, moods, and drugs or alcohol—and following up on any relevant cues emerging in the interview.

Additional Assessment Tools

Assessment of ADDs in adults who are no longer in school is generally more difficult than similar evaluations for children and adolescents because there is no adult equivalent to school grades and related academic measures. There is, at present, no standardized way to measure the effectiveness with which persons organize their personal budget or daily calendar, sustain attention in reading reports or newspapers, attend to communications with friends and colleagues, or keep up initiative on independent work tasks.

Self-report in a clinical interview or in response to ADD symptom screens is probably the most effective and "ecologically valid" (Barkley, 1991) measure of ADD impairments in adulthood. Additional reliability may be added by conjoint interview if the individual has a spouse, offspring, or friend whom they want to include in a portion of the evaluation interview to offer an additional perspective regarding possibly symptomatic behaviors which may not be obvious to the person being evaluated. The Brown ADD scales are set up to include an option for such conjoint assessment.

Some clinicians utilize computerized continuous performance tests, for example, the Test of Variables of Attention (TOVA), or Conners Continuous Performance Test (CPT) to assess problems of inattention and impulsive responding. Such measures have been shown to discriminate between those with ADHD and nonclinical populations; they can also be sensitive to medication-induced changes in symptoms (Greenberg, 1991). However, it is not yet clear how well such "objective" tests can assess the broader range of ADD symptoms.

Another "objective" measure that may be useful in assessing ADD symptoms is subtest factor analysis of standard IQ tests. Overall IQ scores have no value in assessing ADDs because ADD diagnosis is quite independent of intelligence; ADDs occur in individuals at every point in the overall IQ range, from very superior to mentally defective. Yet, there are some IQ subtests that tap into functions impaired in ADDs, such as concentration, sequencing, memory, and speed of information processing. Statistical comparison of an individual's performance on those subtests relevant to ADDs versus a baseline factor of subtests relatively independent of ADD can provide an index of impairment by ADD symptoms which, though not sufficient to make a diagnosis, may be useful as one element of the total diagnostic picture. Biederman and colleagues (1993) recently reported a study in which such IQ measures discriminated adults with ADD from a comparison group; similar IQ measures on adults, children, and adolescents are included in the Brown ADD Scales system (Brown, 1995). (See chapter 7, this volume, for a more complete discussion of the uses of diagnostic tests.)

Integration of Data for ADD Diagnosis

Ultimately diagnosis of ADDs and differentiation of ADDs in various subtypes and comorbidities involve integration and weighing of data from a variety of sources. An evaluating clinician needs to assess findings from clinical interviews including the individual's presenting complaints, health history, school history, work history, social functioning, family history, psychiatric symptoms, and so forth, in the context of developmental history and overall levels of functioning. Using this data as context, the clinician does a wide symptom screen for ADDs (e.g., Brown ADD Scales), and a specific assessment for each of the established DSM- IV symptoms of AD/HD, with a screen for alternative psychiatric diagnoses or possible comorbidities. These data are then weighted and integrated to address the question of whether the individual at this time fits the established diagnostic profile for an ADD sufficiently to warrant that diagnosis. In making such an assessment there is no substitute for the seasoned judgment of a sensitive clinician who has had extensive experience in assessing and treating a large number of persons with ADDs.

DIFFERENTIAL DIAGNOSIS OF BASIC TYPES OF ADDS

Although this chapter addresses differential diagnosis of ADDs with and without hyperactivity, much of the information presented here does not emphasize differences between these two types so much as the centrality of broad-ranging cognitive symptoms in both basic types. One underlying assumption of this chapter is that the core symptoms of ADDs are essentially cognitive impairments, some of which are listed or alluded to on the Inattention list of DSM-IV. Particularly for adults, these cognitive symptoms seem to constitute the central impairments for persons with ADDs with or without significant impulsivity-hyperactivity.

Some adults with ADDs have had and continue to manifest significant impairments due to hyperactivity, but even for these persons, their primary ADD impairments are usually due to cognitive symptoms. In schools, in employment, in social relationships, and in families, there is usually more latitude for persons who are highly energetic, restless, and impulsive than there is for persons who are inattentive, disorganized, forgetful, careless, and unable to sustain effort for work.

Clinicians need to be alert to recognize symptoms of both basic types of ADDs in adults. It is especially important for clinicians to keep in mind the clinical profile of AD/HD, Predominantly Inattentive Type, so they can recognize the AD/HD syndrome when it occurs without the more readily identifiable symptoms of impulsivity-hyperactivity or when it is masked by comorbid symptoms.

Since, at present, the primary treatment intervention most likely to alleviate ADD symptoms in either basic type is stimulant medication, differential diagnosis between Predominantly Inattentive Type and Combined Type is not likely to be very important in choice of initial treatment. Yet, recognition of the broad and more pervasive "silent" ADD symptoms may be critically important for diagnostic assessment and for monitoring of treatment for ADDs of either basic type.

REFERENCES

American Psychiatric Association. (1968). *Diagnostic and statistical manual of mental disorders* (2nd ed.). Washington, DC: Author.

American Psychiatric Association. (1980). *Diagnostic and statistical manual of mental disorders* (3rd ed.). Washington, DC: Author.

American Psychiatric Association. (1987). *Diagnostic and statistical manual of mental disorders* (3rd ed., revised). Washington, DC: Author.

American Psychiatric Association. (1994). *Diagnostic and statistical manual of mental disorders* (4th ed.). Washington, DC: Author.

Barkley, R. A. (1991). The ecological validity of laboratory and analogue assessment of ADHD symptoms. *Journal of Abnormal Psychology, 19,* 149–178.

Barkley, R. A. (1993). A new theory of ADHD. *ADHD Report, 1*(5), 1–4.

Biederman, J., Faraone, S. V., Spencer, T., Wilens, T., Norman, D., Lapey, K. A., Mick, E., Lehman, B. K., & Doyle, A. (1993). Patterns of psychiatric comorbidity, cognition, and psychosocial functioning in adults with attention deficit disorder. *American Journal of Psychiatry, 150*(12), 1792–1798.

Biederman, J., Newcorn, J., & Sprich, S. (1991). Comorbidity of attention deficit hyperactivity disorder with conduct, depressive, anxiety and other disorders. *American Journal of Psychiatry, 148*(5), 564–577.

Brown, T. E. (1995). *Brown Attention Deficit Disorder Scales.* San Antonio, TX: The Psychological Corporation.

Brown, T. E. (Ed.). (in press). *Attention deficit disorders and comorbidities in children, adolescents and adults.* Washington, DC: American Psychiatric Press.

Chess, S. (1940). Diagnosis and treatment of the hyperactive child. *New York State Journal of Medicine, 60,* 2379–2385.

Denckla, M. B. (1991). Attention deficit hyperactivity disorder–residual type. *Journal of Child Neurology, 6*(Suppl.), S42–S48.

Denckla, M. B. (1993). The child with developmental disabilities grown up: Adult residua of childhood disorders. *Neurologic Clinics, 11*(1), 105–125.

Epstein, M. A., Shaywitz, S. E., Shaywitz, B. A., & Woolston, J. L. (1991). Boundaries of attention deficit disorder. *Journal of Learning Disabilities, 24*(2), 78–86.

Gammon, G. D., & Brown, T. E. (1993). Fluoxetine and methylphenidate in combination for treatment of attention deficit disorder and comorbid depressive disorder. *Journal of Child & Adolescent Psychopharmacology, 3*(1), 1–10.

Greenberg, L. M. (1991). *T.O.V.A. Interpretation Manual.* Minneapolis, MN: Author.

Jensen, P. S., Shervette, R. E., Xenakis, S. N., & Richters, J. (1993). Anxiety and depressive disorders in attention deficit disorder with hyperactivity: New findings. *American Journal of Psychiatry, 150*(8), 1203–1209.

Lahey, B. B., & Carlson, C. C. (1991). Validity of the diagnostic category of attention deficit disorder without hyperactivity: A review of the literature. *Journal of Learning Disabilities, 24*(3), 110–120.

Pennington, B. F. (1991). *Diagnosing learning disorders: A neurological framework.* New York: Guilford Press.

Weiss, G., & Hechtman, L. T. (1986). *Hyperactive children grown up: Empirical findings and theoretical considerations.* New York: Guilford Press.

Weiss, G., & Hechtman, L. T. (1993). *Hyperactive children grown up: ADHD in children, adolescents and adults* (2nd ed.). New York: Guilford Press.

Wender, P. H. (1978). Minimal brain dysfunction: An overview. In M. A. Lipton, A. Di Mascio, & K. F. Killam (Eds.), *Psychopharmacology: A generation of progress* (pp. 1429–1435). New York: Raven Press.

Wender, P. (1987). *Hyperactive child, adolescent and adult: Attention deficit disorder through the lifespan.* New York: Oxford University Press.

Wender, P., Wood, D. R., & Reimherr, F. W. (1991). Pharmacological treatment of attention deficit disorder, residual type (ADD-RT) in adults. In L. L. Greenhill & B. B. Osman (Eds.), *Ritalin: Theory and patient management* (pp. 25–33). New York: Mary Ann Liebert.

Zametkin, A. J., Nordahl, T. E., Gross, M., King, A. C., Semple, W. E., Rumsey, J., Hamburger, S., & Cohen, R. M. (1990). Cerebral glucose metabolism in adults with hyperactivity of childhood onset. *New England Journal of Medicine, 323*(20), 1361–1366.

7

Neuropsychological and Psychoeducational Testing in the Evaluation of the ADD Adult

SUSAN H. BIGGS

This chapter explores assessment of Attention Deficit Disorder (ADD) in adults. The previous chapters in this section addressed the differential diagnosis issues that are essential to consider in the assessment of adults with ADD, including neurodevelopmental, neurological, and psychiatric conditions that may accompany ADD. In this chapter, I address how attention deficit can be diagnosed, as well as the assessment of these possible comorbid conditions. I begin by discussing screening information, which will be especially useful for professionals wishing to discern the need for more extensive and specific evaluations. The second part of this chapter details how to test for problems with attention, memory, and executive functions, and includes discussions of specific measures that might be included in an ADD battery. The final part of this chapter addresses an assessment of comorbid psychiatric and neurodevelopmental conditions.

SCREENING FOR ATTENTION DEFICIT DISORDERS

As has been repeatedly discussed in previous chapters, Attention Deficit Disorders in adults can coexist with other disorders. Furthermore, attentional problems in adults may be symptomatic of neurological or psychiatric disorders other than ADD. Therefore, the essential first step when working with an adult who is questioning the presence of ADD is to determine if an in-depth assessment is needed. Several questionnaires described here may be useful in determining the need for more specific testing.

Determining the Need for Further ADD Assessment

With the increasing awareness of the presence of ADD in adults, many professionals in the mental health and education fields are encountering more frequent questions about adult ADD. Among others, college counselors for disabled students, psychologists, psychiatrists, and neurologists will be hearing more and more questions from clients about the possible role of ADD in their lives. Professionals encountering these issues need to be able to distinguish ADD from other disorders in order to treat it appropriately. Questionnaires are probably one of the fastest and easiest ways to rule in or rule out attention-related problems.

Screening for ADD is essential due to the frequency of unrelated disorders that also manifest attentional problems. Although recently, through magazine articles and television coverage, there has been an increase in public awareness of ADD in adults, many adults with ADD will present in mental health clinics or private offices with symptoms of depression and anxiety, leaving the detection of ADD up to a discerning clinician. Clients may initially describe problems with spousal relationships or an inability to maintain friendships. They may state an inability to cope with the stresses of life, difficulty performing competently on the job, or trouble finding and keeping jobs. They may feel frustrated by forgetfulness, poor memory, poor time management, or difficulty staying with tasks for a length of time. Clients may feel depressed or have low self-esteem, despite appearing to be capable individuals. They may describe problems with concentration, organization, self-discipline, tolerance for frustration, or perseverance (Barkley, 1990; Woods, 1986). As Ratey (1991) stated, out of 70 adults with ADD seen in his clinic, 40% "presented with disorders of mood including depression, dysthymia, and bipolar disorder. Others were referred with diagnoses of impulse disorders, obsessive-compulsive disorder, substance abuse or with a range of anxiety symptoms from generalized anxiety to panic" (p. 13).

Screening questionnaires are useful in determining what other kinds of evaluation and treatment may be necessary in addition to (or instead of) evaluation of ADD. For example, the Wender Utah Rating Scale (Ward, Wender, & Reimherr, 1993) has been successfully used in determining the presence of depression in addition to ADD. However, even when ADD is detected by these questionnaires, other disorders cannot be ruled out.

Questionnaires are completed by the client. They may be filled out independently or with the examiner reading the items aloud. Some prefer the latter approach, which gives the opportunity for further questions and discussion. Brown and Gammon (1991) suggest questionnaires also be completed by others who play a significant role in the life of the client (such as parents, spouse, grown children). This is often especially important for ADD clients in that they are not always the best judges of their impact on the lives of those around them (Wender, 1987).

Parents may often be good reporters of childhood experiences (Woods, 1986). One caveat should be mentioned, however, regarding enlisting parents of adults to describe academic or behavioral problems the adult client may have had as a child. In the experience of some clinicians (K. Nadeau, personal communication, 1993), parents of adults, in contrast to parents of children with ADD, sometimes underreport ADD symptoms. Some parents may react defensively, fearing that such a late discovery of a lifelong condition may suggest inadequate parenting on their part. Others may have faded memories or lack of awareness of ADD symptoms. Other parents seem wary of hurting the feelings of their adult offspring by describing them in "negative terms." The clinician needs to be aware that these parents may comprise a different population from the parents currently flocking to clinics seeking treatment for their children with ADD. In at least some parents, the clinician needs to be prepared for minimization or outright denial of childhood difficulties.

Questionnaires typically include questions regarding a range of major issues commonly reported by adults with ADD. These include problems with concentration, impulsivity, interpersonal skills, tolerance for frustration, restlessness, time management, motivation, underachievement, and daydreaming.

Wender Utah Rating Scale

Ward et al. (1993) developed the Wender Utah Rating Scale to identify Attention Deficit Hyperactivity Disorders (ADHD) and to assess their presence in adults. The scale asks adult subjects to describe their own childhood behavior, but it does not address the issues of adult functioning. By comparing scores for adults with ADHD, adults with depression, and "normal" adults, Ward et al. were able to identify 86% of the adults with ADHD. These scales are based on the presumption that for ADHD to exist in adulthood, it had to have been clearly present in childhood. In clinical practice, however, many adults with patterns suggestive of ADD in adulthood report that these patterns were minimal and went unrecognized in childhood. Research is needed to investigate patterns of ADD "emerging" in adulthood as demands for concentration, follow-through, planning, and organization increase. As discussed by Brown (chapter 6, this volume), the Utah Rating Scale emphasizes symptoms of hyperactivity and may be less useful in evaluating a nonhyperactive adult.

The Brown Attention-Activation Disorder Scale (BAADS)

Brown and Gammon (1991) developed the Brown Attention-Activation Disorder Scale (BAADS) to assess Attention-Activation Disorder, which is an expanded version of Attention Deficit Disorder without Hyperactivity. This 40-item questionnaire was designed "for use with adolescents, adults or children who show a pattern of chronic under-achievement marked by attentional and motivational problems without hyperactivity in school or employment" (p. 1). Unlike the Utah scales, this scale focuses on current functioning within the last month.

Adult ADHD Questionnaire

In her Adult ADHD Questionnaire, Nadeau (1991) offers a detailed list of questions for adults. This questionnaire has not received clinical trials, but is based on clinical experience and is meant to be used as a structured assessment interview. Questions are broken down into 19 categories:

Inattention	Impulsivity	Self-esteem/Confidence
Hyperactivity	Distractibility	Substance abuse
Time management	Self-discipline	Family history
Organization/Structure	Memory	Social/Interpersonal
Frustration tolerance	Anger control	Anxiety/Depression
Stimulants	Academics	Oppositional tendencies
Sleep patterns		

Within each category, up to 15 specific questions explore problems. Clients are asked to rate their reaction to each question on a scale of 0 ("I do not feel this statement describes me at all") to 4 ("I feel this statement describes me to a very large degree"). An average is computed for each category, allowing the examiner to evaluate the level of difficulty in each domain. Average scores of 2.75 or greater are considered significant areas of concern meriting further assessment.

The Adult ADHD Questionnaire has been revised as a screening tool in the assessment of college students, recently published in *ADD and the College Student* (Quinn, 1993). These questionnaires differ from other screening tools in that they cover a broader range of issues that the clinician will need to address during the course of treatment, rather than simply focusing on the ADHD triad of distractibility, impulsivity, and hyperactivity.

Copeland Symptom Checklist for Adult Attention Deficit Disorder

As she reported, Copeland's checklist was based on the clinical experience of many experts in the treatment of ADD and Hyperactivity. It has not been normed, and is meant to be used as a screening instrument. The questionnaire consists of 63 items contained in eight different categories. Her questionnaire contains two sets of items that deal with both hyperactivity and underactivity, allowing the clinician to distinguish between the two patterns.

Suggested Diagnostic Criteria for ADD in Adults

In their 1993 article for *ADDult News*, Hallowell and Ratey list 20 possible symptoms reported by adults with ADD. They stress, however, that these criteria are suggested only, and are based on clinical experience rather than field trials. The criteria they posit may be easily posed as questions (for example, "a tendency to be easily bored," "many projects going simultaneously," "trouble with follow-through") for use by the clinician in assessing an adult for possible attention deficits. In addition to offering these criteria, a brief description of each one is offered discussing how the symptom fits into the ADD syndrome.

Self-diagnosis Through the Use of ADD Questionnaires

Many adults are now arriving at the clinician's door having "diagnosed" themselves with ADD through a questionnaire in a book or magazine. While many of these individuals may be correct in their assessment, there are many others who are not. ADD has the danger of becoming the "diagnosis of choice" for a number of reasons. Some may have more serious and limiting neurological disorders but prefer the less stigmatizing ADD diagnosis. A number of adult ADD support group leaders have mentioned a pattern of adults attending such groups, having self-diagnosed ADD, when they clearly have more serious or complicated psychiatric or neurological disorders. Some attorneys (Patricia Latham, personal communication, November 30, 1993) report that individuals who have committed serious crimes are now beginning to contact attorneys intending to use ADD as a factor in their defense. Again, while ADD may play a strong role in the commission of some highly impulsive crimes, the clinician must be alert to the popularization and potential exploitation of the adult ADD diagnosis.

At the opposite end of the self-diagnosis continuum is the "underreporter" of symptoms. Because low self-awareness is often seen in ADD adults, the minimization of symptoms can occur, highlighting the risks involved in putting too strong a reliance on self-report through interview and questionnaires. In some cases, a spouse will become aware of the issue of ADD in adults, recognize such symptoms in his or her partner, and urge the partner to seek an ADD evaluation. The likelihood of underreporting may be higher in these "other-referred" adults because they are not seeking an evaluation out of their own concern about their functioning, but in response to their partner's concerns.

Diagnosis Versus Assessment of ADD in Adults

In this chapter I address the issue of assessment from a broader perspective than a simple "yes-no" response to the diagnosis of ADD. It seems that a complete reliance on clinical interview and ADD questionnaire responses, an approach recommended by some experts in the field of ADD, can be risky. Such reliance presupposes the accuracy of responses to questionnaires, as well as the clinical expertise of the clinician conducting the interview. While an experienced clinician may be able to make highly accurate diagnoses using these assessment tools alone, the possibility of missing the attentional problems of nonhyperactive adults, highly intelligent adults, or those who are only mildly to moderately affected seems high (as discussed further below). (See Brown, chapter 6, this volume, for further discussion of this issue.) The requirement that ADD symptoms must have been present in childhood as reported on questionnaires needs to be moderated by the experience of the clinician. For example, even *with* the benefit of an extensive psychological report diagnosing a college student with ADD, a psychiatrist at a well-respected university did not feel that such a diagnosis was accurate given the student's high academic performance in high school. This psychiatrist apparently believed that a history of marked academic difficulty was essential to a diagnosis of ADD.

Even in those cases where there appears to be little question of the ADD diagnosis, it seems that a more complete assessment can be useful to more fully evaluate not just the global presence of ADD symptoms which warrant the diagnosis, but also the degree of these symptoms, which can be quite variable from one individual to the next. In addition, it will be possible to assess potential comorbid neurodevelopmental, neurological, and psychiatric conditions.

Exceptions to the Rule

Another factor the clinician should be aware of in diagnosing ADD in adults is the role that family structure, personality structure, external environmental structure, and intelligence can play in how ADD is manifested. In adults who were not hyperactive as children, their childhood symptoms of ADD may seem less obvious. This is especially true for females, whose symptoms in childhood may have been viewed through different lenses (see chapter 14, this volume). ADD children whose intelligence was above average, whose parents provided a high level of structure and guidance, and who attended highly structured schools may report few or no symptoms in early childhood. As the demands to provide structure for oneself increased, as these individuals left the family nest and the more structured (often private or parochial) school environment, their ADD symptoms tended to become more evident. These individuals, who were mildly or moderately affected by ADD, in effect, received the environmental supports needed by children with ADD, even though they were not diagnosed as having ADD. Clinicians should also be aware that if symptoms are present later in life, especially in adults of high intelligence, a good school record should not rule out the diagnosis of ADD.

ASSESSMENT OF ATTENTION, MEMORY, AND EXECUTIVE FUNCTIONS

Unless a clinician is highly experienced in working with adults with ADD, questionnaire data alone may not be sufficient for a definitive diagnosis. Further testing can often help confirm diagnostic impressions. Because there is a wide variation in the number and severity of symptoms among adults with ADD, testing can help the clinician assess the degree to which memory, organization, self-discipline, hyperactivity, and so forth affect functioning. It is also helpful in making a differential diagnosis between ADD and other conditions in which attentional problems are symptomatic. Finally, testing is very useful in evaluating the wide range of comorbid conditions discussed in preceding chapters. When administering a battery of tests, however, it is essential for the clinician to note that some adults can compensate sufficiently for their ADD and perform well during brief evaluation sessions. In these cases, clear evidence of ADD is not always seen, but aspects of performance, in combination with questionnaire data, can help highlight attention-related problems.

The empirical research on testing adults with ADD is extremely limited. In the few studies that have been conducted, the sample sizes are relatively small (Greenberg, 1992; Hechtman, 1989; Hechtman, Weiss, & Perlman, 1984; Klee, Garfinkel, & Beauchesne, 1986; Mirsky, Anthony, Duncan, Ahearn, & Kellam, 1991; Shekim, Asnarow, Hess, Zaucha, & Wheeler, 1990; Ward et al., 1993). Furthermore, the results often conflict. Because there is not a definitive battery developed to assess ADD in adults, it is often helpful to approach testing from a flexible perspective. That is, the goal of the examiner is to capture aspects of attention problems by setting up situations in which clients are likely to demonstrate how they approach and solve problems. This approach to testing, like other neuropsychological evaluations, is based not only on standardized test scores, but also uses a variety of formal and informal measures to assess problem-solving style (Johnston, 1986). The interpretation of such testing is a process that requires familiarity with both the test measures and the fundamentals of ADD in adults.

The Importance of Interpretation

For each test given, it is essential to address the level of performance, the quality of performance, the relationship between the level and quality of performance, and the problem-solving strategy used (Rudel, Holmes, & Pardes, 1988). For children, Johnston (1986) advises clinicians to watch for signs of ADD in short latency responses, uncritical and careless performance with frequent false starts, off-task behavior, and concentration problems. Many of these same problems can be seen in adults with ADD. A clinician should also be watching for distractability, auditorily and visually (such as a car in the parking lot, a stopwatch ticking, voices in the hall, a painting on the wall, sights out the window). Clients may alternate between a slow work style and impulsive responding. Many adults are nervous about the testing, perhaps because it reminds them of unsuccessful school days. Some relax as the testing proceeds and others become more anxious. Observation of or report of mental fatigue is important as well. For example, many adults with ADD can perform flawlessly on a continuous performance task, but may report that they feel exhausted afterward due to the mental energy required to maintain concentration. In short, all observations are important. Even noticing nothing out of the ordinary is important, as it points out how well one can compensate under certain conditions.

Asking clients to comment on their reactions to tests can offer further insights. What was easy? What was frustrating? What did you do to remember that? What other activities make you feel the way you did when you did that? Is it easier or harder when you know you have a time limit? And so forth. To gain these insights, a clinician must help clients feel at ease and help them understand what kinds of information are important to gather from the testing. Clinicians should explain how the tests work as much as possible without spoiling the responses. It may be helpful to tell clients what the tests were intended to measure, *following* administration of each test, and then ask for their impressions.

As the research on ADD in adults is growing exponentially, the tests described in this chapter must be considered a sampling of those that might be useful. Many of these are traditionally used for other purposes, but can offer valuable insight when seen through the lens of ADD. Some measures useful in assessing adult ADD are gathered from the cognitive rehabilitation field. These were developed to evaluate head-injured adults with acquired attention deficits.

Measures to Include in an ADD Battery for Adults

Intelligence Tests

As Barkley (1990) states, intellectual abilities in and of themselves do not relate to the presence of ADD. However, administering an intelligence test such as the Wechster Adult Intelligence Scale-Revised (WAIS-R) can offer a wealth of information about how a client copes with a variety of verbal and visual/spatial tasks. In addition, intelligence testing will rule out lack of ability as a cause of unsuccessful school or work experiences. It is also useful in helping clients develop vocational and educational goals. A note of caution should be used in interpreting IQ scores because "children with ADHD may score somewhat lower on intelligence tests than control groups of children or even their own siblings" (Barkley, 1990, p. 632).

Although no research data exist at this point, clinical observation suggests strongly that the more intelligent ADD adults tend to manifest their ADD symptoms later in life when the demands placed upon them (either academically or vocationally) finally exceed their ability to cope, given their attentional difficulties. Nadeau (personal communication, 1993) has worked with several cases of highly intelligent college students with ADD symptoms, whose therapist or physician discounted the possibility of ADD because of the students' good academic history during elementary and high school.

In evaluating the subscale scores on the WAIS-R, some researchers suggest that particular attention should be directed to the Digit Symbol subtest, the Digit Span subtest, and the Arithmetic subtest (Barkley, 1990; Klee et al., 1986). These subtests have shown to be particularly revealing in clients with ADD. Nadeau (personal communication, 1993) has evaluated a number of adults who, due to their professional training in science, math, or the computer field, were able to perform quite well on the Digit Span subtest despite evidence of short-term auditory memory difficulty on other measures. Administering the entire WAIS-R may be preferable over administering just these subtests. Using all of the subtests permits comparison of a range of cognitive skills. Performance on the Digit Symbol subtest was poorer for 12 adult males with ADD in a study by Klee et al. (1986). However, they did not see significant differences in performance on the Arithmetic subtest.

Other patterns should be looked for by the examiner administering the WAIS-R. Although there are no empirical data at this point, clinical experience in administering the WAIS-R to many adults with ADD suggests that many of them show patterns of carelessness or inattention to visual detail throughout. This may result in a low Picture Completion score, or may be observed on Picture Arrangement if the client overlooks important visual clues. Other patterns to look for are repeated forgetting of instructions, requests to repeat instructions, or requests to repeat items on the Arithmetic subtest. The clinician should also note hyperverbalization and tangential speech which impedes the progress of the test administration. Aspects of memory difficulty are very commonly found in ADD adults. As Sohlberg and Mateer (1989b) note, attention is the fundamental underpinning of memory. Some adults with ADD may show a pattern of poor long-term retention, evidenced by a low Information subscale score.

Continuous Process Tests

An electronic diagnostic instrument may be useful when testing for ADD in adults. The Test of Variables of Attention Computer Program (TOVA; Greenberg, 1992), and the Gordon Diagnostic System (GDS; Gordon, 1986) are two that are in widespread use. More recently, a third measure has been introduced, the Continuous Performance Test (CPT) Computer Program 2.0, developed by Keith Connors. These tools administer repetitive tasks and measure responses over a period of time. Continuous performance tasks ask a subject to "respond only to a specific combination of symbols in a stream of irrelevant symbols"(Gordon, 1986, p. 54). "They generally require clients to sustain attention and control behavior over a period of time and with varying degrees of feedback" (p. 54).

The GDS "is a microprocessor-based, portable unit that, without an external microcomputer, allows for the administration of multiple tasks" (Gordon, 1986, p. 56). The GDS includes three separate continuous processing tasks. The first is a delay task measuring the ability to inhibit responses. The second is a vigilance task that taps sustained attention. Finally, the GDS presents a distractibility task (Gordon, 1986). Currently, norms are available for children ages 4 to 16, for adults, and even for the elderly. Examiners should be aware that even adults who score within the normal range on the GDS may experience significant attentional difficulties. Often such adults report extreme frustration and/or boredom with the test.

The TOVA is a 25-minute continuous performance test of attention (Greenberg, 1992). As with the GDS, the TOVA is non-language based. It offers a repetitive task during which clients are asked to watch for a designated target and ignore a nontarget. Unlike the GDS, however, the TOVA offers normative data for ages 4 to 80 (Greenberg & Crosby, 1992). It measures omissions, commissions, correct response time, and anticipatory errors. These offer insight into impulsivity and inattention.

The Connors CPT test, much like the others, is a computer-based electronic continuous performance task. The CPT measures response inhibition. The subject is instructed to respond to every letter but X. It also measures response patterns at various speeds of stimulus presentation, allowing a measure of visual-processing ability at various rates. The CPT provides measures of omissions, commissions, reaction times, and variability of responses during the 14-minute task.

All of the continuous performance tasks presented above involve visual measures only. Another measure not widely known at this point is the

Comprehensive Auditory Visual Attentional Assessment System developed by Becker (Taylor, 1994); it taps both visual and auditory distractibility. This test is an adaptation of the GDS that includes an auditory component. Individuals vary in the degree to which they are affected by visual in comparison to auditory distracters (Taylor, 1994). This variable response to different distracters can be useful information in the assessment of an adult for ADD.

All of the CPT tests mentioned above, with the exception of Becker's, only measure visual distractibility. It can be helpful to observe auditory distractibility by noting unusual sensitivity to environmental sounds, such as a radio playing in another room. Adults who are auditorily distracted may request that the radio be turned off, or may respond to extraneous noises, providing the clinician with valuable information about auditory distractibility. Interestingly, at least one adult with ADD reported that a radio playing quietly in another room helped him to concentrate on the less demanding Vigilance task of the GDS by reducing his boredom. On the more demanding Distractibility task of the GDS, however, this same individual experienced the radio as a distracter (K. Nadeau, personal communication, December 1993).

Other Tests of Attention

The continuous process tests described above measure sustained attention (the ability to maintain a focus of attention over an extended period of time) and selective attention (the ability to intentionally maintain focused attention in the presence of distracters). Less emphasis has been placed on measures of more complex aspects of attention, such as alternating and divided attention. Yet, it is often those more complex aspects of attention that are problematic for individuals in their daily functioning.

Alternating attention refers to mental flexibility, or the ability to intentionally shift the focus of attention between two tasks that have different cognitive requirements. This is the attentional ability required of mothers who are simultaneously cleaning house and supervising children, or that is required of workers who must shift from answering phone calls to doing paperwork. Divided attention refers to the ability to simultaneously attend to multiple task demands, such as driving a car while listening to the radio, or cooking dinner while carrying on a conversation. Divided attention may, in fact, be very rapidly shifting alternating attention, or it may involve one activity that it so overlearned that it places very little attentional demand on the individual while the person is simultaneously conducting the other activity.

Sohlberg and Mateer (1989a) have developed a number of tests for use in attention training of brain-injured individuals which may have merit in the evaluation of an adult for Attention Deficit Disorder. These tests are specifically designed to involve alternating and divided attention tasks. For example, in the Card Sorting task, the subject sorts playing cards according to suit but is also instructed to turn over certain cards if a target letter appears in the name of the card. For example, if the target letter is an e then 1s, 3s, 5s, 7s, 8s, 9s, and queens must be turned over as they are sorted by suit. Sohlberg and Mateer (1986) have developed other interesting alternating and divided attention tasks, available through their Attention Process Training. Although this training package was developed to work with head-injured individuals with severe levels of impairment, the more recently developed Attention Process Training II is more appropriate for those with mild to moderate impairments, and therefore more appropriate for use in an ADD evaluation.

The Trail Making Tests, Parts A and B, of the Halstead-Reitan Neuropsychological Test Battery (Reitan, 1986) can reflect a client's ability to shift attention smoothly. On Part B, clients are asked to quickly complete a connect-the-dot pattern by connecting alternating letters and numbers. Impulsive responses, failure to smoothly shift between letters and numbers, and losing track of the sequences are common problems on this test. The Wisconsin Card Sorting Test (Heaton, 1981) may be included as another indicator of the ability to shift attention flexibly.

Barkley (1990) and Johnston (1986) include the Paced Auditory Serial Addition Test (PASAT) (Gronwall, 1977) in their batteries for ADD. This measure assesses both sustained and divided attention. On the PASAT, a series of digits are presented auditorily at a predetermined rate. The subject is instructed to give the sum of the last digit and the immediately preceding digit. A total of 60 digits is presented. Although the PASAT has made a valuable contribution to clinical practice, it has been criticized because it requires mathematical skills and a rapid motor response.

Weber (1986) found that ability on the PASAT correlated strongly with the ability to add. Weber (1986) developed the Attentional Capacity Test, which places similar demands on the capacity for information processing, but removes the requirements for arithmetic calculation and rapid verbal response. In this test, subjects listen to a tape and are asked to count verbally presented stimuli of increasing complexity. For example, the subject is initially asked to count the frequency of a single digit, but is later asked to count a more complex series, such as the number of 8s preceded by a 5. Weber found that, when this test was used to measure the attentional capacity of brain-injured individuals, their performance was highly correlated with therapists' ratings of the subjects' attentional capacity. The Stroop Color and Word Test is another test commonly included in ADD batteries for both children and adults. The Stroop taps the ability to inhibit automatic overdetermined responses (Rudel et al., 1988).

It is our clinical experience that individuals with ADD experience much frustration and fatigue when placed in common everyday situations that call upon their ability to rapidly process simultaneous sets of information coming from the environment. It is important that we include tests in our assessment protocols which adequately tap these higher levels of attentional capacity (Sohlberg & Mateer, 1989a).

Measures of Impulsivity

Kagan's Matching Familiar Figures Test (MFFT) (Kagan, 1966) has an adolescent and adult form, which asks adults to carefully compare a series of sample pictures with eight nearly identical ones. Klee et al. (1986) included the MFFT as one measure of attention in their study exploring ADD in adults. However, it did not prove a sensitive enough measure to discriminate between adults with and without ADD. Nevertheless, it remains a useful tool. Clinicians should watch for impulsive responses (that is, failure to fully explore all pictures before making a selection). Other ADD adults may compensate for their impulsive tendencies in the testing session by taking extraordinary amounts of time to consider their answers prior to responding.

The clinician can also make very useful assessments of impulsive response style through careful observation of the client throughout testing. Clinicians should look for patterns of "jumping the gun" and beginning a test response prior to being asked to do so, and patterns of interrupting. Nadeau (personal communication, 1993) reports that she often finds a pattern of impulsive responding on the Digit Span subtest of the WAIS-R in which the client, having been presented with, for example, a three-digit sequence of numbers, starts to respond to the next sequence after the third number rather than waiting for the fourth to be read aloud by the examiner.

Memory Tests

Some aspects of memory that are important to assess include rate of learning and stability of recall. However, the clinician should note that memory deficits in adults with ADD may be more subtle than those seen in clients with brain injuries. Deficits commonly seen are those requiring greater organizational abilities, such as retrieving information from memory (Barkley, 1990).

The Wechsler Memory Scale: Revised (Wechsler, 1987) is a battery of memory tests that measures both verbal and visual recall. It also offers a delayed recall index as well as a short-term memory measure called Attention/Concentration. The Wechsler Memory Scale: Revised measures a number of cognitive processes involved in memory. First, it compares the client's ability to remember information presented verbally with the ability to re-member information visually. In treatment planning, the results of this test can suggest ways clients might learn to cope more effectively. For example, clients with a lower verbal memory score might be told to have someone else take notes in a meeting or a class to enable them to focus more fully on the speaker. A second use for these memory scales is behavioral observa-tion. Indications of impulsivity and planning are often evident in perfor-mance. For example, clients with good planning skills will often employ strategies to boost memory (such as visualization or rehearsing).

Other measures of memory that may be included in an ADD battery are the California Verbal Learning Test (Delis, Kramer, Kaplan, Ober, and Fridlund, 1987). This test presents a list of words which are then repeated several times. Memory scores are offered for immediate recall, recall after repetition, recall after interference, recall after a time delay, and recogni-tion within a list of alternative words. A clinician should observe the learn-ing curve, which should be a steady increase. Clients with attention prob-lems often tire of this task quickly and may show a decreasing learning curve as their mental fatigue increases. Barkley (1990) recommends the Verbal and Nonverbal Selective Reminding Tests (Kane & Perrine, 1985) as a another memory assessment for adults with ADD.

While some adults with ADD can demonstrate excellent long-term se-mantic memory, it is the experience of many clinicians working with adults with ADD that aspects of "everyday memory" or "absentmindedness" are commonly problematic. "Absentmindedness" or poor "prospective memory," as it is termed by those who study memory and cognition, (discussed at length in chapter 11, this volume), is the ability to remember to perform certain tasks at a specified future time. This is an area that should be ex-plored thoroughly by the clinician through client interview, and is an area that badly needs more exploration and study. At this point, there are no tests developed to specifically measure prospective memory. One ques-tionnaire developed by Broadbent (Broadbent, Cooper, Fitzgerald, & Parkes, 1982), the Cognitive Failures Questionnaire, may prove useful for the cli-nician in assessing "absentmindedness."

Measures of Strategic Planning and Executive Functioning

This section will review a variety of measures that may be included in a battery of tests for adults with ADD. Some were developed for use with children and have been expanded more recently for adults. Others were developed for assessing cognitive abilities in adults with head injuries or strokes. Still others are often included in neuropsychological evaluations assessing cognitive processing. As mentioned previously, when adminis-tering these measures, clinicians should be observing clients' problem-solving methods, frustration levels, perseverance, impulsivity, restlessness, and distractibility.

Measures of cognitive processing and executive functioning are included in testing for ADD in an attempt to capture problem-solving abilities and work style. Lezak (1993) outlined four basic aspects of executive functioning. These provide a framework for observing adults as they attempt a variety of cognitive processing tasks:

1. Volition, including capacities for awareness of one's self and surroundings and motivational state;
2. Planning, including abilities to conceptualize change (look ahead), be objective, conceive of alternatives and make choices, develop a plan conceptually, and sustain attention;
3. Purposive action, including productivity, and self-regulation; and
4. Performance effectiveness, or quality control (p. 25).

There are a number of tests in standard usage designed to measure executive functions. These include category, sorting, and maze tests, all of which measure planning ability (Sohlberg & Mateer, 1989b). Two of the most common tests measuring ability to sort or classify are the Halstead Category Test (Halstead, 1947) and the Wisconsin Card Sorting Test (WCST) (Grant & Berg, 1984). Another useful test of planning is a maze test, the best known of which is the Porteus Maze Test (Porteus, 1950).

Other tests that can be very useful in measuring executive planning abilities are those that present the subject with an unstructured task and that are evaluated impressionistically rather than through comparison against strict norms. Several of such tasks have been studied experimentally. One of the best known, perhaps, is the Tower of London Puzzle (Shalice, 1982), which requires both sequencing and planning. The subject is presented with a puzzle that consists of three pegs of different heights and three differently colored rings. The subject is instructed to move the rings from a start position to a specified end position in the fewest moves possible. Poor performance on this test has been correlated with poor planning ability.

The Letter Cancellation Task (Lezak, 1983) offers a chance to observe strategic planning in a relatively unstructured task. Clients are presented with a page randomly covered with letters and are asked to circle all of one particular letter as fast as possible. This offers the clinician a chance to observe the ability to develop and maintain an effective search pattern. Clinicians should watch for speed and omissions, as some clients will be fast but inaccurate. Others will be more accurate but inefficient.

The Rey-Osterrieth Complex Figure Task (Lezak, 1983) may be used to assess both strategic planning and memory. Clients are first asked to copy a complicated geometric figure. The execution of their drawing should be carefully observed to evaluate how planned their reproduction is (that is, do they pick a place to begin and proceed from there, do they capture the outline and fill in the details, etc.). After clients have copied the figure, they may be asked to reproduce it again from memory, both immediately after copying it again and after a 20-minute delay (often, they are not told in advance that this will be required). Renditions from memory are evaluated for completeness of general gestalt as well as inner details.

ASSESSMENT OF COMORBID CONDITIONS

As discussed in the preceding chapters, there are three primary types of coexisting conditions to consider when evaluating an individual who is presenting with symptoms suggestive of ADD.

Screening for Possible Neurological Conditions

A first concern is whether ADD-like symptoms may be related to unknown neurological conditions. The clinician who is not medically trained should habitually screen for the possibility of a neurological condition through the use of a questionnaire or checklist. The Neurological Symptom Checklist (Shinka) is one such screening tool in wide use. If the client indicates items suggestive of a neurological disorder, then appropriate referral for a neurological examination is in order.

Psychiatric Comorbidity and Differential Diagnosis

A second concern is whether the ADD symptoms presented are actually due to other psychiatric conditions or to comorbid conditions (see chapter 3, this volume, for a more complete discussion of these). Projective tests are an essential component of an ADD battery in order to screen for the presence of such conditions, including depression, obsessive-compulsive disorder, bipolar disorder, anxiety disorders, and others. There are many tests effectively used as projective measures. Commonly used measures that may be added to an ADD battery include the Thematic Apperception Test (Murray, 1971), the MMPI-2 (Hathaway & McKinley, 1989), Sentence Completion Tests (Rabin & Zlotogorski, 1981), and the Rorschach (Rorschach, 1942). Svanum & Ehrmann (1992) write that they find the MMPI-2 especially useful in assessing and developing a treatment plan for clients with problems of impulsivity. For the sake of efficiency and cost control, we do not recommend that the clinician administer a full psychological evaluation for each client evaluated for ADD. It seems useful to conduct a thorough history and to administer one test as a screening tool. If areas of concern arise during interview or through this screening, then a more complete set of projective tests may be warranted.

It is important to note that both anxiety and depression are common comorbid conditions. Therefore, the presence of anxiety and/or depression does not in any way rule out ADD. However, when there is anxiety or depression accompanied by poor concentration, without a history suggestive of ADD, then a different course of treatment may be indicated.

Hyperactivity versus mania is another differential diagnosis question that sometimes arises. Unfortunately, there remain a number of physicians who can mistakenly diagnose a manic state in hyperactive adults and place their patient on lithium rather than a stimulant medication as a consequence of this misdiagnosis. A thorough history, in addition to psychological and projective testing, can be useful in making a distinction between the two. (See chapter 3, this volume, for more complete discussion.)

Although not reported commonly as an ADD-related condition, Bellak (Bellak, Kay, & Opler, 1987) suggests a diagnosis that he calls ADD Psychosis. It appears related to the schizophrenic syndrome, but shows interesting differences. These "schizophrenics," as they were diagnosed at the time, had problems of impulse control, learning disabilities, difficulty with spatial orientation and, a low stimulus barrier, and showed a hypersensitivity to loud sound and bright lights, which seemed to disorganize and upset them severely. Bellak noted that such patients tended to become worse on neuroleptic drugs, and showed improvement with amphetamine-like drugs. He further reports that psychiatrists who have worked with a highly disturbed population of adolescents on Rikers Island in New York believe that as many as 90% of the juveniles incarcerated there suffer from ADD psychosis. This observation is important for psychologists working within any phase of the correctional system.

The Myers-Briggs Type Inventory in ADD Evaluations

The Myers-Briggs Type Inventory (Myers & Briggs, 1976) does not address psychiatric issues, but may be a particularly useful measure, contributing a different set of information than is provided by other psychological tests. It can be used to highlight personality strengths and weaknesses to develop the best match of career, mate, and work style.

Some clinicians (K. Nadeau, personal communication, 1993) find that the J-P factor of the Myers-Briggs is especially useful to consider in an ADD evaluation. Nadeau finds that "Js," those who prefer a more structured approach to tasks, have often worked quite hard to develop compensatory strategies to combat ADD tendencies, and are quite eager to implement whatever strategies are suggested by the therapist. In effect, ADD symptoms are ego-dystonic for them, and they expend enormous energy in combatting tendencies toward forgetfulness or disorganization. On the other hand, "Ps" on the MBTI are those who tend to prefer a more unstructured, spontaneous approach to life. For "Ps," implementing the strategies needed to improve planning and to provide structure may seem burdensome and undesirable. Nadeau finds that measuring where a client falls on the J-P continuum of the MBTI can help the clinician to develop a set of recommendations for compensatory strategies that may be more appropriate for the client.

Other Neurodevelopmental Disorders

As is discussed at length in chapter 4, there is a strong likelihood that other neurodevelopmental disorders coexist with Attention Deficit Disorder. The client and clinician should undertake a cost-benefit analysis to decide whether undergoing an extensive psychoeducational evaluation seems worthwhile. A thorough understanding of other related disabilities that impair functioning in important areas of life can be extremely valuable. Because psychoeducational testing has been so thoroughly discussed in the educational literature, I will only introduce this topic as an important area to consider as a facet of an ADD evaluation. The clinician should keep in mind that neurodevelopmental disorders, or learning disabilities, as they are commonly referred to, can affect people profoundly, not only in the academic setting but also on the job and in daily life.

Educational Tests

Tests of reading, writing, spelling, mathematics, and broad knowledge may also be included in a battery for ADD in adults. These are especially important if a learning disability is also suspected. Patterns of poor organization, lack of planning, and impulsivity may also be assessed in educational evaluations. Educational evaluations are also useful in treatment planning where weak academic skills may play a role (for example, treatment planning for college or graduate school students or for those with careers requiring academic skills). There are a myriad of educational evaluations available. The Woodcock-Johnson Psycho-Educational Battery–Revised Tests of Achievement (Woodcock & Johnson, 1989) offers a broad-based evaluation of most academic skills and has norms for adults. However, the tasks are often brief and may be a better measure of basic academic skills.

Adults with learning and attention problems may do well on brief tasks and still have greater difficulty applying basic academic skills to more complex tasks. For example, a client may perform well on the Writing Samples subtest of the Woodcock-Johnson (which requires writing only individual sentences) and still have great difficulty organizing ideas for a term paper for school or memo for work. Such an observation parallels findings on tests of executive function that show that individuals, even those with frontal lobe injury, may be able to perform adequately on less demanding measures of executive function (Sohlberg & Mateer, 1989b), but may demonstrate planning impairment in more open-ended, less structured tasks such as the Tower of London Test (Shalice, 1982). A parallel to the Tower of London test might be to require the individual to write an open-ended essay on a topic of choice. The examiner should then evaluate the writing sample for clarity, focus, structure, appropriate sequence, and lack of repetition or circularity.

GOALS OF TESTING

Testing for ADD in adults offers nothing if it is not then communicated carefully to the client in relation to treatment planning. Other chapters in this book detail what kinds of treatment can be helpful to the adult with ADD. Treatments may include medication, therapy, educational support, and/or accommodations in the client's environment. When assembling a battery of tests for ADD, each measure included should be a means to the end of treatment and a happier and more productive life for the client. A good ADD evaluation will not only thoroughly discuss diagnostic issues, but also will offer a set of recommendations that can provide a blueprint for the client and his therapist to follow in treating the Attention Deficit Disorder.

This blueprint for treatment should include a detailed list of recommendations including:

1. Possible recommendation of medical consultation to consider a trial of medication or medications. Comorbid considerations, such as depression and anxiety, should be mentioned here for consideration by the physician, as the presence of such conditions will influence the medications prescribed by the physician.

2. Referrals to other professionals, such as career consultants, speech pathologists, learning disability specialists, neurologists, or specialists in vision or hearing, as needed. Ideally, the examiner develops a network of professionals knowledgeable about ADD in adults and comorbid conditions to whom clients who have been evaluated can be referred.

3. Information about ADD in adults, including the presence of local support groups, the names and addresses of organizations that support the interests of adults with ADD, and the titles of books and publications that deal with the concerns of adults with ADD. Such self-education is a very important aspect of the treatment of ADD in adults.

4. Suggestions regarding accommodations and compensatory strategies that would be useful to the adult who may be in school, or who plans to return to school.

5. Strategies to improve daily functioning (see chapter 11, this volume, for further discussion of these strategies).
6. Issues upon which the client and his therapist should focus in their ongoing work together.
7. Recommendation for psychotherapy with a clinician who is expert in adult ADD issues if the client who has sought evaluation is not currently in treatment.

SUMMARY

The initial step for any clinician should be identifying whether or not ADD is a possible cause for presenting problems. A second question should be, does ADD coexist with any other disorders? Questionnaires developed to highlight characteristics of ADD in adults are useful tools at this screening stage. They may be completed by the client alone or by other close friends and family members. If ADD does surface as a possibility, further testing can confirm the diagnosis as well as offer much information for treatment planning. A battery of tests for ADD in adults may include intelligence tests, continuous process tests, memory assessments, educational evaluations, and personality tests. Measures tapping strategic planning and executive functioning may offer unique insights. Clinician insight and observation plays a special role in diagnosing ADD. The goals of testing include a differential diagnosis and effective treatment planning.

Professionals in a variety of settings are likely to be encountering increasing numbers of inquiries about ADD in adults as awareness of its presence grows. In addition to direct inquiries, clinicians may encounter adults with ADD who often seek help for a variety of related complaints ranging from depression to difficulty with time management. The paucity of research in this area means that much of the information on testing must come from our knowledge of ADD in children and clinical observation. There is a great need for empirical research in this area.

REFERENCES

Barkley, R. A. (1990). *Attention deficit hyperactivity disorder.* New York: Guilford Press.

Bellak, L., Kay, S., & Opler, L. (1987). Attention deficit disorder psychosis as a diagnostic category. *Psychiatric Developments, 3,* 239–263.

Broadbent, D. E., Cooper, E. F., Fitzgerald, P. & Parkes, K. R. (1982). The Cognitive Failures Questionnaire (CFQ) and its correlates. *British Journal of Clinical Psychology, 21,* 1–6.

Brown, T. E., & Gammon, G. D. (1991). *The Brown attention-activation disorder scale: Protocol for clinical use.* Yale University.

Copeland, E. D. (1989). *Copeland Symptom Checklist for Adult Attention Deficit Disorders.* Atlanta: Southeastern Psychological Institute.

Delis, D. C., Kramer, J., Kaplan, E., Ober, B.A., & Fridlund, A. (1987). *California Verbal Learning Test.* San Antonio, TX: The Psychological Corporation of Harcourt, Brace, Jovanovich.

Gordon, M. (1986). How is a computerized attention test used in the diagnosis of attention deficit disorder? *Journal of Children in Contemporary Society, 19* (1–2), 53–64.

Grant, D. A., & Berg, E. A. (1984). A behavioral analysis of reinforcement and ease of shifting to new responses in a Weigl-type card-sorting problem. *Journal of Experimental Psychology, 38,* 404–411.

Greenberg, L. M. (1992, January). Treating attention-deficit disorders in children and adults. *Psychiatric Times,* pp. 18–19.

Greenberg, L. M., & Crosby, R. D. (1992). *Specificity and sensitivity of the Test of Variables of Attention (T.O.V.A.).* Manuscript submitted for publication.

Gronwall, D. (1977). Paced auditory serial addition task: A measure of recovery from concussion. *Perceptual and Motor Skills, 44,* 367–373.

Hallowell, E. M., & Ratey, J. J. (1993). Suggested diagnostic criteria for ADD in adults. *ADDult News.* Winter.

Halstead, W. C. (1947). *Brain and intelligence.* Chicago: University of Chicago Press.

Hathaway, S. R., & McKinley, J. C. (1989). *Minnesota Multiphasic Personality Inventory.* Minneapolis: National Computer Systems.

Heaton, R. K. (1981). *A manual for the Wisconsin Card Sorting Test.* Odessa, FL: Psychological Assessment Resources.

Hechtman, L. (1989). Attention-deficit hyperactivity disorder in adolescence and adulthood: An updated follow-up. *Psychiatric Annals, 19*(11), 597–603.

Hechtman, L., Weiss, G., & Perlman, T. (1984). Young adult outcome of hyperactive children who received long-term stimulant treatment. *Journal of the American Academy of Child Psychiatry, 23*(3), 261–269.

Johnston, C. W. (1986). The neuropsychological evaluation of attention deficit disorder. *Psychiatric Annals, 16*(1), 47–51.

Kagan, J. (1966). Reflection-impulsivity: The generality and dynamic of conceptual tempo. *Journal of Abnormal Psychology, 71,* 17–24.

Kane, R. L., & Perrine, K. R. (1985). *Nonverbal Selective Reminding Test.* Unpublished manuscript.

Klee, S. H., Garfinkel, B. B., & Beauchesne, H. (1986). Attention deficits in adults. *Psychiatric Annals, 16*(1), 52–56.

Lezak, M. (1983). *Neuropsychological assessment.* New York: Oxford University Press.

Lezak, M. D. (1993). Newer contributions to the neuropsychological assessment of executive functions. *Journal of Head Trauma Rehabilitation, 8*(1), 24–31.

Mirsky, A. F., Anthony, B. J., Duncan, C. C., Ahearn, M. B., & Kellam, S. G. (1991). Analysis of the elements of attention: A neuropsychological approach. *Neuropsychology Review, 2*(2), 109–145.

Murray, H. A. (1971). *Thematic Apperception Test.* Cambridge, MA: Harvard University Press.

Myers, I. B., & Briggs, K. C. (1976). *Myers-Briggs Type Inventory.* Palo Alto, CA: Consulting Psychologists Press.

Nadeau, K. (1991). *Adult ADHD Questionnaire.* Annandale, VA: Chesapeake Psychological Services.

Porteus, S. D. (1950). *The Porteus Maze Test and intelligence.* Palo Alto, CA: Pacific Books.

Quinn, P. (1993). *ADD and the college student.* New York: Magination Press.

Rabin, A. I., & Zlotogorski, Z. (1981). Completion methods: Word association, sentence, and story completion. In A. I. Rabin (Ed.), *Assessment with projective techniques.* New York: Springer.

Ratey, J. J. (1991). *Paying attention to attention in adults. Chadder: A Publication by CH.A.D.D.* Fall/Winter, pp. 13–14.

Reitan, R. M. (1986). Theoretical and methodological bases of the Halstead-Reitan Neuropsychological Test Battery. In I. Grant & K. Adams (Eds.), *Neuropsychological assessment of neuropsychiatric disorders.* New York: Oxford University Press.

Rorschach, H. (1942). *Rorschach Psychodiagnostic Test.* New York: Grune & Stratton.

Rudel, R. G., Holmes, J. M., & Pardes, J. R. (1988). *Assessment of developmental learning disorders.* New York: Basic Books.

Shalice, T. (1982). Specific impairments of planning. In P. Broadbent & L. Weisknartz (Eds.), *The neuropsychology of cognitive function* (pp. 199–209). London: The Royal Society.

Shekim, W. O., Asarnow, R. F., Hess, E., Zaucha, K., & Wheeler, N. (1990). A clinical and demographic profile of a sample of adults with attention deficit hyperactivity disorder, residual state. *Comprehensive Psychiatry, 31*(5), 416–425.

Shinka, J. A. *Neurological Symptom Questionnaire.* Odessa FL: Psychological Assessment Resources (PAR).

Sohlberg, M., & Mateer, C. (1986). *Attention process training (APT).* Puyallup, WA: Association for Neuropsychological Research and Development.

Sohlberg, M., & Mateer, C. A. (1989a). The assessment of cognitive-communicative functions in head injury. *Topics in Language Disorders,* *9*(2), 15–33.

Sohlberg, M., & Mateer, C. (1989b). *Introduction to cognitive rehabilitation, theory & practice.* New York: Guilford Press.

Svanum, S., & Ehrmann, L. (1992). Alcoholic subtypes and the MacAndrew Alcoholism Scale. *Journal of Personality Assessment, 58,* 411–422.

Taylor, C. J. (1994). Auditory and Visual Continuous Performance Test: A comparison of modalities. *ADHD/Hyperactivity Newsletter,* Fall/Winter, No. 20.

Ward, M. F., Wender, P. H., & Reimherr, F. W. (1993). The Wender Utah rating scale: An aid in the retrospective diagnosis of childhood attention deficit hyperactivity disorder. *American Journal of Psychiatry, 150,* 885–890.

Weber, A. M. (1986). *Measuring attentional capacity.* Unpublished doctoral dissertation, University of Victoria, Victoria, Canada.

Wechsler, D. (1981). *Wechsler Adult Intelligence Scale-Revised.* San Antonio, TX: The Psychological Corporation of Harcourt, Brace, Jovanovich.

Wechsler, D. (1987). *Wechsler Memory Scale: Revised.* New York: The Psychological Corporation of Harcourt, Brace, Jovanovich.

Wender, P. H. (1987). *The hyperactive child, adolescent and adult.* New York: Oxford University Press.

Woodcock, R. W., & Johnson, M. B. (1989). *Woodcock-Johnson Psycho-Educational Battery-Revised.* Allen, TX: DLM Teaching Resources.

Woods, D. (1986). The diagnosis and treatment of attention deficit disorder, residual type. *Psychiatric Annals, 16*(1), 23–28.

SECTION III

Treatment Issues in Adult ADD

This section addresses general treatment issues in working with adults with ADD and introduces the clinician to broader aspects of such treatment. Kevin Murphy's chapter opens the section. As director of the Adult ADD Clinic at the University of Massachusetts Medical Center, he brings a wealth of experience to his very hopeful message and practical suggestions. A critical message in Murphy's chapter is the importance of recognizing and counteracting the often crippling damage to self-esteem that has occurred for many adults with ADD whose condition remained undiagnosed and untreated into adulthood. This is followed by Edward Hallowell's chapter describing his approach to psychotherapy with adults with ADD, which he has developed as a specialty in his private practice. The third chapter in this section deals with the use of medication as an important aspect of the overall treatment plan for adults with ADD. It is written by Timothy Wilens, Thomas Spencer, and Joseph Biederman, members of one of the premier medical research teams investigating the use of medication in the treatment of adults with ADD, at Massachusetts General Hospital in Boston, affiliated with Harvard University.

8

Empowering the Adult with ADD

KEVIN R. MURPHY

Most adults with ADD have suffered years of feeling demoralized, discouraged, and ineffective due to a history of frustrations and failures in school, work, family, and/or social domains. Many are plagued with a chronic inner sense of underachievement and intense frustration. Moreover, many have repeatedly heard negative messages about themselves either directly or indirectly from teachers, parents, spouses, friends, or employers highlighting their weaknesses and shortcomings. The cumulative effect of such a history can sometimes lead to internalization of these negative messages and can result in an entrenched belief that they are in fact true and unchangeable.

Many of the patients I have seen believe they have been hardwired to fail and have come to expect failure as a natural consequence of their efforts. After all, they usually have had many experiences to validate this perception. This phenomenon is referred to as "learned helplessness," which is the giving-up reaction, the quitting response that follows from the belief that whatever you do doesn't matter (Seligman, 1990). An example I hear frequently from college students is "Whether I spend 5 minutes or 5 hours studying for the test, it won't matter, so why bother?" They are so wedded to this belief system that they often give up believing life could be any different for them.

What is so hard for many adults with ADD is that deep down they know they have the raw materials to succeed and achieve more (i.e., they have intelligence, drive, energy, creativity), but for reasons they often cannot explain, they have great difficulty consistently translating these abilities into positive outcomes. This is the essence of the frustration and even the underlying rage they sometimes feel.

It is important to realize that underachievement is a relative term. What constitutes underachievement for one may represent the pinnacle for another. The common thread is a nagging sense of feeling blocked and thwarted from being as productive or successful as they know they are capable of. Numerous individuals have routinely said to me the following types of statements: "I have lots of great ideas, but I can never follow through on translating them into action"; "If I could only follow through on the little details and paperwork, I'd be far more successful and wouldn't be so far behind"; "I am technically very competent, but sometimes I impulsively say inappropriate things that I immediately regret that get me into trouble"; "I am the best at my job, but my temper and abrasive style have prevented me from getting ahead"; "If I could only be more organized, focused, and less distractible, I would accomplish so much more."

Some of the people who make such comments are highly accomplished professionals. At the ADD Adult Clinic, University of Massachusetts Medical Center, I have treated a variety of people ranging from highly successful to extremely unsuccessful, including physicians, surgeons, lawyers, athletes, business executives, and those who seem unable to hold onto a job. Having ADD does not disqualify one from being "successful," but it can interfere in reaching one's full potential. Assisting people in becoming the best they can be by helping them to focus and build on their strengths and compensate for their weaknesses is a major tenet in working with adults with ADD.

The theme of this chapter is to instill hope, optimism, and motivation in adults with ADD. It represents the philosophy of our clinic to help adult ADD patients view their disorder within a framework that empowers them to believe their lives can be different, and encourages their active and enthusiastic involvement in treatment. Although there are no controlled empirical studies demonstrating the efficacy of these approaches with ADD adults–or any other psychosocial treatment methods for that matter–the methodology appears to have been helpful to many of our clinic population.

SOME COMMON CONSEQUENCES OF HAVING ADD

In addition to learned helplessness, some of the more common correlates of having ADD are low self-esteem, avoidance/anxiety, depression, and substance abuse. It is not surprising that many adults, after years of frustration with their academic, work, and social lives, have developed low self-esteem. Approximately 80% of the clinic's adult population have admitted to having low-self esteem. They often have a nagging sense of knowing something was wrong but never knowing exactly what it was. In many cases, they had sought help with various mental health professionals who overlooked the ADD and never got to the bottom of what was actually troubling these individuals. Consequently, they frequently attribute their problems to a character defect and conclude they simply don't measure up. Helping to rebuild self-esteem and self- confidence is therefore critical in the treatment of adults with ADD.

Another common consequence of having ADD is anxiety and avoidance of situations that historically have been unsuccessful or troublesome for the individual. This often manifests itself in the social realm. Due in part to their impulsivity, interrupting or intruding on others, forgetfulness, inattentiveness, hyperactivity, temper, and mood swings, adults with ADD frequently have difficulty making and keeping friends. Their behavior may be viewed by others as rude, insensitive, irresponsible, or obnoxious, and they may be ostracized by others. Some have come to associate social interaction with either embarrassment, disappointment, criticism, or failure. When confronted with future opportunities for social interaction, these adults will often prefer to stay on the sidelines to avoid embarrassment and prevent another painful experience. They tend to withdraw from people to protect themselves.

Another problematic issue for adults with ADD is the idea of returning to school. A significant number of our clinic population have expressed a desire to return to school but are extremely reluctant because of past school difficulties. They might consider it if they were able to focus and concentrate better, but to them it seems safer not to try. After all, one thing they do not need is another setback. Hence, they avoid school, even though deep down they may have a strong desire to return. In short, some adults with ADD would rather stay in the dugout than get up to the plate to take their swings because they assume they will strike out.

Depression is another relatively common consequence associated with adult ADD (see chapter 4, this volume). Approximately 40% of our adult ADD patients have met criteria for either major depression or dysthymia (chronic low-grade depression) at some time in their lives. Some have become so demoralized over their past failures and over being misunderstood and mistreated by others that they may require additional treatment for the secondary affective component of this disorder.

Finally, a substantial minority of adults with ADD gravitate toward substance abuse, possibly as a way of relaxing or calming the mental restlessness they often experience. Recent studies have suggested that those with ADD are at increased risk for developing substance abuse problems (Mannuzza, Klein, Bessler, Malloy & LaPadula, 1993; Weiss & Hechtman, 1993). Approximately 35% of our clinic population have met criteria for substance abuse or dependence, either presently or in the past. Many of these individuals appear to be self-medicating in an attempt to quell the manifestations of their underlying ADD symptoms. Most report using alcohol and/or marijuana as their primary drugs of choice. They make statements such as "It is the only way I can calm down"; "It is the only way I can relax"; "It helps me to focus better"; "It helps me shut my mind off"; and "It helps me sleep."

Interestingly, our clinic has found that after being treated with stimulant medication, a significant number of our substance-abusing ADD patients report improvement not only in their ADD symptoms but in their substance abuse as well. It is almost as if they get what they need with the medication and feel less of a need to continue to self-medicate. We therefore do not routinely disqualify a substance *abuser* with ADD from medication treatment. To do so may be depriving these patients of a potentially helpful treatment they desperately need. We do not, however, medicate those with active substance *dependence*; they get referred elsewhere for primary substance abuse treatment. Improvements in ADD symptomatology and a reduction in the desire for substance abuse after stimulant medication treatment are a preliminary trend we have found in our clinic, which clearly warrant further investigation.

A major challenge for professionals treating adults with ADD is to address these and any other negative manifestations of having ADD in a way that instills hope and empowers them to believe that with a combination of treatment, support, perseverance, and hard work, their lives can be improved.

COMMUNICATING THE ADULT ADD DIAGNOSIS

Treatment for adults with ADD begins at the time they are diagnosed. How clinicians communicate the diagnosis to these individuals is critical to both their understanding of the disorder and their willingness to engage in and follow through with treatment. If clinicians can help patients understand the disorder, frame it as something treatable, and instill hope and optimism for the future, then patients are more likely to feel motivated to work at and follow through with treatment. This should also result in more positive outcomes. Conversely, if patients are left with only a vague notion of what ADD is, are confused or unsure of how they might be helped, and are not activated to feel hope, then they are far less likely to persevere and achieve a positive outcome.

It is unfortunate but true that many patients who visit our clinic have had prior ADD evaluations but have little, if any, understanding of ADD, do not understand the implications it has on their lives, and do not know how to manage their symptoms. Clinicians can have substantial control over the feedback process and can help determine whether patients become engaged or disengaged from treatment. The following framework can assist clinicians in developing a strategy to effectively communicate the diagnosis to adults.

Explaining ADD and Comorbid Diagnoses

Assuming an accurate diagnosis is made by an experienced professional who understands adult ADD, the first step is to explain the rationale for arriving at the diagnosis and any other comorbid conditions. This can help patients begin to understand ADD, for example, by explaining that they (1) endorsed many of the core symptoms of ADD, (2) had an onset in early childhood, (3) have no other psychiatric or medical condition that could account for their symptoms, and (4) have behavioral, school, and/or work histories that are consistent with the diagnosis. This is not enough, however.

Reframing the Past

The next step in communicating the diagnosis is to continue educating the patient about ADD and how it manifests itself in the person's life. Patients need to have at least a general understanding that they have a neurological condition, not a character defect or moral shortcoming. Often they have internalized negative messages from parents, teachers, spouses, and employers and have come to believe they are either dumb, lazy, incompetent, or unmotivated. They should be told that many of the problems they experienced in many aspects of their life were largely due to a subtle neurological deficit in the brain that they had little control over. Their problems are not and were not the result of willful misconduct, low intelligence, or lack of effort. In short, inaccurate and unhealthy notions should be reframed in a more positive and hopeful light so patients can begin to rebuild their self-esteem and believe successful treatment is possible. Once this happens, patients may be better able to break out of the shackles of feeling stuck, demoralized, and chronically frustrated.

Offering Hope and the Human Element

Patients need to feel hope—whether they are battling a life-threatening illness, facing difficult surgery, recovering from physical or psychological trauma, or learning to cope with ADD. Without hope, there is little chance of significant change, consistent effort, or positive outcome. Moreover, patients need to feel their clinician is a partner with them who also sincerely believes they can be helped. If clinicians are genuine in their desire to become involved in helping, and this attitude shines through to the adult with ADD, this can go a long way toward instilling hope and motivation. Conversely, if clinicians are perceived by patients as merely technicians performing their routine in a relatively uninvolved or distant manner, the opposite is true.

The human element in clinicians' interactions with patients should never be underestimated. A caring attitude, support, and encouragement are crucial ingredients. The message that should come through loud and clear is that with proper treatment–including education, counseling, medication, behavioral strategies, hard work, and the support of family and friends–individuals with ADD can make significant and sometimes dramatic improvements in their lives.

Providing Educational Resources

It can be helpful to provide a packet of literature at the end of the evaluation. This may include a fact sheet on ADD, advice on books that may be useful (e.g., Paul Wender's *The Hyperactive Child, Adolescent, and Adult* [1987]; Kevin Murphy and Suzanne Levert's *Out of the Fog: Treatment Options and Coping Strategies for Adult Attention Deficit Disorder* [1995]; Ned Hallowell & John Ratey's *Driven to Distraction* [1994]; Lynn Weiss's *Attention Deficit Disorder in Adults* [1992]; Kate Kelly and Peggy Ramundo's *You Mean I'm Not Lazy, Stupid, or Crazy?!* [1993]), and copies of newsletter articles on ADD in adults (e.g., Walid Shekim's [1990], Edward Hallowell's [1993], John Ratey's [1991], or my own [1992] articles in CH.A.D.D.'s newsletter). Information on medications may also be given if a medication trial has been recommended (e.g., the fact sheets on medication in the *Journal of Child and Adolescent Psychopharmacology* [see Dulcan, 1992]. Providing this type of immediately relevant educational information can help motivate the individual to engage in ongoing treatment.

Discussing Vocational Issues

Patients with job problems are often poorly matched with their jobs. They rarely fail because of incompetence or poor ability. In fact, most have great strengths and high potential if they find the right job. Pointing out their strengths and communicating a belief that they can succeed if they find the proper fit is another way to instill hope. Sometimes referral to a vocational assessment specialist will generate a more in-depth analysis of patients' interests and abilities and how these might best match with various vocations. If treatment is successful, personal goals that patients always thought were unattainable–such as returning to school or getting a higher level job–may become possible. With support and encouragement, these patients may decide they are willing to undertake the challenge they have avoided for so long. (See chapter 16, this volume, for further discussion of career issues.)

Creating this spark of hope, balanced with the reality that real change requires hard work and sustained effort, can help set the proper tone. Clinicians can go a long way toward setting a therapeutic atmosphere of hope and optimism in patients who are so accustomed to hearing the opposite about themselves. Armed with this combination of hope, knowledge, and awareness of ADD, patients will be in a much better position to benefit from treatment, to learn to adapt better to current tasks and responsibilities, and to lead more fulfilling lives than has previously been the case.

TREATMENT STRATEGIES

Providing some specific examples of treatment strategies relevant to the problems the patient is currently experiencing can be very helpful. For example, patients who are disorganized and forgetful may benefit from being told about making lists, keeping an appointment calendar, posting visual reminders in strategic locations, blocking out time in schedules for priority tasks, breaking long tasks into small units, and building minirewards into projects. Or, if the patient is a college student, it would be useful to describe specific types of classroom modifications, class schedule adjustments, study skills, and other suggestions that could help the student succeed (see chapter 15, this volume, for further information).

As noted above, education about medication is important if medication is being proposed. Explaining how medication might help patients improve their ability to focus and concentrate may provide further hope. Answering questions about side effects and providing enough accurate information so the patient can make an informed decision about trying medication is also important. Patients often have mistaken notions and unrealistic fears about medication that need to be addressed before they are willing to take it. In addition to these explanations, the fact sheets can give them further information to digest and share with significant others following the session.

Psychosocial Treatment Options

A combination of treatments is usually recommended for adults with ADD. Some of these will be briefly described here. A more detailed discussion of treatment strategies including medication can be found in chapters 11 through 16. Initially, when diagnosed, the adult with ADD should be educated about what ADD is, its causes, and its management. Once diagnosed, there is often a sense of relief at finally having an explanation for their long-standing difficulties and realizing they are not at fault. Knowing how the disorder manifests itself in their lives can assist patients in devising specific behavioral strategies to manage their symptoms. Knowledge of the disorder also has implications for making future decisions. For example, knowing one has ADD can influence such things as choice of job, choice of spouse, and the decision to return to school and where to attend (preferably a school with an established program for assisting ADD/LD students).

Some patients in our clinic have stated that if they had known about and understood their ADD earlier, it might have spared them much pain and suffering and is likely to have made a big difference in their lives. Hence, linking education about ADD with immediate and future life circumstances can bring the disorder "closer to home" for patients and their families and help them realize the potential implications it may have on their lives now and into the future. This awareness may assist them in being better able to make choices and decisions that will minimize the negative effects of their symptoms and capitalize on their strengths.

Individual Counseling

Adults with ADD seem to have a tremendous need to talk and emote with someone who understands what they have experienced. Finally finding someone who truly understands them and is willing to listen can be a powerful experience for them. They are tired of being misunderstood and always trying to explain themselves and make excuses for their behavior. When they realize that ADD is largely responsible for much of their difficulties and when they can share this with a knowledgeable therapist or other adults with ADD, it can be extremely cathartic and enlightening. This is one obvious benefit of individual counseling.

Adults with ADD also can benefit from individual counseling by learning more about behavior modification principles and strategies. This can help with their inattentive and impulsive behavior and its effects on their ability to meet the demands of daily work and family and social life. More specifically, training in methods of time management, organizational skills, anger control, self-monitoring and reward, decision-making, cognitive-behavioral techniques for greater emotional control, and communication skills can be helpful.

Preparing patients for the inevitable feelings of disappointment and frustration when setbacks occur by framing setbacks as normal can help prevent excessive demoralization and discouragement—for example, explaining that learning to make lists and use an appointment book to become better organized is not accomplished in one lesson. One does not learn something today and become an expert tomorrow. Many patients say that lists do not work for them because they lose them. Of course they do; this is normal and expected. The goal is to continue practicing until the skill becomes an automatic and natural part of your daily routine, like brushing your teeth or getting dressed. This will require practice, perseverance, and tolerance. Accepting setbacks as normal and applying the knowledge and lessons learned from them to improve in the future can be a useful principle for adults with ADD.

Group Counseling

Many adults with ADD have never known another adult with the disorder. This tends to heighten their sense of isolation and loneliness. Participation in supportive, educational group counseling is likely to benefit many affected adults. Sharing individual coping strategies, learning how others cope and manage their symptoms, realizing others are struggling with similar issues, giving and receiving feedback, having a "laboratory" for learning and trying out new social and interpersonal skills, and learning more about ADD can all be useful. Participating in local support associations such as CH.A.D.D. (Children and Adults with Attention Deficit Disorder) may also be helpful.

Vocational Counseling

This is an area of great need for many adults with ADD. Unfortunately, the need seems to greatly outweigh the availability of skilled resources. A substantial majority of our clinic population have had problems maintaining consistent employment and are often poorly matched to their jobs. They frequently leave jobs due to boredom. They are also sometimes clearly in the wrong type of job for someone with their particular set of ADD symptoms. Vocational counseling aimed at identifying strengths and limitations and matching patients to jobs that fit is much needed for some adults with ADD. If this can be accomplished, it will likely increase patients' chances for success, reduce boredom, and hopefully result in a greater sense of confidence, self-esteem, and personal satisfaction.

Couples Counseling

Couples counseling can sometimes enable ADD-affected couples to look at their difficulties from a new perspective. It can be extraordinarily difficult to live with a spouse with ADD. A significant percentage of the non-ADD spouses that come to our clinic are on the verge of divorce. They are often fed up with what they consider to be willful misconduct, insensitivity, and irresponsible behavior. They are tired of the inconsistency, lack of intimacy, forgetfulness, and not being listened to, and they are tired of feeling sad, angry, and frustrated.

Educating the non-ADD spouse about the disorder and helping the spouse to realize that many of the partner's problems do not stem from willful misconduct may enable the couple to reframe their difficulties, stop blaming, and begin to work together as a team to improve the relationship. Viewing the marriage from this perspective may increase hope and allow for a fresh chance at rebuilding the relationship. To be successful, however, the non- ADD spouse must perceive the patient to be making a sincere and legitimate effort at behavior change in order to better manage the ADD symptoms. If the patient uses ADD as an excuse to justify continued behavioral problems without demonstrating an observable commitment to change, improvement in the relationship will be highly unlikely.

SUMMARY

Most adults with ADD have experienced long-standing frustration, discouragement, and underachievement in school, career, and social arenas. Some have developed a failure identity and have adopted a pessimistic belief system about their ability to improve their lives. Just receiving the diagnosis can be very therapeutic and can provide patients with the valuable knowledge that there is a bona fide name and explanation for their lifelong difficulties. Realizing that ADD stems from a neurological condition and is not their fault can also be immensely helpful. Whatever combination of treatments is used for a given patient, it is likely that intervention will need to be extended over longer time intervals, much like the management of a chronic medical illness such as diabetes (Barkley, 1993). Periodic professional follow-up for support, treatment adjustment, or new interventions as needed will likely be necessary and helpful for most ADD adults in the ongoing management of their disorder.

Beyond this, those professionals working with adults with ADD need to help counteract the ingrained negative self-perceptions, create conditions that empower patients to believe their lives can be different, and activate them to engage in and persist with treatment. Patients need to realize that ADD is a treatable condition. They need to understand that they have some power, control, and responsibility in how effectively they learn to manage it. Instilling hope, fostering in patients a belief that they are potent and can succeed, and demonstrating a sincere and ongoing commitment to helping patients work around their difficulties appear to be important and sometimes overlooked components of treatment for adults with ADD.

REFERENCES

Barkley, R. A. (1993). *ADHD in adults: Manual accompanying videotape.* New York: Guilford Press.

Dulcan, M. K. (1992). Information for parents and youth on psychotropic medications. *Journal of Child and Adolescent Psychopharmacology, 2,* 81–101.

Hallowell, N. (1993, Spring/Summer). Living and loving with attention deficit disorder: Couples where one partner has ADD. *CH.A.D.D.ER,* pp. 13–19.

Hallowell, E., & Ratey, J. (1994). *Driven to distraction.* New York: Pantheon.

Kelly, K., & Ramundo, P. (1993). *You mean I'm not lazy, stupid, or crazy?!* Cincinnati: Tyrell & Jerem Press.

Mannuzza, S., Klein, R., Bessler, A., Malloy, P., & LaPadula, M. (1993). Adult outcome of hyperactive boys. *Archives of General Psychiatry, 50,* 565–576.

Murphy, K. R. (1992, Fall/Winter). Coping strategies for ADHD adults. *CH.A.D.D.ER, 6*(2), pp. 10–11.

Murphy, K. R., & Levert, S. (1985). *Out of the fog: Treatment options and coping strategies for adult attention deficit disorder.* New York: Hyperion.

Ratey, J. J. (1991, Fall/Winter). Paying attention to attention in adults. *CH.A.D.D.ER,* pp. 13–14.

Seligman, M. E. P. (1990). *Learned optimism.* New York: Knopf.

Shekim, W. O. (1990, Spring/Summer). Adult attention deficit hyperactivity disorder, residual state (ADHD, RS). *CH.A.D.D.ER,* pp. 16–18.

Weiss, G., & Hechtman, L. (1993). *Hyperactive children grown up.* New York: Guilford Press.

Weiss, L. (1992). *Attention deficit disorder in adults.* Dallas, TX: Taylor.

Wender, P. H. (1987). *The hyperactive child, adolescent, and adult: Attention deficit disorder through the lifespan.* New York: Oxford University Press.

9

Psychotherapy of Adult Attention Deficit Disorder

EDWARD M. HALLOWELL

Although there is a great deal of available information about Attention Deficit Disorder (ADD) in children, far less literature is to be found that deals with adult ADD. Within this small amount of information, there is very little that addresses psychotherapy with adults with ADD. Thus, the adult with ADD and his or her therapist are left without guidance for psychotherapeutic treatment strategies that are most effective in grappling with this disorder. Clearly, some of the literature about therapy with children and techniques of overcoming the inherent distractibility of the person with ADD can be applied to adults (such as the need for external structure [Wender, 1971]), but the nature of the day-to-day difficulties that an adult with ADD experiences is vastly different from that of a child.

A trend toward increased internalizing behavior and decreased externalizing behavior has been seen as ADD children grow older (Brown, Madan-Swain, & Baldwin, 1991). Thus, adults with ADD often exhibit symptoms of depression and anxiety while being able to control their impulsiveness and hyperactivity (Mann & Greenspan, 1976). Children with ADD who are not diagnosed at an early age are often very intelligent and may come from a supportive environment; hence, it is not until the stresses of adulthood take their toll that the difficulties of ADD become apparent. When treating adults, it is also necessary to keep in mind that they are carrying with them years of ingrained behavior patterns and a reinforced negative self-image that can initially block the path to change.

While therapy with children may focus primarily on behavior modification (Greenhill, 1989), adults need to reconceptualize themselves in light of their disorder. Once the individual understands the nature of his or her disorder, it is easier to deal with the cognitive, emotional, and self-esteem

146

problems that are often inherent. Therefore, therapy with ADD adults should include education regarding their disorder (Bellak, 1977), which removes some of the self-blame (Wender, 1971).

This chapter explores the course of treatment of adults with ADD, focusing on the psychotherapeutic process. While the goal of this psychotherapy is the same as with other disorders, the methodology most effective with such individuals is somewhat deviant from traditional psychotherapy in that the therapeutic relationship is one of more involvement on the part of the therapist, an issue that will be explored later in more detail.

Once the diagnosis of adult ADD has been established, one must decide on treatment. Just making the diagnosis often brings great relief of psychic pain as well as dramatic reduction in symptoms (Barkley, 1990); in that sense, diagnosis becomes a significant part of treatment. The comprehensive treatment of ADD does not, of course, end with diagnosis; it begins. Treatment may be divided into five components, as follows:

1. Diagnosis
2. Education
3. Structure
4. Psychotherapy
5. Medication

The first two components are invariably essential; the third, almost always; each of the final two may or may not be necessary. Here, I discuss the fourth component of treatment—psychotherapy—and suggest when and how it may be useful.

THERAPIST AS COACH

The treatment of ADD is best undertaken by a psychotherapist who knows about both ADD and psychotherapy. The degree the person has does not matter, but experience with ADD is important, as well as experience in doing psychotherapy with other conditions.

The therapist should understand that ADD is not treated just like any other issue in psychotherapy, and should retain a human rather than mechanical view of the syndrome. The therapist must keep several issues in mind. While attending to the patient's neurological problems, the therapist should never forget the human, emotional problems. He or she should remain attuned to the omnipresent therapy issues of hidden meanings, covert signals, concealed motives, repressed memories, and unspoken desires, and leave aside all prejudice or preconceived ideas derived from diagnosis or gut reaction. First of all, seek to know the patient.

I must underscore this point: The treatment of ADD should never over-look that the patient is a person first, and a person with ADD second. While the ADD symptoms may dominate the clinical picture, they should never be allowed to obscure the patient's individuality. The patient needs the chance, as do we all, to be heard and understood as a person first—as an individual with a specific history, an idiosyncratic set of habits and tastes, a personal chest of drawers of memories and mementos; the person is not just another patient who has ADD.

The patient's feeling of being understood can heal more wounds than any medication, kind words, or bits of advice (Shekim, Asarnow, Hess, Zaucha, & Wheeler, 1990). This is true in all therapy but is particularly true in therapy with newly diagnosed adults with ADD. They often have had a secret life, a history of many years of keeping their true selves hidden from others, as they tried to cover up their mistakes, their idiosyncrasies, their absences. Finding out at last that there is a name for what they have, that there is an explanation beyond moral failing for their lifelong struggles comes as a great relief. Feeling understood by the therapist begins the healing process.

Once this human bond has been established, or, really, while it is being established, some kind of external supports can help a great deal toward restructuring the patient's life. People with ADD do very well when given support. While they may never get organized on their own, if they feel part of a team, they will function much better.

While in traditional psychotherapy one tries, usually, to maintain a po-sition of neutrality, in psychotherapy with patients who have ADD it can be useful to be overtly encouraging rather than emotionally neutral, and to be directive rather than withholding of advice.

In this posture the therapist becomes like a coach: that individual stand-ing on the sidelines with a whistle around his or her neck, barking out encouragement, directions, and reminders to the player in the game. The coach can be a pain in the neck sometimes, dogging the player to stay alert, and the coach can be a source of solace when the player feels ready to give up. Mainly, the coach keeps the player focused on the task at hand and offers encouragement along the way.

Particularly in the beginning phases of treatment—the first several months—the therapist/coach can help the patient from reverting to old bad habits: habits of procrastination, disorganization, and negative thinking, the latter being the most damaging and pernicious. Treatment begins with hope, with a jump start of the heart. A coach, someone on the outside, can holler at the ADD mind when it starts down the old negative grooves and bring it back to a positive place.

As simpleminded as this approach may sound—indeed, perhaps even superficial–it works well because the ADD mind has such a difficult time supplying direction and encouragement. While in traditional psychotherapy the therapist would encourage patients to learn how to supply these things for themselves, and the therapist would allow patients to bear the tension of not receiving these supplies from the therapist in the hope that they would learn how to supply them themselves, in therapy with a patient with ADD, it is usually effective for the therapist to supply the direction and encouragement in the therapy session. Rather than teaching patients how to supply these for themselves, the therapist should teach patients instead how to find them from other people beyond the therapist, from other "coaches" on the outside.

This approach takes into account the neurological inability of the ADD mind to focus and organize as efficiently as other minds (Mesulam, 1986). Rather than seeing this inability as based on psychodynamics, this approach sees it as based on neurology (Zametkin et al., 1993).

At the beginning of treatment there should be brief (10–15 minutes), daily check-ins with the coach, in person or over the phone. The discussion should focus on the practical and concrete–What are your plans? What is due tomorrow? What are you doing to get ready for tomorrow?–as well as on the abstract–How do you feel? What is your mood? These questions can be organized by the initials H-O-P-E.

HELP:	Ask the person you are coaching, "What kind of help do you need?" Begin by getting an update and seeing what specific assistance is needed.
OBLIGATIONS:	Ask specifically which obligations are coming up and what the person is doing to prepare for them. You must ask. If you don't ask, the individual may forget to tell you.
PLANS:	Ask about ongoing plans. It is very helpful to remind people with ADD of their goals. They often forget them, quite literally, and so stop working toward them. If they say they don't know what their goals are, try to help them define them. Goals function as a kind of guard against aimlessness, drawing the individual through time toward a desired place.
ENCOURAGEMENT:	This is the most enjoyable part of the coach's job. The coach should really engage

and not be embarrassed to be "rah-rah." The coach is joining a battle against chaos and negativity; the more affirmative he or she can be, the better. Rather than biting one's tongue when the desire to offer encouragement comes up, the therapist can go with that desire and offer encouragement freely.

THE IMPORTANCE OF STRUCTURE AND DIRECTION

There are some elements of traditional psychotherapy that are useful for people with ADD because of their problems with self-esteem (Barkley, Fischer, Edelbrock, & Smallish, 1990; Hoy, Weiss, Minde, & Cohen, 1978), anxiety (Biederman, Newcorn, & Sprich, 1991), and depression (Biederman et al., 1987; Millman, 1979; Wood, Reimherr, Wender, & Johnson, 1976) that build up in the wake of ADD (Ratey, Greenberg, Bemporad, & Lindem, 1992). The emphasis, however, should still be on interpersonal and systems-oriented rather than interpretive therapy. While the primary problem of ADD is best treated with structure (Leimkuhler, in press; Mann & Greenspan, 1976), medication (Wender, Reimherr, Wood, & Ward, 1985), and coaching, the secondary psychological problems sometimes require ongoing psychotherapy. It is a mistake to treat the primary problems related to attention, distractibility, impulsivity, and restlessness and overlook the considerable secondary problems associated with self-esteem, depression, or marital or family discord (American Psychiatric Association, 1987; Heilman, Voeller, & Nadeau, 1991; Hunt, 1988; Safer & Allen, 1976).

When working with adults with ADD, the therapist should help structure the sessions and be quite active. The fundamental rule of psychoanalysis, that the patient is to say whatever comes to mind often leaves the person with ADD at a complete loss. There is so much coming to mind that he or she does not know where to begin or where to resume. Or, once begun, he or she does not know where to stop. The person may become flooded, not with interesting unconscious material, but with bushels of detritus—useless material that risks casting psychotherapy into a kind of aimless monologue, going nowhere, frustrating both patient and therapist.

If the therapist can provide some structure and direction, the patient can often get on track. If the patient has trouble getting started, the therapist might ask a directive question, such as, "How is that problem with your boss working out?" Or, if the patient starts to go off on a tangent that seems to be leading nowhere, the therapist might try to help by bringing the patient back to the original subject. This is quite counter to what a good therapist usually does in open-ended, insight-oriented psychotherapy.

In that kind of therapy, the therapist often wishes the patient would get off track, would let go of conscious control to some extent, in order to uncover what lies beneath the surface. However, in patients with ADD, this approach can backfire, leaving both patient and therapist lost in a meaningless maze of distractions, interruptions, and hiccups of incomplete thoughts and images.

Here, the therapist should act as a guide through thoughts and associations, helping prioritize mental productions so as to pay attention to what is germane while letting go of what is extraneous. If in the process one lets go of a pearl, that is too bad, but it is better than spending the whole therapy shucking pearl-less oysters.

Let me give an example to illustrate this point. At the beginning of a session, one of my patients, a 42-year-old man in treatment for ADD and depression, said, "Well, I sure won't be needing my wife's money anymore." His reliance on his wife's considerable inherited wealth had become a central issue in therapy because the money undermined his sense of independence and self-esteem. In fact, he relied on it only in his imagination, as the couple lived on the combined incomes of both and they earned about the same amount.

In response to his statement, I looked interested and said, "Oh, really, why is that?"

"Because I've had a breakthrough. The store has said it will pay me to get special training that will enable me to take over the whole department probably in about a year."

"Really," I said, hoping for more.

"Yes, but I also want to talk to you about the elevator in this building. Why can't they get it fixed? It's a real pain walking up four flights of stairs."

Now at this point I had a decision to make. In psychotherapy with a patient without ADD, I would probably remain silent, or I would ask more about the elevator, thinking in the back of my mind that the patient was inching in on significant transference feelings, feelings about me, his therapist, through his feelings about the elevator and the pain it caused him to get to me, to our sessions. Why couldn't I make it easier, he might be asking me. Why couldn't I take better care of my building, of my elevator, of my patients, of him? Couldn't I be relied on for that much? Or, looking for past memories or unconscious fantasies, I might ask for my patient's associations with elevators. Sometimes such a question can jar loose an old memory, and lead to a whole new and unexpected vein of material. On the other hand, my patient's bringing up the subject of the broken elevator right on the heels of announcing a big promotion certainly could make me wonder if he did not feel conflicted about the promotion. Did the promotion make him think of things that needed repair, like the elevator, like himself? Was he wondering, in the punning way the unconscious often works, if he were "up" to the job, if he were entitled to "rise" in his field, or if he needed an extra "lift," perhaps from me? With another patient, I might have pursued any or all of these ideas.

With this patient, however, I simply said, "I know the broken elevator is annoying. I am told it will be fixed this week. But I'm interested in hearing more about your feelings about the new development at work." It may be argued that in doing this—essentially redirecting the patient toward what I thought was most important—I lost an opportunity. No doubt I did. But I especially did not want to lose the opportunity the patient had presented at the start of the session in telling about his possible promotion at work. In looking at both opportunities—the opportunity presented by the promotion and the opportunity presented by the elevator—I decided to take over and choose the promotion as the issue to focus on.

Now if the man had responded, "No, I really want to talk about the elevator," of course, I would have let him. But he didn't. Instead he very easily glided back into talking about the promotion, as if that was what he had really wanted to talk about in the first place. If I had let us get into a long discussion about the elevator, it is more than likely we never would have found our way back to the promotion.

I had to decide whether he brought up the topic of the elevator because he needed to, for hidden reasons we had best look at, or if he brought it up just because it popped into his head, for no significant reason, like a distraction, like the sound of a train whistle outside my window or the telephone ringing in the next office. In making the decision I did, I was taking on the role of distraction-censor, a role I often play with my patients who have ADD. The risk inherent in my making such a decision for my patient is that I would unintentionally sidestep important material.

The therapist must make this kind of determination all the time in doing psychotherapy with patients with ADD. Even with people who do not have ADD, the therapist must constantly weigh what is heard and consider what to focus on and what to let slide by. With patients with ADD, however, the therapist has to be more active along these lines than with other patients.

In addition, the therapist should take into account the patient's inherent perceptual problems in understanding social situations. Often people with ADD respond inappropriately or awkwardly with other people (Biederman et al., 1987). Sometimes they appear to be self-centered and remarkably unaware of the needs of others. Consider the following scene as an example:

> Dave, a 35-year-old man with ADD, paused at the office water cooler for a drink. As he was sipping the spring water, a friend joined him at the cooler. "Hi, Dave," the friend said, filling his conic cup. Dave did

not respond. "Be nice to get these estimates out on time, for once, huh? You've done a great job." Dave still did not say anything. "You must have been here late last night?"

Dave, who had been thinking about how to construct a three-dimensional oval, like an egg, for his daughter's science project, threw his cup in the metal trash basket, saw his friend, grunted, and headed back toward his office. His friend called after him, "Nice talking to you, Dave." Dave did not stop. His friend registered this encounter as just another example of "spacy Dave" being "spacy Dave."

It is not that Dave was too selfish or narcissistic to acknowledge or hear his friend; it is that he was mentally elsewhere. It would be important for his therapist to know of this tendency and to give practical advice on how to handle similar social situations. By practical advice, I mean concrete pointers, such as: "When you are at the water cooler, or any central stopping place, keep in mind that other people might walk up to you," "When you see a friend, don't just grunt; say something, give an interested response," or, "When you are in a conversation, it is important to make eye contact and listen before you start to speak." These kinds of counsel—concrete, obvious, perhaps tedious for the therapist—can help a person with ADD immensely.

People with ADD may have trouble making friends or succeeding socially simply because they don't know how to behave. They don't know the rules. They don't know the steps of the dance. They have never been taught—and they were never able to learn—what we all assume everyone learns as second nature. People with ADD may lack this second nature. They may need lessons in how to interact. Social "reading" can be as difficult for these people as the reading of words. As painfully obvious as these lessons may be to the socially adept, to the person with ADD, who can feel as lost in a conversation as he does in the middle of a written page, these lessons can impart the ability to make meaningful contact with other people.

Having stressed the importance of "coaching," and the importance of focusing and directing the psychotherapy in working with patients with ADD, let me reiterate that the work the therapist does is not simpleminded. While coaching may sound simple—and, indeed, at its best, it is simple, deceptively simple—and while focusing the therapy may sound like a kind of traffic control, stopping this conversation, whistling it over there, this work can also be as subtle, unpredictable, and imaginative as any kind of psychotherapy.

While individual therapy marks the starting point for most people with ADD, additional forms of psychotherapy can be extremely helpful, particularly family therapy, couple therapy, and group therapy.

GROUP THERAPY

Group therapy for ADD can mobilize positive energy in ways that are truly remarkable. When groups are properly run, they are a safe, cost-effective, and highly successful kind of therapy for people with ADD, both children and adults. Indeed, with children, individual therapy may not get at the real problems at all, because the problems only come up in group situations (Biederman & Steingard, 1989). The child may sit with his or her individual therapist and happily play games, all the while showing none of the symptoms that cause the big problems at school and at home. Whereas a children's group therapy can address the issues as they come up, head on, in situ, as it were, in the group. For example, a child who cannot pay attention when other children are around will not show this in individual therapy. Or a child who becomes disruptive when asked to share with other children will not demonstrate this symptom in individual therapy. But in a group, these kinds of behaviors will appear.

For adults with ADD, group therapy has several advantages. It gives people a chance to meet and interact with other people like themselves, people who have had to deal with many of the same problems and frustrations in life. The members of the group can teach each other a great deal. They can talk about their own experiences and share tips and pointers that they have found helpful in their own lives, while learning similar information from other group members. In a sense, the best therapist for someone with ADD is someone else with ADD, someone who has been there, someone who knows the place from the inside.

A group can validate its members' experiences in ways that an individual therapist cannot. It can support and understand its members in a powerful way. The acceptance one can find in a group can be uplifting. Groups can supply a tremendous amount of energy, like reservoirs of fuel where members fill up each week.

As with groups for children, adult groups can re-create the very situations with which people with ADD are trying to learn how to cope. Groups can re-create situations like Dave's at the water cooler. Members must listen to each other, wait their turn, share, keep silent for a period of time, stay put, take responsibility for what they say or do not say. And, very important, they can receive feedback as to how they affect others. As the individual learns to bear with the tension of these feelings in the group, that skill can be carried into the outside world.

Groups can also address the problem of disconnectedness. Many people with ADD have trouble finding a place where they feel connected, a part of something larger than the self. Although they tend to be outgoing and gregarious, they can also harbor strong feelings of isolation, loneliness, and disconnectedness. Their stance in life is often one of reaching out but not quite making contact, as if running alongside a speeding train trying to grasp the hand that is being held out to help them board. Groups can bring people on board. Groups can provide a sense of belonging, of connectedness. Once on board, the individual can feel more a part of things in other areas of his or her life.

To illustrate the power of group therapy in ADD, let me tell a story. Some time ago I began to run groups for adults with ADD. I had never done this before and had not read of others doing it, but for all the reasons given above it seemed to me a good idea. I announced the idea at a lecture. From the people who signed up, I selected a group of 10 men and women, and we started to meet once a week. I did not know what to expect. Colleagues I mentioned the idea to rolled their eyes and said, "Ten people with ADD in a group?! How can you run herd on that?" Another colleague asked, "Will they ever show up on time?"

Not knowing what would happen, I sat in my office the evening of the first meeting. We were to meet from 7:00 to 8:15. By 7:15, not one of the ten members had appeared. I began to wonder if my own ADD had led me to write down the wrong day. At 7:20, the first member showed up. He burst into the office ready to apologize for being late, but when he discovered he was the first to arrive, he started laughing and said, "Well, what can you expect?" Seven people eventually arrived for that first meeting. Three others left messages that they had gotten lost on their way to my office.

The ones who did find their way began the most remarkable group I have ever participated in. They came together immediately, united in their desire to find mutual understanding, to tell their various stories, and to "be there" for each other.

I gave the group some basic guidelines: Try to be on time. Don't socialize with each other outside the group. If you are going to miss a session, try to let the group know about it in advance. We contracted to meet for 20 weeks, with an option to continue for another 10 weeks if people wanted to. I also called the members who had gotten lost and gave them directions for the following week.

The next session all 10 members showed up and on time. They laughed about the trouble they'd had with the directions the week before, and started what became a regular practice in the group of giving good-natured kidding as a way of dealing with the problems of ADD. "It's a miracle," they laughed, "that we all got here this week, and on time no less." They looked around at each other, giving nods of approval and looks of recognition as they would identify with one detail or another that was being related. To be with them was to be with people who had spent their whole lives feeling "different," only now to discover in each other that they were not alone. Their exuberance filled the room even before they knew each other. It was as if, in some intuitive part of their minds, they already knew each other and how important the group would become. From the beginning, they were ready for each other.

They began to tell their stories. One by one, not on cue, but spontaneously, tales of humor and tales of pain filled the room. They laughed back tears and faced each other's pain with firsthand understanding, as they told of misunderstandings, frustrations, and lost chances, as well as gave tips and advice, tricks from the ADD trade.

I did not have to intervene. If one member interrupted another, others would say something like, "Now don't interrupt. Since we all have ADD, we have to be really careful about paying attention to each other." They looked out for each other in this kind of way all the time. I sat back and answered factual questions about ADD now and then, but, by and large, the members of the group did all the work. When I had to miss a few meetings due to prior commitments, the group simply met in my office without me. They asked only if I would bill them for sessions I missed. I said of course I would not.

Within a few weeks, the group had developed a powerful sense of cohesion. One member, who was an aspiring actress, turned down a part in a play because rehearsal time conflicted with group time. Another member, who went on vacation, sent us a postcard. Members gave each other permission to call each other in case of an emotional crisis. I worried this might lead to subgrouping or breakdowns in confidentiality. It never did.

When the option to continue the group for another 10 weeks came up, everyone wanted to go on. However, one member stated she could not afford to. Later that week I received a letter without signature or identifying marks. It contained, in cash, the fee for an additional 10 weeks of the group. The person who wrote the letter identified himself or herself as only, "a member of the adult ADD group."

Now I, who was trained in psychoanalytically oriented Boston, went into a snit. What should I do? Do I bring the money into the group? Give it back? To whom? What if the person who had said she could not afford to continue had said that as a way of leaving the group gracefully? Would this put undue pressure on her to continue? What if others felt gypped that they couldn't get a "scholarship" also? What about the group's curiosity as to the identity of the anonymous donor? What about my own curiosity? With these questions swimming through my mind, I called a colleague experienced in group work for advice. He felt a bit perplexed as well, but advised me to bring the matter up in the group and see how they handled it.

At the next meeting of the group, we decided to go on for 10 more weeks and then to stop. At that point I informed the group that I had received an anonymous cash donation to cover the fee of the member who could not afford to continue. Well, thankfully, the group was not psychoanalytically trained. The members' response was to say how generous that someone had donated the money, and then they moved on to other topics. I sat there biting my tongue, thinking, yes, but, don't you want to know more, don't you see the complicated dynamic issues involved here, shouldn't we analyze the implications of this gift, and on and on. Fortunately, I didn't let myself make more of the matter than the group did, so the incident passed into the group's history as this: The group received a generous gift which allowed the group to remain intact for 10 more weeks. In retrospect, I do still have all those questions I had originally. But most of all I see the gift as evidence of just how important it was to those people to be together and, at last, to be understood.

* * *

Having outlined some general considerations on psychotherapy with adults with ADD, let me conclude with specific suggestions that may be given to patients to help them in their day-to-day lives. These suggestions are intentionally directive; it is the hope that they can serve as a kind of behavioral prescription, giving the patient useful suggestions. These tips are culled from years of experience in working with individuals with ADD, hearing their problems and complaints, and learning from the solutions they devised.

I usually hand these suggestions out to patients at the beginning of treatment and explain to them that some of the points will seem irrelevant, obvious, or trivial, but others may be quite useful. I refer back to the tips as the therapy goes on, trying to let them serve as a kind of "home reference" when times are confusing or difficult.

What is printed here is exactly what the patient receives. The "you" mentioned in these tips is the patient.

50 TIPS ON THE MANAGEMENT OF ADULT ATTENTION DEFICIT DISORDER

As you read through the following suggestions, you will probably find that you already use many of them; you will find that some of them are obvious or apply to everybody, with or without ADD; you will find that some of them seem irrelevant to your situation; and you will find, we hope, that some of them are new and quite helpful.

A word of caution: Often when people read these tips for the first time, they become excited about incorporating them into their lives right away.

After an initial burst of enthusiasm and improvement, however, they find that the old habit associated with their ADD starts to creep back into their lives. They find that tips, although "correct," are hard to follow consistently. As one patient said, "If I could follow the tips, then I wouldn't need to follow them, because I wouldn't have ADD in the first place." Or, as another patient said, "I have days when I can follow the tips and days when I can't. It's like the old heartbeat, up and down."

It is important, therefore, to keep in mind that the tips are only one part of a treatment program. Very few people with ADD can implement these tips consistently on their own. They need help, either from what we call a "coach," from a group, from a therapist, or from some other external source. Do not feel intimidated or disheartened if at first you have trouble putting all these tips to work for you in your life. It will take time, it will require hard work, and it will require encouragement (and forgiveness) from the outside world. But, given these things, the tips can offer solid, practical help.

I. Insight and Education

1. Be sure of the diagnosis. Make sure you're working with a professional who really understands ADD and has excluded related or similar conditions such as anxiety states, agitated depression, hyperthyroidism, manic-depressive illness, or obsessive-compulsive disorder.

2. Educate yourself. Perhaps the single most powerful treatment of ADD is understanding ADD in the first place. Read books. Talk with professionals. Talk with other adults who have the disorder. These may be found through ADD support groups or local or national ADD organizations such as CH.A.D.D. You'll be able to design your own treatment to fit your own version of ADD.

3. Coaching. It is useful for you to have a coach, some person close to you to keep after you, but always with humor. Your coach can help you get organized, stay on task, give you encouragement, and remind you to get back to work. Friend, colleague, or therapist (it is possible but risky for your coach to be your spouse), a coach is someone to stay on you to get things done, who exhorts you as coaches do, keeps tabs on you, and in general is in your corner. A coach can be tremendously helpful in treating ADD.

4. Encouragement. ADD adults need lots of encouragement. This is in part due to their having many self-doubts that have accumulated over the years. But it goes beyond that. More than the average person,

the ADD adult withers without encouragement and positively lights up like a Christmas tree when given it. They will often work for another person in a way they won't work for themselves. This is not "bad," it just is. It should be recognized and taken advantage of.

5. Realize what ADD is *not*, that is, it is not conflict with mother, unconscious fear of success, passive-aggressive personality, and so forth. People with ADD, of course, may have a conflict with their mother or an unconscious fear of success or a passive-aggressive personality, but it is important to separate the ADD from these other kinds of problems because the treatment for ADD is completely different.

6. Educate and involve others. Just as it is key for you to understand ADD, it is equally if not more important for those around you to understand it—family, coworkers, schoolmates, friends. Once they get the concept, they will be able understand you much better and help you as well.

7. Give up guilt over high-stimulus-seeking behavior. Understand that you are drawn to high stimuli. Try to choose them wisely, rather than brooding over the "bad" ones.

8. Listen to feedback from trusted others. Adults (and children, too) with ADD are notoriously poor self-observers. They use a lot of what can appear to be denial.

9. Consider joining or starting a support group. Much of the most useful information about ADD has not yet found its way into books but remains stored in the minds of the people who have ADD. In groups, this information can come out. Plus, groups are really helpful in giving the kind of support that is so badly needed.

10. Try to get rid of the negativity that may have infested your system if you have lived for years without knowing that what you had was ADD. A good psychotherapist may help in this regard.

11. Don't feel chained to conventional careers or conventional ways of coping. Give yourself permission to be yourself. Give up trying to be the person you always thought you should be—the model student or the organized executive, for example—and let yourself be who you are.

12. Remember that what you have is a neuropsychiatric condition. It is genetically transmitted. It is caused by biology, by how your brain is wired. It is *not* a disease of the will, or a moral failing. It is *not* caused by a weakness in character, or by a failure to mature. Its cure is not to be found in the power of the will, or in punishment, or in sacrifice, or in pain. ALWAYS REMEMBER THIS. Try as they might, many people with ADD have great trouble accepting the syndrome as be-

ing rooted in biology rather than in weakness of character.

13. Try to help others with ADD. You'll learn a lot about the condition in the process, and feel good to boot.

II. Performance Management

14. External structure. Structure is the hallmark of the nonpharmacological treatment of the ADD child. Structure can be equally useful with adults. Although tedious to set up, once in place, structure works like the walls of a bobsled, keeping the speedball sled from careening off the track. Make frequent use of

> Lists
> Notes to self
> Color coding
> Rituals
> Reminders
> Files

15. Use pizzazz. Try to make your environment as peppy as you want it to be without letting it boil over. If your organization system can be stimulating (imagine that!), instead of boring, then you will be more likely to follow it. For example, in setting things up, try color coding. Many people with ADD are visually oriented. Take advantage of this by making things memorable with color: files, memoranda, texts, schedules, and so forth. Virtually anything in the black and white of type can be made more memorable, arresting, and therefore attention-getting with color.

16. O.H.I.O. When it comes to paperwork, use the principle of O.H.I.O: ONLY HANDLE IT ONCE. When you receive a document or a memo or any kind of written material, try to only handle it once. Either respond to it right away, on the spot, or throw the document away, or file it permanently. Do not put it in a "To Do" box or pile. For people with ADD, "To Do" piles might just as well be called NEVER DONE piles. They serve as little menaces around one's desk or room, silently building guilt, anxiety, and resentment, as well as taking up a lot of space. Get in the habit of acting immediately on your paperwork. Make the wrenching decision to throw something away. Or, overcome inertia and respond to it *on the spot.* Whatever you do with the document, whenever possible, only handle it once.

17. Set up your environment to reward rather than deflate. To understand what a deflating environment is, most adult ADDers only need

to think back to school. Now that you have the freedom of adult-hood, try to set things up so that you will not constantly be reminded of your limitations.

18. Acknowledge and anticipate the inevitable collapse of x% of projects undertaken, relationships entered into, obligations incurred. Better that you anticipate these "failures" rather than be surprised by them and brood over them. Think of them as part of the cost of doing business.

19. Embrace challenges. ADD people thrive with many challenges. As long as you know they won't all pan out, as long as you don't get too perfectionistic and fussy, you'll get a lot done and stay out of trouble. Far better that you be too busy than not busy enough. As the old saying goes, if you want something done, ask a busy person.

20. Make deadlines.

21. Break down large tasks into small ones. Attach deadlines to the small parts. Then, like magic, the large task will get done. This is one of the simplest and most powerful of all structuring devices. Often a large task will feel overwhelming to the person with ADD. The mere thought of trying to perform the task makes one turn away. On the other hand, if the large task is broken down into small parts, each component may feel quite manageable.

22. Prioritize. Avoid procrastination. When things get busy, the adult with ADD loses perspective: Paying an unpaid parking ticket can feel as pressing as putting out the fire that just got started in the waste-basket. Prioritize. Take a deep breath. Put first things first. Procras-tination is one of the hallmarks of adult ADD. You have to really discipline yourself to watch out for it and avoid it.

23. Accept fear of things going too well. Accept edginess when things are too easy, when there's no conflict. Don't gum things up just to make them more stimulating.

24. Notice how and where you work best: in a noisy room, on the train, wrapped in three blankets, listening to music, whatever. Children and adults with ADD can do their best under rather odd conditions. Let yourself work under whatever conditions are best for you.

25. Know that it is O.K. to do two things at once: carry on a conversa-tion and knit, or take a shower and do your best thinking, or jog and plan a business meeting. Often people with ADD need to be doing several things at once in order to get anything done at all.

26. Do what you're good at. Again, if it seems easy, that is O.K. There is no rule that says you can only do what you're bad at.

27. Leave time between engagements to gather your thoughts. Transi-

tions are difficult for ADDers, and minibreaks can help ease the transition.

28. Keep a notepad in your car, by your bed, and in your pocketbook or jacket. You never know when a good idea will hit you or you'll want to remember something else.

29. Read with a pen in hand, not only for marginal notes or underlining, but for the inevitable cascade of "other" thoughts that will occur to you.

III: Mood Management

30. Have structured "blow-out" time. Set aside some time in every week for just letting go. Whatever you like to do–blasting yourself with loud music, taking a trip to the race track, having a feast. Pick some kind of activity from time to time where you can let loose in a safe way.

31. Recharge your batteries. Related to #30, most adults with ADD need, on a daily basis, some time to waste without feeling guilty about it. One guilt-free way to conceptualize it is to call it time to recharge your batteries. Take a nap, watch TV, meditate–something calm, restful, at ease.

32. Choose "good," helpful addictions, such as exercise. Many adults with ADD have an addictive or compulsive personality such that they are always hooked on something. Try to make this something positive.

33. Understand mood changes and ways to manage these. Know that your moods will change willy-nilly, independent of what's going on in the external world. Don't waste your time ferreting out the reason why or looking for someone to blame. Instead focus on learning to tolerate a bad mood, knowing that it will pass, and learning strategies to make it pass sooner. Change sets, for example, get involved with some new activity (preferably interactive), such as a conversation with a friend, a tennis game, or reading a book.

34. Related to #33, recognize the following cycle which is very common among adults with ADD:

    a. Something "startles" your psychological system, a change or transition, a disappointment or even a success. The precipitant may be quite trivial.

    b. This "startle" is followed by a minipanic with a sudden loss of perspective, the world being set topsy-turvy.

    c. You try to deal with this panic by falling into a mode of obsessing and ruminating over one or another aspect of the situation. This can last for hours, days, even months.

To break the negative obsessing, have a list of friends to call. Have a few videos that always engross you and get your mind off things. Have ready access to exercise. Have a punching bag or pillow handy if there's extra angry energy. Rehearse a few pep talks you can give yourself, such as, "You've been here before. These are the ADD blues. They will soon pass. You are O.K."

35. Learn how to name your feelings. Many people with ADD, particularly men, get frustrated and angry because they cannot put their feelings into words. With practice and coaching, this is a skill that can be learned.

36. Expect depression after success. Paradoxically, people with ADD commonly complain of feeling depressed after a big success. This is because the high stimulus of the chase or the challenge or the preparation is over. The deed is done. Win or lose, the adult with ADD misses the conflict, the high stimulus, and feels depressed.

37. Learn symbols, slogans, sayings as shorthand ways of labeling and quickly putting into perspective slipups, mistakes, or mood swings. When you turn left instead of right and take your family on a 20-minute detour, it is better to be able to say, "There goes my ADD again," than to have a 6-hour fight over your unconscious desire to sabotage the whole trip. These are not excuses. You still have to take responsibility for your actions. It is just good to know where your actions are coming from and where they're not.

38. Use "time-outs" as with children. When you are upset or overstimulated, take a timeout. Go away. Calm down.

39. Learn how to advocate for yourself. Adults with ADD are so used to being criticized, they are often unnecessarily defensive in putting their own case forward. Learn to get off the defensive.

40. Avoid premature closure of a project, a conflict, a deal, or a conversation. Don't "cut to the chase" too soon, even though you're itching to.

41. Try to let the successful moment last and be remembered, become sustaining over time. You'll have to train yourself consciously and deliberately to do this because you'll naturally tend to forget your successes as you brood over your shortcomings or pessimistically anticipate the worst.

42. Remember that ADD usually includes a tendency to overfocus or hyperfocus at times. This hyperfocusing can be used constructively or destructively. Be aware of its destructive use: a tendency to obsess or ruminate over some imagined problem without being able to let it go.

43. Exercise vigorously and regularly. You should schedule this into your life and stick with it. Exercise is positively one of the best treatments for ADD. It helps work off excess energy and aggression in a positive way, it allows for noise reduction within the mind, it stimulates the hormonal and neurochemical system in a most therapeutic way, and it soothes and calms the body. When you add all that to the well-known health benefits of exercise, you can see how important exercise is. Make it something fun so you can stick with it over the long haul, that is, the rest of your life.

IV. Interpersonal Life

44. Make a good choice in a significant other. Obviously this is good advice for anyone. But it is striking how the adult with ADD can thrive or flounder depending on the choice of mate.

45. Learn to joke with yourself and others about your various symptoms, from forgetfulness, to getting lost all the time, to being tactless or impulsive. If you can bring a sense of humor to your failings, others will forgive you much more quickly.

46. Schedule activities with friends. Adhere to these schedules faithfully. It is crucial for you to keep connected to other people.

47. Find and join groups where you are liked, appreciated, understood, enjoyed. Even more than most people, people with ADD take great strength from group support.

48. Reverse of #47. Don't stay too long where you aren't understood or appreciated. Just as people with ADD gain a great deal from supportive groups, they are particularly drained and demoralized by negative groups, and they have a tendency to stay with them too long, vainly trying to make things work out, even when all the evidence shows they can't.

49. Pay compliments. Notice other people. In general, get social training if you're having trouble getting along with other people.

50. Set social deadlines. Without deadlines and dates your social life can atrophy. Just as you will be helped by structuring your business week, so too you will benefit from keeping your social calendar organized. This will help you stay in touch with friends and get the kind of social support you need.

REFERENCES

American Psychiatric Association. (1987). Diagnostic and Statistical Manual of Mental Disorders (3rd ed., revised.). Washington, DC: Author.

Barkley, R. A. (1990). *Attention deficit hyperactivity disorder: A handbook for diagnosis and treatment.* New York: Guilford.

Barkley, R. A., Fischer, M., Edelbrock, C. S., & Smallish, L. (1990). The adolescent outcome of hyperactive children diagnosed by research criteria: An eight-year prospective follow-up study. *Journal of the American Academy of Child and Adolescent Psychiatry, 29,* 546–557.

Bellak, L. (1977). Psychiatric states in adults with minimal brain dysfunction. *Psychiatric Annals, 7,* 58–76.

Biederman, J., Munir, K., Knee, D., Armentano, M., Autor, S., Waternaux, C., & Tsuang, M. (1987). High rate of affective disorders in probands with attention deficit disorder and their relatives: A controlled family study. *American Journal of Psychiatry, 144,* 330–333.

Biederman, J., Newcorn, J., & Sprich, S. (1991). Comorbidity of attention deficit hyperactivity disorder with conduct, depressive, anxiety and other disorders. *American Journal of Psychiatry, 148,* 564–577.

Biederman, J., & Steingard, R. (1989). Attention-deficit hyperactivity disorder in adolescents. *Psychiatric Annals, 19,* 587–596.

Brown, R. T., Madan-Swain, A., & Baldwin, K. (1991). Gender differences in clinic-referred sample of attention-deficit-disordered children. *Child Psychiatry and Human Development, 22,* 111–128.

Greenhill, L. L. (1989). Treatment issues in children with attention-deficit hyperactivity disorder. *Psychiatric Annals, 19,* 604–613.

Hallowell, E. M., & Ratey, J. J. (1994). *Driven to distraction: Recognizing and coping with attention deficit disorder from childhood and adulthood.* Pantheon.

Heath, C. T., Jr., Wright, H. H., & Batey, S. R. (1990). Attention deficit hyperactivity disorder: Does it affect adults too? *Southern Medical Journal, 83,* 1396–1401.

Heilman, K. M, Voeller, K. S., & Nadeau, S. E. (1991). A possible pathophysiologic substrate of attention deficit hyperactivity disorder. *Journal of Child Neurology, 6,* s76–s81.

Hoy, E., Weiss, G., Minde, K., & Cohen, H. (1978). The hyperactive child at adolescence: Cognitive, emotional, and social functioning. *Journal of Abnormal Child Psychology, 6,* 311–324.

Hunt, R. D. (1988). Clonidine and treatment of ADHD. *Psychiatric Times, 2,* 10–12.

Leimkuhler, M. E. (in press). Attention deficit disorder in adults and adolescents: Cognitive, behavioral and personality styles. In G. Ellison, S. Weinstein, & T. Hodel-Malinofsky (Eds.), *The psychotherapist's guide to neuropsychiatric patients: Diagnostic and treatment dilemmas.* Washington, DC: American Psychiatric Press.

Mann, H. B., & Greenspan, S. I. (1976). The identification and treatment of adult brain dysfunction. *American Journal of Psychiatry, 133,* 1013–1017.

Mendelson, W., Johnson, N., & Stewart, M. A. (1971). Hyperactive children as teenagers: A follow-up study. *Journal of Nervous and Mental
Disease*, *153*, 273–279.

Mesulam, M. M. (1986). Attention, confusional states, and neglect. In M. M.
Mesulam (Ed.), *Principles of behavioral neurology* (pp. 125–168). Philadelphia: F. A. Davis.

Millman, D. (1979). Minimal brain dysfunction in childhood, outcome in
late adolescent and early adult years. *Journal of Clinical Psychiatry*, *40*,
371–380.

Ratey, J. J., Greenberg, M. S., Bemporad, J. R., & Lindem, K. J. (1992).
Unrecognized attention-deficit hyperactivity disorder in adults pre-
senting for outpatient psychotherapy. *Journal of Child and Adolescent
Psychopharmacology*, *4*, 267–275.

Ratey, J. J., Middeldorp-Crispijn, C. W., & Leveroni, C. L. (in press). The
influence of attentional problems on the development of personality.
In J. J. Ratey (Ed.), *Neuropsychiatry of behavior disorders.* Boston: Blackwell
Scientific.

Safer, D. J., & Allen, R. P. (1976). *Hyperactive children.* Baltimore: University Park Press.

Shekim, W. O., Asarnow, R. F., Hess, E., Zaucha, K., & Wheeler, N. (1990).
A clinical and demographic profile of a sample of adults with attention deficit hyperactivity disorder, residual state. *Comprehensive Psychiatry*, *31*, 416–425.

Wender, P. H. (1971). *Minimal brain dysfunction in children.* New York:
Wiley-Interscience.

Wender, P. H., Reimherr, F. W., Wood, D., & Ward, M. (1985). A controlled study of methylphenidate in the treatment of attention deficit
disorder, residual type, in adults. *American Journal of Psychiatry*, *142*,
547–552.

Wood, D. R., Reimherr, F. W., Wender, P.H., & Johnson, G.E. (1976).
Diagnosis and treatment of minimal brain dysfunction in adults: A
preliminary report. *Archives of General Psychiatry*, *33*, 1453–1460.

Zametkin, A. J., Liebenauer, L. L., Fitzgerald, G. A., King, A. C., Minkunas,
D. V., Herscovitch, P., Yamada, E. M., & Cohen, R. M. (1993). Brain
metabolism in teenagers with attention-deficit hyperactivity disorder.
Archives of General Psychiatry, *50*, 333–340.

BIBLIOGRAPHY

Bellak, L. (Ed.). (1979). *Psychiatric aspects of minimal brain dysfunction in adults.*
New York: Grune & Stratton.

CH.A.D.D.ER. Special Edition: The adult with A.D.D.

Fowler, M. C. (1990). *Maybe you know my kid: A parent's guide to identifying, understanding and helping your child with attention deficit disorder.* Birch Lane Press.

Greenhill, L. L., & Osman, B. B. (Ed.). (1991). *Ritalin: Theory and patient management.* New York: Guilford Press.

Hechtman, L., & Weiss, G. (1986). *Hyperactive children grown up.* New York: Guilford Press.

Kavanaugh, J. F., & Truss, T. J. (Eds.). (1988). *Learning disabilities: Proceedings of the National Conference.* Parkton: York Press.

Levine, M. (1991). *Keeping ahead in school.* Cambridge, MA: Education Publishing Service.

Pennington, B. B. (1991). *Diagnosing learning disorders: A neuropsychological framework.* New York: Guilford Press.

Rapoport, J. (1989). *The boy who couldn't stop washing.* New York: Dutton.

Vail, P. (1987). *Smart kids with school problems: Things to know and ways to help.* New York: New American Library.

Vail, P. (1993). *Learning styles: Food for thought and 130 practical tips.* New Jersey: Modern Learning Press.

Vail, P. (in press). *Emotion: The on/off switch for learning.* New Jersey: Modern Learning Press.

Weiss, L. (1992). *Attention deficit disorders in adults: Practical help for sufferers and their spouses.* Dallas, TX: Taylor.

Wender, P. (1987). *The hyperactive child, adolescent, and adult.* Oxford University Press.

10

Pharmacotherapy of Adult ADHD

TIMOTHY E. WILENS, THOMAS J. SPENCER,
AND JOSEPH BIEDERMAN

Attention Deficit Hyperactivity Disorder (ADHD) is a highly prevalent disorder of unknown etiology estimated to affect 6 to 9% of school-age children (Anderson, Williams, McGee, & Silva, 1987; Bird et al., 1988; Safer & Krager, 1988) (ADHD as used here also refers to previous definitions of the disorder). It is commonly associated with high disability that has an impact on all aspects of life, including work, relationships, and intrapsychic distress. The persistent inability to concentrate, multiple failures, disapproval, and demoralization may also contribute to low self-esteem. Recent studies confirm that ADHD is commonly associated not only with antisocial disorders but also with anxiety and depressive disorders (Biederman, Newcorn, & Sprich, 1991; Biederman et al., 1993). While its etiology remains unknown, family, adoption, and twin studies as well as segregation analysis, have indicated that genetic risk factors may be operant in this disorder (Faraone et al., 1992).

Although historically ADHD has been considered a disorder found only in children, more recent reports have documented the persistence of ADHD into adulthood. Prospective long-term follow-up studies, with blind assessment of probands and controls, have shown the persistence of the syndrome in up to 50% of young adults diagnosed as having ADHD in childhood (Gittelman, Mannuzza, Shenker, & Bonagura, 1985; Mannuzza, Klein, Bessler, Malloy, & LaPadula, 1993; Weiss, 1992; Weiss and Hechtman, 1986). Hence, 2 to 4% of adults may have current symptoms of ADHD, although systematic epidemiological data on rates of adult ADHD are lacking.

The "core" ADHD symptoms in adults appear to be developmentally related to those in children. In addition to the inattention, impulsivity, and occasional hyperactivity characteristics of the disorder, adults with ADHD also have clinical features commonly found in childhood ADHD. These include stubbornness, low frustration tolerance, and chronic conflicts in social relations with peers, spouses, and authorities (Biederman et al., 1993; Spencer, Biederman, Wilens, Faraone, & Li, 1994; Wood, Reimherr, Wender, & Johnson, 1976). These features may be responsible for the high rates of separation and divorce, and poor academic and occupational achievement despite adequate intellectual abilities (Klein & Mannuzza, 1988; Mannuzza et al., 1993; Weiss & Hechtman, 1986). Of interest, adults commonly describe their work difficulties and frequent job changes as stemming from dissatisfaction, easy frustration, boredom, and impulsiveness. Employers of these adults report they have poor levels of work performance, impairment in task completion, lack of independent skill, and poor relationships with supervisors (Weiss & Hechtman, 1986). Hence, adults with ADHD often have a number of ADHD symptoms noted by themselves and others that have a significant impact on major aspects of their lives.

While the validity of the diagnosis of adult ADHD has been questioned, Spencer and colleagues (Spencer et al., 1994) systematically assessed the available literature and reported that ADHD in adults is a reliable and valid disorder. Psychopharamacological treatment trials show that the adult diagnosis of ADHD predicts a positive response to a mostly disorder-specific treatment (stimulants) (Spencer et al., 1994). In addition, family-genetic correlates of ADHD in adults, and similarity in the rates of age-corrected comorbidity in adults and children with ADHD have been reported (Biederman, Faraone, Keenan, Knee, & Tsuang, 1990; Biederman, Faraone, Keenan, Benjamin, & Krifcher, 1992; Biederman et al., 1993). Likewise, neurobiologic findings in adult ADHD have been described, including brain positron-emission tomography (PET scan) that revealed reduced glucose metabolism in areas of the cerebral cortex associated with control of attention and motor activity (Zametkin et al., 1990). These never-treated adults with ADHD had biologic children with ADHD. Taken together, these findings indicate that ADHD is a valid clinical entity in adults.

Despite the increasing recognition that children with ADHD commonly grow up to be adults with the same disorder, little is known about the treatment of this disorder in adults. This is especially of concern given the marked impairment in multiple social and interpersonal domains associated with the disorder (Biederman et al., 1993; Mannuzza et al., 1993; Weiss, 1992). In addition, complicating the diagnostics and treatment strategy, many adults with ADHD seeking treatment have depressive and anxiety symptoms, as well as histories of drug and alcohol dependence or abuse

(Biederman et al., 1993; Eyre, Rounsaville, & Kleber, 1982; Tarter, McBride, Buonpane, & Schneider, 1977; Wood, Wender, & Reimherr, 1983). Thus, with the increasing recognition of the complex presentation of adults with ADHD, there is a need to develop effective pharmacotherapeutic strategies. In the following sections, guidelines for pharmacotherapy will be delineated, the available information on the use of medications for adult ADHD will be reviewed, and pharmacologic strategies suggested for the management of ADHD symptoms with accompanying comorbid conditions.

ASSESSMENT AND DIAGNOSTIC CONSIDERATIONS

Pharmacotherapy should be part of a treatment plan in which consideration is given to all aspects of the patient's life. Hence, it should not be used exclusive of other interventions. The administration of medication to adults with ADHD should be undertaken as a collaborative effort with the patient, with the physician guiding the use and management of efficacious anti-ADHD agents.

The use of medication should follow a careful evaluation of the adult, including psychiatric, social, and cognitive assessments. Diagnostic information should be gathered from the patient and, whenever possible, from significant others such as partners, parents, siblings, and close friends. If ancillary data are not available, information from an adult is acceptable for diagnostic and treatment purposes as adults with ADHD, like other disorders, are appropriate reporters of their own condition. Careful attention should be paid to the childhood onset of symptoms, longitudinal history of the disorder, and differential diagnosis including medical/neurological as well psychosocial factors contributing to the clinical presentation.

In the ADHD adult, issues of comorbidity with learning disabilities and other psychiatric disorders need to be addressed. Because learning disabilities do not respond to pharmacotherapy, it is important to identify these deficits to help define remedial interventions. For instance, such an evaluation may assist in the design and implementation of an educational plan for the adult who may be returning to school, or may serve as an aid for structuring the current work environment.

Because alcohol and drug-use disorders are frequently encountered in adults with ADHD, a careful history of substance use should be completed. Patients with ongoing abuse of or dependence on psychoactive substances should generally not be treated until appropriate addiction treatments have been undertaken and the patient has maintained a period free of drugs and alcohol.

Other concurrent psychiatric disorders also need to be assessed and, if possible, the relationship of the ADHD symptoms with these other disorders delineated. In subjects with ADHD plus bipolar mood disorders, for example, the risk of mania needs to be addressed and closely monitored during the treatment of the ADHD. In cases such as these, the conservative introduction of ant-ADHD medications along with mood-stabilizing agents should be considered.

MANAGEMENT

The patient needs to be familiarized with the risks and benefits of pharmacotherapy, the availability of alternative treatments, and the likely adverse effects. Certain adverse effects can be anticipated based on known pharmacologic properties of the drug (e.g., appetite change, insomnia), while other more infrequent effects are unexpected (idiosyncratic) and are difficult to anticipate based on the properties of the drug. Short-term adverse effects can be minimized by introducing the medication at low initial doses and titrating slowly. Idiosyncratic adverse effects generally require drug discontinuation and selection of alternate treatment modalities.

Patient expectations need to be explored and realistic treatment goals need to be clearly delineated. Likewise, the clinician should review with the patient the various pharmacological options available, noting that each will require systematic trials of the anti-ADHD medications for reasonable durations of time and at clinically meaningful doses. The potential need for adjunctive treatment and agents should also be explained in advance. Treatment-seeking ADHD adults who report psychological distress related to their ADHD (e.g., self-esteem issues, self-sabotaging patterns, interpersonal disturbances) should be directed to appropriate psychotherapeutic intervention with clinicians knowledgeable in ADHD treatment. In our center, for example, we frequently utilize cognitive-based therapies, with generally good patient response and overall satisfaction (S. McDermott, personal communication, October, 1993).

MEDICATIONS IN USE

Stimulant Medications

The stimulant medications remain the mainstay treatment in children, adolescents, and adults with ADHD. The effects of the stimulants in the brain are variable. Preclinical studies have shown that the stimulants block the reuptake of dopamine and norepinephrine into the presynaptic neuron, and that both drugs increase the release of these monoamines into the extraneuronal space (Elia et al., 1990). While not entirely sufficient, alteration in dopaminergic and noradrenergic functions appears necessary for clinical efficacy of the anti-ADHD medications including the stimulants (Zametkin & Rapoport, 1987). Stimulants reach their maximal therapeutic effects during the absorption phase of the kinetic curve, within approximately 2 hours after ingestion. The absorption phase parallels the acute release of neurotransmitters into synaptic clefts, providing support for the hypothesis that alteration of monoaminergic transmission in critical brain regions may be the basis for stimulant action in ADHD (Elia et al., 1990; Zametkin & Rapoport, 1987). There may be differential responses to the chemically distinct available stimulants, as each may have a different mode of action. For example, although methylphenidate (MPH, Ritalin®) and amphetamines alter dopamine transmission, they appear to have different mechanisms on release of dopamine from neuronal pools (Elia et al., 1990).

There are few pharmacokinetic studies of stimulants in humans with most studies limited to children and adolescents (Patrick, Mueller, Gualtieri, & Breese, 1987). Table 10-1 shows the preparations, pharmacokinetic properties, and dosing differences of the stimulants currently available. Dextroamphetamine has a half-life of 3 to 6 hours, achieves peak plasma levels in 2 to 3 hours, with behavioral/cognitive effects usually noted between 30 minutes to 2 hours postingestion, dissipating by 4 hours. Administration of MPH results in a variable peak plasma concentration in 1 to 2 hours postingestion, with an elimination half-life of 2 to 3 hours (Patrick et al., 1987; Sebrechts et al., 1986). Peak behavioral effects generally occur within 30 minutes to 2 hours and wear off by 3 to 5 hours. Pemoline has a longer half-life than that of the short-acting stimulants, reaches peak levels 1 to 4 hours postingestion, and requires daily administration to achieve behavioral/cognitive effectiveness. Of interest, food ingestion appears to have little impact in the pharmacokinetic profile of the stimulants (Patrick et al., 1987), and may assist in reducing the occasional indigestion related to stimulant administration. There is little correlation between stimulant plasma levels and response (Patrick et al., 1987; Spencer et al., 1994).

Both MPH and dextroamphetamine are available in long-acting preparation (see Table 10-1). The longer acting form of dextroamphetamine is preferable to the shorter acting form to reduce the very rapid onset and offset of action, as well as the potential for euphoria and addiction on higher doses of the short-action form. The half-life of the long-acting preparation of MPH (slow release, SR) is between 2 to 6 hours, with peak behavioral effect generally occurring within 2 hours and lasting up to 8 hours postingestion (Birmaher, Greenhill, Cooper, Fried, & Maminski, 1989; Pelham et al., 1987; Pelham et al., 1990). In cross-comparison studies, similar efficacy has been reported for the two preparations of MPH, the sustained preparation of dextroamphetamine, and pemoline (Pelham et al., 1990). There are, however, anecdotal reports of patients who do not respond to the long-

TABLE 10-1

Adult ADHD: Stimulant Preparations and Pharmacokinetics

Medication	Tablet Size and Preparation		Peak Levels	Half Lives	Dosing	Daily Dose Range
	Short-acting	Long-acting				
Methylphenidate (Ritalin-CIBA)	5, 10, 20 mg	20 mg SR (Sustained release)	1-2 hr (reg) 2-3 hr (SR)	2-3 hr (reg) 2-6 hr (SR)	1-5 times daily	0.3-2.0 mg/kg
D-amphetamine (Dexedrive-SK&F)	5 mg	5, 10, 15 mg (spansule)	1-2 hr (reg) 1-3 hr (spansule)	3-6 hr	1-5 times daily	0.1-1.0 mg/kg
Magnesium Pemoline (Cyclert-Abbott)	18.75, 37.5, 75 mg		1-4 hr	11-13 hr	1-2 times daily	1.0-2.5 mg/kg

Adapted from Wilens and Biederman (1992). Trade names and manufacturers are listed in parenthesis.

acting preparations compared to the short-acting forms. The sustained release MPH (MPH 20 mg SR) is approximately equipotent with twice-daily MPH 10 mg-tablets (Pelham et al., 1990).

The increasing usage of psychostimulants has paralleled the increasing recognition of the persistence of childhood ADHD symptoms through adolescence and into adulthood (Wilens & Biederman, 1992). In contrast to more than 100 studies of stimulant efficacy in children and adolescents with ADHD (Wilens & Biederman, 1992), there are only six controlled studies assessing the efficacy of stimulants in adults with ADHD (Gualtieri, Ondrusek, & Finley, 1985; Mattes, Boswell, & Oliver, 1984; Spencer et al., 1995; Wender, Reimherr, & Wood, 1981; Wender, Wood, & Reimherr, 1985; Wood et al., 1976) (see Table 10-2). In contrast to consistent robust responses to stimulants in children and adolescents of approximately 70% (Barkley, 1977; Wilens & Biederman, 1992), studies in adults have shown more equivocal responses to stimulants ranging from 25 to 73% (mean 50%), despite moderate doses of these medications. Both magnesium pemoline (Cylert®) and methylphenidate (MPH, Ritalin®) have been shown to be variably effective in controlled studies of adults with ADHD. Variability in the response rate appears to be related to the diagnostic criteria utilized to determine ADHD, low-stimulant doses, and differing methods of assessing overall response. In a recent double-blind, placebo, controlled crossover study applying DSM-III-R criteria for adult ADHD, Spencer and colleagues at the Massachusetts General Hospital (MGH) found a dose-dependent improvement in symptoms (Spencer et al., 1995).

In this 7-week study of 23 adults with ADHD, a marked 78% response was noted for MPH treatment, whereas there was only a 4% response rate on placebo. This response rate was independent of gender, psychiatric comorbidity, or family history of psychiatric disorders. Of interest, modest improvement in ADHD symptoms with MPH were noted at a total daily dose of 0.5 mg/kg (ca. 30–40 mg/day), whereas improvement of ADHD symptoms was far more robust when higher doses of 1.0 mg/kg (ca. 60–80 mg/day) were attained, suggesting a dose-dependent response to MPH in adults with ADHD (Spencer et al., 1994). These findings are consistent with pediatric studies in which cognitive, behavioral, and academic improvements occur in a stepwise fashion with increasing dose of MPH (Rapoport et al., 1987; Rapoport, Quinn, DuPaul, Quinn, & Kelly, 1989). The results of this study strongly suggest that adults, like younger patients, require robust dosing to attain adequate clinical response.

There is a paucity of data available to guide the dosing parameters of the stimulants. FDA guidelines for dosing reflect general cautiousness and should not be the only guide for clinical practice. For instance, absolute dose limits (in mg) do not adequately consider a patient's height and weight,

TABLE 10-2
Stimulant Efficacy in Adult ADHD

Study (year)	N	Mean age (yrs)	Design	Medication	Duration	Total Dose (Wt-corrected)	Response	Comments
Wood et al., 1976	15	29	Open Double blind	Pemoline MPH	4 weeks 4 weeks	37.5–70 mg (0.5–1.0mg/kg)* 27 mg 0.4 mg/kg*	73%	Diagnostic criteria not well defined Mild side effects
Wender et al., 1981	51	28	Double blind, placebo crossover	Pemoline	6 weeks	65 mg 0.9 mg/kg*	50% in those with childhood onset	Diagnostic criteria not well defined High rate of comorbid dysthymia Moderate side effects
Mattes et al., 1984	26	32	Double blind, placebo crossover	MPH	6 weeks	48 mg 0.7 mg/kg.	25%	Moderate rate of comorbidity Mild side effects
Wender et al., 1985	37	32	Double blind, placebo crossover	MPH	5 weeks	43 mg 0.6mg/kg*	57%	68% dysthymia 22% cyclothymia Mild side effects
Gualtieria et al., 1985	8	28	Double blind, placebo crossover	MPH	2 weeks	42 mg* 0.6 mg/kg	Mild–moderate response	No plasma level-response associations
Spencer et al., 1994	23	40	Double blind, placebo crossover	MPH	7 weeks	30–100 mg 0.5, 0.75, & 1.0 mg/kg	78% response rate, Dose relationship	No plasma level associations; no effect of gender or comorbidity
TOTAL	160	29	Double blind: N=6; Open: N=1	MPH & Pemoline; Pemoline	2–6 weeks	39 mg 0.6 mg/kg* 65 mg 0.9 mg/kg*	Variable responses	Dx not well defined High rate of comorbidity Side effects in 30%

Duration of medication trial includes placebo phase. abbreviation used:
MPH=methylphenidate, Dx=diagnosis
* Weight-normalized dose using 50th percentile wieght for age.

or use in refractory cases or adults. The dose should by individually titrated based on therapeutic efficacy and side effects. Treatment should be started with short-action preparations at the lowest possible dose. Initiation of treatment with once-daily dosing in the morning is advisable until an acceptable response is noted. The half-life of the short-acting stimulants necessitates at least twice-daily dosing with the addition of similar afternoon doses dependent on breakthrough symptoms. Starting doses of MPH and dextroamphetamine in most adults is 5 mg, with a suggested range of 0.3 to 1 mg/kg daily (approximately 20–80 mg daily in the average-sized adult) in 2 to 4 divided doses (Wilens & Biederman, 1992) (see Table 10-1). Pemoline is given once or twice daily starting usually at 37.5 mg in the morning, and increased weekly depending on response and adverse effects. Because of its long half-life, pemoline may need up to 6 weeks for full assessment of efficacy. Once pharmacotherapy is initiated, monthly contact with the patient is necessary during the initial phase of treatment to carefully monitor response to the intervention and adverse effects.

The side effects of the stimulants are generally mild and can be managed with adjustment of timing of administration or dose. In a review of the studies of adult ADHD, the following side effects were reported by frequency of occurrence: insomnia, edginess, diminished appetite, weight loss, dysphoria, and headaches. No cases of stimulant-related psychosis at therapeutic doses have been reported in adults. Likewise, despite the abuse potential of the stimulants, there have been no reports of stimulant abuse in controlled or retrospective studies of adults with ADHD (Spencer et al., 1995; Wilens & Biederman, 1992). The addition of low-dose beta-blockers (e.g., propanolol at 10 mg up to 3 times daily) or busipirone (5–10 mg up to 3 times daily) may be helpful in reducing the edginess/agitation associated with stimulant administration (Ratey, Greenberg, & Lindem, 1991). Rebound has been described as deterioration in behavior that usually occurs in the afternoon and evening following administration of stimulant medication and exceeds baseline behavior. While the prevalence of this effect appears to be low in adults, rebound reactions with excitability, talkativeness, and euphoria have been described in children (Rapoport et al., 1978). While concerns have been raised about cardiovascular adverse effects of stimulants on children, there have been only minimal clinically insignificant elevations of heart rate and diastolic blood pressure in controlled investigations weakly correlated with stimulant dose (Spencer et al., 1995). In ADHD patients with cardiac abnormalities, however, treatment should be carefully monitored with appropriate cardiology consultation obtained.

The interactions of the stimulants with other prescription medications are generally mild and not a source of concern (Wilens & Biederman, 1992). Whereas coadministration of sympathomimetics (e.g., pseudoephedrine) may potentiate the effects of both medications, the antihistamines may diminish the stimulants' effectiveness. Caution should be exercised when using stimulants and antidepressants of the monoamine oxidase inhibitor (MAOI) type because of the potential for hypertensive reactions with this combination. The concomitant use of stimulants and tricyclic antidepressants (TCAs) or anticonvulsants has been associated with an increase in the serum levels of both medications. Thus, when combinations of stimulants with TCAs or anticonvulsants are used, it may be necessary to monitor the levels of these medications more closely.

Nonstimulant Medications

Despite the increasing use of stimulants for adults with ADHD, approximately 30 to 50% do not respond positively to the stimulants, have untoward side effects, or have concurrent depressive and anxiety disorders, which stimulant medication may exacerbate or be ineffective in treating (Biederman et al., 1993; Spencer et al., 1995; Wilens & Biederman, 1992). Hence, the need for nonstimulant pharmacotherapy continues to be an area of ongoing investigation. Reports of nonstimulant treatments for ADHD adults have included the use of antidepressant medications, antihypertensive agents, and amino acids. (See Table 10-3.)

Tricyclic Antidepressants

Within the past two decades, the tricyclic antidepressants (TCAs)–desipramine, nortriptyline, and imipramine–have been used increasingly as an alternative treatment to the stimulants for ADHD in children and adolescents, irrespective of psychiatric comorbidity with the ADHD (Biederman, Baldessarini, Wright, Knee, & Harmatz, 1989; Rapoport, Quinn, Bradbard, Riddle, & Brooks, 1974; Wilens, Biederman, Geist, Steingard, & Spencer, 1993). In part, the usefulness of the TCAs has arisen because of several advantages over the stimulants in the treatment of ADHD. TCAs have a long half-life permitting flexible dosing (once daily), have little risk for abuse or dependence, and appear to be helpful in stimulant-refractory patients (Biederman et al., 1989). TCAs have also been shown to be safe, effective, and well tolerated in adults treated for anxiety, panic, and depressive disorders (Baldessarini, 1989), conditions that commonly co-occur with ADHD in adults (Biederman et al., 1993). Despite experience in children and adolescents, substantial anecdotal information (Ratey et al., 1992), and the theoretical benefits of the TCAs, these agents have not been prospectively assessed in a controlled manner for the treatment of adult ADHD.

Our clinical experience with adults indicates that TCAs may be useful for treating ADHD symptoms. A systematic chart review of 37 adults (mean age 41 years) receiving routine care at our center with TCAs for ADHD indicated a reasonably good response to desipramine and nortriptyline (Wilens, Biederman, Mick, & Spencer, 1995a). The mean dose of desipramine (182 mg/day) was equipotent to that of nortriptyline (92 mg/day). The majority of patients responded to treatment (68%), with 52% manifesting a marked improvement with TCA treatment. The anti-ADHD efficacy of the TCAs appeared to be sustained for an average follow-up period of 1 year. Hence, the results of this pilot investigation indicate that the secondary amines nortriptyline and desipramine may be useful agents for adult ADHD; however, more controlled investigations are necessary to fully evaluate this issue. Currently, a placebo-controlled trial of desipramine up to 200 mg/day for adult ADHD is underway at our center to further investigate the usefulness of TCAs in treatment.

Generally, TCA daily doses of 50 to 250 mg are required, with a relatively rapid response to treatment (e.g., 2 weeks) when the appropriate dose is reached. The TCAs should be initiated at 25 mg and slowly titrated upward within dosing and serum-level parameters until an acceptable response or intolerable adverse effects are reported. Common side effects of the TCAs include dry mouth, constipation, blurred vision, and sexual dysfunction. While cardiovascular effects of reduced cardiac conduction, elevated blood pressure, and elevated heart rates are not infrequent, if monitored, they rarely prevent treatment. As serum TCA levels are variable, they are best used as guidelines for efficacy and to reduce central nervous system and cardiovascular toxicity.

More recently, the atypical, stimulant-like antidepressant bupropion (Welbutrin®) has been reported to be moderately helpful in reducing ADHD symptoms in children (Casat, Pleasants, & Fleet, 1987) and adults (Wender & Reimherr, 1990). In an open study of 19 adults treated with an average of 360 mg of bupropion for 6 to 8 weeks, Wender and Reimherr (1990) reported a moderate to marked response in 74% of adults in the study (5 dropouts), with sustained improvement at 1 year noted in 10 subjects remaining on bupropion. Despite the small numbers of adults studied, bupropion may be helpful with ADHD, particularly when it is associated with comorbid mood instability or is found in adults with cardiac abnormalities (Gelenberg, Bassuk, & Schoonover, 1991). The response of ADHD to bupropion appears to be rapid and sustained, with dosing for ADHD appearing to be similar to that recommended for depression, with a suggested maximal dose of 450 mg/day divided in 3 daily doses. Bupropion appears to be more stimulating than other antidepressants, and is associated with a higher rate of drug-induced seizures than are other antidepressants (Gelenberg et al., 1991). These seizures appear to be dose related (>450 mg/day) and elevated in patients with bulimia or a previous seizure

TABLE 10-3
Nonstimulant Pharmacotherapy for Adult ADHD

Study (year)	N	Mean age (years)	Design	Medication	Duration (weeks)	Dose (mean)	Results	Comments
Wood et al., 1982	8	25–35	Open	L-DOPA (+ carbidopa)	3	625 mg (63 mg)	No benefit at end of trial	Side effects: nausea, sedation, low doses
Wender et al., 1983	22	32	Open	Pargyline	6	30 mg	13/22 moderate improvement, 6 dropouts	7–10-day onset Stimulant-like effect postdosing (4–6hours)
Wender et al., 1985	11		Open	Deprenylanine	6	30 mg	6/9 responded, 2 dropouts	Stimulant-like efffect Patients preferred stimulants
Wood et al., 1985	19	28	Double blind crossover	Phneylalanine	2	587 mg	6/14 responded initially (mood Sx), 6 dropouts	Transient improved mood NO change in ADHD Sxs in open follow-up
Mattes, 1986	13	22	Open Retrospective	Propanolol	3–50	528 mg	11/13 improved	Problematic assessments, part of "temper" study
Reimherr et al., 1987	12	30.2	Open	Tyrosine	8	150 mg	8 initial response, 4 dropouts	14-dayonset of action Tolerance developed
Wender and Reimherr, 1990	19	39	Open	Bupropion	6–8	360 mg	8/14–marked, 6/14–moderate response; 5 dropouts	10 subjects with improvement at 1 year
Wilens et al., 1994b	32	41	Retrospective	Desipramine Nortriptyline	50	160 mg 84 mg	72% response rate (52% marked) response sustained	No effect of comorbidity, gender, on response, 41% receiving stimulants
TOTAL	123	28–41	1–controlled 6–open	Mixed	2–50	Moderate doses	Variable response	Side effects common Often nonsustained effect Dx criteria not consistent

Duration of medication trial includes placebo phase. Abbreviations used: Sxs=symptoms, Dx=diagnosis

history. Bupropion has also been associated with excitement, agitation, increased motor activity, insomnia, weight loss, and tremor.

The MAOI antidepressants have also been studied for the treatment of ADHD. Moderate efficacy of MAOIs were shown in a controlled study of hyperactive children (Zametkin, Rapoport, Murphy, Linnoila, & Ismond, 1985). In open studies of adult ADHD, moderate improvements were reported in 61% of subjects (Wender, Wood, Reimherr, & Ward, 1983; Wender et al., 1985). In these studies with pargyline and deprenyl (not available in the United States), there were numerous adverse effects with relatively high dropout rates during the 6-week trial periods (Wender et al., 1983; Wender et al., 1985). The mean dose of pargyline used in these trials was 30 mg, and it appears that standard dosing of the MAOIs, as for the treatment of depressive disorders, appears necessary for anti-ADHD efficacy. Of interest, the authors reported a delayed onset of action, and a postdosing stimulant-like quality of the MAOIs on ADHD symptoms lasting up to 6 hours (Wender et al., 1983).

The MAOIs may have a role in the management of treatment refractory, nonimpulsive, adult ADHD subjects with comorbid depression and anxiety, who are able to comply with the stringent requirements of the MAOIs. The low tyramine dietary requirements and adverse effect profile of these agents often make compliance difficult. Likewise, concerns of diet- or medication-induced hypertensive crisis limit the usefulness and safety of these medications, especially in a group of ADHD patients vulnerable to impulsivity. Additionally, other adverse effects associated with the MAOIs include agitation or lethargy, orthostatic hypotension, weight gain, sexual dysfunction, sleep disturbances, and edema, often leading to the discontinuation of these agents (Gelenberg et al., 1991).

Antihypertensives

Antihypertensives have been used successfully for the treatment of childhood ADHD, especially in cases with a marked hyperactive or aggressive component. Although clonidine has been shown effective in the treatment of ADHD in children and adolescents (Hunt, Mindera, & Cohen, 1985; Steingard, Biederman, Spencer, Wilens, & Gonzalez, 1993), the potent hypotensive effects of this agent preclude its use in adults. Beta-blockers may also be helpful in adult ADHD. A small open study of propanolol for adults with temper outbursts indicated some improvement in ADHD symptoms at daily doses of up to 640 mg/day (Mattes, 1986). Another small series case indicated that beta-blockers may be helpful in combination with stimulants (Ratey et al., 1991). To date, the efficacy of beta-blockers for adult ADHD needs to be further assessed.

Other Antidepressants

The selective serotonin reuptake inhibitors (SSRIs)—fluoxetine, sertraline, paroxetine, and others—have been used extensively in the past few years for the treatment of depressive, anxiety, and obsessive-compulsive disorders. While there are no controlled studies evaluating the efficacy of these agents for adult ADHD, fluoxetine was reported in one small case series to be moderately effective for children with ADHD (Barrickman, Noyes, Kuperman, Schumacher, & Verda, 1991). In our clinical experience with adult ADHD, the SSRIs have been invaluable in treating concurrent anxiety, depressive, and obsessive-compulsive disorders, but not the core ADHD symptoms. This is not surprising as the pathogenesis of ADHD appears to be more related to the central nervous system's dopaminergic and adrenergic systems, with little direct influence by the serotonergic systems (Zametkin & Rapoport, 1987). A novel antidepressant with both SSRI and noradrenergic properties—Venlafaxine has been reported to be helpful in two adults with ADHD (Wilens et al., 1995)—may be a promising new agent for adult ADHD, but it remains untested.

Amino Acids

The results of open studies assessing the efficacy of L-DOPA, phenylalanine, and tyrosine for adults with ADHD have generally been disappointing. These amino acids were in part utilized with the assumptions that ADHD may be related to a deficiency in the catecholaminergic system, and that administration of precursors of these systems would reverse the neurochemical, behavioral, and cognitive deficits of ADHD. Initial studies with L-DOPA on 8 adults with ADHD yielded an initial response that was lost by the second week of treatment. However, this study was limited by the relatively low doses of L-DOPA administered secondary to sedation and gastrointestinal complaints (Wood, Reimherr, & Wender, 1982). A double-blind study of phenylalanine resulted in an initial transient improvement in the accompanying mood symptoms in almost half of the adult ADHD subjects, but no change in ADHD symptoms was reported in follow-up or in a separate open study (Wood, Reimherr, & Wender, 1985). In an open study using L-tyrosine at moderate doses, there was an initial response to treatment by 2 weeks that was lost by 6 weeks, leading the authors to conclude that tyrosine was not useful in treating adults with ADHD (Reimherr, Wender, Wood, & Ward, 1987). Hence, the available literature suggests that the amino acids studied are not helpful in the treatment of adult ADHD.

Combined Pharmacotherapy

Combined pharmacotherapy may be useful in ADHD adults who have an inadequate response with single agents, or manifest comorbid psychiatric disorders. Whenever possible, monotherapy with single agents is preferable to reduce the possibility of adverse effects and to improve treatment compliance. Adjunctive agents may improve or potentiate the individual effects of both medications in ameliorating ADHD symptoms. For instance, whereas in some adults single agents may not provide acceptable control of ADHD symptoms, we have found that the addition of stimulants (e.g., MPH at 5–20 mg) often improves the anti-ADHD effectiveness of the antidepressants. As coadministration of stimulants and TCAs has been associated with potentiation of adverse effects and TCA levels in children and adolescents, serum TCA levels should be reevaluated when other psychoactive agents are added. Coadministration of adjunctive anti-ADHD medications with the MAOIs is not recommended. In cases of partial response or adverse effects of edginess and anxiety with stimulants, the addition of low-dose beta-blockers or busipirone may be helpful (Ratey et al., 1991).

The use of multiple agents is also helpful in treating disorders concurrent with the ADHD. For example, the combined use of the stimulants or TCAs with SSRI agents may assist in the management of concurrent depressive disorders. Benzodiazepines in combination with anti-ADHD medications are useful in the management of ADHD and comorbid anxiety disorders. Likewise, for individuals with prominent mood lability, mood-stabilizing agents such as lithium carbonate or carbemazepine may assist in reducing impairment of the dysphoria while providing the opportunity to treat the ADHD symptoms. It is important to note that whereas specific individual agents have been evaluated for safety and efficacy, the use of multiple agents simultaneously for adult ADHD remains unstudied.

TREATMENT REFRACTORY PATIENTS

Despite the availability of various agents for adults with ADHD, there appear to be a number of individuals who either do not respond or are intolerant of adverse effects of medications used to treat their ADHD. In managing apparent medication nonresponders, several therapeutic strategies are available (see Table 10-4). If psychiatric adverse effects develop concurrent with a poor medication response, alternate treatments should be pursued. Severe psychiatric symptoms that emerge during the acute phase can be problematic, irrespective of the efficacy of the medications for ADHD. These symptoms may require reconsideration of the diagnosis of ADHD and careful reassessment of the presence of comorbid disorders. If reduction of dose or change in preparation (e.g., regular vs. slow-release stimulants) does not resolve the problem, consideration should be given to alternative treatments. Concurrent nonpharmacologic interventions such as behavioral or cognitive therapy may assist with symptom reduction.

CONCLUSION

Adult ADHD is an important and underrecognized disorder that has adverse impacts on various aspects of a patient's life. Pharmacotherapy serves an important role in reducing the core symptoms of ADHD and other concurrent psychiatric disorders in adults. The administration of these agents should be integrated into a multimodal approach following a thorough assessment and formulation that includes the treatment of related

TABLE 10-4
Strategies in Medication-refractory Adult ADHD

Symptoms	*Intervention*
Worsened or unchanged ADHD symptoms (inattention, impulsivity, hyperactivity)	• Increase medication dose • Change timing of administration • Change preparation, substitute stimulant • Consider adjunctive treatment (add antidepressant, stimulants) • Consider nonpharmacological treatment (e.g., cognitive / behavioral therapy)
Intolerable side effects	• Assess overall response • Evaluate if side effect is drug-induced • Aggressive management of side effects: usually changing timing of dose, preparation; stimulant or antidepressant substitution • Use of adjunctive medication (i.e., propanolol)
Marked rebound phenomena	• Assess overall response • Change timing of administration • Change preparation • Add multiple dosings
Emergence of dysphoria, anxiety, agitation, irritability	• Assess overall response • Assess for toxicity or withdrawal • Evaluate for return of ADHD symptoms • Evaluate for comorbidity • Reduce or change dosing • Change preparations, substitute type of agent • Discontinue stimulants, add antidepressants • Consider alternative treatment
Emergence of major depression, mood lability, marked anxiety symptoms	• Assess for toxicity or withdrawal • Evaluate for comorbidity • Reduce or discontinue stimulant • Adjunctive use of mood stabilizer (i.e., lithium) • Use of antidepressant • Nonpharmacologic intervention (psychotherapy)
Emergence of psychosis	• Discontinue medication • Assess for comorbidity (e.g., bipolar disorder) • Consider alternative treatment

Adapted from Wilens and Biederman (1992).

psychiatric and cognitive disabilities associated with ADHD. There is a paucity of data on effectiveness and dosing parameters of agents for adult ADHD, with many studies limited to open conditions in small numbers of patients.

The stimulant medications continue to be the first-line drug of choice for uncomplicated ADHD in adults, with TCAs and bupropion for nonresponders or adults with concurrent psychiatric disorders. Current clinical findings suggest that multiple agents may be necessary in the successful treatment of some ADHD adults with impartial responses or psychiatric comorbidity. Anecdotal data support that pharmacotherapy may be more effective when combined with specific types of psychotherapeutic and psychoeducation interventions.

REFERENCES

Anderson, J. C., Williams, S., McGee, R., & Silva, P. A. (1987). DSM-III disorders in preadolescent children. *Archives of General Psychiatry, 44*, 69–76.

Baldessarini, R. J. (1989). Current status of antidepressants: Clinical pharmacology and therapy. *Journal of Clinical Psychiatry, 50*, 117–126.

Barkley, R. A. (1977). A review of stimulant drug research with hyperactive children. *Journal of Child Psychology and Psychiatry, 18*, 137–165.

Barrickman, L., Noyes, R., Kuperman, S., Schumacher, E., & Verda, M. (1991). Treatment of ADHD with fluoxetine: A preliminary trial. *Journal of the American Academy of Child and Adolescent Psychiatry, 30*, 762–767.

Biederman, J., Baldessarini, R. J., Wright, V., Knee, D., & Harmatz, J. S. (1989). A double-blind placebo controlled study of desipramine in the treatment of ADD: I. Efficacy. *Journal of the American Academy of Child and Adolescent Psychiatry, 28*, 777–784.

Biederman, J., Faraone, S. V., Keenan, K., Benjamin, J., & Krifcher, B. (1992). Further evidence for family-genetic risk factors in attention deficit disorder: Patterns of comorbidity in probands and relatives in psychiatrically and pediatrically referred samples. *Archives of General Psychiatry, 49*, 728–738.

Biederman, J., Faraone, S. V., Keenan, K., Knee, D., & Tsuang, M. T. (1990). Family-genetic and psychosocial risk factors in DSM-III attention deficit disorder. *Journal of the American Academy of Child and Adolescent Psychiatry, 29*, 526–533.

Biederman, J., Faraone, S. V., Spencer, T., Wilens, T. E., Norman, D., Lapey, K. A., Mick, E., Lehman, B., & Doyle, A. (1993). Patterns of psychiatric comorbidity, cognition, and psychosocial functioning in adults with attention deficit hyperactivity disorder. *American Journal of Psychiatry, 150*, 1792–1798.

Biederman, J., Newcorn, J., & Sprich, S. (1991). Comorbidity of attention deficit hyperactivity disorder with conduct, depressive, anxiety, and other disorders. *American Journal of Psychiatry, 148,* 564–577.

Bird, H. R., Canino, G., Rubio-Stipec, M., Gould, M. S., Ribera, J., Sesman, M., Woodbury, M., Huertas-Goldman, S., Pagan, A., Sanchez-Lacay, A., & Moscoso, M. (1988). Estimates of the prevalence of childhood maladjustment in a community survey in Puerto Rico. *Archives of General Psychiatry, 45,* 1120–1126.

Birmaher, B., Greenhill, L. L., Cooper, T. B., Fried, J., & Maminski, B. (1989). Sustained release methylphenidate: Pharmacokinetic studies in ADHD males. *Journal of the American Academy of Child and Adolescent Psychiatry, 28,* 768–772.

Casat, C. D., Pleasants, D. Z., & Fleet, J. V. W. (1987). A double blind trial of bupropion in children with attention deficit disorder. *Psychopharmacology Bulletin, 23,* 120–122.

Elia, J., Borcherding, B. G., Potter, W. Z., Mefford, I. N., Rapoport, J. L., & Keysor, C. S. (1990). Stimulant drug treatment of hyperactivity: Biochemical correlates. *Clinical Pharmacology Therapy, 48,* 57–66.

Eyre, S. L., Rounsaville, B. J., & Kleber, H. D. (1982). History of childhood hyperactivity in a clinic population of opiate addicts. *Journal of Nervous and Mental Disease, 170,* 522–529.

Faraone, S. V., Biederman, J., Chen, W. J., Krifcher, B., Keenan, K., Moore, C., Sprich, S., & Tsuang, M. T. (1992). Segregation analysis of attention deficit hyperactivity disorder. *Psychiatric Genetics, 2,* 257–275.

Gelenberg, A. J., Bassuk, E. L., & Schoonover, S. C. (1991). *The practitioner's guide to psychoactive drugs.* New York: Plenum Medical Book Company.

Gittelman, R., Mannuzza, S., Shenker, R., & Bonagura, N. (1985). Hyperactive boys almost grown up, I: Psychiatric status. *Archives of General Psychiatry, 42,* 937–947.

Gualtieri, C. T., Ondrusek, M. G., & Finley, C. (1985). Attention deficit disorder in adults. *Clinical Neuropharmacology, 8,* 343–356.

Hunt, R. D., Mindera, R. B., & Cohen, D. J. (1985). Clonidine benefits children with attention deficit disorder and hyperactivity: Report of a double-blind placebo-crossover therapeutic trial. *Journal of the American Academy of Child and Adolescent Psychiatry, 24,* 617–629.

Klein, R., & Mannuzza, S. (1988). Hyperactive boys almost grown up. III. Methylphenidate effects on ultimate height. *Archives of General Psychiatry, 45,* 1131–1134.

Mannuzza, S., Klein, R. G., Bessler, A., Malloy, P., & LaPadula, M. (1993). Adult outcome of hyperactive boys: Educational achievement, occupational rank, and psychiatric status. *Archives of General Psychiatry, 50,* 565–576.

Mattes, J. A., (1986). Propanolol for adults with temper outbursts and residual attention deficit disorder. *Journal of Clinical Psychopharmacology, 6,* 299–302.

Mattes, J. A., Boswell, L., & Oliver, H. (1984). Methylphenidate effects on symptoms of attention deficit disorder in adults. *Archives of General Psychiatry, 41*, 1059–1063.

Patrick, S. K., Mueller, R. A., Gualtieri, C. T., & Breese, G. R. (1987). Pharmacokinetics and actions of methylphenidate. In H.Y. Meltzer (Ed.), *Psychopharmacology: The third generation of progress* (pp. 1387–1396). New York: Raven Press.

Pelham, W. E., Greenslade, K. E., Vodde-Hamilton, M., Murphy, D. A., Greenstein, J. J., Gnagy, E. M., Guthrie, K. J., Hoover, M. D., & Dahl, R. E. (1990). Relative efficacy of long-acting stimulants on children with attention deficit-hyperactivity disorder: A comparison of standard methylphenidate sustained-release methylphenidate, sustained-release dextroamphetamine, and pemoline. *Pediatrics, 86*, 226–237.

Pelham, W. E., Sturges, J., Hoza, J., Schmidt, C., Bijlsma, J. J., Milich, R., & Moorer, S. (1987). Sustained release and standard methylphenidate effects on cognitive and social behavior in children with attention deficit disorder. *Pediatrics, 80*, 491–501.

Rapoport, J. L., Buschsbaum, M. S., Zahn, T. P., Weingartner, H., Ludlow, C., & Mikkelsen, E. J. (1978). Dextroamphetamine: Cognitive and behavioral effects in normal prepubertal boys. *Science, 199*, 560–562.

Rapoport, J. L., Quinn, P. O., Bradbard, G., Riddle, K. D., & Brooks, E. (1974). Imipramine and methylphenidate treatments of hyperactive boys. *Archives of General Psychiatry, 30*, 789–793.

Rapoport, M. D., Jones, J. T., DuPaul, G. J., Kelly, K. L., Gardner, M. J., Tucker, S. B., & Shea, M. S. (1987). Attention deficit disorder and methylphenidate: Group and single-subject analyses of dose effects on attention in clinic and classroom settings. *Journal of Clinical Child Psychology, 16*, 329–338.

Rapoport, M. D., Quinn, S. O., DuPaul, G. J., Quinn, E. P., & Kelly, K. L. (1989). Attention deficit disorder with hyperactivity and methylphenidate: The effects of dose and mastery level on children's learning performance. *Journal of Abnormal Child Psychology, 17*, 669–689.

Ratey, J., Greenberg, M., & Lindem, K. (1991). Combination of treatments for attention deficit disorders in adults. *Journal of Nervous and Mental Disease, 176*, 699–701.

Ratey, J. J., Greenberg, M. S., Bemporad, J. R., & Lindem, K. J. (1992). Unrecognized attention-deficit hyperactivity disorder in adults presenting for outpatient psychotherapy. *Journal of Child and Adolescent Psychopharmacology, 2*, 267–275.

Reimherr, F. W., Wender, P. H., Wood, D. R., & Ward, M. (1987). An open trial of L-tyrosine in the treatment of attention deficit hyperactivity disorder, residual type. *American Journal of Psychiatry, 144*, 1071–1073.

Safer, D. J., & Krager, J. M. (1988). A survey of medication treatment for hyperactive/inattentive students. *JAMA, 260*, 2256–2258.

Sebrechts, M. M., Shaywitz, S. E., Shaywitz, B. A., Jatlow, P., Anderson, G. M., & Cohen, D. J. (1986). Components of attention, methylphenidate dosage, and blood levels and children with attention deficit disorder. *Pediatrics*, *77*, 222–228.

Spencer, T., Biederman, J., Wilens, T. E., Faraone, S. V., & Li, T. (1994). Is attention deficit hyperactivity disorder in adults a valid diagnosis? *Harvard Review of Psychiatry*, *1*, 326–335.

Spencer, T., Wilens, T. E., Biederman, J., Faraone, S. V., Ablon, S., & Ras, J. F. (1995). A double blind comparison of methylphenidate and placebo in adults with attention deficit hyperactivity disorder. *Archives of General Psychiatry*, *52*.

Steingard, R., Biederman, J., Spencer, T., Wilens, T., & Gonzalez, A. (1993). Comparison of clonidine response in the treatment of attention deficit hyperactivity disorder with and without comorbid tic disorders. *Journal of the American Academy of Child and Adolescent Psychiatry*, *32*, 350–353.

Tarter, R. E., McBride, H., Buonpane, N., & Schneider, D. U. (1977). Differentiation of alcoholics. *Archives of General Psychology*, *34*, 761–768.

Weiss, G. (1992). *Attention-deficit hyperactivity disorder*. Philadelphia: W. B. Saunders.

Weiss, G., & Hechtman, L. T. (1986). *Hyperactive children grown up*. New York: Guilford Press.

Wender, P. H., & Reimherr, F. W. (1990). Bupropion treatment of attention deficit hyperactivity disorder in adults. *American Journal of Psychiatry*, *147*, 1018–1020.

Wender, P. H., Reimherr, F. W., & Wood, D. R. (1981). Attention deficit disorder ("minimal brain dysfunction") in adults. *Archives of General Psychiatry*, *38*, 449–456.

Wender, P. H., Reimherr, F. W., Wood, D., & Ward, M. (1985). A controlled study of methylphenidate in the treatment of attention deficit disorder, residual type, in adults. *American Journal of Psychiatry*, *142*, 547–552.

Wender, P. H., Wood, D. R., & Reimherr, F. W. (1985). Pharmacological treatment of attention deficit disorder residual type (ADD, RT, "minimal brain dysfunction," "hyperactivity") in adults. *Psychopharmacology Bulletin*, *21*, 222–230.

Wender, P. H., Wood, D. R., Reimherr, F. W., & Ward, M. (1983). An open trial of pargyline in the treatment of attention deficit disorder, residual type. *Psychiatry Research*, *9*, 329–336.

Wilens, T. E., & Biederman, J. (1992). The stimulants. In D. Shafer (Ed.), *The psychiatric clinics of North America* (pp. 191–222). Philadelphia: W. B. Saunders.

Wilens, T. E., Biederman, J., Frances, R. J., & Spencer, T. (1994). Alcohol and drug abuse: Comorbidity with attention deficit disorders. *Hospital Community Psychiatry*, *45*, 421–433.

Wilens, T. E., Biederman, J., Geist, D. E., Steingard, R., & Spencer, T. (1993). Nortriptyline in the treatment of ADHD: A chart review of 58 cases. *Journal of the American Academy of Child and Adolescent Psychiatry,* *32,* 343–349.

Wilens, T. E., Biederman, J., Mick, E., & Spencer, T. (1995a). A systematic assessment of tricyclic antidepressants in the treatment of adults with attention deficit disorders. *Journal of Nervous and Mental Disease.*

Wilens, T. E., Biederman, J., & Spencer, T. (1995b). Verlafaxine for adult ADHD (letter). *American Journal of Psychiatry.*

Wood, D., Reimherr, J., & Wender, P. H. (1982). Effects of levodopa on attention deficit disorder, residual type. *Psychiatry Research, 6,* 13–20.

Wood, D. R., Reimherr, F. W., & Wender, P. H. (1985). The treatment of attention deficit disorder with d,l-phenylalanine. *Psychiatry Research, 16,* 21–26.

Wood, D. R., Reimherr, F. W., Wender, P. H., & Johnson, G. E. (1976). Diagnosis and treatment of minimal brain dysfunction in adults. *Archives of General Psychiatry, 33,* 1453–1460.

Wood, D., Wender, P. H., & Reimherr, F. W. (1983). The prevalence of attention deficit disorder, residual type, or minimal brain dysfunction, in a population of male alcoholic patients. *American Journal of Psychiatry, 140,* 95–98.

Zametkin, A. J., Nordahl, T. E., Gross, M., King, A. C., Semple, W. E., Rumsey, J., Hamburger, S., & Cohen, R. M. (1990). Cerebral glucose metabolism in adults with hyperactivity of childhood onset. *New England Journal of Medicine, 323,* 1361–1366.

Zametkin, A. J., & Rapoport, J. L. (1987). Neurobiology of attention deficit disorder with hyperactivity: Where have we come in 50 years? *Journal of the American Academy of Child and Adolescent Psychiatry, 26,* 676–686.

Zametkin, A., Rapoport, J. L., Murphy, D. L., Linnoila, M., & Ismond, D. (1985). Treatment of hyperactive children with monoamine oxidase inhibitors I: Clinical efficacy. *Archives of General Psychiatry, 42,* 962–966.

SECTION IV

Specific Treatment Issues for Adults with ADD

Because attention deficit disorder is manifested in all areas of life, and because each of these areas introduces specific concerns, we have attempted to address a number of major life issues for adults with ADD in this section. The chapter on life management skills discusses practical approaches to the problems posed by the cognitive difficulties associated with ADD, including problems with planning, organization, memory, distractibility, and stress management. John Ratey, Edward Hallowell, and Andrea Miller address the neurobiology of relationships, interweaving our understanding of the neurobiology of ADD with widely recognized difficulties in relationships experienced by many adults with ADD. Ellen Dixon expands our understanding of how ADD affects relationships by discussing ADD within the context of marriage and the family. Also included is an important chapter on the special issues pertaining to women with ADD, which discusses the disorder within the context of the social conditioning of women, as well as considering the additional impact of hormonal variations experienced by women.

The last two chapters in this section target ADD issues within two of the most challenging areas for adults with ADD: higher education and the workplace. Although universities have recognized the need for special supports and accommodations for students with learning disabilities, the recognition that students with ADD have similar needs is quite recent. Mary Richard, President-elect of CH.A.D.D., head of the Adult Issues Committee of CH.A.D.D., and a staff member of the office of Services for Persons with Disabilities at the University of Iowa, provides a comprehensive discussion of the needs of postsecondary students with ADD. My chapter on ADD in the workplace completes the section on special topics. Although problems in the workplace are probably one of the most common presenting complaints when an adult seeks assessment for ADD, there had been remarkably little writing and less research on the topic. My chapter here is an attempt to compile and organize my clinical experience on the impact of ADD in the workplace, and, I hope, may provide the starting point for much needed empirical investigation. With the passage of the Americans with Disabilities Act, discussed in detail in section V, the need for accurate documentation about appropriate accommodations in the workplace for adults with ADD is ever more acute.

11

Life Management Skills for the Adult with ADD

KATHLEEN G. NADEAU

The clinician who works successfully with adults who have attention deficit disorder (ADD) needs to view the disorder from a broad perspective, taking into consideration all of the aspects of daily functioning that are affected by the cognitive skills deficits associated with ADD. Zametkin's research (Zametkin et al., 1990) has implicated the frontal lobes as one of the major neurological structures involved in attention deficit. As has been widely documented, the frontal lobes are considered to be the area of the brain that controls "executive functions" (Luria, 1966; Stuss & Benson, 1986). Executive functions are the oversight or managerial functions so often affected in adults with ADD. Luria (1973a) wrote that one of the primary functions of the frontal lobes was the verbal regulation of motor behavior (i.e., thinking and talking about what we do before we do it). The executive functions of the brain include attention, memory, organization, planning, initiation, self-inhibition (self-discipline), ability to change set, strategic behavior, and self-monitoring in relation to time (time management). It is this broad set of concerns—executive functions—that I address in this chapter, considering their effect on practical life management skills.

Just as the assessment of attention deficits (discussed in section II, this volume) requires consideration of problems from a neurological, neuropsychological, educational, psychiatric, and psychological perspective, treatment also requires a multi-disciplinary approach. Other chapters in this volume describe the roles of the psychopharmcologist, the neurologist, the neuropsychologist, the career consultant, and the psychotherapist in treating adults with ADD. In this chapter, the emphasis is on certain aspects of the psychotherapist's role that are more analogous to that of the rehabilitation counselor, that is, focusing on practical ways to enhance daily functioning for the ADD adult.

Executive function disorders (as discussed in chapter 4, this volume) can result from a host of neurological conditions other than ADD. Much of our knowledge about improving executive functioning and developing compensatory strategies is derived from work with individuals whose executive function problems resulted from these other neurological conditions, including head injury. One such treatment model has been adapted for use with adults with ADD (Goodwin & Bolton, 1991). The model suggests a three-pronged approach which emphasizes (1) retraining cognitive functions, (2) developing internal and external compensatory strategies, and (3) restructuring the physical and social environment to maximize functioning. Goodwin and Corgiat (1992) report using this model successfully in their work with a college student with ADD.

In addition to the rehabilitation model, some of the techniques suggested in this chapter are based on my own clinical experience, as well as the reported clinical experience of Hallowell (see chapter 9, this volume), Gabrielle Weiss (Weiss & Hechtman, 1993), Lynn Weiss (1992), and the personal and clinical experience of Kelly and Ramundo (1993). As Weiss and Hechtman write in their newly revised book, "Controlled treatment studies involving medication, psychological therapies and their combination are sorely lacking and urgently needed" (1993, p. 406). The efficacy of these approaches is supported only anecdotally, at this point, and has yet to pass the test of clinical trials.

ROLES OF THE THERAPIST

Numerous adults with ADD have reported to me that psychotherapy of a more traditional insight-oriented type has proved largely ineffective in helping them with their ADD symptoms. In fact, some of them have felt that their previous psychotherapy was demoralizing and destructive due to the therapist's psychological interpretations of neurological symptoms such as forgetfulness or lack of follow-through. Many struggled for years with self-blame and guilt, attempting to understand the psychological basis for their "immature," "passive-aggressive," or "self-defeating" patterns. When receiving psychotherapy that focused on their ADD, these same individuals were able to develop a more hopeful and effective approach to life, after moving through phases of relief (as they relinquished their self-blame) and sadness (as they faced the fact of their lifelong neurobiological disorder).

Therapist as Educator

An essential role for the therapist of a client with ADD is to educate and thereby enable the client to better understand the neurological basis for the ADD symptoms. The process of education can be supported through reading, participation in support groups for adults with ADD, and the ongoing process of therapy. Providing concrete examples from the lives of other adults with ADD and showing how certain patterns relate to the neurobiology of ADD can be helpful. Many clients find that instructive anecdotes about others can help them see their own behavior in a more objective light.

Therapist as Supporter

A critical goal of the therapist should be encouraging the adult with ADD to move from victimization to empowerment in relation to the ADD symptoms. The individual needs to firmly embrace the concept that ADD presents challenges which must be actively managed through a range of strategies. A crucial task for the therapist is to inculcate this attitude and discourage the common hope that medication will eliminate problems without further effort. An ADD diagnosis should not become an excuse for underfunctioning, but rather be a challenging fact of life that requires ongoing active strategic management. As Barbara Fisher so succinctly put it during her Adult ADD Workshop at the first annual conference on adult ADD in Ann Arbor, Michigan, in May 1993, "You need to learn to manage your ADD so that it won't manage you."

Therapist as Interpreter

Because distractibility, absentmindedness, disorganization, and reactivity to stress pose problems for everyone to some extent, adults with ADD may often encounter skepticism as they attempt to explain the disability to coworkers, supervisors, spouses, or others. The clinician can play a therapeutic role by supporting the client in seeing this disability as "valid" and by interpreting the client's ADD patterns to the significant people in the client's life, helping them to accept the validity of the disabling effect of attention deficits. Spouses and employers who recognize the validity of practical problems that result from ADD should not be expected to simply overlook disorganization, forgetfulness, or chronic lateness, but rather, to interpret these behaviors correctly, as the result of ADD, not indifference or low motivation.

The interpretation of ADD symptoms to family members, coworkers, and employers is the first step toward developing accommodations in the home and work environment that can reduce the impact of the symptoms (see chapter 16, this volume, for a more complete discussion of disclosure of ADD in the workplace). Adults with ADD legitimately require certain accommodations and deserve support and understanding as they work to restructure their environment and learn strategies to compensate for dysfunctional patterns.

Therapist as Structurer

In my experience as well as that of others (see Hallowell, chapter 9, and Murphy, chapter 8, this volume), the clinician who wishes to become most effective with ADD adults needs to modify the passive-receptive-interpretive therapeutic role to become more active and directive. Because ADD individuals typically have difficulty with planning, organization, and prioritization, it may be helpful for the therapist in this particular role to begin with the structure of the psychotherapy session itself. Initially, the therapist can play a useful role by providing guidelines within each therapy session, and by helping the client to maintain focus. Later, the therapist can assist the client in developing self-structuring skills. It is often useful for the client to maintain a journal of events between sessions, keeping a log of "homework" completed during the week and jotting down thoughts or observations to discuss in the next therapy session. Without this degree of structure, the client with ADD may tend to skip from topic to topic in the therapy session, just as in daily life, never really staying focused long enough to develop awareness and strategies.

Therapist as Rehabilitation Counselor

Currently, there is no single profession that provides adequate training in the treatment and accommodation of cognitive impairments (Sohlberg & Mateer, 1989). Various aspects of relevant training exist within the fields of neuropsychology, cognitive psychology, educational psychology, and rehabilitative training. There is much work to be done to develop training programs for therapists in cognitive training and environmental restructuring for the ADD adult. Many of the approaches and strategies that seem useful for work with adults with ADD are derived from those of the rehabilitation counselor who focuses very concretely on practical ways to improve aspects of daily functioning. In his role as "rehabilitation counselor" the therapist can suggest many concrete modifications to the client's daily routine and to his or her home, school, and work environments.

ASSESSMENT OF EXECUTIVE FUNCTIONING

Standard psychological and neuropsychological testing is not sensitive, for the most part, to frontal lobe dysfunction (Sohlberg & Mateer, 1989). Stuss and Benson (1986) write that perhaps the greatest confusion regarding the function of the frontal lobes lies in the relationship between the frontal lobes and cognition. Many case studies show that individuals with normal-range cognitive functioning, as measured by the Wechsler Adult Intelligence Scale-Revised, manifest severe deficits in functional ability. Several researchers (Luria, 1973b; Stuss & Benson, 1986) suggest that the frontal lobes do not involve primary cognitive functions, but rather are responsible for coordinating and actualizing cognitive processing through attention, motivation, regulation, and self-monitoring. Lezak (1976) sheds some light on the puzzle of adults with ADD who often test in the average or above-average range on cognitive tests while still manifesting many functional deficits. Lezak writes that cognition refers to how much a person knows and what the person can do, whereas executive functions relate to how or whether the individual performs certain tasks.

Assessment of Executive Functions

There are several standardized tests commonly used to measure executive functioning. They include the Halstead Category Test (Halstead, 1947), the Wisconsin Card Sorting Test (WCST), and the Porteus Maze Test (Porteus, 1950). All three tests investigate planning ability. Other experimental tests have been developed to assess frontal lobe functioning. Shallice (1982) developed the Tower of London Puzzle, which requires sequencing and planning. Lezak (1983) believed that standard tests of executive function were not sensitive to issues of initiation and goal-directed behavior. She developed her unstructured Tinker Toy Test to assess initiation, goal-directed behavior, and planning ability (Lezak, 1982). These tests can be used only impressionistically, however, since norms and standardization are lacking. Sohlberg and Mateer (1989) also describe informal measures of executive functioning through providing the patient with a multistep task, and then observing the patient's performance.

Therapist Assessment of Executive Functions

The neuropsychological instruments discussed earlier may be useful for an initial assessment of executive functions. However, the therapist working with an ADD adult needs to assess executive functions as they occur in daily living. One structured rating scale developed by Sohlberg & Geyer (1986), Executive Functions Behavioral Rating Scale, may prove useful to make such an assessment more meaningful. This rating scale asks the therapist to rate the patient on ability to select and execute a complex, multistep plan, on time management during the execution of the plan, and on ability to self-regulate and self-correct as the execution of the plan evolves.

Self-assessment of Executive Functions

A similarly structured approach can be helpful for the ADD adults themselves. Pollens, McBratnie, and Burton (1988) have developed a sheet that lists the eight executive functions outlined by Ylvisaker, with each function noted along a continuum. Such a sheet could be used as a work sheet for adults with ADD, to assist them in focusing effectively on the areas in which they need to improve functioning and to assist them in monitoring their progress.

Planning and Task Execution

Ylvisaker (1990) outlined the following specific behaviors within the realm of executive functioning:

1. Awareness
2. Goal setting
3. Planning
4. Self-initiation
5. Self-inhibition
6. Self-monitoring
7. Ability to change set
8. Strategic behavior

Pollens et al. (1988) suggest using these stages as a framework within which to assess and treat executive functioning of a client, using real-life situations. In working with adults with ADD, this approach might involve setting up structured assignments of increasing complexity requiring goal setting, planning, organization, and follow-through. Therapy sessions then focus not only on levels of satisfactory completion of these "homework assignments" but also on developing clients' awareness of their level of functioning, self-monitoring skills, and strategic problem-solving skills.

Pollens et al. (1988) report that a structured planning sheet was a useful tool to assist in the development of planning ability. The therapist could develop a sheet for planning multistep activities to be completed by the client between therapy sessions. Cicerone and Wood (1987) found that the client verbalizing plans with the therapist prior to initiating an activity was very successful in reducing the rate of error in task completion. The therapist might employ both of these approaches—verbal rehearsal and a structured planning sheet—to assist the client in developing such planning skills. Later, the dependence on verbal rehearsal during therapy sessions can be reduced, shifting the verbal rehearsal to self-talk or discussion of plans with others. Gradually, the client could complete planning sheets at home and bring them to therapy sessions for review.

ATTENTION

Before addressing ways to improve attention and concentration, a discussion of the concept of attention is in order.

Types of Attention

Sohlberg and Mateer (1989) outline a broad concept of attention which is perhaps useful in thinking of the complex, real-life phenomenon with which the ADD adult struggles. Their model addresses five levels of attention:

1. *Focused attention*: the ability to respond discretely to specific stimuli
2. *Sustained attention*: the ability to maintain a consistent behavioral response during continuous repetitive activity
3. *Selective attention*: freedom from distractibility
4. *Alternating attention*: mental flexibility, the ability to shift focus of attention between tasks having different cognitive requirements
5. *Divided attention*: ability to respond simultaneously to multiple tasks or multiple task demands

The assessment of improved attention in individuals with ADD (through either self-report or the observations of others) has focused primarily or exclusively on "selective attention" (Levine, 1987). Assessment tools such as continuous performance tasks (see chapter 7, this volume) are designed to target focused, sustained, and selective attention. The more complicated attentional tasks of alternating attention or divided attention, however, are often ignored. This is unfortunate, because it is the requirement for alternating and divided attention that typically seems to pose the most daunting challenges in daily functioning for ADD adults. For example, parenting roles and managerial positions at work are both rife with interruptions and competing demands that call for great facility with alternating and divided attention. When focusing on attention issues, the clinician would do well to not address exclusively the issues of distractibility and focused or sustained attention, but also to address the more complex and often unavoidable tasks requiring alternating and divided attention. In my clinical experience I have often observed that highly intelligent, higher functioning adults with ADD are able to focus and sustain their attention, which has allowed them to be academically successful; these same adults, however, often report marked difficulty with the complex demands for divided and alternating attention placed upon them as they are promoted to positions as supervisor, project manager, or department head.

Attention Training

Sohlberg and Mateer (1987) have developed an attention training program designed to enhance attentional abilities in brain-injured individuals. They have also developed a second, modified program—Attention Process Training II (APT II)—to manage attention deficits in persons with milder cognitive dysfunction. The program was based on work with individuals with *acquired* attention deficits; however, it has been modified and used successfully by Goodwin and Corgiat (1992) in their work with an ADD college student.

One of the approaches to enhance alternating and divided attention involved the use of an alarm watch, programmed to ring at set intervals. At the sound of the timer, the ADD student was instructed to assess whether his attention was focused on the appropriate task, and, if not, to reorient.

Other Attention-enhancing Techniques

Parente (Parente & Anderson-Parente, 1991) writes about a number of other strategies for enhancing attention, including

1. Frequent self-monitoring: "What should I be doing now?"
2. Assigning time: setting scheduled time to ponder thoughts that repetitively intrude into thoughts regarding the current task
3. Allowing activity: engaging in physical movement while listening or memorizing
4. Distributing practice sessions: taking frequent breaks
5. Active learning: repeating material heard or read, restating in own words
6. Building incentives for concentration: scheduling small rewards earned by periods of concentrated study

Sensory Overload and Attention

Attentional abilities can be strongly affected by the amount of sensory input that is having an impact on the ADD adult at a given moment. Many ADD individuals seem both drawn to and overwhelmed by a highly stimulating environment. The therapist needs to assist the client to think in terms of a "window" of optimal stimulation. If the individual is understimulated, he or she may feel sleepy, bored, or mildly depressed. If the individual feels overstimulated, he or she may "shut down." Goodwin and Corgiat (1992) noted in their case presentation of an ADD college student that as his stimulus load became too great, he tended to cope with this "flooding" by becoming overfocused on some randomly selected aspect of the environment, or by focusing on nothing at all. Some ADD adults describe this reaction as "zoning out."

The therapist can assist in creating improved attentional abilities by teaching the client to recognize and, if possible, avoid situations of prolonged under-

or over-stimulation. This type of environmental restructuring, through aware-ness and control of stimulation level, can be an essential strategy in atten-tion enhancement.

Suggestions to reduce stimulation overload include living alone, hav-ing a living space large enough to allow periodic isolation, working in a private office, and avoiding overstimulating circumstances such as traffic jams, shopping malls, crowds, noise, and commotion. Because children—especially children with ADD—can often produce overwhelming amounts of stimulation, and because adults with ADD have a strong chance of hav-ing children with ADD (Biederman, Faraone, Keenan, Steingard, & Tsuang, 1990), careful consideration of the number of children one chooses to have may be critical in controlling overstimulation. Improving child man-agement techniques is also an essential skill to help control overstimulation and reduce stress (see chapter 13, this volume).

Strategies to avoid understimulation include (1) taking breaks from nec-essary but boring activity, (2) interspersing low-interest activities with higher interest activities, (3) interacting with other people, (4) engaging in physi-cal exercise, (5) creating challenges to increase interest and motivation, and most important, (6) choosing a career path of high intrinsic interest.

MEMORY

Memory difficulties have received less attention than some other cogni-tive dysfunctions associated with attention deficit disorder. In Hallowell and Ratey's (1993) suggested diagnostic criteria for ADD in adults, memory deficiency is not listed as a diagnostic criterion; Brown (chapter 6, this vol-ume), by contrast, includes memory difficulties as one of the important cognitive deficits experienced by individuals with ADD. Perhaps this lack of agreement regarding memory and ADD has to do with the complexity of the cognitive processes involved in memory. Memory is sometimes mis-takenly thought of as a unitary cognitive function. People speak of having a "good memory" or a "bad memory." Research suggests, however, that memory is quite complex, and that one can have excellent memory for certain types of facts or events while having poor memory for others (Ellis & Hunt, 1988). This variability is true for adults with ADD as well.

It seems logical that memory would be a particularly salient issue for ADD adults, however, because, as Sohlberg and others note, there is an inextricable link between attention and memory. "Attentional capacity is a logical component of any memory model since it is this capacity that al-lows information to have access to the (memory) system to begin with"

(Sohlberg & Mateer, 1989, p. 139). There is much need for research into the types of memory difficulties and frequency of memory difficulties experienced by adults with ADD.

Self-reported "Everyday" Memory Difficulties

In my clinical experience, certain types of memory difficulties seem to be reported more frequently by adults with ADD. Some of these areas include difficulty remembering things they have heard (verbal memory), difficulty recalling where they have placed personal belongings (absent-mindedness), and difficulty remembering to do things they have intended to do (prospective memory). Additionally, there appears to be a subgroup who demonstrate difficulty with long-term semantic memory and retrieval. (This may be reflected by low Information subscale scores on the Wechsler Adult Intelligence Scale-Revised [WAIS-R], see chapter 7, this volume.)

Semantic Memory Problems

Kelly and Ramundo (1993) report that many adults with ADD experience difficulty remembering facts, names, faces, books, movies, and so forth. In discussing the different stages in the memory process that may be affected by ADD, Kelly and Ramundo relate that many adults with ADD seem to have a smaller or less complete fund of general information than their non-ADD peers. This may be partially due to interruptions in the very first stage of memory, *acquisition*. The adult with ADD who may have high distractibility may never make the initial step of paying attention to incoming information, and therefore may never "acquire" it.

During *registration*, the second stage of memory, the individual makes an active effort to secure information for later recall. *Coding* and *rehearsal* are important steps in the registration phase. Coding refers to "filing" information according to category. Coding and rehearsal require an active approach to acquisition of information: active decisions to repeat the information to oneself until it is retained, active decisions about the most effective way to encode the information, active associations between the new information and previously learned information, and a conscious decision about where to file or code the information. Reliable retention of information requires an active process of coding and rehearsal. One approach to improving memory for many adults with ADD may be to teach active learning techniques.

Prospective Memory Problems

Difficulty with prospective memory (remembering to remember) can present the ADD adult with significant problems on a daily basis. It can be very damaging to relationships with coworkers, friends, and family members if an individual frequently forgets to do what she or he has promised to do. While it may be highly desirable to have good factual recall, it is often more essential for daily functioning to remember that you need to keep an appointment at 2:30 P.M., that you intend to stop by the bank on your way home, and that you should purchase your spouse's birthday gift before next Thursday.

Prospective memory differs from retrospective memory or recall in three important ways (Winograd, 1988). First, recall focuses on *what* is remembered while prospective memory is concerned with *whether* a person remembers a task; secondly, recall memory is usually demonstrated verbally while prospective memory is demonstrated by the execution of an action; thirdly, recall is usually initiated by an external cue, while prospective memory requires that the individual cues himself or herself. It is this self-cueing aspect of prospective memory which presents the greatest challenge for the individual with ADD. Constantly distracted by the onrushing flow of external and internal distraction, he or she is very likely to forget to self-cue at the appropriate moment.

Although no research exists regarding the frequency of prospective memory difficulties in adults with ADD, Mateer and Sohlberg (1988) found a very strong association between attention and prospective memory in a population of head-injured patients. Mateer and Sohlberg developed a memory questionnaire which investigated the types and frequency of memory difficulties in head-injured patients compared to normal controls. They investigated memory for facts (semantic memory), memory for events (episodic memory), working memory (ability to maintain a group of facts in immediate memory in order to use and manipulate them), and prospective memory (remembering to do a specific act at a specific point in the future). A factor analysis of their results suggested that attention and prospective memory were closely related and were loaded on the same factor. The authors write: "This suggests that the ability to carry out future intended actions depends heavily on attention, perhaps in the form of vigilance relative to time and situational cues" (p. 206). The Attention/Prospective Memory factor accounted for almost half of the memory difficulties reported. Thus, Sohlberg and Mateer's work supports my clinical observation that there is a strong link between inattention and poor prospective memory. This link would be an interesting and important topic to investigate for adults with ADD.

Memory Assessment

Since prospective memory difficulties appear to be so closely linked to attention and seem to pose the majority of memory difficulties for an individual on a daily basis, it is unfortunate that most of the measures used to assess memory focus on other types of memory tasks. The Wechsler Memory Scales-Revised (WMS-R), for example, is a widely recognized and frequently used measure of memory. The WMS-R measures verbal associative memory (memory for word pairs), verbal narrative memory (memory for a narrative account), and verbal sequential memory for nonmeaningful information (memory for spoken number sequences). It also measures memory for designs, visual associative memory, and visual sequential memory. Many ADD adults who report significant memory difficulty in their everyday life are nevertheless able to perform well on the WMS-R.

Currently, due to lack of appropriate diagnostic instruments, we must rely on self-report and the report of significant others to assess these types of everyday memory problems (Harris & Morris, 1984). One self-report questionnaire that has been developed to investigate aspects of "absentminded-ness" or "forgetfulness" is Broadbent's Cognitive Failures Questionnaire (CFQ) (Broadbent, Cooper, Fitzgerald, & Parkes, 1982). Research is badly needed into the incidence of memory difficulty in adults with ADD, as well as into the types of memory tasks that seem to pose the most difficulties.

Memory Training and Compensatory Strategies

Some attempts have been made to improve prospective memory in brain-injured individuals through patterned memory training. Although there have been some limited positive results reported (Parente & Anderson-Parente, 1991), for the clinician working with the ADD adult, it seems more immediately practical to assist the client in developing compensatory strategies such as lists, alarms, rituals, and visual reminders to serve as external cues. There are a number of compensatory strategies that can be very useful for ADD adults to employ to reduce their level of forgetfulness. A few strategies found useful by some clients are briefly highlighted below.

Daily Calendar

First and foremost in the acquisition of memory strategies is the habit of effectively using a daily calendar or "daytimer" in which the individual can write all appointments, commitments, phone calls to make or return, and tasks to accomplish that day. I have worded this recommendation carefully, not recommending that the client acquire a daytimer, but that he acquire the *habit* of using one effectively. Often ADD adults report to their therapist that they have tried to use a daily appointment calendar but soon gave up its use or only use it intermittently. Taking up this habit requires time and reinforcement before it becomes second nature. It can be useful for the therapist to build into the weekly therapy session a prolonged period of time to support the consistent use of a daily calendar in order to reinforce and streamline its use.

Electronic Reminders

It can be useful for the therapist to assist the client in listing the types of things that she or he repeatedly forgets, in order to help strategize for reminders. A watch that can be programmed for multiple beeps throughout the day is useful to remind the ADD adult to complete routine tasks such as taking medication at set intervals, picking up the kids after school, or attending a regularly scheduled daily meeting. There are also computer programs and voice mail systems designed to provide reminders. The key to the usefulness of an electronic reminder, however, depends on how seriously the person regards the reminder when it is received. Some adults inadvertently thwart their carefully designed reminder system by not immediately responding to the reminder. Typically, if the task for which the reminder was programmed is momentarily postponed, it is forgotten.

Visual Prompts

Visual reminders can also be helpful to prompt memory. Placing an item that should be taken to school or work directly on the stair landing or in front of the door will usually be an effective prompt. Notes should be placed in highly visible spots. Notes written on colored paper are more noticeable. Clients should learn to place an item they are likely to forget next to one they are highly unlikely to forget. For example, place mail that needs posting on top of the briefcase. Then, place both items in the front hall near the front door.

Backups for Essential Items

Losing or forgetting small personal items often poses a daily problem for adults with ADD. Several approaches may be helpful. If reading glasses are essential at work, the client should keep an inexpensive second pair in the desk at work. Extra car keys should be kept at work, as well as hidden strategically in a magnetic container on the car. House keys need to be duplicated and hidden strategically. Selecting cars that require the use of a key to lock the door are an effective prevention of locking keys in the car.

Routines

The development of daily rituals and routines can also greatly reduce forgetting. As long as routines are developed and are unvarying, they fall into the category of "overlearned" behaviors which place very little demand on the attentional and memory systems (Norman & Shallice, 1980). It is only when such routines are interrupted or must be varied due to an unusual set of circumstances that a much greater demand is placed on the attentional system.

This technique of developing routines has been used successfully with children with ADD, and needs to be recognized as useful for ADD adults as well. For children, the parent serves as trainer and structurer while these routines are learned and practiced until they become automatic. For adults, the therapist can assist in the learning process. Both morning routines (preparing for work or school) and evening routines (preparing for the next day and for bed) are generally multistep processes that present many opportunities for forgetting.

Ideally, the evening routine should involve as much preparation for the next day as possible, including selecting and laying out clothes, planning and packing lunches, and clustering items that will be needed in the morning preparation, such as glasses, watch, jewelry, briefcase. Items related to any errands on the way to or from work should be gathered as well.

An essential element here is to develop the habit of completing the routine in a timely manner, allowing for "winding down" and getting to sleep on time. Because daily functioning can be so very taxing for adults with ADD, they may become powerfully drawn to those few hours in the day when they can quit worrying about what they "ought to do" and simply escape into pleasurable activity. Books, computers, and late night television can seduce ADD adults into habitually staying up too late. Such a pattern leads to chronic fatigue, exacerbation of their ADD symptoms, and difficulty getting up on time in the morning. Sometimes a "reverse alarm clock" which beeps or rings when the individual should start to get ready for bed can be a useful aid.

The morning routine should be as brief and uncomplicated as possible. The first key element in the successful completion of the morning routine is to rise at the planned time. This is, of course, linked to successful completion of the evening routine, including going to bed at the planned time. As mundane as it may seem, developing a reliable habit of getting to bed on time, getting up on time, and getting to work or school on time is a key step for ADD clients in learning to manage their life in a more successful fashion.

A second critical element in the successful completion of any routine is the elimination and avoidance of distracters. In the morning, key distracters tend to be the newspaper, television, and attending to the needs of children. For ADD adults who have children, generally the morning routine should be planned to be completed prior to the onset of the child's morning routine, allowing the adults to be available to keep their child structured and on time without disrupting their own routine. Because children with ADD often require a high degree of supervision to complete their morning routine, the adults need to take that into account in planning their own schedule. (See chapter 13, this volume, for more discussion of parenting issues.)

Mnemonic Techniques

If the ADD client has difficulty with semantic memory (memory for facts) which is having a significant impact on school or work performance, the therapist may want to make a referral to a person trained in cognitive rehabilitation or in tutoring adults with learning disabilities. Such a person can train ADD individuals in a number of more efficient and effective learning strategies, including teaching them how to be more active in the acquisition of new information. Some of these techniques for enhancing memory include rehearsal, overlearning, developing acronyms, making rhymes, developing webs of associations with previously learned facts, and "chunking" or grouping smaller bits of information together.

PROBLEM SOLVING

Problem solving is sometimes considered to be a higher order cognitive function rather than an executive function; however, as Goldstein and Levin (1987) write, deficits in problem solving can result from deficits in executive functions, even though general intellectual functioning may be intact. The clinician who is working with an ADD adult who shows poor problem-solving skills can be of great assistance to the client by teaching a structured problem-solving approach such as the following:

1. Define the problem: A careful verbal analysis of the problem, with the clinician's guidance, may lead to a new or modified definition of the problem.
2. Propose alternate solutions: Brainstorming by the adult with ADD, with the assistance and guidance of the clinician.
3. Select the best solution among the proposed alternative solutions.
4. Attempt the selected solution.
5. Analyze the results of the attempt.
6. Propose an alternate solution if the initial results were not satisfactory.
7. Analyze the results of the second solution, and so forth.

While this approach may seem too "simple" for use with bright, higher functioning ADD adults, it provides a structure for them to effectively use their higher cognitive functions. It may be a lack of consistency and focus rather than a lack of reasoning ability that results in poor problem solving for adults with ADD.

TIME MANAGEMENT

Time management is a facet of daily functioning that often poses a tremendous challenge for adults with ADD. Although time management is included among the executive functions discussed above, it is such a critical issue for many adults with ADD that it deserves to be considered separately. As responsibilities increase and structure decreases with adulthood, time management difficulties may become disabling. Time management involves a number of skills that may be deficient in an adult with ADD. Good time management requires planning, prioritization, remembering the plan that has been formulated, thoughtful midcourse correction as unexpected variables come into play during the day, the ability to stick to the plan in the presence of appealing distractions, the ability to accurately predict how much time a given activity will require, the ability to keep track of the passage of time while engaged in an activity, and the ability to shift flexibly from one activity to another as the plan requires.

Each of these aspects of good time management may pose difficulty for adults with ADD. The clinician working with an ADD adult who expresses such difficulty might begin by helping the client analyze where the greatest difficulties lie, in order to develop a plan.

Importance of a Daily Calendar

Learning to make regular, active use of a daily calendar is an essential skill in time management. Use of a daytimer was discussed earlier in the chapter as a tool to aid memory. Using a daytimer for time management is a more complex process than the simple listing of tasks to aid memory. Many adults with ADD report that they have made efforts at using a daily calendar in the past, but have not used it consistently or effectively. The clinician can be helpful in providing some structure as clients begin to introduce the use of a daytimer into their lives. Several rules of thumb are useful:

1. Effective use of a daily calendar or daytimer requires the development of a set of habits. These habits need to be built up over time.

    a. The first habit is simply to keep the daytimer or calendar with one at all times.
    b. The second is to learn to write all plans and commitments in it.

2. The adult with ADD should live by the rule "Do it now or write it down."

3. All such reminder notes should be written exclusively in the daytimer rather than on scraps of paper which are easily misplaced.

4. Dates and times should be specified to complete certain tasks. Estimate time and block that time on the daytimer.

5. Over-estimate how much time each task will require to compensate for inaccurate time estimation. (Adults with ADD are often notorious about underestimating the time any activity will take.)

Difficulty Shifting Focus

Another issue that can lead to poor time management is difficulty in shifting the focus of attention. Many ADD adults report that they have difficulty transitioning from one activity to another, especially if they are highly engrossed in an activity. Setting timers to beep at the planned transition time may be useful. Some activities are so "addictively" engaging that they should be avoided altogether during time periods just before a necessary transition.

The Prevalence of Chronic Lateness

Among time management difficulties, chronic lateness often heads the list of complaints made to adults with ADD. Chronic lateness can be caused by difficulty in shifting focus, just discussed. Other causes of chronic lateness include

1. Overcommitment. Adults with ADD will find themselves frequently late if they overcommit. Try as they might to be on time, they will typically find themselves rushing from one activity to the next, feeling stressed and apologizing once again for their lateness.

2. Distractibility. Some adults with ADD report that they are often late because they find themselves distracted by noticing or recalling one small task after another which "will only take a second."

3. Hyperfocusing. When adults with ADD fall into patterns of overfocusing on certain tasks, they may often find that time has "gotten away from them," and they are late once more. Individuals may hyperfocus on tasks that are particularly enjoyable or those that require intense effort.

4. Living reactively rather than proactively. Rather than controlling the use of their time, some adults with ADD respond to the moment. Such individuals may answer the phone, allow themselves to become engaged in conversation, or may impulsively engage in

some activity that occurs to them rather than departing in time to make a scheduled appointment.

Poor Time Management Through Avoidance, Denial, Procrastination

Patterns of avoidance, denial, and procrastination all wreak havoc on the best laid plans for time management. While these patterns are not the exclusive domain of ADD, adults with ADD frequently operate in these modes. A better understanding of why the avoidance, procrastination, and escape activities are occurring can lead to a more effective solution. At first glance, the client may shrug and say, "I avoid things because I don't feel like doing them." An obvious answer, on one level, but then, why does this happen in some instances and not in others? Why do some people go ahead and do things they "don't feel like," while others wait until crisis looms? The clinician needs to assist the client to sort through the motivation maze.

1. Does he develop avoidance/denial patterns because he has difficulty saying "No" in the first place? Does he routinely agree to do things he doesn't want to do, and then fall into an avoidance pattern later?

2. Does he procrastinate on completing important tasks because he lives in a highly reactive, unplanned mode? Perhaps more structure would be helpful, just as it is for impulsive, disorganized adolescents with ADD.

3. Is chronic procrastination a sign that he is generally overwhelmed by too many demands? Does he need to look at ways to simplify his life, to reduce the number of tasks for which he is responsible?

4. Does he generally procrastinate on tasks he dreads doing because he is not good at them, or does not have the organizational skills to readily complete them? Writing proposals and reports and doing income tax preparation often fall into this category. Possible solutions can range from hiring someone to do the task, to hiring a tutor to assist in improving skills, to moving to a job that requires less of the dreaded activity.

MODIFYING THE PHYSICAL AND SOCIAL ENVIRONMENT

Environmental Restructuring

Let's return for a moment to the "three-pronged" rehabilitation model introduced in the beginning of this chapter. In the preceding sections the focus has been on developing and improving various executive functions (rehab. approach #1), and upon developing compensation strategies (rehab. approach #2). In this final section we turn to the third approach–that of modifying the physical, psychological and social environment to enhance functioning. While ADD is a neurobiological disorder, its symptoms can be exacerbated by placing the individual in a confusing, overstimulating, hostile, critical, or stressful situation. Likewise, ADD symptoms can be reduced through clarity, structure, support, encouragement, and low stress. In this section we will address a number of factors which can be changed in order to minimize the impact of ADD upon the individual.

Just as individuals with a physical disability need to assess their environment and alter it to accommodate their needs, ADD adults should undertake a similar assessment, with the support and guidance of their therapist. As Adrian Sandler discusses in chapter 4, the degree to which an individual is affected by attention deficits is greatly influenced by the "goodness of fit" between that individual and his or her environment. ADD adults need to assess whether alterations, both great and small, in their environment may serve to improve the "fit" and therefore enhance their functioning.

Many psychotherapists have been trained to believe that seeking relief through external changes (in jobs, relationships, place of residence) is merely an avoidance of facing the internal issues with which the individual must grapple in order to achieve "real change." In working with ADD clients, the psychotherapist needs to recognize that there are many forces that can operate to improve the client's functioning, and that guidance in making positive external changes or choices (in employment, in patterns of daily living, in life partner, in living situation) is an appropriate and effective role for the therapist.

ORGANIZING THE ENVIRONMENT

Many ADD adults with whom I have worked in therapy describe their home environment as generally chaotic. Personal items are flung or stacked on every available surface. (In some cases this problem is so severe that clients have brought photographs of their homes, anticipating that the therapist would not comprehend the level of disorder which had been created.) Redundant items are frequently purchased for the kitchen larder because a grocery list was never made or was forgotten when the shopping was undertaken. At the same time, other household items are out of supply. Searches for shoes, car keys, purses, and other personal items are frequently necessary.

Several approaches can help tremendously to reduce the level of chaos but may require outside assistance at first. Hiring a "professional organizer" may be a good initial investment. If such a person is unaffordable or unavailable, enlisting the assistance of a close friend or relative who is a good organizer might serve the same purpose. Many adults with ADD report that they have "gotten organized" many times, but it never lasts. Making such a statement is rather like saying "I've taken showers before, but I never seem to stay clean." Being organized is a habit involving regularly repeated sets of behavior, not a singular event. Experts in cognitive rehabilitation (Sohlberg & Mateer, 1989) recognize that adults with deficits in planning and organization need to be taught new habits slowly and repetitively. Too many ADD adults have taken a one-day course or read a book on organization, then started off with the best of intentions to reorganize themselves, but soon find themselves reverting to old habits of disorganization. The therapist can play a very useful role by recognizing the importance of structure, support, and repetition in the development of better organizational habits.

Specific and *convenient* places need to be assigned for coats, purses, briefcases, keys, and so forth. The general level of household clutter needs to be reduced. Often ADD adults contribute to household chaos through making impulse purchases, subscribing to newspapers and magazines they never have time to read, and leaving an accumulation of half-finished projects. The therapist can assist in this process by helping clients to identify the sources of clutter and chaos specific to their household and then identifying ways to reduce the clutter gradually and systematically. These activities can be supported through the use of a planning sheet and daily diary which are brought to therapy sessions.

Many of the same approaches that are so helpful for children are equally helpful for the ADD adult. Purchase storage containers and label drawers, boxes, and containers for easy memory and organization. Keep the system simple. Use bright colors and convenient storage locations. Identify the categories of items that tend to pile up. Do they have a place where they officially belong? What prevents them from being placed there? Is the container full? Is it inconvenient? Is there no designated place? Does the ADD adult already own too many of a particular item (books, magazines, catalogs, etc.)?

DEVELOPING FILING SYSTEMS

The development of organized, efficient filing systems is often difficult for adults with ADD. This task calls for planning, organization, and attention to detail. Many adults recount with dismay that their filing system— whether at home or at work—is in total disarray, with redundant and missing files and no workable system for deciding what to file where. On top of their organizational difficulties, many adults with ADD also have memory retrieval difficulties. They may create a file under the name of an individual, only to subsequently forget the name of that individual or organization. Then they are faced with scanning their entire filing system in an attempt to find the file they are seeking. One man related that he discovered that he had created three files pertaining to car insurance: One was labeled "car insurance," a second labeled "auto insurance," and the third was listed under the name of the insurance company!

An approach often helpful for ADD adults with memory retrieval difficulties is to establish a filing system by category rather than by name. Categorical filing assists greatly in retrieving the information later. For example, home categories could include Legal, Insurance, Financial, Personal, and Auto. After the broad categories are established, files are created within each category. For example: Insurance-Health; Insurance-Car; Insurance-Life. A master list of file categories should be kept in the front for easy reference and to avoid duplication.

REDUCING DISTRACTIONS IN THE HOME AND WORK ENVIRONMENT

Many adults with ADD have significant difficulty screening out distracters, whether visual or auditory. Attempting to work in a distracting environment can be highly stressful. The clinician can assist the client in identifying distracters and looking for ways to reduce or eliminate them. Some of these approaches might include working in a quiet, uncluttered work space, unplugging the phone, asking your spouse to take the children on an outing while you engage in a task that requires more concentration, or developing the habit of working on certain tasks at quieter times of day.

Stress Management

Stress exerts a strong negative influence on the functioning of the adult with ADD. Times of high stress, including periods of increased demands, fatigue, illness, conflict, or frustration, tend to be periods in which the manifestations of attention deficit are exacerbated. In a stressful period, the ADD adult is likely to be less organized, more absentminded, less efficient, more error prone, and more prone to temper outbursts. Conversely, low-stress times tend to lead to improved functioning. Unfortunately, because many adults with ADD live their life in a reactive rather than a planned mode, periods of high and low stress may occur primarily as a function of outside forces. The therapist needs to assist clients in developing a more planned approach to restructuring their lifestyle and immediate environment to reduce their stress level.

STRESS ASSESSMENT

The initial stage of this process should involve a systematic assessment of stressors. Typical stressors might include

1. Finances
   Indebtedness
   Impulse purchases
   Poor record keeping
   Lack of planning and budgeting
2. Family
   Marital problems
   Child behavior problems
   Inconsistent parenting
   Family crises: illness, death, divorce
3. Career
   Workplace stress
   Interpersonal conflicts on the job
   Poor job match
   Traffic/long commute
   Long work hours
4. Health-related stressors
   Poor health
   Poor diet/exercise habits
   Sleep disturbance
5. General stressors
   Domino effect: unsolved problems creating new problems
   Chronic overcommitment
   Poor time management
   Poor organization
   Too many major life changes
6. Internal stressors
   Fear of failure
   Feelings of inadequacy
   Distractibility
   Disorganization

STRESS REDUCTION

After conducting a thorough stress assessment, the therapist should then assist the client in a structured, problem-solving process aimed at deciding which stressors can be reduced, eliminated, or coped with more constructively. When working with young adults, the therapist's role will be to educate them about the effects of stress, help them to identify the patterns by which they may create stress in their life, and help them to develop plans for the future (career, lifestyle, marriage, children) that are designed for optimal stress level. Paradoxically, some ADD adults, especially those more hyperactive in nature, are attracted to highly stimulating environments, despite the fact that their stress tolerance may be low. Such adults need to develop insight into these patterns and learn to seek stimulation in settings of a limited scope that do not lead to a generally high-stress lifestyle.

Many ADD adults seek psychotherapy at a time in their life when they feel overwhelmed by life stresses. Unfortunately, large mortgages, indebtedness, numerous children, and stressful work environments do not lend themselves to quick, ready solutions.

Stress Reduction Through Simplifying

Some stressors in the life of the ADD adult come from the same high-stress lifestyle that many other Americans find themselves living, with dual-career marriages and children who are involved in multiple extracurricular activities. As the continual flow of articles in women's magazines attests, this lifestyle is highly stressful for non-ADD children and adults. Adults with ADD often arrive home from a day's work exhausted, ill equipped to care for children, prepare meals, and maintain their home, not to mention make a round of carpools for children's activities. Unfortunately, when ADD adults see other families functioning in an overcommitted, frantic fashion, they tend to expect themselves to tolerate such a high stress level, and may consider themselves failures if they are unable to do the same. The role of the therapist is to help clients make lifestyle changes that reduce stress and to view those changes in a positive and adaptive light. Some appropriate adaptations might include

1. Looking for ways to live on one and one-half incomes rather than two, allowing more time at home for the performance of household and family duties
2. Changing jobs to gain a shorter commute
3. Avoiding rush hour commuting through flextime
4. Setting limits on the number of activities that children may become involved in that require carpooling
5. Agreeing to set aside some portion of the dual income to pay for services such as house cleaning, home repairs, and lawn mowing, thereby reducing the demand level at home

Stress Reduction Through Delegating Tasks

Another important technique in stress reduction is to engage in an analysis of daily, weekly, monthly tasks that are most difficult or stressful for the adult with ADD, and those that are enjoyable or performed with ease. Often paperwork or other detail-oriented activities are among the most distasteful. If the adult with ADD is married, he or she can engage in problem solving with the spouse, dividing chores equitably but also according to ability and inclination. It may be best to simply hire someone to perform certain functions, such as preparation of income tax returns or household repairs, if these are difficult or stressful for both partners.

Stress Reduction Through Stimulation Management

While not all ADD adults are alike or find themselves overstimulated by the same circumstances, some patterns of overstimulation seem to be prevalent. Often, these involve situations that are overstimulating either auditorily or visually, situations that require too many choices or involve too many interruptions. For example, shopping malls and grocery shopping may be stressful. Compensatory techniques may involve shopping in off hours or delegating that task to the spouse. Holidays with many guests, car pools with several noisy children in the back seat, and loud music may all be highly stressful. Shopping, filing, or sorting through articles to be given away may prove very stressful due to the large number of decisions that are called for. Compensatory techniques may include shopping in small boutiques rather than large department stores, dividing filing or sorting into small batches, or asking for assistance from someone to complete the task.

One client who found rush hour highly stressful was able to arrange his workday so that he could return home prior to rush hour and complete his paperwork and phone calls from home. Another client who found that he was at his most irritable and angry at the end of his workday developed the habit of stopping by the public library for a few moments of quiet reading before returning to his home full of rambunctious children.

Stress Reduction Through Learning Toleration

The client with ADD should not only seek to reduce or eliminate external stressors but also learn techniques to better tolerate stress. Some of these techniques include regular exercise, relaxation techniques, and meditation. The clinician can assist clients by suggesting that they learn such techniques, and also assist in structuring their days to allow for the regular occurrence of these stress-reducing activities.

SUMMARY

In this chapter, I have attempted to outline for the clinician ways to focus on the more practical aspects of the treatment of attention deficit disorder in adults. In using these techniques, the therapist will need to broaden his or her approach from a focus on the emotional and psychological impact of attention deficit to one that includes structured and directive methods more typical of a rehabilitation counselor. This chapter has stressed the clinician's need to understand the basic aspects of memory, attention, and other executive functions in order to be able to assist the client in the development of skills and compensatory techniques that may be applied to practical problems. Equally important, the clinician should function in a more "psychological" capacity, empowering the adult with ADD to come to terms with the disorder and learn to actively manage the practical problems in daily living that result from attentional deficits.

The great majority of clinicians working with adults with ADD were trained to focus primarily on the behavioral and academic problems of children with ADD. These clinicians have little training or experience to address the difficulties that adults with ADD experience in their everyday life, both at home and in the workplace. There is great need for training clinicians to work effectively with adults with ADD, as well as a need for research into which approaches and strategies are most effective.

REFERENCES

Barkley, R. (1993, October). A new theory of ADHD. *The ADHD Report, V.* I, No. 5.

Biederman, J., Faraone, S. V., Keenan, K., Steingard, R., & Tsuang, M. T. (1990). Family-genetic and psychosocial risk factors in DSM-III attention-deficit disorder. *Journal of the American Academy of Child and Adolescent Psychiatry, 29,* 526–533.

Broadbent, D. E., Cooper, P. E., Fitzgerald, P., & Parkes, K. R. (1982). Cognitive Failures Questionnaire (CFQ) and its correlates. *British Journal of Clinical Psychology, 21,* 1–16.

Cicerone, K., & Wood, J. (1987, February). Planning disorder after closed head injury: A case study. *Archives of Physical Medical Rehabilitation, 68,* 111–115.

Ellis, H. D., & Hunt, R. R. (1988). *Fundamentals of human memory and cognition.* Dubuque, IA: W.C. Brown.

Goldman-Rakic, P. (1983). Specifications of higher cortical functions. *Journal of Head Trauma Rehabilitation, 8,* (1), 13–23.

Goldstein, F. L., & Levin, H. A. (1987). Disorders of reasoning and problem solving ability. In M. Manfred, A. Benton, & L. Diller (Eds.), *Neuropsychological Rehabilitation* (pp. 327–354). New York: Guilford Press.

Goodwin, R. E., & Bolton, D. P. (1991, July–August). Decision-making in cognitive rehabilitation: A clinical model. *Cognitive Rehabilitation,* 12–19.

Goodwin, R. E., & Corgiat, M. D. (1992, September–October). Cognitive rehabilitation of adult attention deficit disorder: A case study. *Journal of Cognitive Rehabilitation,* 28–35.

Grant D. C., & Berg, E. A. (1984). A behavioral analysis of reinforcement and ease of shifting to new responses in a Weigl-type card-sorting problem. *Journal of Experimental Psychology,* 38, 404–411.

Hallowell, E. M., & Ratey, J. J. (1993, Winter). Suggested diagnostic criteria for ADD in adults. *ADDult News: A Newsletter for ADD Adults,* pp. 1–2.

Halstead, W. C. (1947). *Brain and intelligence.* Chicago: University of Chicago Press.

Harris, J. E., & Morris, P. E. (Eds.) (1984). *Everyday memory, actions and absentmindedness.* London: Academic Press.

Kelly, K., & Ramundo, P. (1993). You mean I'm not lazy, stupid or crazy?! Cincinnati: Tyrell & Jerem Press.

Levine, M. D. (1987). *Developmental variation and learning disorders.* Cambridge, MA: Educators Publishing Service.

Lezak, M. D. (1976). *Neuropsychological assessment.* New York: Oxford University Press.

Lezak, M. D. (1982). Tinker Toy Test: The problem of assessing executive functions. *International Journal of Psychology,* 17, 281–297.

Lezak, M. D. (1983). *Neuropsychological assessment* (2nd ed.). New York: Oxford University Press.

Luria, A. R. (1966). *Human brain and psychological processes.* New York: Harper & Row.

Luria, A. R. (1973a). The frontal lobes and the regulation of behavior. In K. H. Pibam & A. R. Luria (Eds.), *Psychophysiology of the frontal lobes.* (pp. 3–26). New York: Academic Press.

Luria, A. R. (1973b). *The working brain.* New York: Basic Books.

Mateer, C. A., & Sohlberg, M. M. (1988). A paradigm shift in memory rehabilitation. In H. Whitaker (Ed.), *Neuropsychological studies of nonfocal brain damage: Dementia and trauma.* New York: Springer-Verlag.

Norman, D. A., & Shallice, T. (1980). *Attention to action: Willed and automatic control of behavior* (CHIP Report 99). San Diego: University of California.

Parente, R., & Anderson-Parente, J. (1991). *Retraining memory—Techniques and applications.* Houston: CSY Publishing.

Pollens, R., McBratnie, B., & Burton, P. (1988, September/October). Beyond cognition: Executive functions in closed head injury. *Cognitive Rehabilitation.*

Porteus, S. D. (1950). *The Porteus Maze Test and intelligence.* Palo Alto, CA: Pacific Books.

Shallice, T. (1982). Specific impairments of planning. In P. Broadbent & L. Weisknartz (Eds.), *The neuropsychology of cognitive function* (pp. 199–209). London: The Royal Society.

Sohlberg, M. M., & Geyer, S. (1986). Executive Function Behavioral Rating Scale. Paper presented at Whittier College Conference Series, Whittier, CA.

Sohlberg, M. M., & Mateer, C. A. (1987). Effectiveness of an attention training program. *Journal of Clinical and Experimental Neuropsychology, 9,* 117–130.

Sohlberg, M. M., & Mateer, C. A. (1989). *Introduction to cognitive rehabilitation.* New York: Guilford Press.

Stuss, D., & Benson, F. (1986). *The frontal lobes.* New York: Raven Press.

Weiss, G., & Hechtman, L. (1993). *Hyperactive children grown up, ADHD in children, adolescents, and adults* (2nd ed.). New York: Guilford Press.

Weiss, L. (1992). *Attention deficit disorder in adults—Practical help for sufferers and their spouses.* Dallas, TX: Taylor.

Winograd, E. (1988). Some observations on prospective memory. In M. M. Gruenberg, P. E. Morris, & R. N. Sykes (Eds.), *Practical aspects of memory: Current research and issues, Vol. 1.* London: John Wiley & Sons, pp. 348–353.

Ylvisaker, M. (1990). Rehabilitative assessment following head injury in children. In M. Rosenthal, E. Griffith, M. Bond, & J. Miller (Eds.), *Rehabilitation of the adult and child with traumatic brain injury* (2nd ed.). Philadelphia: F.A. Davis.

Zametkin, A. F., Nordahl, T. E., Gross, M., King, A. C., Semple, W. E., Rumsey, J., Hamburger, S., & Cohen, R. M. (1990). Cerebral glucose metabolism in adults with hyperactivity of childhood onset. *New England Journal of Medicine, 323,* 1361–1366.

12

Relationship Dilemmas
for Adults with ADD
The Biology of Intimacy

JOHN J. RATEY, EDWARD M. HALLOWELL,
AND ANDREA C. MILLER

"It's the ADD zone, where what I see is not what's really happening. I feel like people around me are laughing and I've missed the joke. It's like the world is based on some secret code that I can't decipher. I'm always on the brink of making sense out of things, but then I lose it again," states an adult with ADD, who, like most, has trouble understanding the intricacies of social behavior and the nuances of social relationships. Even if an ADD adult has not had educational or occupational problems, or has learned how to cope with educational or occupational demands, social relationships can remain a shadowy frontier, muddled with uncertainty and insecurity. And intimate relationships can be the biggest puzzle of all.

At the root of the relationship problems, like the guest who won't leave, is the ADD itself, in its many dimensions: neurological, physiological, psychological, and behavioral. Poor self-esteem, chronic feelings of failure, and demoralization lend themselves to relationship difficulties; but these, too, usually have sprung from the rich soil of the disorder. They can be the result of attentional and cognitive deficits that have impaired the individual's capacity to learn, grow, and change. Yet the interplay between ADD and interpersonal difficulties may be overlooked, usually because ADD in adults remains relatively underdiagnosed. The reasons for this are as multifaceted as the disorder itself: adherence to the belief that ADD is outgrown during adolescence; a tendency toward diagnosing more common disorders, such as anxiety or depressive disorders, which may mask an

218

underlying attentional deficit; an underappreciation of the way in which symptoms other than hyperactivity can influence cognitive and behavioral patterns and processes; and so on.

Thus, many clinicians have begun to clarify and classify the symptoms of ADD in adults, which may be more subtle and more integrated into the personality than the childhood symptoms of ADD. Despite the vast literature that has accumulated regarding the consequences of ADD in the lives of children and their families, relatively little research has investigated the specific symptoms and needs of adults diagnosed with ADD. A number of studies have explored various drug regimens in adult ADD populations, but quality of life issues have been given little consideration, and therapeutic strategies usually have been discussed within the wider context of treating the child with ADD (see Barkley, 1990; Wender, 1987).

The authors (Ratey and Hallowell) have treated upwards of 1000 adults diagnosed with ADD, Residual State, according to DSM-III-R or the Wender Utah Criteria (Wender, 1985). The majority have completed a lengthy questionnaire based on Barkley's (1990) structured assessment form, and many have provided written narratives of their perceived difficulties and talents. Through these many encounters we have begun to understand and conceptualize how the phenomenology of ADD in adults undermines interpersonal relationships and emotional functioning. Behavioral characteristics, typified by problems with impulsivity, distractibility, emotional lability, and generalized maturational lag, compromise the sincere and persistent efforts of these adults to establish and maintain intimacy. For some of these adults, intimate relationships are much like college courses, degrees, jobs, or challenges. Once the thrill of the novel and bold passes, they become bored and move on. They have had many relationships, some have even had many marriages. And sometimes they withdraw from the fray, forsaking relationships altogether, feeling like they have no capacity for them because of their selfishness, narcissism, or immaturity. But most adults with ADD have not had many marriages. Most usually have put real work into their intimate relationships. Thus, the guilt over broken loves or deteriorating relationships adds to their deeply rooted demoralization.

Unbeknownst to them, these adults are being defeated by the "biology of intimacy"–those physiological, behavioral, cognitive, and affective symptoms of ADD that act as barriers to forming healthy interpersonal relationships. Our conceptualization of the biology of intimacy in ADD is based upon research implicating specific neurochemical and neuroanatomical systems in ADD, most of which is coalescing around two complementary models of the disorder. The first, commonly referred to as the catecholamine hypothesis (Kornetsky, 1970), attempts to explain the cognitive, physiological, and behavioral symptoms of ADD by focusing on the role of the dysregulated noradrenergic and dopaminergic neurotransmitter systems. The second model, which we might call the theory of frontal lobe disinhibition (Chelune, Ferguson, Koon, & Dickey, 1986; Douglas, 1984; Gualtieri, Ondrusek, & Finley, 1985), seeks to explain the impulsivity, hyperactivity, and distractibility of the disorder through neuroanatomical substrates and functioning. In this model, the frontal lobes are not doing their job properly– their job being to inhibit inappropriate responses from lower brain systems through "cortical control" and the integration of moment-by-moment experience with current expectations and previous experience. These models probably are complementary, as the frontal lobes are rich in catecholamine. Thus, the dysregulated functioning of the catecholamine in the frontal lobes could compromise the ability to appropriately process information, to inhibit or delay responses, to anticipate and carry out plans, and to modulate emotional reactions.

How can the underlying biology of ADD be brought to bear on our understanding of the interpersonal relationship problems so often seen in ADD adults? Interpersonal relationships, especially intimate ones, demand a high level of emotional maturity and rely on the complex integration of affective, cognitive, and temporal information. Appropriate behavior depends as much on frontal lobe inhibition as on the gradual accumulation of social skills, which can be impaired in the ADD adult due to attentional and information-processing difficulties that interfere with the development and internalization of interpersonal rules and guidelines. Thus, many of the skills and abilities that most of us take for granted just are not available to the adult with ADD. As many partners of ADD individuals know, it is hard, if not impossible, to have a good relationship with someone who is so distractible that he walks out of the room in the middle of an important conversation, or is so disorganized and absentminded that she forgets about plans that were made, or who doesn't call home to say he will be a few hours late, or has temper tantrums, or runs hot and cold, being loving one day and emotionally unavailable the next.

It is not surprising, then, that a majority of adults with whom we have worked report intimate relationships to be the most trying construct in their lives. At one end of the spectrum, we see the clinical syndrome of antisocial personality disorder, with a possible comorbidity rate of 25% in ADD populations (Mannuzza, Klein, Bessler, Malloy, & LaPadula, 1993; Weiss, Minde, Werry, Douglas, & Nemeth, 1971). Yet even much less severe disturbances, like those noted above, can undermine or disrupt relationships. Often the adult has had very few intimate relationships because of an inability to form or maintain such relationships. One patient commented, "I was never one to have many friends. When I was young I spent a great deal of time in my room getting lost in books or listening to records. What friendships I did have were usually short-lived." Another wrote, "I have gone through boyfriends like crazy. I've never been good at getting close to them. The truth is, once the first mad thrill is gone I have a hard time maintaining interest."

A number of adults with ADD are prompted to seek help because of a difficult divorce. Some come in with the significant others who have threatened to leave if patterns of neglect and impulsive outbursts are not discontinued. One man, in psychotherapy for 7 years, broke down in tears for the first time when expressing the pain associated with his inability to form an intimate bond with his wife, a bond he wanted and felt she deserved. Other adults lament their inability to be the parents that they want to be, due to their inability to spend time with, and pay attention to, their children. This was illustrated by a client who wrote, "I couldn't even play catch with my son. After 5 minutes I would be bored and overwhelmed with thoughts and feelings and commitments related to other things."

Treatment of the ADD adult should always include identification of the symptoms and problems, an assessment of the use of medication, psychoeducation, restructuring the environment, and working on issues of low self-esteem, lack of confidence, and self-defeating patterns (Ratey, Greenberg, Bemporad, & Lindem, 1992). And where many ADD adults and their partners seek treatment because of relationship problems, it is worthwhile for the clinician to emphasize and explore the underlying biological barriers to intimacy. Fortunately, the mutual recognition of how ADD symptoms wreak havoc on intimate relationships can help the ADD adult change negative and destructive behaviors and patterns, and can set the couple on a new, more even course.

PHYSIOLOGICAL BARRIERS

The physiological restlessness described by adults with ADD has not been established through standard laboratory measures, although it is noted as an ADD symptom in DSM-IV-R. Nonetheless, the physiological unease characteristic of the syndrome dramatically interferes with the quality of the individual's intimate relationships. Some ADD adults cannot bear to be physically close to another individual for an extended time without feeling trapped. Others feel an urgency to move or to act, which manifests itself in pacing, wandering, or leaving. Still others are hypersensitive to tactile sensations, which might include certain materials, or heat, or hugging. Rhythmic touching, such as stroking, can be interminably annoying (Weiss, 1992). One ADD adult sadly commented, "How can I be heart to heart when I can't even be eye to eye?"

One of the most disturbing consequences of physiological restlessness for ADD couples seems to be that of unsatisfying sexual relationships. Many times, sexual problems are the result of the lack of intimacy (Weiss & Hechtman, 1993) and the inability to communicate with one another about individual needs. But the problems can be very specific, too, with the ADD adult perhaps hurrying through sexual interaction, leading the partner to feel ignored and unloved. Sometimes adults with ADD are hypersexual, constantly needing sexual gratification, which leaves the partner exhausted and feeling used. Other ADD adults are hyposexual, living lives that are nearly celibate, due to their fear of intimacy or their sensitivities. Both subtypes are victims, in a sense, of their ADD; both experience frustration and guilt over their apparent deviation.

In any case, the issue of ADD and sexuality is a complicated one, and one that has not been examined in any depth. At the least, it is another opportunity for intimacy to go awry, as neither partner can meet the other's needs. To alleviate the blame, guilt, and hurt feelings with which these couples present, the clinician can frame the problem as one being driven by the symptoms of ADD. This being done, communication between partners should become a focus of treatment. The clinician might also assist the couple in finding new strategies that will work for them. For example, Lynn Weiss (1992) has suggested that experimentation and variety–in location, position, timing–may help both partners enjoy sexual intimacy and appreciate one another. In this way, the symptoms of ADD are accommodated while the needs of the non-ADD partner are taken into consideration. Weiss also suggests that mutually determined ground rules be established and respected. Thus, the couple can attempt to rebuild a trusting relationship as well as a sexually intimate one.

COGNITIVE BARRIERS

The "organic drivenness" (Kahn & Cohen, 1934) of the ADD syndrome extends from physiological urgency to mental hyperactivity and discomfort with sameness. Like ADD children who crave and perform best with new and varied stimuli (Zentall & Meyer, 1987), adults with ADD generally report an overwhelming desire to move onto the next cognitive frame, the next new idea, the next new thing. The sensation is described by a surprising number of ADD adults as the press to achieve "flow," a physiological, affective, and cognitive state of optimal experience where rewards are gained in each moment, rather than at some future time (Csikszentmihalyi, 1990). One woman described the experience as a "spiritual orgasm," induced by solo, sensory experiences such as a naked swim under a setting sun.

Although many adults with ADD have outwardly competent cognitive styles and social skills, their need to move on to the next frame influences the quality of their close relationships. Their tendency for what we might call "cognitive dishinibition," or a failure to delay a response, propels them toward the formation of premature judgments, black-and-white reasoning, and hasty opinions about people and things. There is a lack of receptivity to, and a lack of reflective awareness about, the other's thoughts, feelings, and behavior. It is as if these adults cannot "study" the person or the situation any better than they could study their textbooks while in school. They cannot deliberate over the messages they receive from others or the cues apparent in their environment, nor can they always make sense of the subtle social cues that can guide interpersonal interactions. They are prone to misreading social cues, perhaps due to the interplay of subtle cognitive deficits and past experiences of failure within the interpersonal domain. As a result of all these factors, ADD adults can too quickly assess the other's verbal and behavioral expressions, lumping the messages into what may be inappropriate categories, while forgetting about context. Subsequently they develop a false perception about the other individual, or unfairly label the other individual, or react inappropriately to the other's needs, feelings, and wishes.

Unfortunately, their premature labels and inappropriate categorizations of people, places, and things take on a life of their own, becoming generalized scripts that get played out throughout the adult's life. The boring interpersonal exchange becomes generalized as a boring partner. The painful event becomes the painful relationship. It is as if their reliance on external structure, a recognized correlate of the ADD syndrome, compels them to turn situations into structures, discrete events into overarching frameworks. To understand this tendency we might borrow the ethological concept of the "sign stimulus," where a member of a species responds to a few characteristics (the sign stimulus) of another member of the species rather than to the whole. For adults with ADD, relationships seem to be reduced to sign stimuli, and a wider appreciation of the other person is lost.

Other cognitive styles may impede the adult's interpersonal efforts. Hopkins and colleagues (Hopkins, Perlman, Hechtman, & Weiss, 1979), using neuropsychological testing, identified the ADD adult's cognitive styles as including cognitive impulsivity (vs. reflective capacity); field dependence (i.e., an inability to isolate figure from ground); and constricted control over attention. The study indicated that adults with ADD are left at a disadvantage when they must choose alternative responses in situations when a response is uncertain and when the *relevant* aspects of a complex stimulus situation must be selected. In addition, the study established that adults with ADD are easily distracted by irrelevant stimuli and less able to inhibit incorrect verbalizations.

224 A Comprehensive Guide to Attention Deficit Disorder in Adults

Psychoeducational psychotherapy allows the adult to identify and recognize his or her own cognitive symptoms or styles, and how these impair relationships. What may be key is the understanding that without reception and reflection, false perceptions are established and maintained.

EMOTIONAL BARRIERS

Just as there is the need to move forward to the next cognitive frame, so there is the need to extinguish an existing affect state and move on to the next. This creates intimate relationships that may alternate from being intense and demanding to distant and cool. Interpersonal situations become events, where emotions must be discharged all at once, to "get it over with." Aside from needing to move on, there may be an inability or unwillingness on the part of the adult with ADD to postpone the internal processing warranted by the situation. They do not feel equipped to study the emotional life of the partner, precluding them from a true sense of empathy. Nor do they consider a particular emotional state or situational dynamic to be accessible at a later time. Thus, the tool with which many of us wield our inner lives—namely, time—is unavailable.

There is some empirical evidence that adults with ADD have difficulties with their emotional functioning. A demographic study by Shekim, Asarnow, Hess, Zaucha, & Wheeler (1990) found that 25% of the adults diagnosed with ADD also were diagnosed with alexithymia. Some studies have shown that children and adolescents with ADD have not only impaired social competence and behavioral maladjustment, but emotional difficulties as well (Barkley, Anastopoulos, Guevremont, & Fletcher, 1991). Our clinical practice indicates that impaired emotional functioning not only persists into adulthood but also may become the most embattled symptom of ADD, severely compromising relationships unless recognized and treated through psychotherapy or self-help support systems.

A phenomenon we have observed that seems to impede the adult's emotional maturation is an *exaggerated temperament*. Researchers have known for some time that temperament consists of genetically based behavioral attributes—such as one's adaptability, emotional expressiveness, or motor behavior—that do not reflect motivation or ability, and influence the person throughout life (Chess & Thomas, 1990). Recently Kagan (1992) has defined temperament as an inherited pattern of physiologic and behavioral reactions to particular situations. His work has shown that children are born with a temperamental proneness toward limbic (emotional) reactivity to unfamiliarity; that is, there seems to be genetic underpinnings to a child's lowered or heightened threshold for physiological and emotional reactions to specific stimuli. He has found that 20% of 4-month-old infants are overreactive to novel stimuli, or "inhibited"; 35–40% are "uninhibited," or accommodating to new stimuli; and the remaining 40% represent some combination.

Citing animal research and his studies with infants, Kagan localizes the threshold of excitability in the limbic structure, called the amygdala, and its projections. He notes that because the amygdala receives and integrates internal and external sensory information, and participates in spontaneous avoidant behavior, it probably modulates reactions to novel stimuli. Because another limbic structure, the hippocampus, initially evaluates the degree to which stimuli are classified as novel, we find in the hippocampus-amygdala complex a potent mediator of information processing and behavior. It seems possible that the apparent dysfunctioning of catecholamine in the hippocampal and amygdala structures (Bloomingdale, Davies, & Gold, 1984; Sagvolden, Wultz, Moser, Moser, & Morkrid, 1989) in ADD could influence an individual's temperamental bias. Thus the "inhibited" temperament construct becomes the withdrawn personality of ADDnoH; the "uninhibited," active temperamental construct could become the disinhibited, hyperactive behavior of ADHD; and the "difficult" child with ADD develops conduct disorder. This hypothesis may be supported by a study by Lambert and Windmiller (1977), which examined temperament in children categorized as normal, poorly adjusted, hyperactive, or achieving. They found that the hyperactive group differed significantly from the others on distractibility; but, more interesting, the hyperactive group showed the most extreme scores on both ends of the measurement tools.

In adults, an amplified temperamental disposition causes a number of personal and interpersonal problems and conflicts. The shy temperament becomes an avoidant personality, a loner, perhaps obsessive-compulsive. The sedate, low-key temperament becomes depressive disorder. Interpersonal problems build upon one another, and include emotional outbursts, temper tantrums, hyperreactivity, excessive distractibility, interpersonal aloofness, and magnified mood states. This hypothesis offers an interpretation for the high rates of depression, anxiety, and other comorbid conditions commonly seen in the ADD population. It may account for the diversity of behaviors and personality constructs evident in the clinical picture of ADD. Yet the exaggerated emotional states or tendencies we see in our patients can be misinterpreted for more debilitating or pathological personality disorders, such as borderline personality disorder or narcissism. Many ADD adults suffer from feelings of shame, humility, and inferiority. In addition, the boredom and emptiness that litters their lives, as well as their inability to evaluate the complex feelings of others, could be viewed as the common features of the narcissistic personality. Although we have found it worthwhile to explore narcissistic issues with ADD adults, it seems most useful to recognize these narcissistic tendencies as exaggerated temperaments or experiences, rather than as personality disorder manifestations.

INTERPERSONAL BARRIERS

We witness the disturbing intersection of physiological, cognitive, and affective barriers to intimacy in the ADD adult's sometimes stormy, sometimes moody interpersonal relationships. Along with specific social difficulties, ADD adults report that there is a need to "finish up" an interpersonal event and move on to the next phase of the relationship, the next level, the next plane, or the next event. Consequently, relationships exist as a series of events, getting chunked down into discrete, nettled encounters, instead of existing as a continuum over time. The quiet times of an intimate relationship, the harbors, do not develop. Interpersonal and emotional safety and warmth can be a scarce commodity.

Under such conditions, downward spirals develop as non-ADD partners begin to experience burnout—an emotional exhaustion related to the many peaks and valleys of the relationship, the temper outbursts, or the lack of communication. And where adults with ADD appear to lack their own sense of history, their own "I" established through context and time— probably because their cognitive and behavioral disinhibition, and their inability to delay responses and reflect about their feelings, have immersed them in an existence that is unpredictable and moment-to-moment—communicating about problems in the relationship is a challenge neither partner may be up to. The non-ADD partner may find it impossible to express needs, due to the misinterpretation or lack of attention to which they are subject. The partner with ADD, too, may find it difficult to express needs, as the lack of an "I" precludes "I need." In fact, the partner with ADD may have no idea what she or he needs, and so cannot ask for it. Anger builds when the non-ADD partner cannot read the other's mind, cannot see what seems to the adult with ADD as intuitively obvious. The concept of reception and reflection can be used as a tool to help couples relate to one another, especially while they are in the midst of an overreaction or an argument. If this concept is shared with both members, and employed by both members, chances are it can become part of their repertoire as they establish new scripts and rules for their relationship.

TREATMENT OF ADD ADULTS IN RELATIONSHIPS
AND TREATMENT OF COUPLES

Although the diagnosis of ADD initially may cause confusion, anxiety, even anger, most adults soon feel relieved that finally there is an understandable reason for their difficulties and interpersonal problems. Thus, identification and psychoeducation may be significant aspects of treatment, but as important in the early stages of treatment may be the use of the stimulants or tricyclic antidepressants. The decreased restlessness and enhanced focus that the right medication affords leads ADD adults to newly appreciate their relationships, and to take steps to listen to, learn from, and love their partners and family members in a way that was not possible before.

Once light is shed on the ADD adult's symptoms, problems are given voice, and appropriate psychopharmacological interventions achieved, it becomes important to include partners in the process, and other family members if needed. Non-ADD partners should be encouraged to share all educational materials. It is hoped that the non-ADD partner will recognize the validity of the ADD symptoms rather than see the diagnosis as just another in a long line of excuses. The couple should be encouraged to meet with the treating clinician several times, so that initial problems can be recognized, identified, and framed within the context of ADD. The couple can decide if they are ready and willing to commit to the new communication, role allocations, and problem-solving strategies that will be needed to manage the ADD within the context of the family (Cunningham, 1990) or the relationship. If willing, there are tangible steps that can be taken, and "tips" that can be used, to restructure the relationship and allow the couple to work on long-term improvements (Hallowell & Ratey, 1994). The therapist can introduce the use of these measures and act as a guide along the way, but much of the work will be carried out by the couples themselves. Of course, these steps are interdependent and ongoing, and should not be considered as rungs on the ladder of "relationship improvement."

The first step in regaining an even footing in the relationship is the development of new models of communication. The couple needs to establish time to talk about their relationship and about the impact of ADD on the relationship. This time should be scheduled, in order to resist the temptation to do the talking between tasks or while on the run. It may be helpful for the couple to begin talking about their impression of the current status of the relationship—what is working, what is not, what should be changed or preserved—without blaming one another or using the ADD as an excuse. Efforts should be made to break the tapes of negative thinking about one another and the relationship, and praise and encouragement should be used freely. We have found that it is useful for the couple to write down the major points of their discussions. That way nothing relevant is forgotten, and the couple's documentation can serve later as a springboard toward creating a "treatment plan," where they attempt to determine strategies to reach their goals. Scheduled "connections" should be built into the relationship in an ongoing and constructive way; that is, it will remain important to communicate even after problems are recognized and rectified.

After a useful, productive dialogue has begun, the couple should start thinking about how to best realign their relationship. Realignment includes the introduction of structure into the relationship and the identification of harmful role patterns. It also includes sharing decisions and power—something that is often difficult for adults with ADD. Perhaps because adults with ADD cannot easily shift cognitive sets, or cannot hold contradicting ideas in working memory (in the frontal lobes) long enough to integrate the two demands, compromise and consensus are difficult to reach. It is typical of adults with ADD to demand that things are done their way, or to forfeit power altogether, giving up, in a way, contending that "we'll do it all your way."

As we recommend to individuals with ADD, lists, bulletin boards, notepads, and similar aids can be introduced into the relationship as a means to keep communication flowing, as well as to keep key issues in mind and activities straight. Each partner can use lists of what she or he wants the other person to do that day or that week, and a master appointment book can be kept which each partner checks on a daily basis. The phenomenon of role identification is more complex, but couples should try to determine whether they fall into the patterns we frequently see: that of the mess-maker and the cleaner-upper, where the non-ADD partner "enables" the ADD partner; that of the pest and the daydreamer, where the non-ADD partner incessantly nags at the ADD partner to pay attention, focus, stop daydreaming; that of the victim and the victimizer, where the ADD partner is helplessly controlled by the non-ADD mate; and that of the master and slave, where the non-ADD partner feels like a slave to the mate's ADD. If these roles sound familiar to the couple, they can try to break the patterns through creative problem solving and dialogue. The goal is to have each partner's needs recognized and appreciated, while using organizational tools whereby both their needs and concerns can be anchored between the two of them. From this springs the ability to diminish black-and-white thinking, make compromises, and reach consensus.

The third step is creative problem solving. Again, the ADD partner's therapist can be useful in coming up with suggestions, but the couple's knowledge of the dynamics of their relationship may lead them to come up with the most effective strategies for managing their relationship. For example, the relationship of one couple with whom we worked was marred by the ADD husband's outbursts of rage at inanimate objects—the toaster wouldn't work properly, the screen door wouldn't shut—and he would immediately escalate into a tirade and tantrum. When brainstorming with the couple about how to ward off such unpleasant situations, a strategy was proposed that might be ridiculous in non-ADD relationships but here made perfect sense: the use of a whistle. As funny as it sounds, the wife kept a whistle on hand, and when the husband began to escalate into a tirade, the shrill shriek of the whistle allowed him to stop, step back from the situation, and manage it. They were both saved the anxiety and chaos of his ADD-driven rages.

Our strategies for treating ADD adults in relationships individually, or with their partner in short-term couples therapy, are captured in Table 12–1.

The following case examples illustrate the ripple effect of pharmacological and psychoeducational interventions in treating previously undiagnosed adults with ADD who present with relationship problems in the forefront of their minds. The cases focus on short-term gains, which are crucial to the future success of the couple or family. These adults are well-educated, somewhat successful, high-functioning individuals who have used various strategies to cope with problems of distractibility, disorganization, and emotional lability. Yet they typify the difficulties and self-incriminations that recur in the lives and relationships of ADD adults. They consulted us when problems in their primary relationships had reached intolerable dimensions, for themselves and their families.

Case #1

Mr. G. is a white male in his late 40s. Mr. G. had an average early academic career and completed a college degree program in 7 years. He is nine years sober, divorced once, and remarried to a woman who is sober. He has a stepdaughter who is 5 years old, and a sister on medication for ADD. He is an architect who has had between 15 and 20 jobs over the course of his career due, he says, to a problem with authority figures.

Mr. G. reported that he is alternately anxious and nervous or depressed and blue most of the time, which leads him to procrastinate or to explode impulsively. A previous therapist had diagnosed him with a narcissistic personality disorder and had prescribed an antidepressant. His major presenting complaint was physical violence against objects and verbal abuse directed at his wife. He was particularly concerned that he was having 20 to 40 tantrums a month, often in front of his small stepdaughter. During these episodes he would punch and kick walls, throw things and break things, even bang his head. He reports that once he banged his head on the floor sufficiently hard enough to give himself two black eyes.

These tantrums are just as likely to be provoked by internal crises—confusion, the sense of being overwhelmed by stimuli or information—as they are to be provoked by external situations. He writes, "All the awareness and work I have been doing has not improved the mood changes and acting-out response of my behavior. Fear, anger, depression, low self-esteem, back to fear, and it goes on and on and on."

After being diagnosed with ADD, RT, Mr. G. was titrated to 30 mg t.i.d. desipramine. After 2 months of being maintained at this dosage, he has reported that he has not had one impulsive outburst (recall that Mr. G. was having up to 40 outbursts per month). He believes that the "press to act has been stilled." He feels cooler, calmer, and less burdened by environmental stimuli. He is spending more time reflecting on situations and problems, whether it be an architectural problem at work or a problem at home. He describes this as having "more space" in his head, between one idea and the next, and between himself and others. He now is able to creatively study the surroundings, including the needs and feelings of his wife and child. His wife is reporting that she is less angry with him. Previous to his being on medication, she felt that either he would not understand what she was trying to express or would "make the decision" about how she was feeling and prematurely end any discussion. They are beginning to listen to each other, and hear each other, in ways that had escaped them prior to the diagnosis and medication.

Case #2

Ms. J. is a woman in her 40s who had just returned to school to pursue an MSW. Her child had been diagnosed with ADD, and she had been an active advocate for him. She was aware for some time that she probably had ADD. She had never felt that she could sit still, had chronic problems with disorganization, was easily distracted, and emotionally labile. She was compelled to seek treatment because of problems related to her academics and her marriage.

Ms. J. seemed unable to study and felt particularly unable to manage her class in statistics. She could not concentrate or focus in the presence of any peripheral noise. More distressing to her was the

TABLE 12-1
Treatment Strategies for ADD Individuals and Their Partners

Treatment Aspect	Benefit	For Couples
Identification	Defining specific attentional and cognitive deficits alleviates guilt and blame. By encouraging the adult to identify how these symptoms are perceived to affect work and relationships, the adult's sense of moral failure and incompetence subsides.	Identification of specific limitations can be used to examine relationship difficulties and self-defeating patterns. Problems in relationships can be reframed using the "lens of attention," which assists in finding solutions. Partners should know that the diagnosis is not just another "excuse" for prior destructive behaviors and patterns.
Psychoeducation	The underlying biology of the disorder is made clear through therapeutic sessions and books, articles, and so forth. The ADD individual is taught to manage mood lability and distractibility. Maladaptive behaviors decrease and self-esteem begins to be restored.	Partners can be encouraged to be active participants in the psychoeducational process by joining in therapy sessions and sharing reading materials. The "biology of intimacy" can be discussed with the partners, illustrating how the ADD symptoms undermine the relationship. Negative patterns and roles can be examined within the context of the ADD.
Structuring the Environment	Coaching, organizational tools, and exercise provide new structure for the ADD individual. The structure and organization become internalized as an internal map for managing daily living and a sense of control and self-confidence grows.	The cooperation of the partner is essential for the success of a newly structured environment. Joint lists, calendars, and daily planners enable the couple to start reinventing their relationship. Relationship problems should be delineated, and their solutions written down according to a mutually determined plan of action.
Medication	Low-dose tricyclics or stimulants decrease the sensation of restlessness and boredom, while enhancing the ability to focus. The adult becomes less impulsive, and more able to receive information and reflect on it without overreacting.	The value of medication should be discussed with the partner. Effective psychopharmacological interventions often allow the ADD individual to be more present, and the partner feels listened to for the first time.
Character rebuilding	Long-term therapy addresses the maladaptive coping strategies and behaviors that the individual has employed, including procrastination, avoiding difficult tasks, and the fear of intimacy.	Long-term therapy usually is indicated for the ADD individual but the partner can keep the long-term gains on track through coaching and having a sense of humor!

impasse she seemed to be experiencing in her marriage. Her sudden explosions had become more frequent, her inability to relax with her husband more pronounced, her mood swings more perilous. Her interactions with her husband had become a series of small crises, with each interaction seeming to provoke her into a testy, nasty, doubting attitude. She described herself as a "bramble bush." She also reported problems with eating behaviors, where occasionally she would binge. Her sense of escalation around her symptoms made her life feel out of control.

Ms. J. was diagnosed with ADD, RT according to the Utah Criteria and placed on 10 mg/day desipramine and maintained at that dose. After a month on the medication, she reported the following: a cessation of panic-like responses, crises and outbursts in her marriage; a diminishment of the "peaks and valleys" in her emotions and fewer crying jags; an increased relaxation, playfulness, and enjoyment within her marriage; the ability to spend more time with her husband, watching television or talking, without jumping to conclusions; an increased control of her eating behavior; and an enhanced ability to study statistics and her other class materials.

Case #3

Mr. K. is a 40ish, attractive white male who was prompted to consult our practice after his son, recently diagnosed with ADD, had a positive response to Ritalin. On the phone he stated that he had the same thing as his son, and it had probably destroyed his marriage.

At the time of his initial consultation, Mr. K. was working as a salesman for a computer hardware firm. He reported he was very successful on the job but had problems with organizing his desk, his tasks, and his time. He would infuriate people with what seemed to be his professional carelessness. Yet, when a big sale was at stake, he would become fully engaged, fully consumed; he stated that this would make the hair on the back of his neck stand up.

His bigger concern was his impending divorce, his relationship with his children, and the fact that he could not be intimate with his new girlfriend. He felt guilty about the divorce, as his wife literally threw him out for his irresponsibility, his lack of help with the children, and his lack of attention to their needs. He felt guilty about his children because he didn't know what to do with them when they arrived for weekend visits. He wanted to be a good father but felt he was the same type of father as his own: distant, always busy, preoccupied when he was with his kids. He saw his children an in intrusion on his life, for which he hated himself.

Mr. K. was diagnosed with ADD, RT and titrated over 6 weeks to 30mg/day desipramine. The most positive response was 20 mg/day. This became the maintenance dose. After 8 weeks on medication he felt like his life and his relationships were changing in many ways. He had balanced his checkbook for the first time and had become organized enough to do his banking via phone. He had begun making lists of things that he had to do and then would do them. He had fewer "tantrums" and remarked on an overall decrease in anger and impulsivity. His moods were much less labile. He also reported an increased sexual intimacy with his girlfriend.

Perhaps his greatest triumph was in his relationship with his children. He had begun looking forward to spending time with his children. Intriguingly, on the medication he began experiencing "flow" during somewhat ordinary experiences with his children, the most noticeable being the occasions when he would need to pick them up for a visit. The anticipation, he commented, would make the hair on the back of his neck stand up! This experience made him attend to, and appreciate, his children in a way that he never had.

Identifying the neuropsychological impact of the disorder enabled these adults to remove some of the blame and guilt with which they had burdened themselves. It gave them a scaffold from which they could understand their problems with intimacy and work to improve them. It allowed them to reframe the patterns that had developed in their intimate relationships in ways that allowed them to become aware of the needs of others. Treating them with appropriate medication assisted them in modulating emotional functioning, enhancing focus, and reducing impulsivity. This made an immediate difference in these adults' ability to recognize interpersonal stimuli for what they are, take in appropriate cues, and reflect on the information received. Exaggerated temperamental biases became less potent mediators of experience, and the adults reacted and responded more appropriately to the environment.

Diagnosis, psychoeducation, and pharmacotherapy are short-term treatment strategies that improve self-esteem by lessening blame and guilt; they have a positive and dramatic impact on the quality of intimate relationships and the overall quality of their day-to-day experiences. Longer term strategies include structuring the environment to rebuild and realign the relationship. Finally, adults with ADD may need to be confronted with the defenses and maladaptive coping strategies that have been employed as survival mechanisms but are harmful to partners and ADD adults attempting to establish and maintain relationships. The goal is for both members of the couple to disassemble the structural phenomena of blame and guilt and take charge of their experience. Thus, they can begin building the lasting positive perceptions and interpersonal experiences that have been missing from their lives.

REFERENCES

Barkley, R., Anastopoulos, A., Guevremont, D. C., & Fletcher, J. (1991). Adolescents with ADHD: Patterns of behavioral adjustment, academic functioning, and treatment utilization. *Journal of the American Academy of Child and Adolescent Psychiatry, 5,* 752–761.

Barkley, R. A. (1990). *Attention deficit hyperactivity disorder: A handbook for diagnosis and treatment.* New York: Guilford Press.

Bloomingdale, L. M., Davies, R. K., & Gold, M. S. (1984). Some possible neurological substrates in attention deficit disorder. In L. Bloomingdale, (Ed.), Attention Deficit Disorder: Diagnostic, cognitive, and therapeutic understanding (pp. 37–66). New York: Spectrum Publications.

Chelune, G. J., Ferguson, W., Koon, R., & Dickey, T. O. (1986). Frontal lobe disinhibition in attention deficit disorder. *Child Psychiatry and Human Development, 16,* 221–235.

Chess, S., & Thomas, A. (1990). The New York Longitudinal Study (NYLS): The young adult periods. *Canadian Journal of Psychiatry, 35,* 557–561.

Csikszentmihalyi, M. (1990). *Flow: The psychology of optimal experience.* New York: HarperCollins.

Cunningham, C. E. (1990). A family systems approach to parent training. In R. A. Barkley, *Attention deficit hyperactivity disorder: A handbook for diagnosis and treatment.* New York: Guilford Press.

Douglas, V. I. (1984). The psychological processes implicated in ADD. In L. Bloomingdale (Ed.), *Attention Deficit Disorder: Diagnostic, cognitive, and therapeutic understanding.* New York: Spectrum Publications.

Gualtieri, C. T., Ondrusek, M. G., & Finley, C. (1985). Attention deficit disorder in adults. *Clinical Neuropharmacology, 8*(4), 343–356.

Hallowell, E. M., & Ratey, J. J. (1984). *Driven to distraction: The human story of attention deficit disorder in adults and children.* New York: Random House.

Hopkins, J., Perlman, T., Hechtman, L., & Weiss, G. (1979). Cognitive style in adults originally diagnosed as hyperactives. *Journal of Child Psychology and Psychiatry, 20*, 209–216.

Kagan, J. (1992). Behavior, biology, and the meanings of temperamental constructs. *Pediatrics, 90*, 510–513.

Kahn, E., & Cohen L. H. (1934). Organic drivenness: A brain stem syndrome and an experience. *New England Journal of Medicine, 210*, 748–756.

Kornetsky, C. (1970). Psychoactive drugs in the immature organism. *Psychopharmocologia, 17*, 105–136.

Lambert, N. M., & Windmiller, M. (1977). An exploratory study of temperament traits in a population of children at risk. *Journal of Special Education, 11*, 37–47.

Mannuzza, S., Klein, R. G., Bessler, A., Malloy, P., & LaPadula, M. (1993). Adult outcome of hyperactive boys. *Archives of General Psychiatry, 50*, 565–576.

Ratey, J., Greenberg, M. S., Bemporad, J. R., & Lindem, K. (1992). Unrecognized attention-deficit hyperactivity disorder in adults presenting for outpatient psychotherapy. *Journal of Child and Adolescent Psychopharmocology, 4*, 267–275.

Sagvolden, T., Wultz, B., Moser, E. I., Moser, M., & Morkrid, L. (1989). Results from a comparative neuropsychological research program indicate altered reinforcement mechanisms in children with ADD. In T. Sagvolden & T. Archer (Eds.), *Attention deficit disorder: Clinical and basic research.* (pp. 261–286) Hillsdale, NJ: Lawrence Erlbaum.

Shekim, W. O., Asarnow, R. F., Hess, E., Zaucha, K., & Wheeler, N. (1990). A clinical and demographic profile of a sample of adults with attention deficit hyperactivity disorder, residual state. *Comprehensive Psychiatry, 31*(5), 416–425.

Weiss, G., & Hechtman, L. T. (1993). *Hyperactive children grown up* (2nd ed.). New York: Guilford Press.

Weiss, G., Minde, K., Werry, J., Douglas, V., & Nemeth, E. (1971). Studies on the hyperactive child: VIII. Five-year follow-up. *Archives of General Psychiatry, 24*, 409–414.

Weiss, L. (1992). *Attention deficit disorder in adults: Practical help for sufferers and their spouses.* Dallas, TX: Taylor.

Wender, P. H. (1987). *The hyperactive child, adolescent, and adult.* New York: Oxford University Press.

Wender, P. H. (1985). The Utah Criteria in diagnosing attention deficit disorder. *Psychopharmacology Bulletin, 21*, 222–231.

Zentall, S., & Meyer, M. J. (1987). Self-regulation of stimulation for ADD-H children during reading and vigilance task performance. *Journal of Abnormal Child Psychology, 15*(4), 519–536.

13

Impact of Adult ADD on the Family

ELLEN B. DIXON

It is often the case in clinical enterprises that treatment has proceeded without the underpinnings of empirical data and often without the confidence that would be provided by a sound research base. This has certainly been the case for all of us working in the field of adult Attention Deficit Disorders. Many of us began only a few short years ago to evaluate adults with attention disorders whose problems were recognized because we had worked with their clearly ADHD children. At that time, we were developing diagnostic protocols that approximated our clinical needs but were not anchored in research data. For that matter, there was not even consensus as to what kinds of behavior patterns were characteristic of adults with Attention Deficit Disorders.

While we await empirical information, clinical data has accumulated about the challenges of family living for this population, and the demand has increased for strategies to assist ADD adults with the various areas of their lives that have been impacted by this condition. Not the least of these are the couple and family relationship issues, areas in the individual's life that are nearly always affected by this persistent neurodevelopmental pattern. All of us who work with this population have been besieged by requests for help in dealing with children and spouses. Additionally, there are the many requests from ADD adults for help in managing the incessant march of detail that makes up daily family life. Thus, many of us as clinicians find ourselves in the position of working with adults with ADD in the family and marital areas, and doing so in the absence of the research that one day will strengthen our understanding and streamline our interventions. This chapter then, dealing with the ADD adult and the family, is necessarily based on the opinions and observations of the frontline clinicians who have been working closely with this population, and it provides a preliminary look at the behavioral and clinical patterns that are emerging.

MODERATING FACTORS FOR ADD IN ADULTS

How well the ADD adult copes with the dailiness of family life seems related to a number of factors or moderator variables, the first of which is the severity of the attention deficit disorder. From Weiss and Hechtman's 15-year follow-up of hyperactive children, Hechtman (1991) reports that 66% of their subjects continued to exhibit "at least one disabling symptom of ADHD" (p. 416). From their review of the available studies, Weiss and Hechtman (1993) conclude that one third to one half of previously diagnosed ADHD children grow up to be essentially normal. They go on to conclude further that most studies indicate that about one third to one half of subjects studied at the time of young adulthood continue to be plagued by ADHD symptoms. Barkley (1993a) writes that over 75% of children with ADHD grow up to be adults with "significant social adjustment problems" (p. 3). Extrapolating from childhood incidence measures of 3–5% of the general population, this would suggest that from 1 to 3 adults out of 100 experience troubling levels of ADHD symptoms. On the other hand, many clinicians believe their experience suggests that the childhood incidence figures may be as high as 15%, leaving perhaps as many as 5 to 7 adults in 100 attempting to cope with family life in spite of significant ongoing ADHD symptoms.

Where the symptom pattern is mild, the individual functions well, troubled by little more, for example, than the frustration of a recalcitrant memory for the children's activity schedule, the need to make lists of daily tasks, an impatient personality, or a restless dissatisfaction with the level of housekeeping. The more severe the ongoing ADD, however, the more areas of family life are affected, and the more overwhelmed the individual feels. Not surprisingly, most of the adults seen in clinical practice fall in the moderate to severe range; it is primarily this group described in this chapter.

Other important moderator variables found clinically to predict the smoothness of family functioning for ADD adults include (1) comorbid conditions such as depression, anxiety, alcoholism, learning disabilities, and obsessive compulsive disorder; (2) the cognitive ability of the individual; (3) socioeconomic status; (4) degree of stress tolerance of the individual; (5) level of functionality of the spouse and amount of support available from the spouse; (6) number and severity of additional stressors such as job, commute time, need to care for aging parents, chronic illness; (7) number of children and the nature of their individual needs; (8) sources of outside support such as parents and close friends; and (9) whether the ADD has been identified and effectively treated.

According to Shekim (1990), ADD in adults is rarely present without coexisting conditions. The increased threat to organization and emotional stability that can be posed by these conditions is considerable.

> Current research suggests that ADHD, RT rarely occurs alone. Typically there is an associated diagnosis present–alcohol and drug use problems can complicate the picture in one third of the cases– minor chronic depression can occur in one quarter of the cases. Similarly, mood swings, highs and lows in mood and energy is also present in one quarter, anxiety problems with nervousness, sleep difficulties, concentration difficulties, muscular tension can be present in half of the cases. (p. 16)

The clinician working with an adult with ADD needs to carefully assess all of these moderating factors, especially the possible presence of comorbid conditions, in order to develop intervention strategies that are appropriate for that particular client. Keeping these multiple moderating factors in mind, the clinician can proceed to assess his or her client's functioning on the home front in terms of three major domains: household organization, parenting, and marital relationship issues. Of course not all adults with ADD are married, or have children, but our primary focus in this chapter is upon the functioning of the family unit as it is affected by ADD. Many adults with ADD regard their family life as a confusing, undifferentiated blur in which parenting issues, marital communication patterns, and the endless rush of chores and responsibilities all mix together. The therapist may provide a helpful framework for developing strategies and for seeking solutions by guiding his or her client to consider household management, parenting, and marital issues each in turn.

HOUSEHOLD ORGANIZATION

Organizing a household requires coordination of many unrelated parts and activities, and entropy is a constant threat. We are told by our ADD clients that they lose or forget their lists, fail to leave time for disruptions in the various routines, fail to anticipate how long things will take, fail to maintain and file paperwork and therefore can't find the papers they need to file insurance forms, pay bills, and maintain necessary correspondence. Organizational problems extend beyond overflowing desks and misplaced lists to poorly planned housekeeping schedules, piles of unsorted laundry, delays in important home repairs, and inefficiency in running Saturday errands.

Of course, these problems are not unique to persons with ADD. Just as the behavioral characteristics of ADD contain nothing that is not also true to a lesser degree in normals, so do the kinds of problems described above also reflect an intensification of those with which all adults have had experience. The problems evolve not from experiencing the normal demands of a busy life, but from the fact that the tasks must be accomplished *despite* problems of memory, attention, and organization and in spite of procrastination, overwhelmedness, inconsistency, and lack of stick-to-itiveness, and often in spite of marked impulsivity, difficulty with delayed gratification, restlessness, and low frustration tolerance. Also, there is an order of magnitude difference between the impact of occasional disarray and the effects of chronic inability to manage the daily routine of family life. The degree of chaos in some homes of adults with ADD is so marked that a number of adults or their spouses have brought photographs to therapy sessions, feeling that the severity of the problem would not be properly understood without such graphic evidence!

It does not require a great leap of imagination to understand how the daily "to do" list of a household becomes a quagmire for the individual with ADD whose weak suit is often the very adaptability and organization so needed to successfully fulfill the demands of the day. For example, a look at a hypothetical basic daily routine for a working mother of two might well include the following:

1. Up at five, make bed, shower, dress, fix hair and makeup.
2. Wake up kids, get them dressed.
3. Fix breakfast, pack lunches, clean up kitchen.
4. Get kids' teeth brushed and hair combed.
5. Be sure both have their coats and backpacks, check that both have their homework, and that one has his signed permission slip for the field trip.
6. Jot down the grocery items needed after work and pocket the list, put new book of checks in wallet, check to be sure of having the phone numbers of the insurance agent and exterminator to call on lunch hour.
7. Get kids, coats, backpacks, briefcase, and dry cleaning items into the car.
8. Stop and get gas, deliver kids and backpacks to before-school sitter, drop off dry cleaning, go to work.
9. Leave work, stop at grocery store, pick up kids.
10. Fix dinner, set table, help the kids eat.

11. Clean up, help kids with homework, referee sibling fights.
12. Call a friend about the charity bake sale.
13. Get kids bathed, teeth brushed, pajamas on and into bed, read them stories.
14. Run a load or two of laundry, balance the checkbook, pick up the family room.
15. Get ready for bed, collapse.

Of course, this is a very basic, pared-down list and includes only a few of the "required" activities that are demanded of parents. The list does not mention yard work, managing investments, finding time to be on a softball team, exercise, visits to the orthodontist, dentist, and doctor, scrubbing floors and cleaning out refrigerators, washing or repairing cars, quiet time with spouses, taking out the garbage, going to PTA meetings, maintaining schedules, buying clothes, soccer practice, or birthday parties.

Our clients tell us that they are frazzled, overwhelmed, and feel constantly on the verge of being unable to cope with the demands of family life, a fact that springs to life in the following vignette. Describing an attempt to straighten her living room, a client reported:

> I started out with my vacuum cleaner except for all the kids' toys which I had to stop and push over by the TV. Of course my 2-year-old kept bringing them back, plus she was crying because she hates the sound of the vacuum cleaner. But I had to do it. And then I was stacking up the newspapers, but I saw an article with a recipe I liked, so I went to the kitchen to see if I had coriander like it needed and boy, what a mess my spices were in! So I cleaned them up a little, which reminded me that my canister set was a mess. Pretty soon my husband came home and the living room was still a disaster which he was not very happy about, and pretty soon we were fighting.

This client was in tears when she told this story, which she felt was representative of her whole life. Fortunately, she suffered relatively little from coexisting conditions, although she was certainly at high risk for depression. If she had also struggled with a comorbid condition, as many ADD adults do, the additional impairment in concentration, focus, alertness, and organization brought about by depression, anxiety disorders, or certainly substance abuse would have rendered her nearly dysfunctional.

Another vignette offered by Ashlaw (1992) describes her own experience while performing a simple household task—ironing.

Set up board - get out iron, turn on - begin ironing - *no steam* - forgot to put water in iron - unplug, then turn iron off - at sink noticed faucet was very loose - bumped head while crawling under sink to investigate - finding loose part, went to get wrench - couldn't find wrench - remembered it is still under Christmas tree from tightening stand two days before - at the tree, noticed no water in the stand - forgot the wrench - looked for pitcher to get water in - found pitcher in dishwasher - filled with water, set on counter - continued to empty dishwasher. . . (p. 9)

When we consider these stories of relatively limited tasks fraught with such confusion and inefficiency, and then refer back to our hypothetical daily schedule, it is plain to see how many opportunities exist within the most simple and ordinary day for the ADD adult to experience failure. It is crucial for both the clinician and the non-ADD spouse to appreciate the level of effort and subsequent exhaustion experienced on a daily basis by adults with ADD as they struggle to fulfill their obligations.

ADD homemakers (usually women), have particularly difficult roles to maintain, as described by Nadeau (1990b) (see chapter 14, this volume, for further discussion of women with ADD).

The job of mother and housewife is a particularly difficult one for the ADHD adult because of its inherent lack of structure. Many women diagnosed as ADHD report that they performed well in high- functioning professional positions, but find themselves falling apart after the birth of their first, or sometimes second, child. Stress and irritability increase as the number of interruptions and crises increases. On the job they were able to shut their office door, quit accepting phone calls, and focus on their work for periods of time. At home they are awakened frequently at night, interrupted constantly while talking on the phone, and called by crying children in the next room while trying to write a grocery list. It is often when these women feel at the breaking point that they seek treatment for what they may label depression. (p.1)

Another vignette from my own practice, illustrates a female client who had reached such a "breaking point":

Mrs. L. arrived for her therapy session at 6:00 P.M. looking visibly exhausted. She had set herself the modest task of straightening and cleaning a guest room, but by 10:00 A.M., had succeeded only in stripping the bed and removing one box of stored items (this due to her remembering that she ought to water her plants, and to her beginning to reorder her linen closet before a call from a friend reminded her of her original task). At 10:00 her (also ADD) husband called from his office to ask her to bring his briefcase, which he had forgotten. She did so (a round-trip of 75 minutes) and arrived home to find a phone message from him saying that he couldn't make his joint tennis lesson at 1:00 with their adult son and asking that she please stand in for him. Angry but compliant, she showered, pulled on tennis togs, and went off to a lesson that ended at 1:45. On her way home she was attracted to a produce stand with a large display of tomatoes and decided to stock up on some fresh vegetables. Arriving home around 3:00, she remembered that she had agreed to pick up her daughter and a friend after school for a prearranged sleepover and dashed to the school, arriving 20 minutes late and finding the girls waiting worriedly in the principal's office. Her complaint, as always, was that she never could get anything done.

All of the stories related thus far feature females with ADD, perhaps because the greater share of household management responsibilities continue to fall on the shoulders of women, despite these "liberated" times. The problems, however, are certainly not unique to women. One man with ADD related, with discouragement, his inability to complete household projects:

> I seem to be able to get started on doing repairs or remodeling around the house, but I just never seem to get them finished. The bathroom in our master bedroom has been "under construction" for almost a year now. There are just a few more things I need to do, but other things seem to get in the way. Then there's the garage. My wife and I have been trying to clean out closets and give things away to charity. We get started and make piles of things in the garage, but I never remember to call Goodwill or take things to the dump, so now we can't even get into the garage. And paperwork, forget it! My wife took over paying the bills years ago after I bounced one too many checks.

Difficulties caused by poor organization in adults with ADD tend to create their own multiplicative trouble spots: bills paid late create cash flow problems; late meals push homework later into the evening and lead to disruptions in bedtime routines; lost keys mean getting to karate late which can lead to an angry or anxious child; forgetting to put gas in the car until you have to be somewhere in 20 minutes pushes the schedule back further, particularly if you forgot to get cash and left your credit card at home on the desk.

The problems with household management described above often lead to chronic marital stress, as described later in this chapter.

PARENTING

Ready or not, the young couple will typically progress from the management of a house or apartment to the management of a family. Here the burden is still more likely to fall upon the mother. If she is also employed, then even more flexibility, initiative, stamina, and planning are required. If either or both partners have ADD, the demands on their coping resources have just multiplied. Kelly and Ramundo (1993), writing in their popular book *You Mean I'm Not Lazy, Stupid, or Crazy?!*, have emphasized the importance to ADD couples of planning when to have children, taking into account spacing, personal and financial resources, the extra effort and expense that might be required if the child is ADD, and such issues as outside resources and ways to build in breaks and relief for each parent.

The adult whose ADD has been identified and treated early in adulthood has the opportunity to learn of the need for planning, simplification, and stress management, as he or she makes crucial life decisions. All too often, however, the adult with ADD seeks treatment after having made decisions earlier in life, either impulsively or with lack of awareness, which greatly increases their stress level and makes good parenting and household management that much more difficult.

For many adults with ADD, the problems of parenting center less around the increased organizational demands, although these are significant, and more around the requirements for managing behavior, setting limits, providing discipline, maintaining family harmony, accomplishing specific tasks such as mealtimes and bedtimes, and meeting the emotional needs of both the child and the parent. Threats to the accomplishment of these goals come primarily from two sources: the inherent ADD traits of the parent, and the 30–80% probability, reported by Biederman (cited in Barkley & Murphy, 1993), that one or more of the children will also have an attention deficit disorder. Adding to the confusion is the greater number of sibling conflicts that are present in families where there is ADHD (Barkley, 1990). Barkley (1990) also cites several studies suggesting that mothers of ADHD children are more likely to report higher levels of depression; he also presents empirical support from a study that documents not only greater depression in these mothers, but also lower parenting self-esteem and greater self-blame and social isolation (Mash & Johnston, 1983).

ADD Parents of ADD Children

Even children who are not naturally difficult to manage can become more so when reared by a parent who is impatient, inconsistent, easily frustrated, or moody. Similarly, even normal children respond poorly to a parent's inconsistency in discipline, erratic emotional availability, and inability to maintain boundaries or keep the peace. When the child (or children) also has ADD, the ADD adult must now develop the stamina, patience, and flexibility to parent a child who may be hyperactive, inattentive, impulsive, demanding, defiant, aggressive, overreactive, and undercontrolled. Not only will such a child be challenging to the parent, but he or she also will be less likely to meet the parent's expectations for a reciprocally nurturing and noncoercive relationship. Instead of realizing their image of quietly reading stories to their child, many ADD parents present clinicians with tales of exhaustion, embarrassment at their child's loud and noncompliant behavior, anger and bewilderment over their demanding nature and willfulness, confusion over how to discipline, frustrations over calls from teachers, and bitter disappointment over their inability to be the kind of parent they had hoped to be.

When an ADD adult must parent an ADD child, the sources of difficulty are seemingly endless. In such frequently seen situations, the problems are not merely additive, but also create their own synergy, as illustrated in the following vignette:

> Ms. P., a single parent, is a restless, perfectionistic, reactive individual with diagnosed Attention Deficit Disorder. Her 8-year-old daughter has been diagnosed with ADD with hyperactivity. After dinner, Ms. P. tries to help her daughter with homework, but admits that she hates to "waste" the whole hour. To save time, she tries to read the newspaper and cook a batch of chili for use later in the week. Her daughter, Jennifer, angry, tired, frustrated, and peeved that she does not have her mother's full attention, begins to cry and refuses to proceed with the homework. Ms. P. begins to threaten Jennifer with an early bedtime if she doesn't get back to her math problems immediately. Jennifer returns to her homework, makes a mistake on the next problem, then wads up the paper and throws it away. Ms. P. retrieves the work sheet, but Jennifer refuses to work on the now-crumpled paper, pushes her book on the floor, and then ignores her mother's repeated and angry demands that she recommence the homework. Ms. P., now thoroughly frustrated herself, throws her newspaper on the floor and stalks off. She comes back later to offer Jennifer some cookies if she will do her math. Jennifer sullenly accepts the cookies. After eating the cookies, Jen-

nifer will only do two more problems and then quits. At this point, Ms. P. gives up and orders Jennifer to bed. After a brief tantrum, Jennifer is wrestled into bed, where she tosses and turns for about an hour before falling to sleep. In the meantime, Ms. P. has forgotten the chili on the stove, which is now scorched.

Such a story illustrates how some of the emotional characteristics of ADD can negatively impact a parent's ability to set up necessary accommodations, to structure interactions, and to provide appropriate consequences to behavior. The inner resources of these parents are strained continually as they fight to maintain their own precarious equilibrium. These parents, who struggle so with self-discipline and who are themselves so forgetful, inconstant, and impatient, have enormous difficulty with the unrelenting demands for consistency and constancy presented by their ADD children. In fact, they are typically unable to apply child management principles with the necessary consistency and creativity and therefore sometimes find themselves contending with households that at times approach anarchy, further overwhelming the ADD parent.

Potential for Abuse in the ADD Family

A concern that the clinician needs to watch for is the possibility that a parent with ADD may become so overwhelmed by prolonged struggles with an ADD child that verbal or physical abuse may occur. Combining the low frustration tolerance and short fuse of an adult with ADD with a defiant, reactive child has the potential for unintended disaster. In addition to teaching consistent and effective parenting techniques, the clinician needs to teach such a parent explicit tactics to defuse potentially dangerous interactions before they reach the danger zone. Such parents need quiet time away from their child, need the active support and intervention of another parent or adult relative during times of high stress, and need to learn to strategically separate themselves from their child before they lose control.

Kelly and Ramundo (1993) stress that adults in the household should continually keep their finger on the pulse of the family's emotional status, with the premise that awareness of mounting stress levels at least provides an opportunity to back down on the expectations of family members, thereby preventing potentially damaging explosions.

Establishing and Maintaining Boundaries

Kelly and Ramundo (1993) address the need for mutual respect of boundaries and the opportunity for individual family members to be able to create what they refer to as "rest and relaxation zones." Although these strategies, as well as others they suggest, appear to presuppose relatively well-functioning parents in spite of their presumed ADD, the strategies are nevertheless useful in outlining a core of basic concepts which, if parents could learn to implement them, could help in containing the natural chaos that often prevails in families with ADD.

In order to accomplish setting boundaries and establishing "R&R" zones, Kelly and Ramundo suggest designating areas in the house for quiet activities, such as reading and studying, while noisy activities be conducted as far away from the quiet places as possible. They also suggest that some of these activities may perhaps be conducted with headphones so as not to disturb other family members. They emphasize that members of the family should each have their own retreats, where they will not be disturbed.

Recognizing the need for more specific means of enforcing these boundaries than might normally be necessary in a family, they suggest a number of ways to achieve the goals of providing for family members' emotional needs. These include setting aside specific quiet times, instituting a brief period of mandatory silence if the noise level has exceeded certain limits, requiring all family members to ask permission when borrowing any item belonging to someone else, imposing a "stop-look/listen-speak" procedure for interactions, and setting up a well-stocked message center in a highly frequented area of the household (Kelly and Ramundo, 1993).

Family Communication Patterns

Kelly and Ramundo (1993) also recognize the importance of special attention being given to the communication patterns within such households, and they specifically recommend rules against all communications that require yelling and that are conducted while scrambling to complete another task. Both of these rules recognize (1) the difficulties that individuals with ADD have in splitting attention and (2) the opportunities for missed communication that can occur when communication is done on the run or accomplished at high volume in order to get the attention of someone in another part of the house. They also suggest that there be rules against inappropriate teasing of family members, which is reflective of the literal interpretation of comments often made by individuals with ADD, and of the difficulty that some individuals with ADD have in discerning the effect of their comments on others. With regard to their stop-look-and-speak procedure, they urge that family members be enjoined against interrupting anyone in the household who is engaged in a task requiring concentration. They do recognize that for young children such a discrimination might be difficult, particularly in light of events that they may personally interpret as emergencies. If necessary, Kelly and Ramundo even recommend going so far as to set up a list of events that might or might not be considered emergent to the child.

Family Management Strategies

In order to develop some general rules for managing difficult situations, Kelly and Ramundo (1993) have chosen meal times as an example of a common family crisis point. In the case of discordant and disorganized mealtimes, the authors suggest a brief set of rules which include:

1. Reduce or eliminate unnecessary distractions; that is, turn off radios, televisions, and stereos, put away newspapers, and put the telephone on the answering machine
2. Establish a family signal that includes a predetermined cue that noise levels are getting out of control
3. Make a "no arguments at the dinner table" rule
4. Plan a weekly work detail ahead of time in order to reduce arguments, disorganization, and last-minute confusion
5. Maintain order by establishing a structure (here they refer to any rituals that are useful for the individual family, such as storytelling, individually relating the events of the day, etc.)
6. Change the rules (which refers to the appropriateness of giving an individual family member permission to leave the table if he or she is having a particularly troublesome day)
7. If all else fails, eliminate family meals (pp. 223–224)

This last suggestion is a particularly poignant one, in that it implies the reality which some families have experienced that it is not possible to have relaxed or congenial family meals in the usual sense of the word. When smaller units of the family are fed at different times, harmony is sometimes easier to maintain, and the authors wisely recognize that in a family where there are members with ADD, sometimes normal family conventions must be adapted as they no longer serve the function of family cohesiveness.

Reframing ADD Within the Family

Hallowell (1993b) suggests setting the stage for smoother functioning by redefining the ADD as a set of no-fault characteristics that include special gifts as well as difficulties. He also exhorts families to emphasize that ADD is not a moral issue, and that an individual should not be blamed for having this disorder. In line with his focus on redefining the individual with ADD, Hallowell strongly proposes that the family begin to see the problems caused by members' ADD as being family issues rather than issues of the individuals who exhibit the difficulties. He rightfully points out that because of the nature of ADD, fallout from this disorder becomes a matter affecting everyone's life in the family quite intimately. In similar manner to Kelly and Ramundo, Hallowell urges families to "normalize" the disorder by treating it as they would any other condition within the family and by not letting these problems dominate the family process. In a final conceptual piece of advice, Hallowell emphasizes the very important need for families with ADD members to maintain hopefulness about their future.

Defusing Conflicts Within the ADD Family

Hallowell (1993b) uses the term "the big struggle" generically to refer to the potential for frequently occurring major battles and blowups that occur in the day-to-day lives of individuals with ADD, especially those whose disorders have not been fully defined or treated. The primary tool suggested for the avoidance of the big struggle is negotiation—spouse with spouse, parents with children, and siblings with siblings. It is suggested that the terms of these agreements and settlements be put in writing whenever possible. Like Kelly and Ramundo, Hallowell also suggests the use of therapists when problems appear resistant to solution by the family members themselves. Other specific suggestions from Hallowell include agreeing to temporary deliberate disengagement in the face of growing emotionality, giving everyone a chance to be heard in the family, focusing on positive approaches rather than negative ones, being clear about who in the family has responsibility for what, making time for spouses to confer with each other, creating specific plans for target problem areas, remembering the value of negotiated agreements, holding family brainstorming sessions, and remaining attentive to the many boundary issues that arise within the families of individuals with ADD. He also makes the important point that parents need to be on guard against the expression of extreme accepting and loving behavior one day and a negative, rejecting attitude the next. Hallowell recognizes the difficulty in maintaining emotional equilibrium within a family that has individual members with ADHD, but he stresses making a conscious effort to keep parental overreactivity and fluctuation at a minimum.

Parent Training

Kelly and Ramundo (1993) have taken a position of "normalizing" the family with ADD members, and certainly there are a great many households in which such an approach to family management will be extremely useful. For those of us in clinical practice, however, these suggestions are a good starting spot and a good way of organizing oneself conceptually; but we find that parents with ADD often need, in addition, a more strategic set of guidelines for working with their challenging families.

Because the ADD parents themselves have such enormous difficulty with consistency, self-discipline, and understanding the subtleties of the rules they are attempting to implement, Barkley's (1987) more strategic approach to parenting has much to offer. Although we recognize that the levels of consistency and planning required for the implementation of these strategies are not natural for any parents, much less parents with ADD, nevertheless, proper training in these techniques and proper support and implementation until the necessary principles and flexibility have been learned can be crucially important to the successful running of a household where there are both parents and children who suffer from ADD. These strategies include carefully specified approaches to reinforcement and time-out, as well as other skills for parenting challenging children.

Differences Between Mothers and Fathers in ADD Families

Another aspect of adult ADHD functioning within families, which has repeatedly presented itself clinically, is the too-frequently-seen lack of support given by one spouse to another, especially when that spouse is not responsible for requiring the types of child behavior that precipitate manifestations of the attention deficit disorder in the child. For example, a father who works until dinner time or later will often not see the kinds of reactions with which the mother must contend when she requires a child to come in from play, do his homework, or pick up his room. The father may wrongly conclude that the problem is not as significant as is reported by the mother and may fail to support her in her request for assistance. This creates not only parenting difficulties but also spousal conflict.

Another frequently seen variation is that although both parents are aware that they may have a child who is difficult to parent, one parent, more typically the father, will discover that he is able to elicit a much higher level of compliance from the child than is the mother. He may, again wrongly, assume that if the mother were to address the child in the same manner that he does, then the problems would no longer exist. In fact, there is extensive anecdotal support for what seems to be the reality that a great many children do respond more appropriately to their fathers than to their mothers. Whether this is because, as has been variously proposed, of the father's more commanding voice, his more immediate insistence upon compliance, his lesser degree of familiarity to the child, or because he is making different kinds of requests of the child, has not been adequately researched. It is valuable to point out, however, that children do respond differently to individuals and situations in their lives, and parents, particularly those who are themselves struggling with attention deficit disorders, need to be taken seriously in their concerns, and supported.

Overidentification with the ADD Child

Another issue for ADD parents who are raising children with attention deficit disorders is the sensitivity of many of these parents to what they perceive their child to be going through, as they relate the child's difficulties to their own experiences. Such sensitivity is a powerful motivator in helping a parent modulate what might otherwise be more frequent expressions of exasperation and anger. It can also interfere with appropriate parenting when a parent becomes fearful of the necessary structure and discipline in the mistaken belief that this will be harmful to the child. When a parent's own insecurities, low self-esteem, and unhappy memories of childhood prevent him or her from exercising needed controls, then not only does the child suffer, but the household can suffer as well.

One family that contacted our clinic illustrated this pattern in the extreme:

> The mother, who had experienced much unhappiness as a child in school due to learning disabilities and to a very shy, sensitive temperament, decided to "home school" her shy, awkward, ADD/LD daughter. The mother sought an educational evaluation following conflicts with her husband over whether the daughter should continue to be home-schooled or enter a private-school environment. To the mother's enormous dismay we informed her that her daughter was several years behind her age-mates academically and had signs of anxiety and extremely poor social adjustment as well. In her attempts to protect her child, the mother had created even more difficulties.

A variant of this overidentification is the undiagnosed ADD father who sees his child's behavior as "all boy" and just like himself, and who refuses to see the problems as meriting special intervention.

> In one extreme situation, a boy with ADHD whose parents were divorced, moved between his mother's house, where he was taking Ritalin and was parented in a highly structured fashion, to his father's house, where the father refused to give him medication and where he spent his weekends largely unsupervised. The benefits of helpful and appropriate interventions at school and at his mother's home were rapidly undone by his father on a regular basis.

It is useful to point out that many adults with ADD were themselves products of households in which their own parents did not understand or parent them very well, and therefore they often bring inadequate skills and expectations to the business of parenting.

Sibling Issues in the ADD Family

The matter of sibling relationships is beginning to be addressed clinically. Repeatedly we see families in which the non-ADD sibling, by virtue of being easy to manage, not only receives less parental attention but also finds that he or she must frequently subjugate personal wishes in the interest of placating or getting along with an ADD sibling. These children must cope with the chaos that can be created by an ADD child, the disruptions to routines that occur because of the ADD child's special needs, the emotional outbursts that often come with such children, the invasions of their own privacy and the insensitivity to their own needs that they frequently experience at the hands of an ADD sibling. Consider the following vignette:

> Joan is the ADD mother of a 7-year-old hyperactive ADD son and two non-ADD children (ages 4 and 6). She has never learned to manage her son's behavior and describes a recent trip to the community pool with her children.
>
> "We hadn't been there 10 minutes before Jeremy started begging for money to buy candy. When I wouldn't give it to him, he got angry and started pushing and dunking his brother. I kept telling him to leave him alone, but he wouldn't, so I made him come out of the pool. He was so mad at me that he was yelling, and I couldn't watch Evan and Missy, so I had to make them leave the pool while I tried to calm Jeremy down. I ended up offering him the money for candy just to stop the scene, but I know the other two don't understand. It wasn't fair for them to have to leave the pool, and it wasn't fair that they didn't get candy until later just because they were willing to wait."

It is essential that the clinician working with an ADD family not overlook the needs of the non-ADD siblings. Just as the parents can easily become caught up in the demands for crisis management posed by the ADD child, it can happen in the clinical setting as well. Parents can support their non-ADD children by recognizing their frustration as valid, by trying to arrange space in the household to allow the non-ADD children a more quiet, ordered space to which to retreat, such as a private bedroom, and by making a special effort to regularly spend time alone with their non-ADD child.

COUPLES' ISSUES

Persons with ADD often take with them into adulthood derivative problems of self-doubt, low self-esteem, personal sensitivity, and interpersonal skill deficits. Coupled with specific ADD traits, this mix substantially raises the probabilities that marriages with an ADD individual are loaded with potential pitfalls. Again, there are not yet empirical data, but clinicians engaged in the treatment of such high-risk couples have begun to write about their experiences with this phenomenon. Some have begun to describe the patterns they observe in the dynamics of these couples, and others have begun to report the kinds of interventions they have found useful.

Recognizing and Identifying ADD Patterns in Couples

Hallowell (1993a) refers to the inherent unpredictability of life with an ADD spouse and the emotional responses of the non-ADD spouse, and refers to the fact that the non-ADD spouse often mistakenly assumes that the forgetfulness, irresponsibility, behavioral variability, emotional reactivity, and so on, are under the voluntary control of the spouse. With such misapprehension, opportunities abound for worsening of the spousal relationship. Again, as is so often the case, emphasis is placed on the necessity for accurate diagnosis to provide a baseline for a common understanding among the individuals who are involved. Hallowell makes an often stated but very important point: The behavioral characteristics of the adult with ADHD often mimic other disorders, and misattributions are easily and frequently made. He gives as an example:

> A husband comes home and tunes out by reading the newspaper, has trouble paying attention when talking about feelings, drinks too much, and struggles with self-esteem while not paying attention to his wife's repeated attempts to get close to him. Or a wife daydreams chronically, feels depressed, complains of never having reached her potential and feels trapped at home. (p. 13)

As the author points out, these symptoms do not automatically suggest an attention deficit disorder to most individuals, yet to professionals who work with this disorder, it is a familiar pattern.

Like others writing in this field, Nadeau (1990a) stresses the necessity for accurate diagnosis and treatment, and describes the value of psychotherapy in combination with possible medication treatment. The dynamics of the relationship between spouses in an ADD couple can be quite complex, with members needing to understand fully not only the roles that they play but also the ways in which they can learn the necessary problem-solving skills. Writing in *ADDendum*, Nadeau (1991b) has done a particularly good job of articulating observations from her experiences in working with such couples and has begun to organize these experiences into a schema that could be useful as a model for exploring ADD couples issues with new clients. In another piece, Nadeau (1991a) focuses on couples issues, and addresses marriages where both individuals have ADD and those where only one spouse is thus impaired. The dynamics of these two relationships are seen by Nadeau as somewhat different.

The Dual ADD Marriage

In marriages where there are two ADD adults, both contributing to confusion and disorganization, Nadeau (1991a) describes a tendency toward mutual blaming. She also mentions the easily imagined, more extreme level of dysfunction that could be present in such families when neither spouse is able to attend adequately to the necessary nuts and bolts of family operation. On the more positive side, these couples may be more likely to forgive and overlook each other's shortcomings, with neither expecting or demanding high functioning from the other. Nadeau also reports that in her experience when "both spouses are relatively comfortable with confusion and crossed signals, then the tension level between them is much lower" (p. 2). This is not to minimize the realities of the problems with day-to-day functioning, however. Here is a clinical example from my own practice:

> Both Mr. and Mrs. Y. have ADD. They were able to laugh in a counseling session when telling a recent story about their lives together, when in fact, life has been quite frustrating, as neither is able to organize the household. They recently decided that they needed counseling after an outing to a local dinner theater. They had expected to leave home together at 7:00 P.M., but Mrs. Y. called to say that she had forgotten an important report that had to be finished at work and would therefore be a few minutes late. She came home at 7:30 to find a frustrated husband who could not locate the small binoculars that he wanted to take with him. She helped locate the binoculars (inexplicably left in a bathroom drawer), and they dashed out of the house, now 35 minutes late. They soon discovered that neither knew the location of the dinner theater, so they had to call for directions. Arriving breathless but only about 15 minutes late, all would have been well except that neither had remembered to bring the tickets.

Spouse "Burnout" and Codependency

More commonly, Nadeau finds herself dealing with couples in which only one spouse has the ADD, while the partner is more organized and orderly. In fact, Nadeau reports that in her clinical experience, individuals with ADD tend to be attracted to more organized spouses as a form of needed complementarity. She reports that sometimes these marriages can evolve from complementarity into a more unbalanced parent-child relationship, where one becomes responsible for the other to such an extent that it pervasively affects the dynamics of the relationship. She describes a common dynamic that develops when the organized spouse takes on increasing responsibility, perhaps even encouraging the dependency of the

ADD spouse, leading to increased tension and disequilibrium within the relationship, as in the following vignette:

> Marie sought psychotherapy several years after her midlife marriage to a highly intelligent, but totally disorganized husband. Since his recent retirement she noted that without the structure of a daily work schedule his disorganization had reached intolerable levels. Despite good intentions, his days seemed to be frittered away performing meaningless, nonessential activities while he was unable to consistently perform even the most basic and necessary household tasks. Marie, a few years younger than her husband, continued to work full-time, with mounting anger and resentment toward her spouse with ADD. Through her psychotherapy she recognized strong codependent patterns in herself which had motivated her to marry and "save" her charming, but dysfunctional husband.

Weiss (1992) introduces the concept of codependency as a way of understanding the unbalanced relationships that can develop within ADD couples. In so doing, she highlights the issue of failure to take personal responsibility, resulting, as in the case just described, in the bifurcation of roles between the more scattered and seemingly irresponsible ADD partner who presents as helpless and needy and the responsible non-ADD partner who begins to take responsibility for the shortcomings of the spouse. Weiss also proposes mutual inadequacy as the conceptual glue holding these unbalanced relationships together. In her own clinical experience, she has found that the ADD partner often responds positively to considerate questioning by the non-ADD spouse, particularly in situations where the partner is feeling flooded and overwhelmed. Weiss sees this as one of the ways out of a codependent relationship: The spouse helps the ADD partner to focus through the questioning process, but does not take responsibility for that person's feelings or actions.

Nadeau (1993) finds that in her experience the codependent relationship tends to be an essentially unstable one, with increasing frustration and difficulties experienced by both spouses. She focuses not only on the need for diagnosis of and treatment for the ADD spouse, but also on the need for specifically targeted support for the non-ADD partner, who has often been carrying more than his or her share of the load within the relationship. She states: "It is also critical that the therapist appreciate the level of chronic stress and resentment the spouse may be feeling, and pay adequate attention to the needs of this highly fatigued support system" (p. 1).

Spouses of ADD adults struggle with feeling resentment. Having to always be available to meet the needs of the ADD partner, feeling unhappiness at the requirement that their own needs often go unmet, feeling unappreciated, and feeling overburdened in the day-to-day management of the household and relationship are also common concerns of the spouses of ADD adults (Miller & Stephens, 1993; Nadeau, 1993). The clinician working with such a couple needs to help the non-ADD spouse recognize his or her contribution to the marital imbalance, and help the couple to develop clearer roles, boundaries, and a healthier degree of separation. Hallowell (1993a) makes a particularly useful point in his multiple references to the roles and dynamics involved in spousal ADD relationships. These couples need to make an important distinction between the value of dividing tasks and expectations based on individual strengths and weaknesses and allowing roles to develop that are dynamically unstable and perpetuate and strengthen the dysfunctional aspects of the relationship.

Denial Patterns in Spouses with ADD

An example of both the disorganization and the denial, or lack of awareness, that can characterize ADD adults is reflected in the following vignette:

Cindy was attracted to Mike because of his great enthusiasms and his wonderful sense of fun. Once they were married, however, she found that Mike was not able to translate his appealing energy into usefulness in the day-to-day operation of their household. He regularly had wonderful ideas, such as a do-it-yourself remodeling of the bathroom. On that project, he got so far as to strip the old wallpaper, take off the cabinet fronts, and remove the medicine chest before losing interest and diving into a new project. Cindy reports with exasperation that the bathroom is a wreck, the dining room table has been covered with his files and papers for weeks, and her cheerful and high-energy husband has in the meantime begun a woodworking project in the garage which requires them to park the cars in the driveway.

Cindy came into our clinic, the final straw being the need for her to get up 15 minutes earlier in order to scrape her windshield and warm up her car. Once she was here, she also mentioned her impatience and exasperation over the fact that Mike had not only forgotten to make a very important annual insurance payment for the two of them but also for the last 4 months had been 2 or 3 days late with the mortgage payment. Cindy was beginning to be worried that the family's security could be jeopardized by Mike's disorganization. When she had offered to take over some of the paperwork for the household, Mike had, again quite cheerfully, asserted that he was able to handle that part of the household operation and did not need assistance.

It is not unusual for the initial contact with a clinician to be made by the spouse of the ADD adult, such as the one described in the preceding example. The clinician then needs to work to bring the spouse with ADD into the treatment process, to help him or her work through their defensiveness and denial, and then to treat the ADD as well as address the marital issues.

Intimacy Issues

Clinical information is also surfacing about physical intimacy and sexuality issues in ADD couples. (See chapter 12, this volume, for more discussion of intimacy issues.) Hallowell (1993a) reports, "The impact of ADD upon sexuality is poorly understood. However, we have seen many people in our practice, both men and women, who complain of either an inability to pay attention during sex well enough to enjoy it, or the opposite: a hyperfocused sexuality. How these traits relate to ADD is hard to say" (p. 13).

Nadeau (1993) also reports observing physical and emotional intimacy problems among the ADD couples she treats. She attributes these difficulties essentially to the poor communication patterns common within such marriages, and she states, "The ADD adult may be so wrapped up in his own thoughts that he is rarely able to establish the closeness and communication which can lead to good sex. The spouse may eventually reject a sexual relationship because she feels that there is little intimacy or gratification for her in the sexual act" (p. 2).

A degree of tactile defensiveness has been reported to Weiss (1992) by her clients, and this has obvious implications for intimate relationships. She reports clients who find touch uncomfortable, even painful, and annoying. She also refers to the tendency of individuals with ADD to seek novelty, and states that an intimate routine which has been pleasurable on one or more occasions may not continue to be pleasurable to the ADD adult, who may find himself or herself needing more variety. Like Nadeau and Hallowell, Weiss emphasizes the importance of skillful and persistent verbal communication, and she also stresses the value of experimentation and flexibility.

Other Issues in ADD Marriages

Nadeau (1991a) outlines specific areas in which she has observed chronic dysfunction within ADD couples. She highlights the areas of money management, clutter and disorganization, imbalance in roles, forgetfulness, chronic lateness, frequent moves and job changes, and social and interpersonal problems. These are the issues around which the couples with whom she works have developed the stress and dissatisfactions that lead them to therapy. Similarly, Weiss and Hechtman (1993) present a representative couples vignette highlighting frequently seen problems of poor problem solving, failure to finish things, impatience, poor communication and difficulty in listening, lack of planning, and sexual problems (p. 396).

Myers, writing in *ADD-Vantage* (1993), reports on a recent meeting of a local support group for spouses and significant others of ADD adults. He describes the problems presented by these individuals as including:

1. Learning to ascertain the degree to which their spouse's problems are attributable to ADD versus normal life problems
2. Being made to feel at fault themselves as a result of a long-standing relationship with an ADD individual
3. Having feelings of anger
4. Needing to look at the intent of the ADD spouse rather than the actual behavior
5. Learning how to encourage the ADD spouse to accept help
6. Dealing with the process of denial of the illness—a pattern seen in both the ADD adult and the partner

This list of concerns generated by a group of adults with ADD and their spouses broadly covers the concerns addressed in this chapter, succinctly communicating to the clinician the heart of the difficult struggles they face as couples and families.

SUMMARY

In summary, clinical experience with ADD adults who are coping with households, families, and partner relationships reveals patterns of adaptation that all too often fail to satisfy and are in themselves cause for frustration. Often these difficulties are directly traceable to the core ADD characteristics as described by Hallowell and Ratey (1994); sometimes they are clearly derivative from these core characteristics, at other times (such as in the sensitivity to touch described by Weiss) other psychological or neurological factors may be involved.

This chapter has attempted to impart an awareness of the common patterns described to clinicians by their ADD adult clients who are coping with family life. As is true of other psychological disorders, the clients who are seeking help and from whom these patterns derive are suffering from moderate-to-severe levels of ADD. These clinical impressions clearly highlight the need for field and experimental research that could refine and quantify the clinically described patterns, and provide models for intervention and evaluation.

258   *A Comprehensive Guide to Attention Deficit Disorder in Adults*

REFERENCES

Ashlaw, J. (1992). Adult ADD: A two-front war. *ADDendum, 9,* 9.

Barkley, R. A. (1987). *Defiant children: A clinician's manual for parent training.* New York: Guilford Press.

Barkley, R. A. (Ed.). (1990). *Attention deficit hyperactivity disorder: A handbook for diagnosis and treatment.* New York: Guilford Press.

Barkley, R. A. (1993). An update on draft of DSM-IV criteria for ADHD. *The ADHD Report, 1,* 7.

Barkley, R. A., & Murphy, K. (1993). Differential diagnosis of Adult ADHD: Some controversial issues. *The ADHD Report, 1*(4), 1–3.

Goldstein, S., & Goldstein, M. (1990). *Managing attention deficit disorders in children.* New York: Wiley.

Hallowell, E. M. (1993a). Living and loving with attention deficit disorder: Couples where one partner has ADD. *CH.A.D.D.ER, 7,* pp. 13–15.

Hallowell, E. M. (1993b). Twenty five tips on the management of ADD within families. *Challenge, 7,* p. 3.

Hallowell, E. M., & Ratey, J. J. (1994). *Driven to distraction.* New York: Pantheon Books.

Hechtman, L. (1991). Resilience and vulnerability in long term outcome of attention deficit hyperactivity disorder. *Canadian Journal of Psychiatry, 20,* 415–421.

Kelly, K., & Ramundo, P. (1993). *You mean I'm not lazy, stupid or crazy?!* Cincinnati: Tyrell & Jerem Press.

Mash, E. J., & Johnston, C. (1983). Parental perceptions of child behavior problems, parenting self-esteem, and mothers' reported stress in younger and older hyperactive and normal children. *Journal of Consulting and Clinical Psychology, 51,* 68–99.

Miller, B., & Stephens, S. M. (1993). Working it out: The challenges of relationships. *LDA/Newsbriefs, 28,* 11.

Myers, R. (1993). Spouses premier meeting review. *ADD-Vantage, 2,* 6.

Nadeau, K. G. (1990a). ADD in adults: Diagnosis and treatment. *Chesapeake Bulletin, 2,* p. 3.

Nadeau, K. G. (1990b). The ADHD adult from the inside out. *Chesapeake Bulletin, 2,* 1.

Nadeau, K. G. (1991a). If your spouse has ADHD...*Chesapeake Bulletin, 3,* 2–4.

Nadeau, K. G. (1991b). Till ADD do us part? Maybe not. *ADDendum, 6,* p. 3.

Nadeau, K. G. (1993). Partners of ADD adults. *Chesapeake Bulletin, 5,* p. 1.

Shekim, W. (1990). Adult attention deficit hyperactivity disorder, residual state (ADHD, RS). *CH.A.D.D.ER, 4,* p. 16.

Weiss, L. (1992). *Attention deficit disorder in adults.* Dallas, TX: Taylor.

Weiss, G., & Hechtman, L. T. (1993). *Hyperactive children grown up* (2nd ed.). New York: Guilford Press.

14

Special Diagnostic and Treatment Considerations in Women with Attention Deficit Disorder

JOHN J. RATEY, ANDREA C. MILLER,
AND KATHLEEN G. NADEAU

Attention Deficit Disorder (ADD) in women can be like the wolf in sheep's clothing. The recognition of attentional problems and the diagnosis of ADD in women escapes even the best clinicians, because these women often lack the typical symptoms of hyperactivity and impulsivity in childhood or adulthood, and because the social filters through which we view women's behavior often are brought to bear upon our interpretation of symptoms.

Women with ADD may be prone to exhibit symptoms of depression and anxiety, and it is not surprising that these symptoms mislead clinicians away from an underlying attention deficit. Their anxiety and depression, whether comorbid with the ADD or a consequence of it, can be made that much more salient by the manner in which ADD symptoms interfere with their attempt to live up to social norms and role expectations. The biologically driven problem of not being able to maintain focus, attention, and connection can be a hammer hitting away at the hearts of these women. Their emotional lability and affective over- or underresponsiveness, in conjunction with their pain over not being able to maintain connection, and their inability to maintain a groundedness, can be mistaken for borderline personality disorder or phobic disorders. Thus, the common clues we have guiding us toward diagnosis are not obvious, while other symptoms and comorbid disorders serve to disguise the real problem. Yet, there the ADD still lurks, with its internal reality of restlessness, boredom, cognitive and affective impulsivity, disorganization and distractibility, and, of course, an inability to pay attention.

This chapter discusses the specific theme of attentional and organizational problems in women, based on our clinical experience in evaluating and treating these women, and on reports in the literature. It is an attempt to illustrate the phenomenology of ADD in women through the eyes of these women, as well as to discuss particular issues that may add to, or detract from, our ability to detect the ADD. These issues are neurobiological, as gender-related neurobiological tendencies may make diagnosis more difficult; they are psychological, as a woman's trend toward internalization rather than externalization and acting out makes diagnosis more complicated; and they are social and cultural, as our gender-related norms and expectations not only color our own ability to recognize the ADD but also influence and complicate the lives of ADD women in ways that are damaging and painful, leading to low self-esteem and a global sense of failure.

THE CLINICAL PICTURE: SYMPTOM DIFFERENCES BETWEEN MEN AND WOMEN AND THE RISK OF DELAYED DIAGNOSIS

It is generally believed that the prevalence of ADD in males is 3 to 9 times as great as that in females, based on epidemiological and clinical studies (Barkley, 1990). However, girls and women with ADD may be underreported and underdiagnosed. Even when ADD is identified in girls or adolescents, the diagnosis is made at a much later age than in their male counterparts (Huessy, 1990; Silver, 1992). The increased probability of ADD males to engage in aggressive and antisocial behavior makes it more likely that they will come to the attention of a clinician. Their more overt hyperactivity leads to significant problems in school and in the home, which also contributes to the likelihood that a teacher, parent, or someone else will notice behaviors that seem inappropriate for the child's age (Breen & Altepeter, 1990). Girls show a trend toward less comorbid conduct disorders than boys, have less behavioral problems, and are not as impulsive as boys (Berry, Shaywitz, & Shaywitz, 1985; Faraone, Biederman, Keenan, & Tsuang, 1991). And, although girls and boys with ADD show equal degrees of inattentiveness, parents of inattentive boys seek help more frequently than parents of inattentive girls (McGee, Williams, & Silva, 1987).

As one might suspect, a recent study (Brown, Abramowitz, Madan-Swain, Eckstrand, & Dulcan, 1989) found that girls with ADD had more internalized symptoms than boys, usually manifested as anxiety and depression, and were more socially withdrawn. As Silver (1992) states, "A girl with ADHD who is doing poorly in school and feeling frustrated might withdraw and appear disinterested or depressed. A boy with the same problems might misbehave and get into trouble. The boy is more likely to be recognized and diagnosed" (p. 57). It has been suggested that girls "suffer silently" with the disorder (Brown, Madan-Swain, & Baldwin, 1991). And yet their problems with peers and with academic work grow more pronounced as they make their way through school-age years, in contrast to ADD boys, whose hyperactivity and agressiveness are not unacceptable to their male peers (Berry et al., 1985).

For many girls with ADD, true behavioral problems begin after puberty, and it also seems that emotional overreactivity, mood swings, and impulsivity increase in severity during the teenage years (Huessy, 1990). The worsening of many conditions at or near puberty—for example, anorexia nervosa in adolescent girls—may be due to the spurt in sex hormones (Geshwind & Galaburda, 1985). Many women with ADD report that their adolescent years were troubled, as they embarked upon painful and destructive paths of promiscuity, fights with parents, and running away from home. Other ADD women, whose ADD is not accompanied by hyperactivity, report that adolescence was a period of isolation and utter compliance. In fact, many experts in the field now believe that ADD without hyperactivity is probably much more common in women than in men. This subtype, which DSM-IV calls AD/HD, Predominantly Inattentive Type, is more prone to anxiety disorders (Lahey, Schaughency, Hynd, Carlson, & Nieves, 1987) and is more difficult to diagnose. Unfortunately, as researchers and clinicians have noted, it appears that the group of ADD children and adolescents most often missed is composed of females who are only distractible.

Peer rejection increases as the behavior of ADD adolescent girls appears more and more aberrant. By the time the adolescent reaches adulthood, she often is depressed, anxious, and lonely, even if she is socially active. Or she might be withdrawn, passive, overly submissive, and unable to advocate for herself or find ways to have her needs met. She has low self-esteem and a lack of self-efficacy, often stemming from an unsuccessful or nontraditional personal life. Men with ADD have low self-esteem as well, but this can be due to employment and achievement problems rather than lifestyle choices or rejection by others.

The older the woman is at the time of diagnosis, the more serious her negative self-image and depressive symptomatology. She feels misunderstood and does not understand her own self. She can be highly reactive and emotional and consider herself a "closet borderline." She has a pattern of impulsive or problematic relationships, and may feel like she is not getting anywhere in life, just treading water despite her own and others' expectations. Her feelings of guilt and failure may be more severe than her male counterparts' even if symptoms have not been as extreme. Frequently, she has been socialized to believe that her success as a person rests in her ability to form and maintain relationships with others, including children—and sometimes ADD women have delayed having children, or don't have them at all, because of the activity in their lives, their disorganization, or the inability to stay put for very long. One woman poignantly described a wish for a long-term, caring relationship, and a comfortable home from where to seek solace and belonging, yet she felt compelled to live her life somewhat like a "gypsy, prepared to bolt at a moment's notice, voracious for experience."

In addition, the woman with ADD may be grappling with issues of hyper- or hyposexuality. According to some reports, women with ADD can be hypersensitive to sensory stimuli, including touch and smell, and this may bear upon their sexual desires. Touching can be annoying, and the constant need for experimentation or, in contrast, total submissiveness may create many problems in the sexual lives of ADD women and their partners. This may be a manifestation of the subtypes of ADD, where the high-stimulation seeking of women with ADD and hyperactivity compels them to seek out many and varied sexual experiences; or where the apathy and withdrawal of ADD woman without hyperactivity imposes on them the need for celibacy. Both types of ADD woman likely are disturbed by their situation: Hypersexual women might have developed reputations that fill them with shame and guilt; hyposexual women see themselves as cold and frigid. Stereotypes such as these are deeply embedded in the woman's psyche, reinforced by societal attitudes, and are a source of constant self-rebuke.

NEUROPSYCHOLOGICAL, NEUROBIOLOGICAL, AND NEUROENDOCRINE CONSIDERATIONS

The biological underpinnings of ADD can have a subtle or profound impact on a woman's physiological, psychological, and social well-being. Distractibility, impulsivity, emotional lability, hyperactivity, and information-processing problems interfere with a woman's attempt to achieve positive relationships and self-fulfillment. These symptoms may be displayed through such behaviors as impulsive shopping, emotional outbursts, or disorganization. Of course, instead of suspecting ADD, these woman and, often, their spouses, just think that they are stereotypical, soap opera women who shop a lot, are irresponsible with money, are at "that time of the month" too often, cry too much, and get lost all the time. Women with ADD without hyperactivity fall prey to the same stereotypical thinking but may amplify it, as their innate passivity is easily translated into their inability to be "assertive" and in charge.

Stereotypes shared by women and clinicians, as well as the different manifestations of ADD symptoms, preclude or delay the diagnosis of ADD in girls and women. It is usually because of neuropsychological deficits that girls with ADD are identified. Studies have found that ADD girls with or without hyperactivity have more pronounced cognitive deficits than their male counterparts, and more variability in their academic work (Berry et al., 1985; James & Taylor, 1990). Keeping in mind that many girls with ADD go unidentified, it is possible that only those with more pronounced neuropsychological difficulties are being diagnosed when they are children or adolescents. Indeed, some research has indicated that differences in academic achievement, intelligence, and measures of concentration and attention (Barkley, 1990) do not exist between ADD girls and boys. It has also been suggested that ADD girls tolerate their deficits more easily (Berry et al., 1985), implying that even when neuropsychological problems exist, they are likely to escape detection.

What might be most informative for clinicians is that although males in the general population suffer from learning disabilities at much higher rates than females (Geshwind & Galaburda, 1985), no differences in the prevalence of learning disabilities have been found between ADD girls and boys (Brown et al., 1991; Horn, Wagner, & Ialongo, 1989). These findings underscore the plight of women whose ADD has gone unrecognized: The women may not have had conduct problems or histories of severe impulsivity; but they may have had less noticeable struggles, and these struggles increasingly mar their social relationships, attempts at achievement or conformity, and their self-esteem.

Is there an explanation as to why girls and women with ADD manifest their symptoms differently, tolerate their deficits more easily, and experience their ADD differently? Certainly socialization and psychological processes contribute to the differences. But it may very well be that the brain contributes the most. Neurobiological differences between girls and boys, men and woman, probably impede our ability to diagnose ADD in women for several reasons. It appears that the lateralization of the brain, wherein males develop "stronger" right hemispheres and females develop "stronger" left hemispheres, influences both the higher rate of ADD in boys and their more overt symptoms. Geshwind and Galaburda (1985) have richly documented the influence of testosterone on the developing male brain, and have concluded that testosterone influences right-hemispheric dominance, which is highly correlated with higher rates of left-handedness, Tourette's syndrome, and hyperactivity in boys versus girls. Testosterone simultaneously suppresses left-hemispheric growth (Kimura, 1992).

In general, boys may be more prone to the ADD syndrome due to a greater vulnerability of the male's central nervous system to developmental failures (Berry et al., 1985). But more intriguing still is the suggestion that a rise in testosterone levels may slow the formation of later-developing regions (Geshwind & Galaburda, 1985), including the frontal lobes. In contrast, the frontal regions of the cortex in women apparently are more finely developed and important. Speech, visual guidance skills, fine motor movements, and language organization all seem localized and dependent on the frontal lobes, especially on the frontal regions of the left hemisphere, whereas the same skills in men appear more dependent on posterior regions such as the parietal lobe (Kimura, 1992).

The primary task of the frontal lobes is to inhibit behaviors and impulses of lower brain structures. They play an important role in allowing us to anticipate, plan, and modulate our responses appropriately. The functioning of the frontal lobes in ADD may be compromised by a dysregulation of the catecholamine system (Chelune, Ferguson, Koon, & Dickey, 1986); and compromised functioning has been "seen" in PET scans which indicate that adults with ADD have lower glucose metabolism in the frontal regions, suggesting a less efficient use of the brain's energy (Zametkin, Nordahl, Gross, et al., 1990). Thus, the current model of ADD is one of disinhibition, where the inability of the frontal lobes to delay response to external and internal stimuli causes cognitive, affective, and behavioral impulsivity, as well as information-processing and attentional problems.

The more robust functioning of the frontal lobes in women possibly makes the symptoms of ADD less overt, less debilitating, and more easily tolerated, whereas the preexisting lack of rich networks in the male's frontal areas makes men more prone to disinhibitory symptoms and behavior. The reliance of a woman's cognitive skills on the frontal regions may even explain why cognitive deficits are more prevalent. In addition, PET scans on adolescent boys and girls (Zametkin, Liebenauer, Fitzgerald, et al., 1993) have indicated that although both sexes have lower glucose metabolism in frontal regions, ADD girls had a 17% lower absolute glucose metabolism when compared to girls from the control group. This was in contrast to the boys where absolute differences between ADD and non-ADD boys were not found. This does not suggest that the girls had more severe metabolic deficiencies than the boys. But it does imply that the ADD may be more distributed throughout the girl's brain, thereby subduing overt manifestations of the disorder. More certain is that the neurobiological disparity between ADD girls and their non-ADD counterparts is more prominent than in male adolescents, setting the stage for the girls' estrangement from their peers and amplifying the girls' inability to meet social norms, roles, and expectations.

Finally, clinical evidence suggests that the dysregulation of the catecholamines in the ADD syndrome in women has a unique and serious consequence related to an exacerbation of premenstrual symptoms. Premenstrual symptoms are likely due to decreased central serotonergic activity (Menkes, Taghavi, Mason, & Howard, 1993), which has been linked to fluctuating levels of estrogen and progesterone during the premenstrual phase (Wood, Mortola, Chan, Moossazdeh, & Yen, 1992) through complex feedback mechanisms with certain brain regions. That is, pituitary trophic hormones set in motion the fluctuations of estrogen and progesterone, made in the ovaries. The pituitary is under the influence of hypothalamic-releasing hormones, the release of which is regulated by serotonin and the catecholamines; estrogen and progesterone, in turn, can influence not only the activity of brain neurons (i.e., serotonin activity), but also the release of the hypothalamic hormones (Meltzer & Lowy, 1986). It is the finely tuned interplay between the neural and endocrine systems that allows an individual to respond appropriately to internal and external stimuli. Thus, it has been speculated that women with severe PMS may have cyclic, hormonally induced changes in brain chemistry (Elks, 1993).

In the ADD syndrome, this picture grows even more complicated. Women with ADD suffer from debilitating mood swings, depression, anxiety, and anger during the premenstrual phase. We could speculate that the dysregulation of the catecholamines influences the interplay of the neural and endocrine systems and destabilizes it. The fluctuations in estrogen and progesterone during the premenstrual phase, and their link to decreased central serotonergic activity in women with PMS, would further dysregulate the feedback loops through which the neural and endocrine systems maintain their necessary coordination. It has been suggested that a loss of serotonergic neurotransmission, especially in the frontal regions of the brain, might seriously compromise an individual's behavioral inhibitory system (Teicher, Glod, & Cole, 1991). Needless to say, in a woman whose inhibitory system is already impaired, the cyclic, disorganizing endocrine storm would make everything worse.

THE ADD WOMAN'S STRUGGLE WITH SOCIAL NORMS AND ROLE EXPECTATIONS

At times, the most painful challenge for a woman with ADD can be an overwhelming sense of inadequacy, as she cannot seem to fulfill what she envisions her duties to be—whether she is a professional trying to juggle career and home, a mother trying to give her child what she thinks the child deserves, or a partner trying to offer patience and support to her significant other. Problems with attention, focusing, and organization seriously impair her ability to carry out what she feels should be natural and innate tasks: remembering to go grocery shopping, keeping a clean house, showering her loved ones with "quality time," giving as much of herself as she can to her job, her community, her home.

In addition to feelings of inadequacy, many women with ADD experience a deep sense of shame in recounting impulsive behaviors, either in their current lives or in their tumultuous adolescence and early adulthood. Research suggests that women are much more likely to feel shame or humiliation regarding their impulsive actions than are men (Johnson, McCown, & Booker, 1986). This sense of shame is not just internally derived, but is very much a product of the culture in which these women live. Saakvitne and Pearlman (1993) report that generally both the media and the popular culture stigmatize women who behave impulsively, while tolerating or even celebrating impulsivity as an attribute in males. This marked gender difference in the way society views certain types of ADD-related behavior has important implications for treatment. Johnson (in press) examined recovery in both men and women from "nonpharmacological addictions" such as compulsive shopping or excessive sexual behavior. Successful treatment of women with these behavioral problems was correlated, by self-report, with their feeling that the treatment program viewed their behavior nonjudgmentally as a product of "disease" rather than as evidence of a flaw in their character. In other words, treatment was successful when the clinician treating the impulsive women did not blame or judge them, and in fact helped them to cease blaming and judging themselves.

CASE HISTORIES ILLUSTRATING ISSUES FOR WOMEN WITH ADD

The case histories that follow are representative of the struggles women with ADD face in varying life situations. For the older women in these cases, ADD went undetected during childhood and adolescence due to either intelligence, parental support, or simply because the symptoms went unrecognized, although most had histories of hyperactivity along with distractibility. Predictably, they suffered from poor self-esteem and confusion over their problems and perceived inadequacies. Complaints about memory lapses abound, as do concerns about depending too strongly on others to maintain stability and order. Significantly, most of these women have children with ADD. And as often happens, some of them initially sought treatment for their children, only to have their own attention deficit unearthed during parent skills counseling. By contrast, two younger women whose case histories are presented were saved from years of negative experiences further assaulting their fragile self-images because their ADD and LD issues were diagnosed earlier.

First, let us examine the cases of these two young women, each of whom had the good fortune of having her ADD identified relatively early in life, one while in high school and the other in her 20s. As discussed earlier, because ADD is manifested somewhat differently in girls than in boys, girls whose ADD is identified in childhood or adolescence tend to be those with accompanying "learning disabilities" or neuropsychological disorders. This pattern was reflected in the histories of these two young women: Heather's ADD was diagnosed in high school due to accompanying learning disabilities, whereas Marcie's ADD was not diagnosed until after she had graduated from college and had entered working life.

Heather

Heather was in the ninth grade when she was referred for evaluation by her mother. Heather's older sister and younger brother were both good students and generally well behaved. By great contrast, Heather presented her parents with challenges at every turn. Although she tested with an IQ well above average, her grades were mediocre, with failing grades in math and foreign languages. Heather was energetic, impulsive, highly social, and moderately rebellious. Her presence at home kept her otherwise quiet household in a state of constant disruption. Psychological and psychoeducational testing was administered which strongly suggested the presence of ADHD with learning disabilities.

Heather was placed on stimulant medication, was seen in both individual and family therapy, and was referred to a tutor who worked with her throughout her high school years. The stimulant medication decreased but did not eliminate her impulsive, rebellious behavior. It seemed to increase her ability to observe her own behavior and, at times, to inhibit undesirable impulses. Medication also increased her ability to focus and concentrate when studying; however, distractibility in class was reduced but not eliminated. Some of this distractibility may have been as much the result of her lively, social nature as the result of distractibility from ADD. Despite improvements, her combination of ADD and LD, and the chronicity of family conflicts, led her progress through high school to be variable.

After high school Heather gained admission to a less competitive state college where she denied any further need for ADD and LD treatment and services. (This pattern of denial—a wish for a "clean slate"—is very common in students with ADD and/or LD when entering college.) By the end of her freshman year, she was on academic probation; discouraged, she returned home to a summer of family conflict. At the urging of her parents, Heather reentered treatment at this point. Through her therapy Heather was able to recognize her self-defeating behavior during her freshman year, and to reach an acceptance of her need for ongoing treatment and support services for her ADD and LD. She decided to transfer to a school near home that offered more comprehensive support services for students with learning and attentional problems. Heather resumed taking her stimulant medication and continued regular weekly psychotherapy sessions. It was decided that living independently from her family would be best, given the pattern of conflict and underfunctioning that Heather demonstrated whenever she lived at home. Therapy focused on problem solving, on learning to inhibit impulsive decision making, on setting priorities, and on making better choices of friends and boyfriends.

Four years later she was graduated from college with a B average, a stable relationship with a boyfriend, and a much calmer, mature relationship with her parents. Due to early identification of her ADHD, and with the benefit of multimodal treatment which included medication, structured counseling on study skills and other academic issues, and structured, strategic psychotherapy which focused on life management skills and on improving her relationships with family members, Heather entered her adult life on firm footing, and with a positive self-image.

Marcie

Marcie, unlike Heather, had no history of learning disabilities. Due to her high IQ and lack of other learning problems, Marcie's ADD was not discovered until somewhat later. After successfully graduating from college, Marcie sought an evaluation when she was dismissed from her job. She presented as a very lively, engaging, expressive young woman, despite her current crisis. The youngest daughter of two college professors, she described herself as very different from her two older sisters. Whereas they had been "mature" and good students, Marcie had been energetic, overemotional, erratic in her schoolwork, disorganized, and more dependent on her parents. It seemed that she always had crises, fights with her sisters, and last-minute panics over incomplete school assignments.

With a gift for mathematics, she followed her mother's footsteps, studying computer science in college. Despite emotional ups and downs and an erratic academic record, she graduated from college and found her first job in the computer field. To her dismay, she found the work boring, confining, and very unsuited to her outgoing personality. Her work quality was unpredictable and she was often late to work. Meanwhile, her private life flourished. She had many friends and interests, and was involved in many activities. She lived in a large house with other young people who enjoyed her enthusiasm and did not object to her messiness, disorganization, and erratic sleep patterns.

Marcie had lost her job, partially due to an economic downturn, but also as a result of her work record. Testing showed that she was highly intelligent, with symptoms very suggestive of ADD including distractibility, impulsivity, poor organization, and difficulty with planning. It also became evident through interview and personality testing that she was very poorly matched with her chosen career. Stimulant medication, brief structured counseling, and career counseling all led to a rapid improvement. With the benefits of medication, which helped her feel calmer and more focused, Marcie learned to use her daily planner to help schedule and organize herself, and she settled into her new job which allowed more flexibility and contact with people. Although she ruefully admitted that medication had not transformed her into an orderly person, it had helped her to the extent that she could clean and organize her living space once a week, an unheard of accomplishment in earlier days!

Marcie improved to the point that, while she continued to take stimulant medication, she no longer needed regular psychotherapy sessions. Marcie become a very active member of a local adult ADD support group and found that this level of support was beneficial. Her relatively early identification of ADD allowed her to make a career change at a time in her life when it was a less costly and drastic decision. Learning about ADD helped her to reframe painful childhood experiences, and allowed her to restructure her life in a way that supports her and lets her take full advantage of her strengths.

Now let us review the cases of four women whose ADD was diagnosed later in their adult lives. As parents of children with ADD, all four women became aware of their own ADD issues as a result of their child's diagnosis. In examining these cases we have the opportunity to explore how societal roles and expectations have an impact on the lives of women with ADD. The first woman is a full-time mother and housewife; the second is a professional woman who juggles responsibilities for children, husband, and career. The third woman is a single parent who struggles with a stressful job and a hyperactive son. The final case is a woman with ADD struggling to cope with the complex demands of stepfamily life.

In considering these cases, keep in mind that the job of primary parent and homemaker has many of the work features that seem to present the greatest difficulty for an adult with ADD: lack of structure, lack of guidance or supervision, multiple simultaneous demands, and frequent interruptions.

Pat

Pat was a young mother and full-time homemaker. Issues concerning Pat's ADD emerged during parent counseling regarding her very lively 7-year-old daughter, Lisa, who was diagnosed with ADD. Pat frequently lost her temper with Lisa, and sometimes resorted to making destructive verbal comments. Pat recounted a painful childhood history. The younger of two daughters, Pat was always viewed as the "problem child." She recalled being boisterous, loud, messy, and much less feminine than her "perfect" sister. Pat's grades were mediocre. She had little interest in academics, and little patience for the strict rules of the Catholic school she attended. In her teen years, battles with her parents escalated. Pat entered a world of alcohol, promiscuity, and school truancy, barely graduating from high school despite an above-average IQ. She had no desire to attend college. Pat went to work, and spent her money very impulsively. After a series of relationships, Pat accidentally became pregnant. She married the father of her unborn child although she had known him only briefly.

At the time of her evaluation, Pat commented that she had never planned anything in her life. Things "just seemed to happen" to her. To her surprise she reported that she was happily married. She described her marriage to Brian as a "lucky accident." Brian was good-natured, relaxed, and seemed to enjoy his noisy household. He was able to cope with Pat's loud voice and hot temper.

Patterns of depression became clearer as she spoke of feeling overwhelmed and confused as she went through her days. A treatment approach for Pat involved antidepressant medication, stimulant medication, and individual psychotherapy which also focused on parent counseling. After a few weeks on antidepressant medication, Pat's mood began to lift. She reported feeling more energetic and less irritable. Stimulant medication was added. She responded well to stimulants, and reported that tasks such as taking all three children in the car seemed less stressful. She noted that she yelled at her children less often. Pat began to think about her own needs and goals, a new concept for her. As her planning and organization improved, she had more energy for friendships and for time with her husband in the evening. She began to relate humorous and appreciative stories about her children, in great contrast to the chronic feelings of irritation toward her children she had reported earlier.

Although her response to medication and short-term treatment has been positive, she still has a long way to go to overcome her self-image as a woman who is messy, not very smart, and has no real talents.

If we look back to Heather's case, her adolescence was not dissimilar; however, it seems likely that Heather's life, as she enters her 30s, will be markedly different from Pat's due in large part to her earlier treatment for ADD. This earlier identification allowed her to go further with her education than she might have otherwise, and allowed Heather to move beyond some early, self-defeating patterns to set a more positive course for her young adult life; whereas Pat's life is typical of women from earlier generations, working as a full-time mother and homemaker.

The next three cases represent the complications and challenges many modern women face: juggling work and family, divorce and single parenthood, and the complex demands of stepfamily life.

Danielle

Danielle struggled with competing desires to pursue her profession and to be a full-time mother. An attractive, well-educated mother of two, her children were both diagnosed ADD. She humorously commented that she believed that she and her husband were ADD as well. Danielle and her daughter tended toward the quiet, dreamy, nonhyperactive form of ADD, while her husband and son were constantly "on the go." She sought treatment for herself a few months after quitting her professional job to devote herself to the needs of her children. She was near tears as she described her seeming inability to structure, she felt overwhelmed and exhausted; she and her husband had nightly squabbles as he came home to a disordered house and an unhappy wife. Several months after quitting work, she sought treatment feeling herself a failure as a mother and homemaker.

Danielle's treatment involved a combination of medication and counseling. In Danielle's case, her discouragement, caused by her inability to function well at home, had led to significant depression.

Initially, she was placed on an antidepressant. As her depression showed signs of lifting, she was subsequently given a psychostimulant medication. With the addition of a stimulant, Danielle reported that she felt much calmer, less distractible, and better able to manage her daily responsibilities.

As she learned about her neurological and psychological makeup, she could better understand, in a nonjudgmental fashion, why she was more suited to the quiet, ordered work environment than to the confusion, noise, and interruptions of a home with a hyperactive child. With greater self-acceptance, she began to approach her problems in a more pragmatic fashion. Her husband, Ken, was brought into psychotherapy sessions so that he could come to understand the issues Danielle faced. He recognized his contribution to her overload and agreed to cut back on some of his commitments and spend more time at home.

With initial reluctance, Ken agreed with Danielle's plan for her to return to part-time work. Danielle hired a cleaning lady, using some of the money she earned by returning to work. Ken adjusted his schedule to become a more active parent. These changes left Danielle with more manageable responsibilities. Her psychotherapy had involved improving self-esteem through a better understanding and acceptance of her ADD, a restructuring of her environment through delegation of some tasks, a better balancing between the competing needs of work and home, and gaining increased support from her spouse. Danielle's medication had improved her organizational skills and allowed her to complete tasks, both at home and at work, with less distractibility.

Sharon

Sharon, a divorced single parent, diagnosed with depression, had spent years in psychotherapy before seeking treatment for attention deficit disorder. She had two children: a son, diagnosed with ADD and learning disabilities, and a daughter. Sharon had dropped out of college to marry at age 20. Highly intelligent, her adolescence was marked by mediocre academic performance and intense, volatile clashes with her parents. Her marriage rapidly deteriorated after the birth of her second child. Following her divorce, she found herself working full-time and still unable to meet her expenses, despite the child support she received. Her daily stress level was intense, her parenting was highly erratic, and during the week prior to her menstrual period she was so emotionally reactive that she missed work regularly. She had dated a number of highly unsuitable men since her divorce. As a result of her poor choices, she periodically felt suicidal as these relationships predictably ended. She had been prescribed a wide variety of antidepressants with little or no positive effect.

Sharon's treatment involved a number of facets. She was evaluated by a physician who prescribed anticonvulsant medication, which very successfully stabilized her angry outbursts and emotional lability. Her mood came under such control that friends and co-workers commented she was "a different person." The effect of stimulant medication was less dramatic, but seemed to improve her ability to get to work on time and to become somewhat more organized at home. Despite the benefits of medication it became clear that she was not able to handle the multiple stresses of working full-time and parenting full-time. After a discussion with her ex-husband, it was agreed that he would take a greater responsibility for the two children while Sharon pursued treatment for her emotional and attentional difficulties. A temporary schedule was worked out in which the two children spent weekends with their mother, and weekdays with their father.

As she improved through medication and structured, ADD-focused psychotherapy, her involvement with her children gradually increased again. Counseling focused on parenting skills and on developing consistency in setting limits with the children. Treatment also addressed her patterns of binge eating and impulsive spending. She maintained better emotional control throughout her ADD treatment than in any of the preceding dozen years of intermittent psychotherapy and antidepressant medication. Due to the intensity of her ADD symptoms, and to the high degree of built-in stressors in the life of a single parent, continued treatment is likely to be needed for a number of years.

Judy

Recently remarried, Judy entered psychotherapy with no concerns about adult attention deficit disorder. Like so many ADD women, she was unaware that such a disorder existed in adult women, even though her son had been diagnosed earlier with learning and attentional problems. Judy sought help in coping with the stresses and conflicts within her new stepfamily. Her second husband, Herb, was widowed with two teenagers. She felt totally overwhelmed by the requirement to build some semblance of family life in her new stepfamily with three children, as well as manage a large house.

Prior to her remarriage, Judy had lived a quieter life. Although she had worked, in addition to having responsibility for her child, she had been able to manage better. The two of them had lived in an apartment. During her single-parent days she often took her son out for a fast-food dinner if she was tired after work. Her approach to child raising was relaxed, loving, and disorganized. Following her remarriage, Judy was thrown into a much more complex life. She had to coordinate schedules of after-school activities for three children. While her son had been thrilled with a carry-out pizza for dinner, her new husband expected a hot meal at night. This meant meal planning and more organized, large-scale grocery shopping than she had ever done before. Judy began to feel depressed, angry, and inadequate within the first year of her marriage. Meanwhile, Herb was continually frustrated with her disorganization. The laundry was never finished, meals were last-minute affairs, and the children, as in all newly forming stepfamilies, were rebelling, demanding attention, and unhappy as they vied with one another to establish a pecking order in their new family.

Only a year after being swept off her feet by Prince Charming, Judy began to feel more like Cinderella before the ball. No matter how hard she tried, she could not keep up with the workload. She felt that everyone was angry with her. Her new stepchildren did not accept her as a replacement for their deceased mother; her own son felt he suddenly had to compete with three other people for his mother's attention; and her husband complained that he came home to upset and chaos each evening.

Judy's treatment had a dual focus. Both the complicated stepfamily issues and Judy's problems with distractibility, planning, and organization needed attention. Because stepfamily work would require much stronger planning and follow-through abilities than Judy seemed to have at her disposal, initial treatment focused on her attentional and executive function difficulties. A thorough evaluation was completed which served to confirm suspicions of problems with memory, distractibility, and planning. Judy was referred for a medication evaluation and was placed on a typical combination of antidepressant and stimulant medication. After a period of adjusting the dosage of her medication, Judy reported that she no longer felt tearful and overwhelmed. As stimulants increased her ability to concentrate, plan, and follow through with her plans, we began to pinpoint areas of organizational difficulty at home and ways to solve those problems.

Meal planning presented a particular challenge for Judy. Many women with ADD find the multistep task of planning meals, shopping for groceries, cooking meals, and monitoring provisions during the week to be a very daunting one. The result is often large grocery bills, wasted food, multiple trips to the store for forgotten items, and fast-food meals because poor planning and poor time management did not allow for meal preparation. Judy had never particularly enjoyed cooking and had never, prior to her remarriage, lived in a household that expected full-scale, balanced hot dinners. Judy and I developed a simple 2-week menu of six dinners, assuming that at least one night in seven the family would order a pizza or eat out. We developed a grocery list for each week's menu, for which she shopped on alternate weeks after checking to see if she already had some necessary items in her larder. Judy learned to cook in quantity and freeze one-dish meals so that she did not need to cook every evening. While this did not become a perfect, foolproof system, she felt more control over meal planning, and this became a less stressful area of her life.

As Judy developed a better sense of internal organization and control, psychotherapy then began to address some of her stepfamily issues. Sometimes only her husband would attend with her, while at other times all of the stepfamily siblings would attend for family sessions. In addressing the stepfamily problems, solutions always were looked at in the light of Judy's ADD. Judy's interpersonal strengths allowed her to develop decent lines of communication with both of her stepchildren, as well as with her new husband. As new family patterns were established, Herb, with his great organizational skills, became the list maker and planner, while Judy, with her people skills, helped the family to come together to work out their feelings and frustrations. Herb became more accepting of Judy and quit expecting a replica of his first wife. He no longer expected the same structure at home or the same elaborate social life as he had had in his first marriage; now he was able to appreciate the special warmth and enthusiasm that Judy brought to his household.

Each of the four women just described were diagnosed with ADD during the most complicated, high-demand portion of their lives, right in the thick of child rearing and family life. The treatment plan for each of these women involved reaching a more comfortable acceptance of their limitations, devising strategies for improved functioning, and, perhaps most important, gaining the increased support and greater sharing of responsibilities with spouses, and even with ex-spouses. The next and last case involves a woman in middle age who has suffered through a divorce and a very fearful reentry into life as an older single person.

Alice

Alice sought psychotherapy for depression, triggered by an impending marital separation. She had been married more than 20 years. Both her son and daughter were away at college. Alice reported, tearfully, that her husband, a patient, quiet, sensible man, had finally and reluctantly reached a decision to end their marriage. Alice had been hyperemotional throughout their marriage, losing her temper at the slightest provocation, and breaking into tears frequently. Ron had dealt with her emotional storms stoically, avoiding her when she was at her worst, and attempting to calm her when he was able. Looking back at the marriage, she described a relationship that was more father-daughter than husband-wife. Alice had tried but was unable to keep the checkbook accurately. Ron had paid the bills, managed their finances, and made all large financial decisions. Finally, weary of Alice's dependence, emotionality, and disorganization, Ron departed, seeking a life of peace and quiet, leaving a terrified Alice behind.

Despite the fact that Alice had been home full-time, she had difficulty managing her household efficiently. Dinner was rarely served on time and groceries were bought several times a week because she had such difficulty planning menus and keeping track of supplies. Despite her hyperemotionality and disorganization, Alice was clearly an intelligent, caring, and likable person. She had lifelong friends who always called on her for sympathy and support. She might spend the afternoon with a friend who was going through a difficult time, only to realize that she was late starting dinner or late to pick up her children from lessons or practice.

Much of the early work in psychotherapy focused on very practical issues. Alice had no confidence and felt completely intimidated by the prospect of building an independent life for herself. Her first major step was to seek employment. Though she had not worked in many years, she brushed up her typing skills and sought a job as an office manager in a local insurance firm. It was only as Alice began to settle into her new job and to develop more confidence and assertiveness skills that her attentional and organizational skills became more evident. As Alice progressed in her job at the agency, her intelligence and caring demeanor were valued, but her memory difficulties and poor organizational skills began to cause notice. At that point, her educational history was explored in greater depth. Fortunately, her elderly mother was still alive and could provide Alice's history during her elementary school years. Her mother depicted a little girl who was highly forgetful, absentminded, and disorganized. Teachers considered her bright, but commented that she needed to apply herself more. Her mother noted a pattern of low frustration tolerance and tantrums from early childhood.

Armed with this history, we undertook a thorough neuropsychological and psychoeducational evaluation. Alice demonstrated significant attentional and memory problems, had difficulty with visual-spatial tasks and with organization and sequencing. Alice was referred to a neuropsychiatrist for a medication evaluation and was first placed on antidepressants. Gradually Alice's agitation and tearfulness decreased. Because her organizational problems were significantly interfering with work performance, which served to increase Alice's anxiety level, a trial of psychostimulant medication was suggested. She responded very well to stimulants, and soon reported that she felt much calmer, better able to plan and organize her day, and was functioning more efficiently at the office.

Luckily for Alice, she had a supervisor who was the parent of a learning disabled child. Alice was able to discuss her difficulties openly with this supervisor, who helped Alice develop a filing system that worked well for her. Because Alice had a significant "retrieval problem" (a difficulty in recalling specific names or facts), the filing system was set up according to broad categories using the names of individuals or organizations as subcategories. Both Alice and her supervisor were pleased with the new system, and Alice's anxiety level was reduced, allowing more improvement in her level of functioning.

Several months after Alice's ADD/LD diagnosis, she was feeling and functioning so much better that psychotherapy was reduced to monthly problem-solving sessions. One year later she terminated treatment. Looking back on her marriage, now that she was feeling more competent and confident, she had mixed feelings. On one hand, she felt her marriage may have survived had her ADD been diagnosed and treated many years earlier; on the other hand, Alice was discovering a lively, adventuresome, and playful side to her nature. She wondered if she would have ever chosen to marry such a phlegmatic man if she had developed her own coping skills earlier in life.

THE DIAGNOSIS OF ADD IN WOMEN

Considering the complicated presentation of ADD in women, and the many ways in which the syndrome can be disguised by other psychiatric symptoms, how can the clinician be "tipped off" to the diagnosis of ADD in women? Of course, a thorough evaluation should include an academic history and a complete medical history to rule out medical contributory factors. In addition to DSM-IV criteria, measurement tools such as the Wender Utah Rating Scale (Ward, Wender, & Reimherr, 1993) can be helpful, as can the Copeland Symptom Checklist for Adult Attention Deficit Disorder (Copeland, 1989), as it allows for the diagnosis of ADD with or without hyperactivity. In addition, neuropsychological testing can effectively reveal significant attentional problems.

The most valuable diagnostic tool is the capacity to listen. The clinician needs to listen carefully for evidence of inattention, impulsivity, mood swings, and subjective experiences of failure, frustration, restlessness, boredom, and disorganization; to note neurological soft signs such as migraines, sleep disturbances, left-handedness, or history of defiant behavior; and to recognize that while anxiety disorders, depressive disorders, and substance abuse disorders may be comorbid, they may just as likely be consequences of unrecognized ADD. The longitudinal development of the syndrome over the life of the woman with ADD is both diagnostic and therapeutic, as the therapist and the ADD woman are both engaged in detailing how ADD has affected her life. In addition, the clinician needs to note those phenomena associated with ADD in women, including problems with sexuality, premenstrual syndrome, poor self-esteem due to the inability to live up to role expectations, descriptions of troublesome passivity and dependency, and neuropsychological problems such as memory problems, spatial-relationship difficulties, and hypersensitivities to sensory experience.

CONCLUSION: TREATMENT CONSIDERATIONS FOR WOMEN WITH ADD

The previous cases illustrate the value in investigating the childhood history of a woman who complains about not being able to manage household and children or make important life decisions, and suffers a great deal of depression and anxiety as a result. They underscore the need to use psychoeducation and psychotherapy to discover what works best for each woman in the context of her own strengths and limitations, her life situations and concerns. We would like to suggest that treatment with the ADD woman should be as centered around gender-related issues as it is around the ADD, since the two can become so intermingled and play off one another. The themes of intimacy, relationships, connectedness, and families must be central, if warranted; if these themes are not applicable or apparent in the woman's life situation, the issues of independence, self-sufficiency, and career management may be most important. Some women with ADD, especially those who have internalized guilt and failure, can feel helpless, powerless, and unable to advocate for themselves, as if they are letting their life pass them by, or their disorganization has made them overly dependent on others and unable to reciprocate.

This strategy could be viewed as a melding of the psychoeducational, managerial approach to treatment with the more dynamic self-in-relation theory set forth by Jordan and Surrey (1986). Their theory recognizes that women tend to organize their sense of identity, find meaning, and achieve a sense of coherence and continuity in the context of relationships. And, as Carol Gilligan (1982) has claimed, a woman's sense of development, maturation, and morality might arise from her ability to affiliate and connect with others. Women with ADD can feel a great sense of loss around their seeming inability to maintain this connectedness and relatedness. At times their sense of self is jeopardized, and always they are trying to live up to standards that seem out of reach.

In addition, psychopharmacological interventions are useful more often than not. The combination of antidepressants and stimulants seems effective for many women. We have also found low doses (10–30 mg/day) of the tricyclics imipramine and desipramine to be effective in ADD women who may not suffer from serious depression (Ratey, Greenberg, Bemporad, & Lindem, 1992). These medications improve focus and attention, quiet inner noise, and lessen emotional lability and outbursts of rage. In addition, buspirone, fluoxetine, and sertraline as adjuncts seem to diminish the debilitating symptoms of PMS that ADD women can experience due to its interaction with the serotonergic system (Menkes et al., 1993; Wood et al., 1992).

As the neurophysiological and biological symptoms of ADD diminish, and the neurochemical systems become stabilized, the ADD woman is well equipped to utilize short- or long-term psychotherapy and to begin constructing her personal truths and meanings. Armed with a knowledge of the biological and neuropsychological ramifications of ADD, a strategy for managing the ADD, effective medication, and an understanding of the psychological, interpersonal and sociocultural pressures that complicate the ADD, women with ADD overcome ADD symptoms. They can become enriched by the challenges and quirks inherent in the disorder, but also can forgive themselves for what they have seen as their failures and inadequacies, breaking free from the many molds into which they have felt they must fit.

REFERENCES

Barkley, R. A. (1990). *Attention deficit hyperactivity disorder: A handbook for diagnosis and treatment.* New York: Guilford Press.

Berry, C. A., Shaywitz, S. E., & Shaywitz, B. A. (1985). Girls with attention deficit disorder: A silent minority: A report on behavioral and cognitive characteristics. *Pediatrics, 76*(5), 801–809.

Biederman, J., Newcorn, J., & Sprich, S. (1991). Comorbidity of attention deficit hyperactivity disorder with conduct, depressive, anxiety, and other disorders. *American Journal of Psychiatry*, *148*(5), 564–577.

Breen, M. J., & Altepeter, T. S. (1990). Situational variability in boys and girls identified as ADHD. *Journal of Clinical Psychology*, *46*, 486–490.

Brown, R. T., Abramowitz, A. J., Madan-Swain, A., Eckstrand, D., & Dulcan, M. (1989, October). *ADHD gender differences in a clinic-referred sample*. Paper presented at the annual meeting of the American Academy of Child and Adolescent Psychiatry, New York.

Brown, R. T., Madan-Swain, A., & Baldwin, K. (1991). Gender differences in a clinic-referred sample of attention-deficit-disordered children. *Child Psychiatry and Human Development*, *22*(2), 111–128.

Chelune, G. J., Ferguson, W., Koon, R., & Dickey, T. O. (1986). Frontal lobe disinhibition in attention deficit disorder. *Child Psychiatry and Human Development*, *16*, 221–235.

Copeland, E. D. (1989). *Copeland Symptom Checklist for adult attention deficit disorders*. Atlanta, GA: Southeastern Psychological Institute.

Elks, M. L. (1993). Open trial of fluoxetine therapy for premenstrual syndrome. *Southern Medical Journal*, *86*(5), 503–507.

Faraone, S. V., Biederman, J., Keenan, K., & Tsuang, T. (1991). A family-genetic study of girls with DSM-III Attention Deficit Disorder. *American Journal of Psychiatry*, *148*(1), 112–117.

Geshwind, N., & Galaburda, A. (1985). Cerebral lateralization: Biological mechanisms, associations, and pathology. *Archives of Neurology*, *42*, 428–459.

Gilligan, C. (1982). *In a different voice*. Cambridge, MA: Harvard University Press.

Horn, W. F., Wagner, A. E., & Ialongo, N. (1989). Sex differences in school-aged children with pervasive attention deficit hyperactivity disorder. *Journal of Abnormal Child Psychology*, *17*(1), 109–125.

Huessy, H. R. (1990). *The pharmacotherapy of personality disorders in women*. Presented at the annual meeting of the American Psychiatric Association (symposia), New York.

James, A., & Taylor, E. (1990). Sex differences in the hyperkinetic syndrome of childhood. *Journal of Child Psychology and Psychiatry*, *31*, 437–446.

Johnson, J. (in press). Shame and sex bias in the impulsive behaviors of women and men: Four empirical studies. *Contemporary Psychodynamics: Theory, Research and Application*.

Johnson, J., McCown, W., & Booker, M. (1986, April). *MMPI profiles of multiply abused and sheltered women*. Paper presented at the meeting of the Midwestern Psychological Association, Chicago, IL.

Jordan, J. V., & Surrey, J. L. (1986). The self-in-relation: empathy and the mother-daughter relationship. In T. Bernay & D. Cantor (Eds.), *The psychology of today's woman: New psychoanalytical visions.* Hillsdale, NJ: Analytic Press.

Kimura, D. (1992). Sex differences in the brain. *Scientific American, 267*(3), 110–117.

Lahey, B. B., Schaughency, E. A., Hynd, G. W., Carlson, C., & Nieves, N. (1987). Attention deficit disorder with and without hyperactivity: Comparison of behavioral characteristics of clinic-referred children. *Journal of the American Academy of Child Adolescent Psychiatry, 26*(5), 718–723.

McGee, R., Williams, S., & Silva, P. A. (1987). A comparison of girls and boys with teacher-identified problems of attention. *Journal of the American Academy of Child and Adolescent Psychiatry, 26*(5), 711–717.

Meltzer, H. Y., & Lowy, M. T. (1986). Neuroendocrine function in psychiatric disorders and behavior. In P. Berger & K. Brodie (Eds.), *American handbook of psychiatry, Vol. 8. Biological psychiatry* (pp. 111–150). New York: Basic Books.

Menkes, D. B., Taghavi, E., Mason, P. A., & Howard, R. C. (1993). Fluoxetine's spectrum of action in premenstrual syndrome. *International Clinical Psychopharmacology, 8*(2), 95–102.

Ratey, J., Greenberg, S., Bemporad, J. R., & Lindem, K. (1992). Unrecognized attention-deficit hyperactivity disorder in adults presenting for outpatient psychotherapy. *Journal of Child and Adolescent Psychopharmocology, 4,* 267–275.

Saakvitne, K., & Pearlman, L. (1993). The impact of internalized misogyny and violence against women on feminine identity. In E. P. Cook (Ed.), *Women, relationships, and power: Implications for counseling* (pp. 247–274). Alexandria, VA: American Counseling Association.

Silver, L. (1992). *Attention-Deficit Hyperactivity Disorder: A clinical guide to diagnosis and treatment.* Washington, DC: American Psychiatric Press.

Teicher, M. H., Glod, C., & Cole, J. O. (1991). Teicher and associates reply. *American Journal of Psychiatry, 148*(9), 1261–1262.

Ward, M. F., Wender P., & Reimherr, F. W. (1993). The Wender Utah rating scale: An aid in the retrospective diagnosis of childhood attention deficit hyperactivity disorder. *American Journal of Psychiatry, 150*(6), 885–890.

Wood, S. H., Mortola, J. F., Chan, Y. F., Moossazadeh, F., & Yen, S. S. (1992). Treatment of premenstrual syndrome with fluoxetine: a double-blind placebo-controlled, crossover study. *Obstetrics and Gynecology, 80*(3), 339–344.

Zametkin, A., Liebenauer, L., Fitzgerald, G., King, A., Minkunas, D., Herscovitch, P., Yamada, E., & Cohen, R. (1993). Brain metabolism in teenagers with attention-deficit hyperactivity disorder. *Archives of General Psychiatry, 50,* 333–340.

Zametkin, A., Nordahl, T. E., Gross, M., King, A. C., Semple, W., Rumsey, J., Hamburger, S., & Cohen, R. (1990). Cerebral glucose metabolism in adults with hyperactivity of childhood onset. *New England Journal of Medicine, 323*(20), 1413–1415.

15

Students with Attention Deficit Disorders in Postsecondary Education
Issues in Identification and Accommodation

MARY McDONALD RICHARD

"Everyone told me I'd grow out of it . . . but here I am at college, still struggling to concentrate, taking my medicine, and trying to get along with my ADD."
—A junior biology major

"If you learn how to ask for the accommodations you need, and follow through, it makes a big difference."
—A college sophomore

Author's Note. Over my 20 years of listening to students and other educators, I have placed a number of their comments into various notebooks and journals. Much of my work as a practitioner is informed and guided by what my students have told me about their lives and educational experiences. Writing down their comments has allowed me to reflect on, and often savor, what they are saying to those of us who are their partners in personal and academic development. The quotations at the beginning of each section and inserted within the text of this article are taken from my personal journals during my years with the office of Student Disability Services at the University of Iowa. In order to maintain the privacy of my students and former students, I have not identified the speakers by name.

> *"Academic accommodations for students with ADD*
> *aren't just a nice thing to do, or the right thing to do—*
> *it's the law!"*
>   *—A disability counselor*

Attention deficit disorders (ADD) are starting to receive notice on college campuses partly as the result of the renewed focus on students with disabilities and the continuing quest to understand factors of student persistence. ADD is the "new kid on the block," eliciting uncertainty about how to assist or proceed on the part of many postsecondary faculty and student services providers. Support services related to ADD are just becoming available on college campuses. Their development is fueled by requests from students and their advocates, and by the requirements for academic accommodations under Section 504 of the Rehabilitation Act of 1973. These services are generally extensions of programs previously offered to students with specific learning disabilities (McCormick & Leonard, 1993). Under the law, students have both rights and responsibilities, for example, a student's request for accommodation must be made in an appropriate and timely manner.

Colleges with support programs do not reduce their standards for students with ADD; rather they offer services designed to provide program access related to the needs of individuals with disabilities (Association for Higher Education and Disability, 1992). Institutions are not required to waive specific courses or academic requirements considered essential to a particular program or degree. Rather, the law mandates that they modify requirements so that they do not discriminate against individuals on the basis of disability. Examples of accommodations include arranging for students with ADD to take their tests in a distraction-free room with extended time, or allowing those who have difficulties with note taking to use note-taking services or bring tape recorders to class (Richard, Chandler, & Wu, 1993). Decisions of appropriate adjustment consider that they

1. Must be made on a case-by-case basis
2. Must not advocate that the exercise of one individual's rights supersede the rights of another
3. Must see that the faculty member's right to academic freedom does not outweigh the student's right to appropriate accommodation

At the elementary and secondary levels, schools are responsible for identifying and serving students with disabilities. At the postsecondary level, this role shifts to students, who become primarily responsible for self-identification and initiating requests for services. If students choose not to do this, then the institution is under no obligation to provide support. Many first-year college students who were accustomed to procedures used in high school are unprepared for this abrupt change. Professionals guiding students in undertaking this new role must not only help them to become more articulate in discussing their disability, but also teach them to recognize and understand the attitudinal barriers they may face, and to adopt strategies for coping with them (Association for Handicapped Student Services Programs in Postsecondary Education, 1987).

The Rehabilitation Act's provision that college students with disabilities must self-identify and request appropriate accommodations may pose a stumbling block for some students with ADD. For a student using a wheelchair or a white cane, the decision to self-identify and request accommodations is relatively straightforward. Since others can see the disability, there is no loss of privacy involved in acknowledging it and requesting legally mandated support. For students with ADD, however, the decision is more complex. They may hesitate to request accommodations when they do not look as though they need them and may even be placed in the position of having to prove that they have a real disability and are making appropriate requests.

Cultural attitudes may magnify concerns about self-identification of a disability and be reflected by the underrepresentation of culturally diverse populations in the caseloads of college disability services providers. Some cultures have especially negative views of disability; within their frame of reference, "disability" may be equated with restricted opportunities or low personal value. These students are less likely to seek assessment services, and are more likely to reject self-identification and participation in support services. Without support and encouragement, the participation of culturally diverse populations in campus programs for the assessment and accommodation of ADD will likely remain limited.

Just as there is no typical student with ADD, there is no universal model for services for these students. Each institution that provides academic accommodations to students with disabilities has its own programs and services. Staff sizes and qualifications, philosophies and practices may differ widely. A number of programs only provide information about accommodations and content-based tutoring. Fewer institutions offer comprehensive programs that provide individual and group counseling, training in advocacy, and study strategies pertinent to the needs of students with ADD (Vogel, 1987; Kravets & Wax, 1992).

While nondiscrimination for college students with ADD is mandated by law, the moral commitment of the college to educational access for students with disabilities is critical. If postsecondary institutions say they value diversity and social mission, then they should be doing all they can to provide an accessible learning environment for students with disabilities. Studies that have examined the persistence and success of students with learning disabilities provide encouragement. When qualified students with learning disabilities were provided accommodations, the majority of those students persisted and did well in college (Vogel & Adelman, 1993).

Disability advocacy groups have promoted the increased attention being paid to college students with ADD. The growth of national organizations such as Children and Adults with Attention Deficit Disorders (CH.A.D.D.) and the Association for Higher Education and Disabilities (A.H.E.A.D.), public recognition of ADD as a significant disability, and increased media attention to ADD have contributed to the growing awareness of its symptoms in adults. As this occurs, postsecondary institutions are becoming more aware that ADD can continue into the college years and that they are obliged to provide accommodations to students who self-identify.

WHY ARE SOME STUDENTS WITH ADD UNIDENTIFIED UNTIL COLLEGE?

"I was in college before I found out why I've been told to pay attention all my life."
                                                                —*A college freshman*

"I guess I was smart enough to sort of fake my way through high school. At college, however, I had another thing coming!"
                                                                —*A college sophomore*

Professionals working with college students frequently ask how students with significant disabilities in the areas of attention and learning have passed undetected through the educational and health care delivery systems. A number of issues, beyond the folk tale that "they outgrow it," contribute to this. Although the symptoms of ADD appear before age 7, like students with other "hidden disabilities," most "fall through the cracks" of the systems charged with their identification and treatment. This is attributed primarily to a lack of preservice and inservice training for educators and health care providers in the identification of children at risk for disorders of learning and attention (Johnston, 1991).

Nontraditional-age college students completed secondary school prior to the enactment of laws that require the evaluation of children demonstrating educational problems. Those who were in primary or secondary school after the implementation of these laws did not fall below grade level substantially enough to meet state standards for eligibility for assessment. Nor did they display behavioral problems to the extent that the system was activated to deal with these symptoms. Of those students who were professionally evaluated, many were missed or misdiagnosed owing to service provider lack of information about ADD. State standards for eligibility commonly require that students be two to three years below grade level in math or reading in order to qualify for school-based assessment. Since students with ADD who select themselves into college are generally of average and above intelligence, they seldom meet this criteria. Thus, it is not surprising that these individuals have gone undiagnosed.

Even when demonstrating school failure, some students, identified as having ADD without the presence of specific learning disabilities, may not have been previously considered eligible for educational services under either Section 504 of the Rehabilitation Act of 1973 or Public Law 94-142. Although some were served through regular and special education on account of academic impairment related to coexisting disabilities (such as specific learning disabilities), it was not until September 16, 1991 that the law was clear on the point that students whose educational progress is impaired as a result of ADD are eligible for accommodations and services. Since the issuance of the Memo of Clarification from the U.S. Department of Education Office of Special Education, which offered definitive guidance to state and local education agencies regarding the eligibility of students with ADD for services under Section 504 or 91-142, advocates have endeavored to meet the challenge of seeing that its contents are implemented.

IDENTIFYING COLLEGE STUDENTS AT RISK FOR ADD

> *"I have a tendency to just put things off, and it just caught up with me."*
> —*A college freshman*

> *"My classes just seemed boring after a couple weeks."*
> —*A college freshman*

A study published in 1992 of full-time college freshmen with self-disclosed learning disabilities documented prior to college admission by the Higher

Education and the Handicapped Resource Center of the American Council on Education (H.E.A.T.H.) (1993) indicated that this group comprises 25% (about 35,000) of all freshmen with disabilities. ADD had never been categorized alone but as a part of this category. Since ADD has also been categorized at times with psychological disabilities, it is reasonable to believe that the actual figure is greater. Additionally, college programs that serve students with ADD and LD note that many of the students they serve are identified after they enroll in college (Smith, 1991).

The prevalence of ADD in adults is unknown; very few have been studied. Studies of children indicate that 3–5% have ADD. About two thirds of the children who are diagnosed in or before elementary school continue to have behavioral symptoms in adolescence. Approximately 40–70% of the children continue to have symptoms of ADD during their adult years (Children and Adults with Attention Deficit Disorders, 1993). ADD is seldom seen in a vacuum; while it may occur alone, it frequently appears comorbid with other neurobiological disabilities (Barkley & Murphy, 1993; Gersh, 1993; Stein, 1993). The majority of college students who have ADD are undiagnosed, their disabilities impairing their academic progress as well as their social and emotional development. It is important for professionals working with college students with ADD to recognize that this group includes traditional-age undergraduates in the process of "making it to adulthood," as well as adults who are enrolled in undergraduate or graduate programs.

Symptoms of ADD in college students are often obscured by problems of stage development common to many students. However, under examination, they experience these problems more intensely and with greater frequency than other students. The following list of characteristics is based on the observation of presenting concerns by the counseling staff of the office of Student Disability Services (SDS) at the University of Iowa (Richard, 1992). SDS practitioners note that among those students who are diagnosed with ADD while in college, many are first referred for problems of academic failure or college adjustment. Not all of the following characteristics apply to every college student with ADD; each individual has his or her own presentation. College students may self-refer or may be referred by staff or faculty to the designated office for services to students with disabilities. Following an interview with a counselor, the student may be referred to either or both private or institutional resources for formal assessment.

Common presenting concerns include:

- Distractibility
- Forgetfulness
- Boredom
- Disorganization
- Procrastination
- Restlessness

- Test anxiety
- Low self-esteem
- Substance abuse
- Relationship problems

- Depression
- Mood swings
- Chronic tardiness or inattendance
- Academic underachievement or failure

A multifactored evaluation is important in the diagnosis of ADD. Both medicine and psychology are represented in the assessment process. The evaluation of a college student or of an individual who plans to enter postsecondary education will vary somewhat in focus from an adult ADD evaluation of someone in the workforce. Special attention must be paid to academic history and academic functioning (Barkley & Murphy, 1993; Gersh, 1993).

Recommendations in the summary report should focus on academic needs. They may include statements concerning a student's eligibility for services such as note takers, extended time for test taking, or recommendations that the student be permitted to substitute approved courses for the general education requirements in such areas as mathematics or foreign language (Mangrum & Strichart, 1984; Richard & Chandler, 1994; Sedita, 1989; Vogel & Adelman, 1993). Most institutions request that the student provide a copy of the summary to the college disability counselor for the purposes of providing evidence of eligibility and arranging for appropriate academic accommodations.

When attention deficit disorders are not diagnosed and understood, the emotional toll may be high. Students may have struggled to control or hide their symptoms to avoid embarrassment. They have often developed low self-esteem and negative perceptions of themselves as a result of academic and social failures (Weiss & Hechtman, 1993). Many have been labeled as "having a bad attitude," "a slow learner," "lacking motivation," "immature," "lazy," "spacey," or "self-centered" (Children and Adults with Attention Deficit Disorders, 1993). Social withdrawal and isolation are strategies employed by some students who are seeking to avoid criticism or hurt (Werry, Reeves, & Elkind, 1987). Some manifest cynicism or aggressive behavior in response to chronic anger and frustration related to the effects of their learning problems.

Identification of college students who have ADD and appropriate assistance improve their chances for a successful outcome. Effective intervention can improve self-esteem, academic achievement, and general adjustment. An accurate diagnosis of ADD can help students to put their difficulties into perspective. Rather than viewing their difficulties as the result of an inherited or acquired neurobiological disorder, many college students with ADD have come to accept the erroneous belief that they are to blame for their problems. Related to this, many also experience a sense of relief following diagnosis. The uncertainty over what was "wrong" or what led to the referral is replaced with information and hope for the future (CH.A.D.D., 1993).

ISSUES IN COLLEGE PREPARATION AND SELECTION

> *"My high school teachers told me I wasn't college material and placed me in classes which were so diluted that I didn't have the chance to become as academically prepared as my peers. This has made things tough, but now that I know about my ADD and take medication regularly, my college cumulative average is well above a 3.0."*
>
> —*A college junior*

> *"Our experience has been that students who have successfully acted on early diagnosis while in high school and continue to seek the support of counseling professionals while in college fare better in their academic pursuits than those who feel they have licked it and no longer seek assistance."*
>
> —*Michael Barron, Director of Admissions*

It is crucial for professionals assisting high school students with ADD to be aware of high school preparation issues that may be affected by the disorder. In addition to the myriad of risks faced by adolescents, these students may be jeopardized by discontinuous development in the areas of academic, social, and emotional functioning related to ADD. Professionals need to understand that these students' consequent vulnerability to underachievement, interpersonal problems, low self-esteem, stress intolerance, and depression may hamper independent long-term planning. Symptoms manifested by many adolescents with ADD, such as procrastination and disorganization, may further compromise a student's progress toward self-determination.

Some students with ADD need counseling with respect to the sufficiency of their preparation for college. Few have an adequate concept of the nature or difficulty of the college experience. They may have a poorly developed understanding of their disability and how it affects them in the classroom and in their daily life. They may not relate academic performance in high school to their future performance at college in a realistic manner. Thus they may either underrate or overrate themselves with respect to their ability to function in college and/or careers.

Professionals who are assisting these students should involve them in a preparatory process that supports student development. The following case study synopsis illustrates a team approach designed to involve a young person with ADD who has college potential in understanding herself, developing academic competencies, generating a vision for her postsecondary education and career, and working through the related issues in a sequential manner.

"Mary Ellen began preparing for college in her first year of high school," her high school counselor said. With her team, which included her parents, high school counselor, and a favorite teacher, Mary Ellen began to work on a number of tasks which helped her develop awareness, understanding, and skills for independence, as well as gain information about her postsecondary options.

As a freshman, she drew up her 4-year plan and began participating in her own I.E.P. (individualized educational plan for special education) meetings. She learned more about her areas of weakness and how to use her strengths to compensate for these areas. She signed up for extra study and computer skills sessions. She met regularly with her counselor and teachers to develop self-monitoring and organizational strategies related to homework and daily life. Her parents were regularly informed by teachers about her progress. She toured her parents' college alma mater.

In her sophomore year, Mary Ellen participated in a self-advocacy workshop and served as a member of a self-advocacy panel at a later workshop facilitated by her counselor, speaking to high school students about being a student with disabilities as part of a schoolwide awareness program. She began using tutoring services for algebra and Spanish. She toured a local junior college and attended a college fair.

During her junior year, Mary Ellen visited several friends who were enrolled at colleges around the state. She applied for and took the ACT's with extended time. She requested application forms and information from three 4-year liberal arts colleges. Together with her team, she investigated the financial aid programs, and services for students with disabilities. She made campus visits. Her psychoeducational testing was updated, and the school psychologist added recommendations for college academic accommodations to her report. Mary Ellen participated in a careers program; she interviewed and observed professionals in work settings.

Early in the fall of her senior year, Mary Ellen submitted applications to the three schools, and was admitted by all of them. She continued in the careers program doing a 4-week, 2-hour per week practicum each trimester in different work settings. She discussed her career goals with her counselor. Mary Ellen had two different majors in mind as she went to register for college classes. She was particularly anxious about registration. These concerns decreased after an interview with her college disability counselor and academic advisor, who gave specific information to assist her in problem solving.

During the summer before she matriculated, Mary Ellen spent quite a bit of time talking with her college disabilities counselor about questions regarding college adjustment. She needed a doctor to write her medication prescriptions. She was also concerned about such issues as where to study, how to make new friends, and how to stay organized in a shared residence hall room.

Professionals may also facilitate student preparation by involving them in building a personal transition file. A transition file should contain the following:

1. The student's high school transcript
2. ACT and/or SAT college testing scores
3. A diagnostic report and summary of treatment recommendations related to the student's ADD (and any other disabilities)
4. Copies of recent educational plans if the student has been served under 504 or IDEA
5. A copy of the most recent (within 3 years of college matriculation) psychoeducational evaluation, including a statement regarding the diagnosis of ADD (and any other disabilities), results from assessment of cognitive abilities and academic achievement levels, and recommendations for academic accommodations
6. A student writing sample, such as a personal statement or essay
7. Copies of newsclippings or other evidence of extracurricular achievements or honors
8. Copies of any letters and applications to colleges completed by the student

Secondary education delivery systems for students identified with ADD and/or LD vary in regard to preparing these students for college. This sometimes accounts for high school requirement deficiencies. Some high school students with ADD and/or specific learning disabilities are not encouraged to take all of the classes that are usually part of a college-bound curriculum. This may place them at a disadvantage when they enter college. Generally, any unit deficiencies (missing high school requirement courses) must be made up at college without benefit of credit toward graduation. While placement in mainstream classes with appropriate accommodations and support services is desirable for most students with ADD, some may benefit from other educational placements, provided they substitute the same information and learning experiences through alternative classes. Generally, high school graduation plans for college-bound students with ADD should include the following:

English	4 years	Science	3 years
Social Science	3 years	Math	3 years
Arts	2 years	Foreign Language	2 years
Computer Science	½ year	Study Skills	

It is important to mention that some students with ADD may be unable to successfully complete the required courses in such areas as mathematics and foreign language. Psychoeducational testing may demonstrate that ADD alone, or in combination with specific learning disabilities, prevents a student from mastering these subjects. If this is the case, it is important that this information be contained in the psychoeducational report along with a recommendation that the student be allowed to complete the requirement through the substitution of approved courses.

A number of other student and institutional issues are raised when professionals work with these high school students in the college admissions process. Many influences–including parents, friends, teachers, location, academic programs, size, and cost–generally guide college selection. Professionals who work with students with ADD should also be aware that the availability of related institutional support services may be a significant factor in college choice (Richard, 1992; Vogel, 1993). Whether it is a personal objective or an I.E.P. transition goal, college-bound students and those who assist them should investigate the service delivery system at each institution under consideration and determine whether the system would meet their anticipated needs. Assessment of services as a part of college selection also supports students' development of self-advocacy skills.

Postsecondary institutions should extend appropriate accommodations to students who have self-identified at first contact with the school. Questions directed to college offices of admissions should include:

1. What are the regular criteria required in the application for admission process (ACT/SAT, class rank, grade point)?

2. Are there special considerations for admission for students who have documented ADD? Is there a deadline for applications that request special admissions considerations?

3. Is the applicant's current diagnosis accepted? What kind of verification is needed?

4. How many credit hours must be taken at the school to be a "full-time" student? Are students with disabilities such as ADD permitted to take reduced course loads and still be considered full-time students?

5. Is there an office of disabilities services at the school? If so, what is the name, address, and phone number of the contact person?

In the course of obtaining more specific information, students and those assisting them should ask campus offices of student disability service the following:

1. What are the qualifications and size of your staff?

2. How many students with ADD are currently actively receiving services from the office?

3. What training and/or experience does your staff have in assisting students who have ADD?

4. Are the professional staff members of CH.A.D.D. or A.H.E.A.D.?

5. Are students assigned an individual staff counselor or advocate? How available are counselors to see students?

6. How willing are faculty members to provide appropriate academic accommodations?

7. What specific programs and services are available to students who have ADD? How are services delivered?

8. Is there an additional cost for participation in services and/or programs?

9. What are the student's responsibilities in obtaining needed services?

Students with ADD served by support programs have diverse profiles of strengths and areas of need for improvement. Modified arrangements for students who have attention deficit disorders must be addressed and planned to meet individual needs. The following "menu of services" lists accommodations pertinent to the needs of students with ADD (Richard, 1992):

Special orientation sessions	Recorded textbooks
Priority registration for classes	Course substitutions
Alternative testing arrangements	Assistance with academic skills
Advocacy with staff and faculty	Support groups
Tutorial services	Counseling

Note-taking services   Disability information
Assistance with time management   Professional referrals
Extended deadlines for course work   Technological assistance

Colleges and universities may not discriminate in their admissions policy on the basis that a student has ADD. Generally, students with ADD are considered for admission to college on the same basis as all other applicants and must meet the same academic requirements. However, some departments of admission work in cooperation with their institution's office of disability services to recognize extenuating circumstances that would affect a student's admissibility. They carefully evaluate the overall performance of these applicants for evidence of ability needed to successfully pursue studies at their college or university (Barron, 1993).

Students are not asked on the application form to provide personal information about whether they have a disability; in fact, such preadmission inquiries are illegal. However, supplying this type of information is useful if a student wants to be referred for related services or does not meet admissions requirements. In order to initiate the application process, a prospective student should go to the office of admissions at the school of his or her choice and inquire about that institution's procedures. To initiate a request for special consideration, the student should submit a letter to the director of admissions, self-identifying his or her ADD (and any other disabilities) and including the following:

1. A statement requesting special consideration in the admissions process
2. A description of how the student is affected by ADD
3. A description of how the student has compensated for any academic deficits
4. Information regarding resources used to compensate for these deficits (such as resource room, tutors, word processing, calculators, extended time for testing, taped text books, etc.)
5. Information about how the student has been involved in self-advocacy
6. A description of why the student was unable to complete the required high school course work (if this is the case), which should be verified by a psychologist's written assessment or by a letter from the student's high school guidance counselor

In addition, most postsecondary institutions require specific evidence from other individuals to initiate special consideration, including:

1. A written assessment of ADD (and any other disabilities), including a list of all criteria that clearly indicate that the student has ADD, updated by a certified school or clinical psychologist or made within 3 years of the application for admission

2. Letters of support, including teacher recommendations, from individuals who have firsthand knowledge of the student's academic abilities

It is the experience of disability services counselors that students who self-identify at the time of application, seek assistance early, and use appropriate accommodations are more likely to achieve academic success (Richard, Carstens, & Chandler, 1992a, 1992b). However, the decision to self-identify a disability is a personal one, and a student's decision not to do so should be respected.

ISSUES IN GRADUATE EDUCATION FOR STUDENTS WITH ADD

"I kept losing interest in my topics so I changed programs several times."
          —An M.A. candidate

"Thank goodness for the software programs which helped with my dissertation!"
          —A new Ph.D. recipient

In many ways, a successful undergraduate career prepares students with ADD to meet the academic challenges of graduate school. During the bachelor's degree program, students develop skills to manage large amounts of work outside of class, assimilate new vocabulary, and manage time. In a graduate program, the demands multiply to use these skills and to increase the use of higher order thinking and synthesis skills. Academic competition increases; and graduate school faculty expect a higher level of student proficiency.

In preparation for graduate school, students with ADD can apply for extended time when taking the Graduate Record Examination (GRE) and other standardized graduate school tests. Instructions and deadline information regarding this are printed on the test application instruction booklets. Even if a student does not plan to enter graduate school immediately following college, professionals should recommend that students take the ap-

298 *A Comprehensive Guide to Attention Deficit Disorder in Adults*

propriate exams because scores are higher when tests are taken near the time of college graduation. If applicants with ADD do not score at the minimum level for admission, they should check the program materials for information on conditional admission of "otherwise meritorious" candidates. If they choose to apply in this category, they should follow the departmental procedures for submitting such a request for admission. They may be asked to provide the following:

1. A statement requesting special consideration in the admissions process emphasizing areas of demonstrated strengths
2. A description of how ADD affects the student with respect to standardized examinations
3. A description of how the student has compensated for any academic deficits in past course work
4. Information about accommodations the student has made use of and found to be effective in the past

The applicant may also need to provide the institution's student disabilities office with specific evidence from other individuals in order to initiate special consideration. This would specifically include a diagnostic summary that clearly indicates that the student has ADD. The assessment should be made or updated within 3 years of the application for admission, and be completed by a clinical psychologist and/or medical doctor. These records should not be sent to the academic department. Disability documentation is confidential and should not be interpreted by persons who are unqualified to interpret such information. The disability office should release information or recommendations contained in an individual's documentation only by his or her written consent.

An optimal transition into a graduate or professional degree program is facilitated by planning which includes:

1. Selecting an institution that provides support services
2. Selecting a suitable degree program
3. Obtaining copies of documentation of the student's ADD (and other disabilities) for the student disability services office
4. Prearranging any accommodations needed, such as

Lighter class load	Alternative exam accommodations
Letters to professors	Tutoring
Note-taking services	Taped textbooks

5. Locating related medical and psychological services
6. Locating appropriate counselors and support groups

Preparation for the graduate school experience is not only a matter of academic background, resources, and personal commitment for a student who has ADD. An understanding of ADD and any coexisting disabilities, and the degree of success the student has attained in living and coping with them, is significantly related to positive academic and personal outcome. Additional factors that support student progress include the availability of supportive advising, academic accommodations, and medical and psychological treatment resources.

THE SUCCESSFUL COLLEGE STUDENT WITH ADD

> *"I couldn't get a handle on my studies until my counselor sat down with me and explained thoroughly how learning happens and what specific areas are affected by my ADD and learning disabilities."*
> —*A junior history major*

> *"Everyone talks about how this affects school, but what really helped was for me to be in a group which discussed how ADD affects the rest of my life. Believe me, this helped me more with school than anything else."*
> —*A college sophomore*

> *"Everyone used to tell me what to do until I learned about my rights. I can't believe the way I was run over until I learned about the laws which protect my educational rights and learned when and how to speak for myself."*
> —*A graduate student*

Postsecondary students with ADD and those who assist them must address a variety of social, emotional, and academic issues. Counseling goals should facilitate the development of a base of information about the effect of ADD on each area in order to equip students to cope with ADD and meet the demands of college. It is vital that students do the following:

1. Understand ADD and its personal impacts
2. Understand and use their best learning styles and strengths
3. Understand their rights and become effective self-advocates

4. Develop strategies for social interactions
5. Learn to use effective learning strategies
6. Learn and implement methods for time management
7. Develop a realistic sense of personal competence and confidence
8. Know and use university and community services that provide counseling, health, and academic accommodations

Interviews with college graduates with ADD reveal they have used a number of cognitive strategies for helping themselves regulate their attention and productivity. While most describe difficulty with stress intolerance and periodic burnout, and many say that they had continuing problems with inconsistency, they felt that using structured note taking and time management were especially helpful (Adelman & Olufs, 1986).

Many successful college students, working with professionals, have written personal essays about growing up and living with ADD. Through this method of "telling one's story," students may reflect on where they have been and where they are going in terms of their personal as well as academic development. This is a valuable developmental exercise, especially for students who process information well through writing. A year after she was diagnosed with ADD, a junior wrote:

> Now that I know how ADD affects me I no longer feel like an inadequate person. It is such a relief! Learning about ADD, taking medication for my symptoms, and visiting with a knowledgeable counselor has given me a new confidence in my future. I still have ADD, but my grades are better and I find it much easier to get along with others. One good thing I gained from having a disability which I hope will stay with me is a real feeling of acceptance of others who are different in some way. Since I paid a high price for learning this, I hope it will stay with me for a lifetime.

The traditional system of guidance in which a professional serves as the "expert" does not offer students with ADD appropriate developmental opportunities to become their own best expert. Emphasis should be placed on increasing the students' own procedural skills and self-understanding, so that they may advocate for themselves (Mangrum & Strichart, 1984). The role of the professional includes offering resources and logistical support, facilitating and monitoring the students' follow-through with plans to obtain information, and assisting the student in identification of the issues that contribute to decision making. The following table (Richard, Chandler, & Wu, 1993) displays situations that are appropriate times for self-advocacy and advocacy by others.

TABLE 15-1
Self-Advocacy Versus Advocacy by Others for Students with ADD

Situation	What the Student May Do	What Student Disability Services Counselor May Do
The student needs academic accommodations in a class.	Make an appointment to request accommodations with the instructor early in the semester at an appropriate time.	At the student's request, the counselor could send a letter to his or her instructors describing the student's disability and eligibility for appropriate services.
The student has an appointment to explain his or her disability and discuss accommodations.	The student should be prepared to talk about: 1. What is ADD and/or LD. 2. How does it affect him or her. 3. What he or she does to compensate for the disability. 4. What accommodations he or she needs to use to complete the course. 5. What accommodations will help him or her demonstrate mastery of this course.	1. At an appointment with a counselor the student could prepare for discussing these issues with faculty. Sometimes role playing is a helpful way of doing this. 2. If the instructor would like more information, he or she might call your counselor.
The student needs to have class materials and books on cassette tape.	1. Contact Student Disability Services to obtain a Books-on-Tape application. 2. Follow the directions for obtaining books on tape.	The counselor can assist with establishing procedures for contacting instructors in advance to make plans for obtaining taping services. It the student is not already a member of Recording for the Blind (RFB), the counselor can assist in filing the application.
The student needs accommodations for tests.	1. Obtain an alternative exam form from Student Disability Services to arrange for the test to be proctored through their office. Complete the form	The Student Disability Services may supervise or schedule quiet testing rooms and other accommodations that are appropriate for students, *(Continued)*

TABLE 15-1 (Cont.)
Self-Advocacy Versus Advocacy by Others for Students with ADD

Situation	What the Student May Do	What Student Disability Services Counselor May Do
	and return it to the exam service by the deadline on the form. 2. Arrange with the instructor for him or her to provide accommodations.	including, but not limited to, readers, clarification, writers, word processing.
The student needs to withdraw from a course and this affects his or her financial aid.	Contact the office of financial aid regarding an appeal.	If the student's withdrawal is based on reasons related to disability, the counselor may be able to advocate for the student regarding the appeal.
The student wants to apply for a major, but does not meet the GPA requirement.	By far the best is to achieve the required GPA. If the student's disability was first diagnosed during the college years, he or she may calculate what the overall GPA and GPA in your major have been since diagnosis and use of accommodation services.	The counselor may be able to advocate for the student in letter form concerning the application.
After class the student is unsure of the objective of an assignment or what to study for a test.	1. See the instructor after class. 2. Ask the instructor for an appointment (either in person or call during his or her office hours). 3. At the appointment ask for clarification; take notes.	The counselor may be able to provide you with a standardized list of assignment and essay question term definitions.
The student is experiencing difficulties writing papers, doing math required for his or her major/minor, etc.	1. Contact the writing lab regarding the availability of assistance with writing. 2. Become familiar with reference library research assistance services. 3. Contact departments about labs, i.e., the chemistry department	Assistant with study skills and strategies may be available from counselors, but may not be directly applicable to specific course work. The counselor may direct the student to an instructional technology lab for

Situation	What the Student May Do	What Student Disability Services Counselor May Do
	about chem tutorial labs, etc.	assistance in learning to use computer software that performs the needed function, for example: spelling or grammar checking.
The student is experiencing emotional, social, or family difficulties which hamper ability to function personally and/or study.	Assess the situation and talk about it with an appropriate person. Appropriate people may be friends, family, a Student Disability Services counselor or another counselor, residence hall staff, physician, clergy, etc.	The counselor is available to talk with students about these issues. He or she may make referrals to another service that can provide additional assistance.
The student is having difficulty managing his or her schedule of classes, studies, work hours, social life, activities, appointments, due dates for assignments, etc.	1. Obtain as much class information as possible for schedule building. 2. Allotting blocks of time for classes, study, etc. 3. Learn to use a comprehensive planner to schedule and plan each day. 4. Record on the planner all of the important college dates including withdrawal and drop-add deadlines, events, holidays.	The counselor may offer training in time management skills for students. He or she will be available to review the schedule for the next semester. In the event of questions that relate specifically to academic advising, the counselor may encourage the student to obtain assistance from an academic advisor.
The student is having extreme difficulty with a course.	1. Determine what aspects of the course are causing problems. 2. Contact Student Disabilities Services.	The student's counselor will assist in analyzing the situation according to the student's disability information. He or she may offer assistance with study strategies, tutoring services, or examine the possibility of need to withdraw from the course, apply for a course substitution, or another course of action.

CONCLUSION: CREDIT TO STUDENTS AND COLLEGES

*"Who are the New Students of the '90s? What issues
drive their agendas for education? What services will
they need in order to have the opportunity to succeed?
What will they contribute to the institution and later, to
society?"*

—A campus lecturer

Students with ADD who are successful in academic programs may give
a certain amount of credit for their success to the lessons they have learned
in life. They have learned that "the buck stops" with them, and have taken
responsibility for their own lives. This indicates they are moving on from
a history of painful memories, and are now following procedures to relieve
and compensate for the symptoms of ADD. They have stopped looking
for a quick fix to their difficulties and have determined that what lies between them and their aspirations consists of dedication and work. They
have learned not to fear making mistakes and to manage their impulses to
the extent that they do not live entirely "on the edge."

The impact of the Americans with Disabilities Act is likely to be felt as
more students with disabilities choose to participate in higher education,
and there is an increased focus on disability services and programs. Campuses benefit from the increased participation of persons with disabilities
in academic life. The increasing number of qualified students with disabilities on campus can enhance higher education's cultural diversity and
expand the pool of college-educated workers with disabilities who will have
the opportunity to lead productive lives and contribute to society.

Credit for student success may be given to the colleges and universities
who provide appropriate support services and accommodations for students with ADD. These are growing in number as a result of parent, student, and professional advocacy, as well as a desire on the part of the academic community to support student development and maintain ethical
and legal standards with regard to students with disabilities. Those institutions that have developed proactive programs for students with ADD, by
going beyond "paper compliance" and offering individuals understanding
and services, are to be especially respected for their integrity regarding
their educational mission and mandate.

Many colleges and universities tout the value of diversity in their academic environment and campus life. If indeed they mean this, then they
must value students who are not representatives of the young, nondisabled
majority. In terms of the richness of human experience, students with ADD
may have a good deal to offer academic communities. Their presence on

campus shows they are taking charge of their lives and are bringing their abilities to bear on their education and future careers. They have learned to avoid situations that work against their symptoms of ADD, and to create and follow their own methods for achieving success. After all, this resourcefulness is a good deal of what education and student development are all about.

REFERENCES

Adelman, P.B., & Olufs, D. (1986). *Assisting college students with learning disabilities: A tutor's manual.* Lake Forest, IL: Barat College.

American Psychiatric Association. (1987). *Diagnostic and statistical manual of mental disorders* (3rd ed.). Washington, DC.

Association for Handicapped Student Services Programs in Postsecondary Education. (1987). *Unlocking the doors: Making the transition to postsecondary education.* Columbus, OH: Author.

Association for Higher Education and Disability. (1992). *Title by title: The ADA's impact on postsecondary education.* Columbus, OH: Author.

Barbaro. F. (1982). The learning disabled college student: Some considerations in setting objectives. *Journal of Learning Disabilities, 15,* 599–604.

Barkley, R. (1990). *Attention deficit hyperactivity disorder.* New York: Guilford Press.

Barkley, R. (1991). *Attention deficit hyperactive disorder: A clinical workbook.* New York: Guilford Press.

Barkley, R., & Murphy, K. (1993, October). Guidelines for a written clinical report concerning ADHD adults. *ADHD Report, 1*(5), 8–9.

Barron, M. (1993, March). Admissions decisions. In materials for National Association of College Admission Counselors workshop, *Understanding Learning Disabilities.* Evanston, IL: Northwestern University.

Brinckerhoff, L. (1993). Developing a summer orientation program for college students with learning disabilities: Issues and considerations. *Support services for students with learning disabilities in higher education: A compendium of readings, 3,* 121–124. Columbus, OH: AHEAD.

Brinckerhoff, L., Shaw, S., & McGuire, J. (1993). *Promoting postsecondary education for students with learning disabilities: A handbook for practitioners.* Austin, TX: PRO-ED Publishers.

Cantwell, D., & Baker, L. (1992). Association between attention deficit hyperactivity disorder and learning disorders. In B. Shaywitz and S. Shaywitz (Eds.), *Attention deficit disorder comes of age: Toward the twenty-first century,* pp. 145–164. Austin, TX: PRO-ED Publishers.

Children and Adults with Attention Deficit Disorders. (1993). Not just for children anymore: ADD in adulthood. *CH.A.D.D.ER,* pp. 19–21.

Gersh, F. (1993, November). Treatment of ADD in college students. *CH.A.D.D.ER Box, 6*(11), 10–11.

Hallowell, E., & Ratey, J. (1994). *Driven to distraction.* New York: Random House.

Higher Education and the Handicapped Resource Center. (1993). College freshmen with disabilities. *Information from HEATH, 12*(2), 4.

Javorsky, J. & Gussin, B. (1994). College students with ADHD: An overview and description of services. *Journal of College Student Development, 35,* 170–177.

Johnston, R. B. (1991). *Attention deficits, learning disabilities, and Ritalin* (2nd ed.). San Diego, CA: Singular.

Kravets, M., & Wax, I. (1992). *The K and W guide to colleges for the learning disabled* (2nd ed.). New York: HarperCollins.

Mangrum, C., & Strichart, S. (1984). *College and the learning disabled student* (2nd ed.). Orlando, FL: Grune & Stratton.

McCormick, A., & Leonard, F. (1993). Learning accommodations for ADD students. In P. Quinn (Ed.), *ADD and the college student: A guide for high school and college students with attention deficit disorder* (pp. 75–83). New York: Magination Press.

Murphy, K. (1992). Coping strategies for ADHD adults. *CH.A.D.D. Special Edition.* Plantation, FL: CH.A.D.D.

Richard, M. M. (1992). Considering student support services in college selection. *CH.A.D.D.ER Box, 5*(6), pp. 1, 6, 7.

Richard, M. M., Carstens, J. B., & Chandler, D. (1992a). *College students with attention deficit disorders: A guide for students.* Iowa City: University of Iowa Student Disability Services.

Richard, M. M., Carstens, J. B., & Chandler, D. (1992b). *College students with attention deficit disorders: A guide for faculty.* Iowa City: University of Iowa Student Disability Services.

Richard, M. M., Chandler, D., & Wu, X. (1993). *Student handbook: Student disability services.* Iowa City: University of Iowa Student Disability Services.

Richard, M. & Chandler, D., (1994). *Student handbook: Student disability services.* Iowa City: University of Iowa Student Disability Services.

Sandperl, M. (1993). Toward a comprehensive model of learning disability service delivery. *Support services for students with learning disabilities in higher education: A compendium of readings.* 3, 67–68. Columbus, OH: AHEAD.

Scheiber, B., & Talpers, J. (1987). *Unlocking potential: College and other choices for learning disabled people–A step-by-step guide.* Bethesda, MD: Adler & Adler.

Sedita, J. (1989). *Landmark study skills guide.* Pride's Crossing, MA: Landmark Foundation.

Smith, S. (1991). *Succeeding against the odds: Strategies and insights from the learning disabled.* Los Angeles: Tarcher.

Stein, M. (1993, November). Has hyperactivity grown up yet? *CH.A.D.D.ER Box*, *6*(11), pp. 6–7.

Vogel, S. A. (1987). Issues and concerns in LD college programming. In D. Johnson & J. Blalock (Eds.), *Adults with learning disabilities: Clinical studies* (pp. 239–275). Orlando, FL: Grune and Stratton.

Vogel, S. A. (1993). *College students with learning disabilities: A handbook for college students with learning disabilities, university admissions officers, faculty, and administration* (4th ed.). Pittsburgh: LDA (Learning Disabilities Association).

Vogel, S. A., & Adelman, P. B. (Eds.). (1993). *Success for college students with learning disabilities.* New York: Springer-Verlag.

Weiss, G., & Hechtman, L. T. (1993). *Hyperactive children grown up* (2nd ed.). New York: Guilford Press.

Werry, J., Reeves, J., & Elkind, G. (1987). Attention deficit, conduct oppositional, and anxiety disorders in children: 1. A review of research on differentiating characteristics. *Journal of the American Academy of Child and Adolescent Psychiatry, 26*, 133–143.

Wren, C., & Segal, L. (1985). *College students with learning disabilities: A student's perspective.* Chicago, IL: DePaul University Project Learning Strategies.

Zentall, S. (1993). Research on the educational implications of attention deficit hyperactivity disorder. *Exceptional Children, 60*, 143–155.

16

ADD in the Workplace
Career Consultation and Counseling for the Adult with ADD

KATHLEEN G. NADEAU

The manifestations of attention deficits in adults are often most evident in the workplace environment, for it is at work that the greatest demands for planning, memory, organization, teamwork, and precision are placed on us. The ADD career consultant has a crucial role to play in enabling the ADD adult to achieve success in the workplace. In this chapter, a model is proposed for the ADD career counselor as the integrator of complex sets of information, who makes appropriate referrals and accommodations based on that information as well as on her or his own assessment, and who serves, in an ongoing capacity, as coach, advocate, and counselor while the adult with ADD works to improve his or her workplace functioning. Career selection or career change, workplace performance, issues relating to promotions or job transfers, disclosure of the ADD diagnosis at work, reasonable on-the-job accommodations, and success strategies in the workplace for the adult with ADD will be addressed in this chapter. Because practitioners, such as myself, are on the "front line" serving newly diagnosed adults with ADD, without the benefit of guidance from empirical evidence, much of the information in this chapter is necessarily derived from clinical experience.

FACTORS TO CONSIDER

In my observation, as well as the observations of others, the population of adults with ADD that tends to seek treatment at clinics, universities, and private offices represent the high-functioning end of the adult ADD continuum. Because of the very recent, and not yet widespread, recognition of ADD in adults, those who are currently aware are likely to be among the relatively well educated who have read articles, watched television documentaries, and attended presentations regarding Attention Deficit Disorder.

Because of this skewed population of adults seeking assistance for ADD, and given the lack of empirical evidence, we should assume that many of the observations contained in this chapter are most relevant to that higher-functioning subgroup of adults. It seems most likely that a large percentage of adults with ADD are to be found also within the prison population, within the various groups of substance abusers, and among the ranks of unemployed or marginally employed, who may not be aware of or have access to treatment for ADD. There is a critical need for research to document work issues among the broad range of adults with ADD, as well as to investigate the efficacy of the accommodations and compensatory strategies suggested in this chapter.

ADD-LD Distinctions

You will notice that many citations in this chapter reference articles and studies regarding learning disabilities (LD) rather than attention deficits in the workplace. This emphasis upon LD as opposed to ADD is due to the very recent recognition of ADD in adults. Much of the literature referring to LD in the workplace is relevant, however, to ADD concerns. In fact, the Rehabilitative Services Program Policy Directive states that *"characteristics such as attention, memory, and social interactions have...greater implications for vocational planning and employment than those associated with poor academic performance"* (Rehabilitation Services Administration, 1981, p. 3). This report goes on to say that academic difficulties are "just the tip of the iceberg" when considering the areas of functioning in the workplace that are affected by learning disabilities. In essence, the very issues associated with ADD are the central issues for learning disabled adults that affect employment success.

Attentional problems and the cluster of problems commonly associated with ADD are a subset of the larger group of issues typically considered to be learning disabilities. It would be more accurate and appropriate to use the medical term *neurodevelopmental disorder* rather than the educational term *learning disability*. However, the majority of research to date focuses on neurodevelopmental dysfunctions as they affect academic performance, thus the term learning disability. The Rehabilitation Services Administration Program Policy Directive (RSA-PPD-885-7, March 5, 1985) defines a learning disability as a disorder that manifests itself with a deficit in: *attention*, reasoning, processing, memory, communication, reading, writing, spelling, calculation, coordination, social competence, and emotional maturity [emphasis mine].

Career Patterns in Adults with ADD

Research is badly needed to investigate the full range of career patterns found among adults with ADD. The following comments are based upon observations of adults who have sought consultation for their ADD. Many of these adults seem to have chosen their career with little organized, planned consideration for their ADD characteristics. ADD adults who are hyperactive and impulsive may present a career pattern of a wide array of short-lived jobs. Weiss, Hechtman, Milroy, and Perlman (1985) found that hyperactive adults generally experienced more employment difficulties than adults with other types of learning and attentional problems.

Because ADD adults range across a broad spectrum with regard to the degree to which and the manner in which their workplace performance is affected by ADD (Lucius, 1991), there are a number of other work patterns that appear to be common among ADD adults. Those less impulsive or less hyperactive in nature may present themselves for career counseling when they have been promoted to a position whose demands exceed their managerial or organizational capacity. Still others have been chronic underachievers. They may have intelligence and talent, yet their wavering motivation, disorganization, or tendency to procrastinate has caused them to be permanently relegated to job assignments below their intellectual capacity. A few, through luck or intuition, find themselves well matched with their career.

Positive Traits Associated with ADD

It is important that career consultation not focus primarily on the traits in ADD adults that have a negative impact on job performance, but also should give attention to positive traits that appear to be associated with ADD. Because of the variety of ways in which ADD manifests in adults, it is impossible to make general statements about strengths and positive traits that would apply to all adults with ADD. Some popular books may tend to make such sweeping, positive generalizations about adult ADD, which does great disservice to those adults who do not have the good fortune to share these positive traits. Paul Jaffe (1993) warns against the use of such generalizations about positive attributes associated with ADD, suggesting that they tend to deny and trivialize a serious disorder.

Nevertheless, there is much to gain by recognition that some traits associated with adult ADD may, in fact, be beneficial in certain work environments. In my clinical experience, I find that some ADD adults make excellent salespeople, promoters, and lobbyists due to their social skills and boundless energy. Still other ADD adults are blessed with an endless flow of creative ideas and associations which make them marvelous brainstormers and catalysts. Many hyperactive adults use their enthusiasm effectively in entrepreneurial activities. Although planning and long-term follow-through tend to be difficult for many ADD adults, some are able to respond superbly to situations calling for crisis intervention or immediate problem solving.

THE ROLE OF CAREER CONSULTANT
WITH THE ADD ADULT

The usual role of career counselor involves an evaluation of (1) interests, (2) strengths and skills, (3) temperament and personality type, and (4) values and needs, to guide the individual to a better sense of "career self." Gloria Monick (personal communication, 1993), a career consultant experienced in working with adults with ADD, suggests that this sense of a "career self" is a key issue for adults with ADD. She finds that "this process serves to build self-esteem and often establishes a positive career identify for the first time for the adult with ADD." The ADD career consultant should fulfill these traditional functions of career counseling; the consultant's work is further challenged, however, by the variety of ways that attention deficits are manifested and affect performance on the job, by the range of other neurodevelopmental issues which often accompany attention deficits, and also by the variety of comorbid neurological and psychological conditions which may be present. (See chapters 3, 4, and 5, this volume, for a more complete discussion of these accompanying conditions.)

Additionally, the ADD career consultant must be aware of the chronic emotional toll these "invisible disabilities" take on the ADD adult. The consultant should be prepared to serve as coach and counselor in assisting the individual to reach a more positive and adaptive level of functioning. Although there is rapidly growing awareness and provision of services to children with attention deficits, contemporary adults have typically received no support or accommodations for their difficulties. A survey of professional and graduate programs (Parks, Antonoff, Drake, Skiba, & Soberman, 1987) found that almost 15 years after the passage of the Rehabilitation Act of 1973, the attitudes of educators and administrators toward students with learning and attentional difficulties continued to be very negative, with little willingness to accommodate their needs. Other studies have shown a similarly negative attitude among employers, particularly those on the professional level (Minskoff, Sauter, Hoffman, & Hawks, 1987).

In the face of such ignorance and bias, many adults with learning and attentional difficulties have developed significant self-esteem problems.

Murphy (1992) stresses that one of the most important functions in career counseling with ADD/LD adults is to rebuild self-confidence and self-esteem following their prolonged academic struggles and years of facing the prejudices of educators and employers. Monick (personal communication, 1994) suggests that this increase in self-esteem allows the adult to channel energy forward in a positive direction. Murphy also emphasizes that vocational counseling with ADD adults needs to match them with jobs that maximize their strengths, giving them a sense of mastery and accomplishment.

ADD adults are now eligible for services through the Department of Rehabilitation Services. The *Memorandum from the Task Force on Learning Disabilities* (Rehabilitation Services Administration, 1981) recognizes learning disabilities as a handicapping condition, making a person eligible for services. Attention deficit disorder is considered a handicapping condition under the broader category of learning disabilities.

It is critical that the career counselor familiarize himself with both the Rehabilitation Act of 1973 and the Americans with Disabilities Act in order to advise clients of their rights to services and accommodations. The career consultant may be called on to serve as advocate for clients as they pursue their rights, and may need to refer clients for legal advice if the consultant feels that clients' rights are not being met. (See chapter 17, this volume, for a more complete discussion of legal issues pertaining to the ADD adult.)

Integrative Role of the ADD Career Consultant

Johnson and Blalock (1987b) wrote that many learning disabled adults received career counseling that was not particularly helpful to them. Most had been presented with reports that did not specify aptitudes, or were given a list of interests that did not take ability or achievement into account. Some reports focused on an area of strength, guiding the learning disabled adult onto a vocational path that was inappropriate for the person because of cognitive difficulties that had not been considered. The most successful vocational guidance that Johnson and Blalock (1987b) encountered with learning disabled adults involved a collaborative effort between psychologists, learning disability specialists, and vocational counselors. Rarely were these individuals found working together. Rather, they were brought together by the dogged effort and persistence of the learning disabled adult. It is exactly this type of task, one requiring organization, planning, and persistence, that poses great difficulty for the adult with ADD. Furthermore, those adults who may be successful in their attempt to find qualified professionals to evaluate the various aspects of their abilities, disabilities, and comorbid conditions are not usually equipped to interpret the results and to develop an action plan based on those results.

In this chapter, I suggest a comprehensive model for ADD career counseling in which the ADD career consultant takes responsibility for the integration of test results from evaluations of ability, achievement, interests, personality traits, and specific problematic LD and ADD concerns. Depending on the background and training of the career consultant he may administer much of this testing himself, he may refer pieces of this comprehensive evaluation to other appropriate professionals, or he may review and interpret previously administered evaluations. If several professionals are involved, it is crucial that the interpretation and integration of the results be done by the ADD career consultant. Although career consultants may not be trained to administer all facets of the evaluation themselves, it is essential that they be very familiar with ability testing and interest testing, in addition to the complex batteries of neuropsychological, psychological, and psychoeducational tests used to evaluate ADD/LD issues. The consultant needs to be able to interpret the results of the evaluations, and integrate the results into a comprehensive plan for clients. Consultants should be familiar enough with possible comorbid conditions to make appropriate referrals to psychiatrists, neurologists, psychotherapists, speech pathologists, educational specialists, vision specialists, or other appropriate professionals as the possible need for their services becomes apparent.

The end point of this evaluative and integrative process should be the presentation not only of suggested career tracks but also, most importantly, of a comprehensive list of specific, practical recommendations. These recommendations might include:

1. Referral to other professionals for treatment of ADD and related conditions that are outside of the expertise of the career consultant
2. Suggested areas for remediation, and referral to appropriate professionals who can undertake such remediation
3. Reasonable accommodations to be requested from an employer
4. Compensatory strategies to be undertaken by the client
5. Recommendations for issues on which to focus in follow-up counseling with the ADD career consultant

The real work of the career consultant has only begun with the presentation of these recommendations. From this point, the consultant's role shifts from evaluator to that of counselor, coach, and advocate. The consultant will need to help educate the ADD adult in self-advocacy skills, but may also need to consult with employee assistance personnel or supervisors regarding reasonable accommodations in the workplace. In the following sections of this chapter, I address, in much greater detail, each of the suggested aspects of the work of the ADD career consultant: assessment, interpretation, and integration of test results; development of recommendations to formulate an action plan; and finally, counseling, coaching, and advocacy as the action plan is put into effect.

COMPREHENSIVE ADD CAREER EVALUATIONS

During this phase, the ADD career counselor will be involved in an assessment process, while interpreting and integrating those aspects of a comprehensive evaluation that may be undertaken by other professionals. Ideally, the career counselor will develop a working relationship with other professionals who are expert in adult ADD issues and who can provide those aspects of the evaluation that are beyond the purview of the career consultant.

Some Considerations when Testing an Adult with ADD

The career counselor should take the individual's attentional difficulties into account when administering any tests. These difficulties could include impatience, distractibility, motor restlessness, a tendency toward careless errors, and inattention when reading, any of which could render the test results inaccurate to some degree. To combat this, the career counselor could consider the following:

1. Because many adults with ADD have a strong tendency to make careless errors, the examiner can accommodate for this by allowing clients to mark their answers next to the questions in a question booklet rather than requiring them to transfer answers to an answer sheet. The examiner can transfer the answers to the answer sheet later to allow for computer or template scoring.

2. Reading difficulties should be carefully considered when administering paper-and-pencil tests. For those who experience difficulty concentrating, frequent breaks may improve performance. For those who have an accompanying learning disability leading to reading problems, it may be appropriate to have the test or questionnaire read aloud to the client by a technician or by the career counselor.

3. Restlessness, mental fatigue, and distractibility need to be considered. It may be appropriate to break testing into 1 hour segments, and to allow breaks within each hour. Testing should take place in a quiet, nondistracting environment.

Psychoeducational Evaluations with a Workplace Perspective

If the ADD adult has had ADD or LD evaluations within the past 2 to 3 years, further testing may not be necessary. However, those evaluations need to be reviewed and reinterpreted in order to develop a list of recommendations that pertain to functioning in the workplace. Just as all good

ADD/LD evaluations during school years will include recommendations to improve academic performance, including remediation (tutoring), coping strategies, and accommodations (in the classroom and in testing situations), a good evaluation for the ADD adult in the workplace should contain parallel recommendations to enhance workplace performance.

A list of recommendations has been developed (see Tables 16–1 and 16–2 later in this chapter) for the use of the diagnostician or career consultant. The clinician/career counselor can refer to this list with the client to collaboratively determine which recommendations may be most appropriate and helpful. These recommendations include those that have been developed through career counseling with ADD adults, as well as job accommodations for adults with learning and attentional difficulties recommended by others (Brown, 1993; Jacobs & Hendricks, 1992; President's Committee on Employment of People with Disabilities, 1993; Vocational Rehabilitation Center of Allegheny County, 1984).

If the ADD adult has not had adequate evaluation of attention, concentration, organization, memory, and learning patterns, this evaluation should be done as an integral part of the career counseling process. Simpson and Umbach (1989) emphasize that such an evaluation is crucial because it will enable the adult to make well-informed choices, as well as to establish rights and eligibility for accommodations under the Americans with Disabilities Act. With adequate documentation, the ADD adult may be eligible for special test accommodations (usually untimed testing, administered individually, in a nondistracting environment), if she or he is required to take an entrance or qualifying test to gain acceptance into a postgraduate school, to obtain licensure in a profession, or to demonstrate competence to enter a skilled craft or trade. (See chapter 7, this volume, for a more complete discussion of these legal rights issues.)

An ADD/LD evaluation is helpful not only in day-to-day functioning on the job but also in helping ADD adults maximize their success in training settings. In today's job market, many workers are trained and retrained, even as they remain in the same position. Training may include short workshops on new policies and procedures, management training seminars as the individual is prepared for promotion, short courses on the operation of new technical equipment, or courses on the use of new software systems. ADD adults will need to have a thorough understanding of their learning style and learning needs in order to keep up with this ongoing expectation for training and development. For example, some ADD adults may have difficulty concentrating sufficiently in daylong seminars, a typical format for training in the business and professional world. Others may have problems with sequential memory which could result in difficulty learning new complicated procedures. Still others may have difficulty processing, storing, and retrieving complicated new information. Just as in the traditional classroom environment, there are ways that these difficulties can be accommodated, but having an understanding of their own needs is essential for ADD adults to request and receive accommodations.

Ability Testing

A second type of testing that can be very helpful to the ADD adult, aside from the "disability testing" just discussed, is ability testing. There are a variety of test batteries in existence, some of which may be available through local offices of rehabilitative services or vocational rehabilitation. Other ability test batteries are available privately. This series of tests can cover a far broader range of abilities than are investigated in a standard psychoeducational test battery. Ability testing typically includes the measurement of "realistic abilities" (the ability to work with things as opposed to people), mechanical and physical abilities (the ability to understand the laws and relationships of the physical world), spatial abilities, investigative (research) abilities, social, artistic, enterprising, and conventional (clerical) abilities (Lowman, 1991). Much research has been done on clusters of abilities from particular test batteries as they relate to likely success in careers with specific task and ability demands. The combination of *ability* testing and disability testing can provide a positive counterbalance to the focus on dysfunction that is an inevitable part of the process of working with an adult with ADD.

Monick (personal communication, 1994) describes another process often employed by career counselors, which involves a "skills assessment" that looks at not just what one *can* do, but also what one *enjoys doing*. By assessing these "motivated energy and strengths" ADD individuals are better able to develop a realistic and positive view of themselves and their potentials in the workplace. Perhaps one of the best known ability tests is offered by the Johnson O'Connor Research Foundation, available in major cities throughout the United States. Another similar and widely respected ability test battery is Highlands Ability Battery. These batteries measure aptitudes including problem-solving ability, classification ability, concept organization, idea productivity, spatial relationships, design memory, observation skill, verbal memory, tonal memory, pitch discrimination, rhythm memory, manual speed and accuracy, time frame orientation, and strength of grip. These abilities are then considered in clusters that have been related to types of career paths.

Personality Testing

Yet a third type of testing that can prove highly useful is personality testing. Personality factors play a major role in the types of positions for which a particular individual is well suited. The Myers-Briggs Type Inventory (MBTI) is a simple, paper-and-pencil test that can be completed by an individual in 30–40 minutes. Investigations have been done (Golden & Provost, 1987) correlating MBTI personality types with particular career paths. The MBTI can help individuals consider personality traits that may suggest that certain broad categories of work may be satisfying to them. Taking personality traits into account, through use of the MBTI, in conjunction with ability and disability testing can be very beneficial.

We are not always drawn to activities simply because we have the capacity to perform them well. Personality factors can have a crucial effect on whether an individual is suited to a particular type of work. Studies of personality types of individuals with attentional or learning disorders have found that there is no typical LD personality type (Hinkebein, Koller, & Kunce, 1992). In my experience working with ADD adults, those with MBTI personality types ending in J (who prefer order and structure) typically implement compensatory strategies more effectively than those whose personality types end in P (who prefer a less structured, more spontaneous approach). Through evaluating the client's personality type, the career consultant can "develop a framework for emphasizing the client's natural gifts and potential blind spots" (Monick, personal communication, 1993), leading the consultant to make recommendations that will be helpful and more likely to be implemented by the client.

Other useful instruments in evaluating personality factors include the California Psychological Inventory (CPI), the Sixteen Personality Factor Questionnaire (16PF), and the Guilford-Zimmerman Temperament Survey (GZTS). Among numerous studies of personality factors relevant to job performance, five tend to be outstanding: achievement orientation, introversion-extroversion, ascendance-dominance, emotional stability-neuroticism, and masculinity-femininity (Lowman, 1991). Other factors that seem to warrant further study include conscientiousness, agreeableness, need for affiliation, energy and general activity level, and the MBTI factors of intuiting versus sensing, thinking versus feeling, and judging versus perceiving.

In addition to considering these career-relevant personality traits, the ADD career consultant needs to carefully consider the possibility of comorbid psychological conditions such as anxiety, depression, bipolar disorder, obsessive-compulsive disorder, and substance abuse. If the career counselor is a trained psychologist, he or she can administer personality tests to screen for these conditions. ADD career consultants who are not clinicians would be well advised to refer their clients for such psychological testing as a part of the comprehensive evaluation.

Interest Testing

Yet another type of career guidance instrument is the interest test. These tests do not measure ability or personality type, but indicate how an individual's self-reported interests match with individuals who are successful in a variety of fields. Lowman (1991) notes that three of the most commonly used measures of interests are the Self-Directed Search (Holland, 1979), the Vocational Preference Inventory (Holland, 1985), and the Strong Vocational Interest Bank (SVIB) (Campbell & Hansen, 1981). In the context of advising adults with ADD, interest tests may be especially pertinent since interest is so strongly linked to motivation, and motivation is such a critical factor in determining success for adults with attention deficits. While all adults function best in a job assignment that interests them, some adults with ADD find themselves almost incapable of functioning well in a job that does not hold their interest.

Evaluation of ADD Traits from a Workplace Perspective

Up to this point, we have considered testing to determine an ADD diagnosis, evaluate learning styles and learning difficulties, consider general personality factors, and measure abilities and interest patterns. While it may seem that the adult with ADD has been evaluated from almost every possible aspect, perhaps the most important area of evaluation is yet to come. None of the test instruments previously discussed deals directly with ADD in the workplace, although all are relevant and provide useful information. To date no instrument or questionnaire has been developed to directly assess ADD traits as they affect workplace performance. In order to conduct a thorough, structured interview regarding ADD issues in the workplace, the ADD career counselor needs to be thoroughly familiar with ADD traits, especially as they may be manifested in the work environment. It may be useful for the counselor to refer to Adult ADD questionnaires and trait lists discussed in chapter 7, this volume, for guidance in conducting such an interview.

Again, although there is no research-based data available regarding ADD and workplace performance, a number of "crisis points" have been observed that may be typical in the work lives of adults with ADD. These "crises," which often become the point at which the adult with ADD seeks career consultation, can emerge in the following situations:

1. A new position requires tracking and coordination of multiple events
2. A new position requires rapid processing of detailed paperwork

3. A promotion to a position requires the supervision and management of others

4. The organization for which the client works is taken over by a new management team that is detail oriented and inflexible

5. An immediate supervisor is critical, detail oriented, and inflexible

6. A new position involves juggling and coordinating work assignments from multiple sources

The common threads among these job crises is an overload situation in which the demands for planning, organization, time management, and attention to detail exceed the individual's ability to cope.

Unfortunately, many ADD adults do not seek consultation until they have received repeated poor performance reviews and fear that they may lose their job. ADD adults will generally find their employer more willing to accommodate their needs if the employer is approached in a constructive manner long before problems become chronic. In order for earlier self-identification of adult ADD and for earlier employer accommodation of adult ADD issues to occur, much public education is needed.

Components of the Integrative Report

An integrative report following such a multifaceted career is essential to the client with ADD. The career consultation process here is much more complex than with other clients, involving the interpretation and integration of information from a variety of sources. Such information is too detailed, technical, and complex to commit to memory. Also, because memory and auditory processing so often pose a problem for adults with ADD, a purely oral presentation of results and recommendations may be quickly forgotten. The recommendations, which ideally should be included in such a report, are numerous and detailed, also necessitating written documentation. This report may become the basis for eligibility for accommodations in the workplace. A written record of the numerous compensatory strategies that may be generated by such a report should exist for the client to repeatedly refer to as he or she gradually learns to implement them. An integrative report should include the following components:

1. A discussion of areas of weakness that may lead to specific difficulties on the job

2. A discussion of areas of strength, including types of work-related activities in which the individual should excel

3. A list of workplace conditions that may prove difficult and should be avoided, if possible

4. A list of recommendations for remediation, accommodation, and coping strategies (discussed in detail in the following section)

This proposed evaluation is an extensive one. The majority of individuals will not receive such an evaluation. It is essential, however, no matter what other factors are considered, that the counselor be aware of and thoroughly evaluate ADD issues in the process of making career recommendations, and assist the client in integrating information received from other professionals or from earlier evaluations.

RECOMMENDATIONS

While the role of assessment, interpretation, and integration of test results is critical, this process is all for naught if it does not lead to a plan of action which is then implemented. In this section, the types of recommendations that should be provided are discussed; the following section addresses how these recommendations are developed into an action plan implemented by the client in ongoing work with the career counselor.

Recommended Remediation

Remediation refers to the process of improving skills in areas of deficit. Remediation involves tutoring and training. The career counselor may want to refer the ADD adult to an expert in vision therapy, speech and language therapy, or educational tutoring for consultation to determine whether it would be useful to attempt to improve the ADD adult's skill level in areas such as reading, writing, mathematics, memory, or verbal expression. If a particular skill is critical for job performance, and if the ADD adult strongly desires to remain in or to seek that job position, then remediation may be essential.

Bencomo and Schafer (1984), in writing about their work with learning disabled adults, indicate that few services are available to remediate areas of weakness in adults because most educators have tended to focus on remedial work with children. It can be difficult to find tutors who are experienced in working with adults, but as learning disabilities are more recognized and identified in adults, it is gradually becoming easier to find such experts. It is essential that ADD adults recognize the limitations of remediation. Training and tutoring can assist them in skill development, but areas of weakness can only be assisted, not eliminated.

Recommended Accommodations

The Job Accommodations Network (JAN), a service of the President's Committee on Employment of People with Disabilities, was established in

1984 to provide information about job accommodations to individuals with all types of disabilities. Jacobs and Hendricks (1992) conducted research on the types of disabilities for which information was requested from JAN. Their results showed that only slightly more than 4% of cases involved learning disabilities, and less than 10% of those LD cases involved attention deficit disorder issues. As the awareness of adult ADD is exploding, the number of ADD individuals requesting JAN information will likely show a dramatic increase. A marked distinction between ADD and LD issues is debatable, however. Cantwell and Baker (1991) found that ADD was present in 63% of the LD children in their study. Many lists of LD traits include ADD traits (Dowdy, 1992; Jacobs & Hendricks, 1992; Johnson and Blalock, 1987b).

Currently, guidelines are being developed for reasonable accommodations for employees with attentional difficulties (Adelman & Wren, 1990; Brown, 1993; Brown, Gerber, & Dowdy, 1990; Jacobs & Hendricks, 1992; Vocational Rehabilitation Center of Allegheny County, 1984). In all of these studies, attentional difficulties are presented as a subtype of learning disability.

We are in a very early phase of seeking reasonable accommodations for attention deficit issues. Much public and employer education is needed. Research is needed on the efficacy of various accommodations. See Table 16-1 for a list of suggested reasonable accommodations which may be useful to the client.

Recommended Compensatory Strategies

In recommending compensatory strategies to the adult with ADD, the career consultant is setting the stage for the clients' acknowledgment that they must take charge of their attentional difficulties and learn to manage them rather than falling victim to them. No matter how accommodating an employer may choose to be, the lion's share of the work involved in compensating for attentional difficulties remains with the ADD individual. With the help of medication, and with the ongoing coaching, support, and guidance of a counselor or therapist, ADD individuals have many tools at their disposal to work against the negative effects of their attentional difficulties.

Table 16-2 provides an extensive, but not exhaustive list of strategies that may be useful to the ADD adult. These recommendations are suggestions based on clinical practice and experience, and have not been tested for efficacy in clinical trials. They are written to be used as recommendations for the adult with ADD, and can be selectively included by the career counselor among other recommendations made to the client in a report following assessment. The career consultant should selectively choose among these compensatory strategies depending on which issues the ADD adult struggles with in the workplace.

COACH, COUNSELOR, AND ADVOCATE

Completing the report, integrating the findings of a multifaceted evaluation, and developing a set of recommendations is only the beginning of the career consultant's work. Because goal setting, prioritization, planning, and long-term follow-through are the very issues with which most ADD adults are struggling, in most cases, it will be quite ineffective for ADD career consultants to simply present their impressions and recommendations to the ADD adult. The consultant's report should function as a blueprint which the consultant and the client will follow in their continuing work together. At this point, the consultant's role changes from evaluator to coach, counselor, and advocate. If the client is prescribed medication for attentional difficulties, is engaged in psychotherapy, or is working with someone to remediate particular deficits, the consultant will need to communicate and coordinate efforts with the other professionals involved.

Counseling the Midcareer Client with ADD

The ADD adult in midcareer should try not to allow discouragement over past job difficulties to completely color the process of charting a future career direction. Often a troubled work history results from lack of information regarding ADD, poorly considered choices, and poor job matches. Seeking professional career consultation should greatly increase the likelihood that the next job choice will be a much better experience. While all career counseling involves consideration of past employment history, with the ADD adult it is important to conduct this review with a particular consideration of ADD issues. Such a review would ideally be an "experience analysis" rather than simply a review of employment history, allowing all past experience, whether paid or unpaid, to be taken into consideration.

Many adults with ADD who seek counseling in midcareer have experienced much career success prior to their "crisis point." Such persons may have college and even graduate degrees, and may have been perceived as hardworking, creative, and competent. Only after their success has elevated them to a supervisory level in their profession do their ADD traits begin to significantly impair their job functioning. In their new position they are expected to track the activities of other individuals, as well as their own. They are expected to be organized, focused, and able to manage long-term, complex, multistage problems.

Some adults with ADD who are experiencing difficulty in midcareer see other individuals handling similar positions, and they unrealistically expect themselves to do the same. Often these individuals are only recently aware of their attentional difficulties, or become aware of them in their attempt to understand their workplace performance difficulties. The focus of career counseling should be on helping them to understand their real strengths, and to learn coping strategies to compensate for their weaknesses. Gaining acceptance of the limitations brought about by their ADD is critical to their making realistic career choices. The best assurance of career success comes when adults with ADD have clear insights into how their disabilities affect them on the job, as well as an understanding of how to compensate for their disabilities (Adelman & Vogel, 1990).

Role of Coach in Teaching Success Traits

Beyond assisting clients to accept their disabilities and develop compensatory strategies, the counselor should also work toward empowering clients by acquiring positive traits. As Murphy emphasizes (see chapter 8, this volume), it is essential for the adult with ADD to feel empowered in order to make the changes necessary to achieve a positive workplace adjustment. Gerber, Ginzberg, and Reiff (1992) conducted a study of highly successful learning disabled adults in an attempt to identify traits and conditions common among them that could be associated with their success. He found that they all shared a strong desire for success, a tremendous level of determination, a powerful need to control their own destiny, and an ability to reframe their learning disabilities in a more positive and productive manner. They also shared a number of external conditions in common. Most had a mentor and had surrounded themselves with positive, supportive people. They had arranged experiences strategically designed to develop or enhance their skills, and were willing to seek out, appreciate, and accept help appropriately from others without becoming dependent. They knew to plan, were highly goal-oriented, and tended to have a high "goodness of fit" between their particular strengths and weaknesses and the jobs in which they were employed.

Guidance Regarding the Disclosure of the ADD Diagnosis in the Workplace

Disclosure of ADD to an employer is a complex and potentially risky process. Career counselors can provide important assistance to their clients by helping them to assess all aspects of their particular situation in order to come to the best decision. Individuals must each decide when, how, or if they wish to disclose to their employer that they have attention deficits or any other learning disabilities.

Dale Brown, of the President's Committee for Individuals with Disabilities, recommends as a general rule that individuals not disclose learning or attentional problems unless such a disclosure is required to obtain essential accommodations. One study of employer attitudes toward learning disabled employees (Minskoff, Sauter, Hoffman, & Hawks, 1987) found that of all employer categories, employers in high-level positions (professional, technical, managerial) were least willing to hire LD employees. This is a discouraging finding, given that these employers are the most highly educated and presumably the best informed about learning and attentional problems. This study predates the passage of the Americans with Disabilities Act (ADA). It is not clear whether employer attitudes have improved since the passage of this law. It seems likely that these negative attitudes persist, though they may be carefully veiled since the passage of the ADA.

The issue of disclosure goes beyond making a simple statement to an employer about an ADD diagnosis. A formal statement accompanied by written documentation may be necessary under certain circumstances, such as when an adult seeks to obtain special test accommodations. Other approaches may be preferable, however, in different circumstances. Even though an ADD adult may determine, with legal advice, that he is within his rights to request a certain accommodation, after examining all factors, he may decide that it is not in his best interest to file a discrimination suit against an employer. (See chapter 17, this volume, for a more thorough review of the legal rights of an ADD adult in the workplace.)

Disclosure of ADD during a job interview or during the hiring process does not seem advisable as it may lead to a company's decision not to hire the ADD adult. Even after obtaining employment, a formal disclosure, using the ADD or LD label, may not bring about desired results. There is a strong need to educate employers. In the meantime, it is necessary for each ADD adult to function in the work environment as it currently exists. A disclosure could lead an employer to assume that the ADD adult is more disabled than he or she actually is. An employer is only bound to provide accommodations if the individual is "fully qualified" to perform the job. Attention deficit traits can so directly influence job performance that it can become debatable whether a person with attentional problems is qualified to perform a particular function.

Often a much less formalized approach is in order. Rather than announcing an ADD diagnosis, Brown (1984) recommends that individuals could discuss with their employer specific problems and proposed solutions. For example, an adult who is highly distractible could request relocation to a desk in a less trafficked area without claiming a specific diagnosis. Another solution could be to request permission to work in a quiet, nondistracting environment when working on difficult or detailed material.

ADD adults need to learn to state their needs in a positive light, by making requests in the spirit of dedication to the job and a desire to improve work performance. Several articles (Hirshfield & Brown, 1992; Stuart, 1992) emphasize the importance of employers' considering the possibility of a person having learning and attentional difficulties when dealing with an employee with productivity problems. While the focus here is on workplace problems from the employee's perspective, it is important to realize that it is in the employer's best interest to identify, understand, and reasonably accommodate the learning disabled employee in order to improve overall performance and productivity.

Possibly the most negative and least constructive manner by which to disclose an ADD diagnosis is for an individual to use it as an explanation when reprimanded for unacceptable performance. One young man with attention deficits announced his diagnosis to his boss in response to a reprimand he had received for repeated late arrivals to work. Introduction of a diagnosis at such a juncture will appear to be merely an excuse for inexcusable behavior.

In my experience, it seems that those adults who disclosed their ADD diagnosis and received a positive, supportive response from their employer were those whose performance ratings were already high. For example, one man was a talented systems analyst for a private firm. He found that his performance was highly variable from day to day, and even within the course of a single day. Protracted meetings posed daunting challenges for his limited ability to remember and process auditory information. He had a chronic problem remembering casual verbal requests or comments made to him by his supervisor or coworkers. After experiencing a positive response to psychostimulant medication, he approached his boss to explain his difficulties. He requested that he be required to attend only the most essential meetings, and also requested that his coworkers send him messages by E-mail so that he would have written records of all requests. Because he had established a positive work record, his boss met his requests with a supportive attitude. Here was a productive employee who was developing strategies to become even more productive!

Ongoing Role as Counselor and Coach

The greatest challenge to adults with ADD comes about during the process of implementing recommendations made by the professionals they have consulted. It is critical that career counselors who elect to specialize in working with adults with ADD realize that their role should appropriately be an extended one. Regular weekly counseling sessions may be necessary when the client is in a crisis state, and possibly in danger of losing her or his job. Continued regular counseling may be appropriate as the client learns to develop better habits and attitudes. There are many important and appropriate issues to be addressed by the ADD career consultant in order to assist the ADD adult in making an optimal career adjustment. These issues will include habits and attitudes that affect workplace performance, patterns of interpersonal reaction in the workplace, and self-esteem as it has an impact on workplace functioning. In the final stages of workplace adjustment, the counselor may serve as an occasional consultant as issues arise for the client in the workplace.

When Psychotherapy Is Needed to Address Career Issues

The ADD career counselor needs to be carefully attuned to issues other than neurodevelopmental difficulties that may lead to problems in the workplace. As is discussed extensively in the chapters on differential diagnosis, many ADD adults have comorbid conditions including chronic anxiety, depression, obsessive-compulsive personality disorder, bipolar disorder, and substance abuse problems, among others. Unless career consultants are also trained psychotherapists, they should not attempt to deal with these or other psychotherapeutic issues.

For some ADD individuals, psychotherapy is essential in addition to the very comprehensive career counseling outlined in this chapter. Some ADD adults need to embark on a course of psychotherapy, for example, that address destructive patterns in workplace functioning. Such therapy would focus on repetitive patterns leading to problems in the workplace, and would work toward gradual improvement and change. While some ADD problems can be effectively dealt with by making specific environmental changes, others can only be changed through the slow, hard process of self-awareness, personal growth, increased self-esteem, and gradual changes in old, destructive patterns.

SUMMARY

Career counseling the ADD adult is a very complex process which requires knowledge of career issues, of neurodevelopmental issues as they affect workplace performance, of psychological disorders that may be related to attention deficit, and of personality factors that interact with attentional difficulties. There is no single course of training that can provide this level of expertise in such a broad range of disciplines. The National Joint Committee on Learning Disabilities (1987) speaks of the urgent need to train vocational and rehabilitative counselors in the needs of adults with learning and attentional difficulties. Interdisciplinary training is essential, as well as consultation with other professionals.

Counselors need to provide education and guidance to the ADD adult; they need to carefully integrate information from a complex evaluation or set of evaluations and present this integrated information to the ADD adult in a clear and supportive way that provides concrete strategies and direction.

Because implementation and follow-through often are areas of weakness for ADD adults, the career consultation process will need to evolve into ongoing, structured, supportive counseling to help the individual implement coping strategies recommended in the initial evaluation. If the counselor suspects that other psychological issues are involved, a referral to a psychotherapist who is expert in working with ADD adults may be called for.

Although we can offer no magic solutions, through a combination of good career counseling, medication, psychotherapy, and a commitment to a patient process of learning and problem solving, many ADD career dilemmas can be successfully challenged.

TABLE 16-1
Reasonable Accommodations to Be Provided by Employers for Adults with ADD

Reasonable accommodations suggested in a variety of articles include:

1. Provision of a private office or nondistracting work space
2. Allow the employee to do some work at home
3. Day-planner computer software to assist in organization and planning, with visual and auditory alarms as reminders to improve time management
4. Video or audiotape equipment to assist with auditory memory difficulties
5. Checklists to provide structure in multistage tasks
6. Give instructions slowly and clearly
7. Write down instructions or communications so the employee has a written record
8. Excuse the disabled person from nonessential tasks
9. Restructure job if necessary
10. More frequent performance appraisals
11. Reassignment to a vacant position that better matches the individual's strengths
12. Extra clerical support

Other accommodations that have proven helpful to some adults with ADD in the author's clinical practice include:

1. A nondistracting environment (such as the supervisor's office when not in use). In particular, make this available for work that requires more intense concentration if space restrictions do not allow an individual office.
2. "Flextime." Highly distractible individuals generally are most productive if they come early, stay late, or work on weekends when fewer distractions are present.
3. More structure and intermediate deadlines. Often a regularly scheduled 15-minute meeting with the supervisor once or twice a week can provide the ADD adult with enough external structure to stay on track.

(continued)

4.   Assistance in setting up a filing system from someone who is skilled at organizing and categorizing.

5.   Structure, guidelines, and intermediate deadlines. When the ADD adult is involved in team projects, the project coordinator should establish these for the entire team. While these are essential for the ADD adult, they will also benefit everyone involved.

6.   When work assignments come from a variety of sources, the supervisor or some other appropriate person should serve as a funnel so that the adult with ADD only needs to interface and set priorities with one person.

7.   Memos and E-mail. Coworkers should use memos or E-mail to communicate with the ADD adult so that he automatically has a written record of their communications.

TABLE 16–2
Recommended Workplace Strategies for the Adult with ADD

Hyperactivity / Motor Restlessness

1.   Work in a job that allows a high degree of physical movement.

2.   If your job requires prolonged desk work, take frequent breaks that allow movement. A simple walk to the water fountain and back every 20 to 30 minutes could be helpful.

3.   Arrange for activity on your coffee breaks and lunch breaks. Consider going for a walk rather than having a cup of coffee.

4.   Bring your lunch so that you can spend the lunch hour walking or exercising in some other fashion.

5.   The more sedentary your work is, the more important it will be to engage in physical activity after work.

6.   When considering a job change, look for a job that allows you to be on your feet more, that allows movement from room to room, that calls for frequent interpersonal interaction, or that allows you to travel from one job site to another.

7.   Work that requires long meetings, or consists of sedentary, detailed desk work is less suited to your needs.

Distractibility

1.   Set aside periods of your day when you will not be interrupted, except in case of emergencies.

2.   Explain to your supervisor and coworkers how important it is for increased productivity that you have uninterrupted time.

3.   Schedule your intensive work in time-limited chunks. Daydreaming may be more likely if you have set aside a long period of time in which to work on a task.

4.   If internal distraction is severe, you may need to carefully analyze how suited you are to the work you have been assigned. Daydreaming may be more likely when engaged in tedious or low-interest work.

5.   When you are distracted by a rapid flow of ideas related to the project at hand or to other work projects, develop the habit of writing down the intruding thought. A note can allow you to return to it efficiently, when appropriate, but also allows you to continue with the immediate task.

6.   A rapid flow of ideas can present difficulties in meetings. If you tend to ramble

or to become tangential, make brief notes about what you want to say and refer to them.

7. Learn to frequently reorient. Ask yourself, "Am I on task?"

8. An orderly work space may be very useful to improve concentration. Try not to surround yourself with piles of paperwork and notes.

9. If your work space is messy, don't allow clearing your desk to turn into a major project. Simply clear your desk of all papers except those on which you are working. Then schedule a later time to reorganize your work space.

10. Poor follow-through can be caused by distractibility. As you are engaged in one task, another suggestion, proposal, idea comes along which captures your interest. Learn to catch yourself and go back to the original task until it is completed. Use new interests or projects as a reward for completion of previous projects.

Organization

1. If organization and follow-through are weak points, try to work as a team with someone more organized.

2. Develop the habit of setting aside 15 minutes at the beginning of each day for planning. An overview of your day will make it more likely that you can set priorities throughout the day.

3. Long complicated projects may be incompatible with your short-term interests. If you find lack of follow-through is a major difficulty in performing your current position, you may want to strongly consider this issue when choosing your next job. You may want to find a job that involves immediate, short-term issues.

4. Try to avoid jobs in which you are assigned work by a number of different people. Such a position is difficult, even for persons with good organizational skills.

Time Management

1. Learn to think proactively rather than reactively. Plan your day and follow your plan. Don't react to events, impulses, and moods as they occur.

2. Don't overschedule your day.

3. Build "slack time" into your day. This can allow you to remain less stressed and be more likely to be on time, even when the inevitable interruptions occur.

4. Break large tasks into chunks. You may find yourself more productive if you give yourself concrete assignments to complete by specified times.

5. Keep your daily schedule with you at all times. When you take on a new task, schedule it; that is, don't just say "I'll call you," or "I'll get it to you later this week," without scheduling an actual time to complete that task. If you can't assign the task an exact time, then put it on your "to do" list on a specific day.

6. If you tend to lose track of time when you are engaged in conversation or in intensive work, it may help to set a timer to beep when you need to terminate the conversation or task.

7. Learn not to say "yes" when you ought to say "no." While hard work, motivation, and a willingness to accommodate the needs of your supervisor and coworkers are positive traits, you need to set reasonable limits so that you are not overly stressed and frequently running late or missing deadlines. Develop the habit of saying "Let me think about it" rather than responding with a reflexive "yes."

(continued)

8.   Avoid last-minute impulses unless they are true emergencies. Many ADD adults are chronically late due to a series of impulses to attend to some brief task that occurs to them as they are on their way out the door to a meeting.

9.   Remind yourself as you are leaving for a scheduled meeting not to get caught in hallway conversations that will throw off your best laid plans.

10.   Planning to be early may help you to be on time. Take some work or reading material with you so that the time isn't wasted.

11.   Try to end phone calls or conversations a few minutes early. Ending a conversation often takes longer than you had planned, making you late for your next commitment. Always try to leave yourself a little leeway.

Procrastination
1.   Give yourself deadlines.

2.   Build in rewards for yourself. (For example: Say to yourself, "When I finish this letter, I'll go downstairs for a cup of coffee.")

3.   Make a commitment to someone about when you will complete the work.

4.   Ask yourself whether your job involves too many tasks that you simply don't enjoy, have difficulty doing, or find tedious. Severe procrastination may be a sign of a poor job match.

Low Frustration Tolerance
1.   Analyze the situations that recur at work that are the most stressful for you. Is there a way to reduce or minimize such occurrences?

2.   Take your frustration level seriously. Don't wait until you "can't take it" before you leave the frustrating situation. Leaving before you reach your "boiling point" may help avoid explosions.

3.   Avoid working for intense, high-stress organizations or individuals.

4.   Develop relaxation techniques to use at the office. Some techniques that involve muscle relaxation or guided imagery may be useful.

5.   Long hours and time pressure may increase your tendency to feel stressed. Avoid these situations whenever possible.

6.   Look for work that allows autonomy, which lets you set your own pace and allows you time alone.

Interpersonal Conflicts on the Job
1.   If you have a history of interpersonal conflicts on the job, there may be issues you need to explore in counseling. A counselor can assist you in developing strategies for avoiding such conflicts in the future.

2.   Some ADD adults "don't know when to stop." They may keep on at something, missing nonverbal cues from others. You may need to learn strategies to try to become better attuned to social cues.

3.   Some ADD adults have been called stubborn or argumentative. It may be helpful to practice "active listening"–that is, pay attention to and try to fully understand what is being said to you rather than immediately responding with a negative or contradictory remark.

4.   If being hot-tempered plays a role in your interpersonal conflicts on the job, you may need to become a better judge of your mood and frustration level in order

to avoid interpersonal confrontations. Develop an "early warning system" to judge your mood and exit the situation temporarily before you explode. Cool off before reengaging in discussion or negotiations.

5.   Work that allows a high degree of autonomy and personal freedom may be best for individuals who find they have little patience or tolerance for the inevitable problems that arise when working with others.

Prioritization

1.   Try not to "dive into" projects at work. Develop the habit of planning your day and doing your plan.

2.   Learn to stop yourself when you fall into the "reactive mode." A reactor abandons his priorities, allowing random events or the priorities of others to take precedence.

3.   Learn to categorize tasks in A-B-C fashion:

      A–has to be done today

      B–would like to get done today

      C–will do today if all As and Bs are completed

4.   Don't say "yes" to a request without consideration of your established priorities. Set limits diplomatically by saying "I'd like to, let me think about it."

Memory

1.   Use tape recorders at important meetings and seminars.

2.   Take notes during the meetings you are recording. If there is a point of particular importance, reference the "counter" on your tape recorder so that you can "fast forward" to this point on the tape for review. This prevents the need to listen to the entire tape in order to refer to particular points.

3.   Take notes during meetings, even brief casual meetings with your supervisor or coworker. Try not to rely on memory, but always keep a written record of things you or your coworker has agreed to do or has communicated to you.

4.   After important meetings or agreements, it may prove useful to provide other individuals with a written copy of your interpretation of agreements made so that you can double check for accuracy.

5.   Keep your daytimer with you so that you can write brief notes regarding decisions and commitments you make. Don't rely on your memory until you get back to your office.

This list of recommendations has been developed by the author for use in her clinical practice. They are based on clinical experience. No field trials have been conducted to test their efficacy. They should be considered selectively, by the career counselor and the client with ADD, and are meant to be included among other recommendations in a report to the client following a comprehensive career assessment.

REFERENCES

Adelman, P., & Vogel, S. (1990). College graduates with learning disabilities–employment attainment and career patterns. *Learning Disability Quarterly, 13*, 154–166.

Adelman, P., & Wren, C. (1990). *Learning disabilities, graduate school, and careers: The student's perspective.* Lake Forest, IL: Barat College; Chicago: De Paul University Press.

Bencomo, A., & Schafer, M. (1984, April-May-June). Remediation and accommodation for clients with specific learning disabilities. *Journal of Rehabilitation,* 64–67.

Brown, D. (1984, April-May-June). Employment considerations for learning disabled adults. *Journal of Rehabilitation,* 1984, 74–77.

Brown, D. (1993, May/June). Job accommodation ideas for people with learning disabilities. *LDA Newsbriefs,* p. 7.

Brown, D., Gerber, P., & Dowdy, C. (1990). *Pathways to employment for people with learning disabilities: A plan for action. Recommendations of a consensus-building conference (April 30–May 1, 1990).* Washington, DC: President's Committee on Employment of People with Disabilities.

Campbell, J. P., & Hansen, J. I. C. (1981). *Manual for the SVIB-SCII.* Stanford, CA: Stanford University Press.

Cantwell, D., & Baker, L. (1991). Association between attention deficit-hyperactivity disorder and learning disorders. *Journal of Learning Disabilities, 24,* 88.

Dowdy, C. (1992). Identification of characteristics of specific learning disabilities as a critical component in the vocational rehabilitation process. *Journal of Rehabilitation, 58,* 51–54.

Gerber, P., Ginzberg, R., & Reiff, H. B. (1992, October). Identifying alterable patterns in employment success for highly successful adults with learning disabilities. *Journal of Learning Disabilities, 25,* pp. 475–487.

Gerber, P. (1988). *Highly successful learning disabled adults: Insights from case interviews.* Paper presented at the Annual AHSSPPE Conference, New Orleans.

Golden, V. J., & Provost, J. A. (1987). The MBTI and career development. In J. A. Provost & S. Anchors (Eds.), *Applications of the Myers-Briggs Type Indicator in higher education* (pp. 151–180). Palo Alto, CA: Consulting Psychologists Press.

Hechtman, L., Weiss, G., & Perlman, T. (1980). Hyperactives as young adults: Self-esteem and social skills. *Canadian Journal of Psychiatry, 25,* 478–483.

Highlands Ability Battery. The Highlands Program, Inc., 999 Peachtree Street NE, Suite 1790, Atlanta, GA 30309.

Hinkebein, J., Koller, J., & Kunce, (1992). Normal personality and adults with learning disabilities: Rehabilitation counseling implications. *Journal of Rehabilitation, 58,* 40–46.

Hirshfield, C., & Brown, D. (1992, Spring). Uncovering learning disabilities can enhance job performance. *Employment Relations Today,* 39–41.

Holland, J. L. (1979). *Professional manual for the self.* Palo Alto, CA: Consulting Psychologists Press.

Holland, J. L. (1985). *Vocational preference inventory (VPI) manual.* Odessa, FL: Psychological Assessment Resources.

Jacobs, A., & Hendricks, D. (1992). Job accommodations for adults with learning disabilities: Brilliantly disguised opportunities. *Learning Disability Quarterly, 15,* 274–284.

Jaffe, P. (1993, Summer). Can this fantasy be saved? ADDendum, #13, pp. 10–12.

Johnson, D., & Blalock, J. (1987a). Summary of problems and needs. In D. J. Johnson & J. W. Blalock (Eds.), *Adults with learning disabilities* (pp. 277–293). Orlando, FL: Grune & Stratton.

Johnson, D., & Blalock, J. (1987b). Primary concerns and group characteristics. In D. J. Johnson & J. W. Blalock (Eds.), *Adults with learning disabilities* (pp. 31–45). Orlando, FL: Grune & Stratton.

Johnson O'Connor Research Foundation Human Engineering Laboratory, 347 Beacon St., Boston, MA 02166.

Lowman, R. (1991). *The clinical practice of career assessment.* Washington, DC: American Psychological Association.

Lucius, M. (1991). ADD adults: Common pitfalls in the workplace. *Challenge–A Newsletter of the Attention Deficit Disorder Association, 5,* pp. 5–8.

Minskoff, E., Sauter, S., Hoffman, F. J., & Hawks, R. (1987). Employer attitudes toward hiring the learning disabled. *Journal of Learning Disabilities, 20,* 53–57.

Murphy, K. (1992, Fall–Winter). Coping strategies for ADHD adults. *CH.A.D.D.ER,* pp. 10–11.

National Joint Committee on Learning Disabilities. (1987). Adults with learning disabilities: A call to action. (A position paper of the National Joint Committee on Learning Disabilities, February 10, 1985). *Journal of Learning Disabilities, 20,* 102–106.

Parks, A., Antonoff, S., Drake, C., Skiba, W., & Soberman, J. (1987). A survey of programs and services for learning disabled students in graduate and professional schools. *Journal of Learning Disabilities, 20,* 181–187.

President's Committee on Employment of People with Disabilities. (1993). *Work-site accommodations for people with cognitive disabilities.* Washington DC: Author.

Rehabilitation Services Administration. (1981). *Memorandum from the task force on learning disabilities.* (Information Memorandum RSA-IM-37, July 14, 1981). Washington, DC.

Rehabilitation Services Administration (1985). Rehabilitative Services Program Policy Directive (RSA-PPD-885-7). Washington, DC.

Rawson, M. R. (1968). *Developmental language disability: Adult accomplishments of dyslexic boys.* Baltimore: Johns Hopkins University Press.

Silver, A. A., & Hagin, R. A. (1985). Outcomes of learning disabilities in adolescents. In M. Sugar, A. Esman, J. Looney, A. Schwartzberg, &

A. Sorosky (Eds.), *Adolescent psychiatry: Developmental and clinical studies* Vol. 12 (pp. 197–213). Chicago: University of Chicago.

Simpson, R., & Umbach, B. (1989). Identifying and providing vocational services for adults with specific learning disabilities. *Journal of Rehabilitation,* 55, 49–55.

Stuart, P. (1992). Tracing workplace problems to hidden disorders. *Personnel Journal,* 71, 82–95.

Thomasson, M. (1991). Attention deficit in adults. *Challenge–A Newsletter of the Attention Deficit Disorder Association,* 5, pp. 1–5.

Vocational Rehabilitation Center of Allegheny County. (1984). *A comprehensive vocational service model for persons with specific learning disabilities.* Pittsburgh, PA: Author.

Weiss, G., Hechtman, L., Milroy, T., & Perlman, T. (1985). Psychiatric status of hyperactives as adults: A controlled prospective 15-year follow-up of 63 hyperactive children. *Journal of the American Academy of Child Psychiatry,* 24, 211–220.

Wolkenberg, F. (1987, October 11). Out of a darkness. *New York Times Magazine.*

SECTION V

Other Issues and Future Directions

In this final section we discuss some very important issues related to the development of the field of adult ADD. Because there are significant legal implications to the diagnosis of attention deficit disorder that pertain to both the fields of education and employment, it is critical that the clinician working with adults with ADD understand those implications so that they may advise their clients of their rights and of services available to them as a result of those rights. Peter Latham and Patricia Latham, pioneers in the field of ADD and the law, and cofounders of the National Center for Learning Disabilities and the Law, bring their considerable knowledge to bear in their informative chapter on legal issues. Their chapter is followed by a chapter on the role of support groups for adults with ADD, written by Kate Kelly, coauthor of *You Mean I'm Not Lazy, Stupid, or Crazy?!* a professional in the field of adult ADD, and an ADD adult herself. Kelly's chapter highlights the important functions that can be served by the rapidly growing number of support groups for adults with ADD which are springing up all over the country. Finally, Paul Jaffe, who opened this volume with an illuminating history of the recognition of ADD as a disorder that affects adults, closes the volume with a thought-provoking discussion of current research and areas of concern for adults with ADD that have not yet been addressed, including advocacy and the need for increased public recognition of ADD in adults.

17

Legal Rights of the ADD Adult

PETER S. LATHAM AND PATRICIA H. LATHAM

The legal rights of adults with ADD stem basically from three sources: (1) the Constitution, (2) statutes and regulations that prohibit discrimination, and (3) cases decided by the courts. In asserting these legal rights, it is important in advocating for adults with ADD to use authoritative material to define ADD clearly and promote understanding of this multifaceted and elusive disorder.

THE CONSTITUTION, STATUTES, AND CASES

The rights of individuals with ADD derive historically and logically from the 5th and 14th amendments to the Constitution, which are the most important sources of the rights of individuals with disabilities. The 14th Amendment provides in pertinent part that "No State shall...deny to any person within its jurisdiction the equal protection of the laws" or "deprive any person of life, liberty or property, without due process of law." Section 5 of the 14th Amendment provides that the "Congress shall have the power to enforce, by appropriate legislation, the provisions of this article." The 5th Amendment contains the identical due process language and has incorporated the "equal protection" concept.

The Constitutional requirements of due process and equal protection are made specific and uniform by statutes that are authorized by and implement these Constitutional provisions. In general, statutes do one of three things: (1) prohibit discrimination, (2) require affirmative action, or (3) provide funds for specific activities and programs. In the latter case, the recipient is required to agree that it will conduct its programs without discrimination.

The two statutes that matter the most to the adult with ADD are (1) the Rehabilitation Act of 1973 (RA) and (2) the recently enacted Americans with Disabilities Act (ADA). A statute of significance to children with ADD is the Individuals with Disabilities Education Act (IDEA). These statutes serve generally as a model for state statutes. State laws may set higher standards than the federal ones, but they may not set them lower. The RA and ADA essentially outlaw discrimination in education, employment, and access to goods and services, while the IDEA ensures that a free, appropriate public education is provided at the elementary and secondary levels.

The RA prohibits discrimination in employment by the federal government, government contractors, and federal grant or aid recipients, and prohibits discrimination in access to the programs and activities conducted by them with federal funds. Most colleges receive federal funds, and, therefore, most are subject to the RA. In addition, the RA requires affirmative action in employment by the federal government and by federal government contractors.

The RA differs from the IDEA. The former is intended to prohibit discrimination, while the latter is intended to ensure a free, appropriate education. The RA is more general in nature and employs a definition of disability that is broader than that of the IDEA. Therefore, it is perfectly possible for a school district, for example, to violate the RA by failing to provide an individual with a disability with a free, appropriate education even though the individual was not entitled to services under the IDEA. The RA is closely similar to the ADA in that both outlaw discrimination against persons with disabilities in employment, education, and access to publicly available programs. Their differences are discussed below.

ADD of sufficient severity is a disability giving rise to certain legal rights. In order to obtain the protections of the RA or ADA, it is necessary to establish that (1) you are an "individual with a disability"; *and* (2) you are "otherwise qualified"; *and* (3) you were denied a job, education, or other benefit "solely by reason" of the disability; *and* (4) the individual, firm, or governmental agency that refused you is covered by the RA or ADA *(Fitzgerald v. Green Valley Area Education Agency,* 1984). We will consider each of these in turn.

INDIVIDUAL WITH A DISABILITY

Under both the RA and ADA, an individual with a disability is any individual who

(i) has a physical or mental impairment which substantially limits one or more of such person's major life activities,

(ii) has a record of such an impairment, or

(iii) is regarded as having such an impairment. (Rehabilitation Act of 1973, § 706[8][B]).

Physical or Mental Impairment

The definition of a physical or mental impairment includes "any mental or psychological disorder, such as mental retardation, organic brain syndrome, emotional or mental illness, and specific learning disabilities" (29 CFR § 1613.702[b][2]). This formulation appears in numerous regulations.

As ADD has been recognized as a "mental or psychological disorder," the RA and ADA apply to individuals with this disorder. In *Letter of Findings (LOF) OCR Docket No. 04-90-1617* (1990), the Department of Education's Office of Civil Rights ruled that the Gaston County School District of North Carolina (which received federal funding) failed to identify, evaluate, and provide the complainant's ADD child with a free public education appropriate to his disorder and thereby violated the RA (1973, § 794). There are similar holdings under the ADA.

Substantially Impairs

The impact of the disability must be severe enough to result in actual substandard performance. Regulations that implement the ADA provide that the term "substantially limits" means either that an individual is (1) "unable to perform a major life activity that the average person in the general population can perform," or (2) is "significantly restricted as to the condition, manner or duration" of the major life activity in question, when measured against the abilities of the "average person in the general population" [29 CFR ¶¶ 1630.2[j][1][i]-[ii]). In assessing the impact of limitations, the following factors must also be considered: (1) the nature and severity of the impairment, and (2) the actual or expected duration of the impairment and the permanent or long-term impact of the impairment (29 CFR ¶¶ 1630.2[j][2][i]-[iii]).

Case law has also defined the term. For example, a machinist whose back injury prevented him from performing normal physical movements but not clerical work was substantially limited in his occupation as a laborer. However, a stock clerk whose job is to manage an inventory of toxic chemicals is not substantially limited in his occupation if he is allergic to and unable to work with particular chemicals.

Major Life Activity

The major life tasks are considered to be caring for oneself, performing manual tasks, walking, seeing, hearing, speaking, breathing, learning, and working. As noted above, the disability must represent a substantial impairment to one of these activities. ADD attentional problems can be said to interfere with one's ability to perform any of these activities except breathing, while the impulsivity and motor restlessness typical of many ADD individuals most clearly have an impact on learning and working.

For our purposes, the most important major life activities are learning and working. In assessing whether there is a substantial limitation on learning, one should consider the actual academic performance or school behavior. In assessing whether there is a substantial limitation on working, one should consider (1) the type of work involved, (2) the number of jobs from which the individual is barred, and (3) the number of jobs from which the individual is barred in a reasonably accessible geographical area *(Macaranas v. United States Postal Service, 1991).*

These tests are required to ensure that the individual with a disability is barred from significant *classes* of jobs, and not just a *particular* job. Only disabilities with the former (and broader) impact are considered to substantially limit working. Consideration of the impact on working need not be undertaken where a substantial impact on another major life activity can be shown. Let's consider each in turn.

Learning

The ADD symptoms must either (1) impact directly on academic performance, or (2) impact indirectly through the problems arising from inappropriate behaviors. The impact must be severe enough to result in actual substandard performance in either the classroom or other school situations. An ADD child who must struggle with her or his work but whose classroom performance is adequate, and who exhibits no disruptive behavior, may be found not to have a disability that interferes with learning! (See *Letter of Findings (LOF) Docket No. 15-93-1016,* 1993.)

Working

Working is the other major life activity of major concern to individuals with ADD. In general, the disability must (1) preclude a substantial number of jobs of the type the individual would otherwise be qualified to hold but for the disability, and, at the same time, (2) be one that is capable of being addressed by reasonable efforts on the part of the employee and reasonable accommodations on the part of the employer. While no cases directly set standards applicable to ADD in the workplace, the following example might be helpful to ADD individuals.

To begin with, it is important to consider just what is meant by job requirements. Most job "requirements" fall into least five separate categories. These are (1) academic qualifications, (2) required on-the-job experience, (3) competence in the work itself, (4) general standards of cooperativeness in the work situation, and (5) compliance with "good citizenship" rules, such as being on time and no unauthorized absences. Moreover, requirements 3–5 become increasingly subjective as the seniority and pay of the positions increase. All of these factors must be considered in selecting a job and deciding whether and how to deal with a disability.

In *Dazey v. Department of the Air Force* (1992), a GS-12 auditor was removed in major part for using abusive language in the office. She suffered from mood changes caused by manic depression and an "apparently irrational dislike for her supervisor." Her psychiatrist prescribed lithium and Prozac, and testified that the treatment would prevent bizarre disruptive behavior if she returned to the workplace even without accommodations. Despite being on the medication, however, the auditor displayed some of her symptoms at the trial. The administrative judge found that the auditor had not shown that medication was a sufficient answer. Accordingly, the judge found that she "could not perform the essential functions of her position because such essential functions included not engaging in the bizarre behavior previously engaged in, and getting along with her supervisor." Clearly, having the (1) academic qualifications, (2) required on-the-job experience, and (3) competence in the work itself, while failing to (4) meet general standards of cooperativeness in the work situation and (5) comply with "good citizenship" rules was not sufficient.

Testing

Testing is used for education, as well as job placement, retention, and advancement. Testing that relies on a single criterion is unlawful if that criterion can be shown to be an inaccurate predictor of performance. In *Stutts v. Freeman* (1983), a dyslexic laborer applied for a job as a heavy equipment operator and was rejected solely on the basis of a low score on written tests, when independent tests showed he possessed an above-average intelligence, coordination, and aptitude for the apprenticeship training program. The Eleventh Circuit held that the Rehabilitation Act of 1973 had been violated, stating:

> When an employer like TVA chooses a test that discriminates against handicapped persons as its sole hiring criterion, and makes no meaningful accommodation for a handicapped applicant, it violates the Rehabilitation Act of 1973. (*Stutts v. Freeman*, 1983, 669)

The Law School Aptitude Tests (LSATs) are potentially such a test for one with attentional and organizational problems. Accordingly, while law schools may require a person to take the test (under modified conditions), they are precluded from basing their acceptance decisions with respect to applicants with disabilities on those tests. Indeed, some law schools give lesser weight to the LSAT results and base their acceptance decisions primarily on (1) grade point averages, (2) undergraduate transcripts and curricula, (3) letters of recommendation, and (4) LSAT writing samples (see *Letter of Findings (LOF) OCR Docket No.02-91-2074*, 1992).

The Department of Education (DOE) has provided guidelines for testing in the context of the IDEA which are generally helpful. The DOE requires that tests and other evaluation materials (1) must be "validated for the specific purpose for which they are used," (2) must be "administered by trained personnel," (3) must "include those tailored to assess specific areas of educational need," and (4) "the test results [must] accurately reflect the student's aptitude or achievement level" rather than his disability, unless specific justification is provided. While these requirements are specifically applicable under 34 CFR §104.35 to school districts receiving federal funds under the IDEA, they express general principles.

While use of a single testing criterion or method is suspect, it may be defensible where the aptitude measured is important to the educational institution or job requirements.

In *Wynne v. Tufts University School of Medicine* (1991), Wynne, a dyslexic student, was held to have been properly dismissed from medical school after failing numerous courses (including failing biochemistry three times) during successive attempts to complete the first-year program. Tufts had refused him permission to take multiple-choice examinations orally. On appeal from the District Court's rejection of Wynne's claim, the First Circuit reversed the District Court's determination, finding that the record did not show that alternative testing methods had been explored and found unsuitable (there was evidence that Brown University permitted oral testing in place of written multiple-choice testing), or that Wynne's academic problems resulted from causes other than dyslexia. On remand, Tufts supplemented the record and showed that it "clearly evaluated alternatives to its current testing format and concluded change was not practicable."

The District Court found in favor of Tufts, holding that the school's decision was rationally justified, and that the accommodations actually provided were reasonable, and the First Circuit affirmed that decision in *Wynne v. Tufts University School of Medicine* (1992). The United States Supreme Court refused to review this case when asked to do so, and consequently the lower court's ruling stands.

In *Pandazides v. Virginia Board of Education* (1991), the courts considered the extent and nature of accommodations that could be extended to a learning disabled applicant for a teacher's certification. Pandazides was given a probationary certification which required that she pass the National Teacher Exam (NTE). Pandazides was given accommodations by the NTE, none of which enabled her to pass the test. She then proposed that she be given the following accommodations: (1) an untimed test, and (2) interaction with the testing examiner. Alternatively, she requested that the NTE be waived. She was denied all of these proposed modifications, brought suit under the RA, and lost in the District Court. On appeal, the Fourth Circuit reversed the trial court and remanded the case with instructions for the trial court to conduct an individualized inquiry as to (1) whether the NTE requirements were essential to the job, (2) whether she could perform the essential functions of the position, and (3) whether a test waiver was a reasonable accommodation.

The District Court considered the case on remand in *Pandazides v. Virginia Board of Education* (1992), and held that Pandazides was not an "otherwise qualified" individual with a disability because (among other things) her learning disabilities prevented her from meeting the essential requirements for a teaching position:

> Plaintiff is not "otherwise qualified" under § 504 because she cannot perform "essential functions" of public school teacher in Virginia. (sic) The ability to read intelligently, to comprehend written and spoken communication accurately, effectively and quickly, and to respond to written and spoken communication professionally, effectively and quickly, are "essential functions" of a special education, public school teacher in Virginia. Moreover, the ability to manage a classroom is an "essential function" for a public school teacher in grades 1 through 12 in Virginia. Plaintiff has failed to prove competence in this essential function. (804 F. Supp. 794 at 803)

Proceedings are ongoing in this case. *Pandazides* and *Wynne* show that the courts will give great deference to the judgment of those charged with testing and educating professionals, even when the academic requirements generated by that judgment are debatable.

OTHERWISE QUALIFIED INDIVIDUAL

Essential Job Features

An "otherwise qualified" individual is one who, though possessed of a disability, would be eligible for the job, education, or program benefit, with or without a reasonable accommodation. The institution or employer must either provide the accommodation or justify in detail the refusal to provide it. A case that should be considered is *Fitzgerald v. Green Valley Area Education Agency* (1984). In that case, a multiply handicapped individual applied for an elementary school teaching position. He suffered from (1) left-side hemiplegia due to cerebral palsy which did not prevent him from walking or preclude him from driving his own vehicle, and (2) from dyslexia which limited his reading at a third-to-sixth-grade level but did not prevent him from teaching reading to first and second graders, the teaching position for which he was applying. However, the school district to which he applied held that bus driving was an essential part of the teaching job and hired a less academically qualified teacher. Fitzgerald sued under the RA (as one basis among several) and the court held that he was "otherwise qualified" because with reasonable accommodations–for example job restructuring–he could perform the teaching duties. Specifically, the court found that bus driving was not an essential element of the teaching job and that the school could have made arrangements to have the bus transportation provided by (1) another district, (2) another teacher, or (3) a private company, and that his application for a teaching position could not be rejected on the ground that he was unsuitable as a bus driver.

An "otherwise qualified" individual is one who can perform the essential functions required by the job with or without a reasonable accommodation. As shown above, bus driving is not an essential part of teaching. These distinctions are relatively easy to draw when the job position is an entry-level one or when the work does not involve the public health or safety. However, as the job level increases, or as the work becomes more safety related, it becomes increasingly difficult to decide which elements are or are not essential. Let us consider *DiPompo v. West Point Military Academy* (1991). There, DiPompo sought employment as a structural firefighter, a job for which West Point required an ability to read at a 12th-grade level. DiPompo was a dyslexic who when stressed was illiterate, but when calm could read at a first-grade level. West Point justified its 12th-grade reading requirement by showing that it required "housewatch" duties–for example, dispatcher duties of its firemen. Those duties consisted of telephone answering, information recording, computer reading, manual and form reading, and other duties. Firemen were assigned the duty on a rotational basis. The court rejected DiPompo's argument that the duty to provide "reasonable accommodations" meant that (1) housewatch duties should be assigned to others and (2) readers should be provided. The United States Court of Appeals for the Second Circuit affirmed the trial court (*DiPompo v. West Point Military Academy*, 1992).

Reasonable Accommodations

In *Lynch v. Department of Education* (1992), a GS-13 trial attorney was dismissed for unsatisfactory work and excessive absences. She suffered from an epileptic condition that was treatable with medication. The medication, however, affected her memory and ability to concentrate. As a reasonable accommodation she requested (1) training in legal drafting, (2) specific structured assignments including clear written assignment instructions and increased supervisory assistance, and (3) the opportunity to make up hours missed by late arrivals. The record contained evidence that prior to medication her work behavior was good. The individual was found to be a "qualified handicapped person" under the RA whose proposed accommodation was reasonable, and she was ordered to be reinstated.

Reasonable accommodations can include any of the following:

- Providing or modifying equipment or devices
- Job restructuring
- Part-time or modified work schedules
- Reassignment to a vacant position
- Adjusting or modifying examinations, training materials, or policies
- Providing readers or interpreters
- Making the workplace readily accessible to and usable by people with disabilities (U.S. Equal Employment Opportunity Commission [EEOC], 1991, p. 3)

Despite this sweeping description, the accommodations actually required for individuals with ADD are probably not extensive or expensive. For example, the President's Committee on Employment of People with Disabilities has pointed out the following:

- Thirty-one percent of accommodations cost nothing.
- Fifty percent cost less than $50.00.
- Sixty-nine percent cost less than $500.00.
- Eighty-eight percent cost less than $1,000.00. (President's Committee on Employment of People with Disabilities, 1993)

The President's Commission also gave these examples, which may be helpful.

Problem:	A person with a learning disability worked in the mail room and had difficulty remembering which streets belong to which zip codes.
Solution:	A rolodex card system was filed by street name alphabetically with the zip code. This helped him to increase his output. ($150.00)
Problem:	An individual with dyslexia who worked as a police officer spent hours filling out forms at the end of each day.
Solution:	He was provided with a tape recorder. A secretary typed out his reports from dictation, while she typed others from handwritten copy. This accommodation allowed him to keep his job. ($69.00) (President's

Committee on Employment of People with Disabilities, 1993)

While federal law contains little specific guidance concerning reasonable accommodations for individuals with ADD, it appears probable that the following would be required in appropriate cases:

1. Providing a structured learning/working environment
2. Repeating and simplifying instructions about work assignments
3. Supplementing verbal instructions with visual instructions
4. Adjusting class or work schedules
5. Modifying test delivery
6. Using tape recorders, computer-aided instruction, or work methods
7. Using other audiovisual equipment

These accommodations track closely those outlined in the 16 September 1991 Memorandum of the Office of Special Education and Rehabilitative Services, issued by the Department of Education as guidance to school districts in educating children with ADD under the IDEA.

SOLELY BY REASON OF THE DISABILITY

An individual with a disability must also show that he or she has been denied employment, education, or access to a public accommodation solely by reason of the disability. In *Ross v. Beaumont Hospital* (1988), a hospital terminated the privileges of a surgeon who suffered from narcolepsy despite the fact that her narcolepsy was largely controlled through medication. However, the surgeon also engaged in verbal abuse of nurses over a 7-year period. There was no evidence that the abuse was related to the narcolepsy. Accordingly, the termination was held to be lawful under the RA because it was based in major part on her unacceptable conduct.

THE RA OR ADA IS APPLICABLE

Finally, an individual with a disability must show that the RA or ADA is applicable to his or her case. The RA is closely similar to the ADA in that both outlaw discrimination against persons with disabilities in employment, education, and access to publicly available programs. The RA differs from the ADA in three principal respects, however. First, the RA follows federal dollars. It applies to the federal government, federal government contractors, federal grant recipients, and certain federal program beneficiaries. In the case of contractors and grant recipients, compliance with the RA is a condition of receiving federal contracts and grants. The ADA applies directly and its application does not depend on the agreement of the recipient. Second, the RA requires affirmative action in federal government and government contractor employment, while the ADA does not. Third, the ADA applies to virtually all public accommodations, while the RA does not.

INDIVIDUALIZED INQUIRY

The bottom line of all these requirements is simply this: Is the individual whose disability substantially limits a major life activity qualified for the education or job he or she seeks with or without a reasonable accommodation? In order to answer this question, businesses, educational institutions, governmental licensing authorities, and firms offering public accommodations must undertake an "individualized inquiry."

In *Ward v. Skinner* (1991, 1992), a truck driver was denied a license to drive a truck by the Department of Transportation (DOT). Although the driver had a history of epileptic seizures, he had not experienced one since 1984 and had driven without incident until May 1989 when his employer discovered his condition and suspended him. The driver showed that his seizures were controllable with anticonvulsant medication, and submitted convincing medical evidence (including expert testimony) that he was fit to drive. However, the DOT revoked his license on the basis of a regulation that prohibited the operation of a commercial motor vehicle by one who has an "established medical history or clinical diagnosis of epilepsy." The DOT refused to waive this regulation (though authorized to do so) based on a DOT Medical Task Force recommendation that the rule be enforced unless an epileptic (1) had no seizures *and* (2) did not take anticonvulsant medication. The driver brought suit under Section 504 of the RA. The United States Court of Appeals for the First Circuit held that the DOT denial was justified because (1) the DOT conducted an individualized inquiry into the driver's circumstances, (2) the DOT based its ruling on the Task Force Report, (3) the Task Force Report was reasonable, (4) further evaluation of the driver's ability could not demonstrate a driving capability greater than he had already shown, and (5) the DOT was in the process of reevaluating its regulation to see if it could be liberalized.

The heart of the matter lay in the Task Force Report, which the court found to be reasonable. The Task Force concluded that although diagnosed epileptic drivers as a group had low accident rates, their irregular work hours could lead to stress, irregular eating habits, and a sporadic lack of access to medical care. These factors, the Task Force found, alone, or if combined with a tendency to lose or forget one's medication, posed a driving risk that could be met only by a rule barring all epileptic drivers except those who (1) had had no seizures *and* (2) did not take anticonvulsant medication.

The process of an individualized inquiry also has a positive side. In *Lynch v. Department of Education* (1992), discussed above, a GS-13 trial attorney was dismissed for unsatisfactory work but was reinstated when she demonstrated that her unsatisfactory work resulted from a disability for which she had a proposed an acceptable accommodation.

The lesson of these cases is clear. The rights afforded by federal law are real, but they have to be asserted. In a sense, we all must become advocates. Rights under the RA and ADA may be enforced by private civil suit and by various other enforcement mechanisms.

FAMILY LAW AND CRIMINAL LAW

ADD may arise as an issue in the courts in the context of family law and criminal law matters. Most laws are not intended to address disabilities as such. Of course, these laws apply to individuals with ADD just as they do to others. In applying the laws, however, courts have taken notice of ADD when it is legally relevant. There are also issues as to accommodations to which ADD individuals may be entitled in connection with testifying in court proceedings.

Family Law

Parents have a legal duty to provide treatment for ADD as part of their general legal obligation to provide medical care for their children. The cost of special tutoring, counseling, and medication is a factor that is considered in establishing the amount of child support to be paid in a divorce action. The needs of a child with ADD will be considered in custody proceedings, both those between divorcing spouses and those initiated by the state on the basis of neglect.

Criminal Law

ADD is not a mental illness that excuses criminal conduct, although it is a factor that may mitigate an offense and reduce its severity. For example, a crime of intentional misconduct might be reduced to one of reckless behavior. The presence of ADD may justify trying a juvenile as such rather than as an adult. ADD is a factor that may mitigate a sentence imposed for a crime or for professional misconduct.

Unfortunately, ADD has also been considered as a factor that will justify an aggravated sentence. In *Zurfluh v. State* (1980), the court approved the imposition of the maximum (5-year) sentence for burglary on a 19-year-old offender with ADD, whose only prior crime had been a misdemeanor committed while a juvenile, saying, "deterrence of borderline criminals is an essential purpose of sentencing" (620 P. 2d 690 at 692).

ADD is also a factor that may be considered in deciding whether an individual has waived his constitutional rights during pretrial interrogation, whether he has the capacity to stand trial or the capacity to testify, and whether he is a credible witness.

Advocacy for ADD adults–whether in education, employment, or other civil cases of criminal matters–poses unique challenges.

ADVOCACY FOR ADULTS WITH ADD

ADD is a disability different from many others. Unlike mobility, hearing, or speech impairment, it is not obvious on first meeting. Therefore an individual with ADD is faced with the decision whether to declare his disability. In the case of education or licensing based on testing, it is probably essential that the individual do so. In the case of employment, the decision is less clear.

The EEOC advises as follows:

> Q. Should I tell my employer that I have a disability?
>
> A. If you think you will need a reasonable accommodation in order to participate in the application process or to perform essential job functions, you should inform the employer that an accommodation will be needed. Employers are required to provide reasonable accommodation only for the physical or mental limitations of a qualified individual with a disability of which they are aware. Generally, it is the responsibility of the employee to inform the employer that an accommodation is needed. (EEOC, 1991, p. 7)

It is wrong to assume that the general public knows or understands ADD. While public awareness is growing, it is prudent to plan on the assumption that the educator, employer, or judge you face is not fully "up to speed" on the topic. It is therefore essential to supply him or her with authoritative discussions of ADD.

One of the most compelling discussions of ADD was issued by the Department of Justice, not by those agencies and educational professionals more obviously interested in the field. On December 16, 1988, the Administrator of the Drug Enforcement Administration of the Department of Justice issued a final ruling on the proper 1986 production quota of Ritalin, following a hearing held for that purpose. The discussion focused on children but has applicability to adults, for the childhood behaviors have their counterparts in adult life (DEA Docket No. 86-52, 1988, paras. 5–9).

ADD is recognized by the American Psychiatric Association in its *Diagnostic and Statistical Manual of Mental Disorders* (DSM). Indeed, so well regarded is the DSM by the courts that the inability of the plaintiff in *Pandazides v. Virginia Board of Education* (1992) to show clearly that her learning disabilities were covered by the DSM was a major factor in the court's ruling against her!

Another authoritative source for a definition of ADD is *Learning Disabilities: a Report to the U.S. Congress* (Interagency Committee on Learning Disabilities, 1987). The value of this text is that it contains a major discussion of ADD and may be regarded as an authoritative recognition of the disorder by the federal government.

Still another source is regulations applicable to Social Security programs. Titles II and XVI provide for benefits and supplemental security income for disabled persons. The disabilities covered include attention deficit hyperactivity disorder. 20 CFR § 404, Subpart P, App. 1, ¶ 112.11, lists Attention Deficit Hyperactivity Disorders and defines them as ones "manifested by developmentally inappropriate degrees of inattention, impulsivity and hyperactivity." For an in-depth understanding, there are numerous informative and comprehensive texts.

Finally, in informing others about ADD in the course of advocating, it could be beneficial to point out positive traits often seen in ADD individuals: high energy, intensity about interests and people, creativity, innovation, attractiveness, and colorfulness. Certain career sectors that may allow more success than others include owning a business (which allows innovation and control); fire protection and law enforcement (which provide structure, stimulation, and opportunity for physical movement); and the media and arts and crafts (which offer creativity and hands-on activity).

In asserting legal rights, it is advisable for an individual with ADD to use a team of medical, educational, and testing professionals who will address the following question: Is the individual whose disability substantially limits a major life activity qualified for the education or job he or she seeks with or without a reasonable accommodation? Ordinarily, this involves consideration of all facets of the job or education and careful evaluation of the individual, including strengths and deficits.

ADD of sufficient severity is a disability that confers legal rights on those affected by the disorder. Those legal rights stem from the 5th and 14th amendments to the Constitution. They provide for equal protection of the law and due process. Statutes and cases further define those rights. The law is a valuable tool that may assist the individual with ADD in an effort to cope with and succeed in life. It should be used appropriately and wisely.

REFERENCES

American with Disabilities Act, 42 U.S.C. §12101 et seq. (1990).

Dazey v. Department of the Air Force, 54 MSPR 658 (1992).

DEA Docket No. 86-52, 53 Fed. Reg. 50591, 1988

DiPompo v. West Point Military Academy et al., 770 F. Supp. 887 (S.D.N.Y. 1991).

DiPompo v. West Point Military Academy et al., 960 F.2d 326 (2nd Cir. 1992).

Fitzgerald v. Green Valley Area Education Agency, 589 F. Supp. 1130 (S.D. Iowa 1984).

Individuals with Disabilities Education Act, 20 U.S.C. §1400 et seq. (1990 [formerly known as the Education for All Handicapped Children Act]).

Interagency Committee on Learning Disabilities. (1987). *Learning Disabilities: A Report to the U.S. Congress.*

Letter of Findings (LOF) Docket No. 15-93-1016, 23 March 1993, Forrest Hills Local School District (1993).

Letter of Findings (LOF) OCR Docket No. 02-91-2074, 5 March 1992, Cornell University Law School (1992).

Letter of Findings (LOF) OCR Docket No. 04-90-1617, 17 September 1990, Gaston County School District (1990).

Lynch v. Department of Education, 52 MSPR 541 (1992).

Macaranas v. United States Postal Service, 48 MSPR 323 (1991).

Pandazides v. Virginia Board of Education et al., 946 F2d. 345 (4th Cir. 1991).

Pandazides v. Virginia Board of Education, 804 F. Supp. 794 (E.D. Va. 1992).

President's Committee on Employment of People with Disabilities. (1993, October). *Job Accommodation Ideas.*

Rehabilitation Act of 1973, 29 U.S.C., §701 et seq. (1973).

Ross v. Beaumont Hospital et al., 687 F. Supp. 1115 (E.D. Mich. 1988).

Stutts v. Freeman et al., 694 F2d. 666 (11th Cir. 1983).

U.S. Equal Employment Opportunity Commission. (1991). *The Americans with Disabilities Act: Your Rights as an Individual with a Disability* (EEOC-BK-18).

Ward v. Skinner, 943 F.2d 157 (1st Cir. 1991), cert. denied, 188 L.E.2nd 207 (1992).

Wynne v. Tufts University School of Medicine, 932 F2d. 19 (1st Cir. 1991).

Wynne v. Tufts University School of Medicine, 976 F2d. 791 (1st Cir. 1992).

Zurfluh v. State, 620 P.2d 690 (Alaska 1980).

18

Adult ADD Support Groups

KATHLEEN M. KELLY

Support groups for adults with attention deficit disorder (ADD) have a short history. Because existing support groups initially developed independent of any national coordination, it is difficult to know precisely when the first group was founded. According to L. Poast, National Coordinator of ADD Adult Support Groups, the first group was probably formed in California in 1989 (personal communication, August 20, 1993).

Since 1991 ADD adult support groups have sprung up so rapidly it has been difficult for persons trying to provide referrals on a national level. The referral list needs constant updating, and this task is made more difficult because those persons attempting to compile and publish a list of groups do not yet have the support of a unified national organization to act as a clearinghouse for information.

The accomplishments of the people who have been organizing a self-help movement for ADD adults are impressive. In a few short years they have established a number of excellent national newsletters, formed a network of key organizers, and orchestrated a highly successful national ADD adult conference. This grassroots self-help movement appeared literally overnight. As of this writing, there are approximately 70 ADD adult support groups in the United States. A few groups have also formed in Canada and England.

Some of the problems encountered, as well as the strengths apparent in attempts to organize ADD adults both on a national and a local level, are related to the characteristics of persons with ADD. Many of the difficulties are not unique to ADD adult groups but are experienced in all self-help organizations. Since this chapter will focus on local organizations, that is, support groups, a more detailed description of national efforts has been left for other chapters in this book.

ADD adult support groups are forming and growing rapidly, but their development has not been a smooth and orderly process. This is to be expected. Dory and Gartner (cited in Mallory, 1984) stress that self-help groups should not expect that their mission and structure will develop overnight, as traditions will take shape gradually. ADD adult support group leaders report that problems often surface after an initial honeymoon period, characterized by burgeoning membership and high enthusiasm. Jaffe (1992) reported that the Manhattan support group disbanded after 9 months, due to problems with finding a place to meet and dealing with much diversity among members. Some groups have coped well with the potential problems and have emerged as potential models for the others. However, according to Poast, many group leaders struggle with chronic problems for which they have found no easy solutions (personal communication, August 21, 1993).

Before the specific issues of ADD adult groups are explored, it will be useful to include some general background information about the characteristics of a functional group. In addition, the self-help movement will be discussed, including its principles, strengths, and the typical problems encountered.

CHARACTERISTICS OF A HEALTHY GROUP

All types of groups must attend to certain functions in order to remain viable. Boards of directors, therapy groups, and political action organizations can flounder and die due to lack of structure. On the other hand, dysfunctional groups often manage to survive, but they are functionally impotent, prevented from accomplishing their purposes because of the disorganization. In this section, the characteristics of a healthy group or organization will be reviewed.

Groups need to address both task and process functions if they are to be successful. Task functions are related to the purpose and work of a given group, while process functions involve the interactions between group members. Some groups, such as committees, focus primarily on the tasks they are charged with. Other groups, such as support groups, are more concerned with the relationships between members. However, if the support group leader fails to make the group's purpose clear to the members, the resulting confusion will undermine the group process. Similarly, if a committee chair fails to deal with warring factions within the group, those relationships will sabotage the committee's work.

A healthy group develops and communicates a clear mission statement to its members. The statement of mission or purpose becomes the backbone supporting the other aspects of a group's structure. For example, if the primary mission of a group is to impart information to members, the format and rules will be different from those of a group whose purpose is to make decisions about the running of an organization. The informational group may use a lecture format with members expected to quietly listen until the question and answer period. The decision-making board, on the other hand, expects continual input from board members.

Well-structured groups have clear boundaries, articulated rules, defined roles, and some provision for the psychological safety of members. Attention to boundary issues usually provides for member safety. Boundaries define the personal and psychological space of individual members as well as the dimensions and limits of the whole group. An example of a boundary problem in a work group occurs when two members have an affair that goes sour and the resulting conflicts get played out at work.

Confidentiality in a support group is both a boundary and a safety issue. A rule of confidentiality defines the group boundaries by stating that "what goes on in this room stays in this room." Further, it gives members a sense of security when they choose to disclose personal information. Personal attacks on individual members violate boundaries on more than one level. The attacker violates the psychological space of the individual and also steps over what should be a clear line drawn between task and personal issues. Another group boundary issue revolves around the decision of who is included in the group. Functional groups have clear criteria defining who is and is not a member.

Boundary issues are complicated and often difficult to define. Well-articulated rules and procedures provide the structure necessary to prevent chaos. On a board, for example, it is a standard rule that the chairperson must recognize a member before she or he is allowed to speak. In a support group, an egg timer may be used to ensure that members do not monopolize the conversation. In any group, procedures for the making of decisions should be developed. For example, it must be determined whether decisions are to be made by committee, group consensus, or majority rule.

Roles within a group should be clearly delineated. The duties of officers in an organization must be well defined, or the officers will find themselves duplicating efforts and engaging in conflicts over the division of labor. A support group requires a designated leader or leaders, at least for each individual session.

Having a designated leader, however, does not mean that all the leadership functions and power rest with one individual. In a healthy group, some of the leadership functions are shared. Turquet (1985) describes the "deskilling" of members that occurs when a group treats the leader as an all-powerful being who will take care of the members. In such a group, the dependency of the members cripples the group, interfering with its task. If, for example, a support group leader is the only one making supportive comments to individual members, the group will not become cohesive or form the network of relationships necessary to do its work. The overly powerful leader will also have a hard time finding someone to take on his or her job when it is time to move on, as the members will not possess the necessary leadership skills.

Ultimately, the glue that binds a healthy, functional group is clear communication. An organization may do a masterful job of setting up its structure, but it is all for naught if the planners fail to communicate pertinent information to all members. The person who is not given an important memo, for example, will be understandably upset and will not know how to proceed without the new information.

In the following section the self-help model will be described and discussed. Since most ADD adult support groups adhere to this model, examining the issues of self-help groups in general will be useful background information for a discussion of the particular problems and successes of ADD adult groups.

THE SELF-HELP MODEL

The following is a list outlining the principles of self-help philosophy:

1. Each person has the ability to make appropriate use of the available resources to meet needs. Some persons may utilize this ability more fully than others, but it is present in everyone.
2. All of us together know more than any one of us.
3. Everyone has value and has something to add to a group process.
4. Each person is the ultimate authority on what he or she needs and on what will work for him or her.
5. Open and honest communication is important to a positive group experience. (Mallory, 1984, pp. 13–14)

Basically, this belief system rests on the premise that the group as a whole has the necessary power and expertise to help itself. There is no one healer or leader that the group looks to for salvation. This is in contrast to professional therapy groups, where the therapist is cast in the most powerful helping role. Therapeutic aspects of the self-help group include the empowerment of members, the fact that all members are equal (at least theoretically), the sharing of ideas and coping skills, and the mentoring relationships that benefit both parties.

The difference between self-help and therapy groups is often not clearly understood. Briefly, the differences between these two types of groups are as follows:

1. Therapy groups seek to change personality or behavior, while support groups focus on helping members cope.
2. The professional therapist works for a fee, while support group leaders volunteer their services.
3. The support group leader is a full member, while the therapist is in the role of the expert.
4. In a therapy group, the therapist is the final authority; in a self-help group, no one is the final authority.

Both mental health professionals and lay persons are often confused about the function and structure of support groups. This confusion creates problems when the boundaries between the two types of groups are blurred.

In fact, one of the biggest problems encountered in self-help groups is in dealing with conflicts between self-help and professional models. Gartner and Reissman (1977) report that mental health professionals and self-help groups often have an uneasy relationship, with both groups fearing invasion of their turf. Members of self-help groups fear that professionals will take over and dominate the group. Many professionals are concerned about the ability of self-help groups to run the groups safely. Gartner and Reissman (1977) point out that while there are advantages to involving professionals in self-help groups, there is always the danger that the groups will be co-opted, becoming mere appendages of the professional structure and thus losing their vitality.

Mental health self-help group members' disabilities can have an impact on the functioning of the group. Communication and leadership skills may be scarce, and the members may lack the experience and contacts needed to secure funding or a place to meet. A self-help group without experienced leadership may begin without adequate planning or structure. The loosely structured group can become further stressed by the open-ended nature of support groups, if the group becomes too large to handle or is derailed by disruptive members.

Nonetheless, self-help groups successfully meet the needs of members, as evidenced by their rapid growth. The prototypal self-help organization is Alcoholics Anonymous (AA), with its much emulated 12-step program. AA has been criticized by some who view it as too rigid a model, but it has thrived largely because the organization has paid very close attention to detail in structuring the program. AA (1952) has a single, clearly articulated mission, stating that each group has but one primary purpose: to carry its message to the alcoholic who still suffers. It stays out of the business of political advocacy, endorsement of other enterprises, and other issues that would diffuse its purpose.

AA meetings are tightly structured, with clear rules governing potentially disruptive behavior. Leaders are trained, essentially by serving an apprenticeship, "working the program." Leadership is rotated and shared. The strengths of the AA 12-step model are apparent to many other types of self-help organizations, who have borrowed and adapted it for their own groups.

PROBLEMS AND LESSONS

ADD adult support groups in this country are in an early stage of development, with most having been in existence for only a year or two. The leaders of these groups are still experimenting, trying various ways to structure the groups in the hope of finding a workable model. In most cases the success of individual groups seems to depend on the skills and energy of the leader(s), rather than emerging from a particular structure that guides a group, independent of who is in the leadership position. As a group, ADD adult support group leaders are groping for solutions to common problems they have encountered. While ADD adult support groups do not need to adhere to a single coherent model on a national level, ways to enhance the functioning of individual groups should be found if these groups are to survive on a long-term basis.

The following section will describe how particular ADD adult support groups have been run, and some of the lessons that have been learned during their development. Information about the functioning of existing support groups was obtained through telephone interviews with group leaders across the country as well as through informal conversations with leaders and from the taped proceedings of sessions at the 1993 ADD adult conference, The Changing World of Adults with ADD.

Many of the problems encountered in ADD adult support groups seem to be related to inadequate structure and leadership skills. Others are the result of trying to deal with a group that is extremely diverse. The disabling aspects of ADD symptoms also have an impact. In addition, ADD adult support groups struggle with issues common in self-help groups, such as turf battles between professionals and laypersons. Finally, there are problems due to inadequate communication skills among both leaders and members.

Structure

Groups without structure are counterproductive. They also have the potential to be anxiety producing and destructive to members. Rioch (1975) cites the story in the novel *The Lord of the Flies* as an extreme example of what can happen in a group when the task aspects are weak and the group energy unharnessed, allowing irresponsible and primitive group forces to take over. This does not mean that support groups are too dangerous to be led by any but trained professionals. There are models for successful self-help groups, which are run, by definition, by those who have the same problem as the other group members. As previously discussed, Alcoholics Anonymous is the classic example of an effective self-help group.

ADD adult support groups struggle with providing enough structure for a number of reasons. The groups, like the ADD individuals who comprise them, may suffer from the failure to adequately plan, a lack of focus, insufficient resources, and a general ambivalence about the value of structure itself.

Lack of focus or planning results in the formation of a group without a clear direction. As was previously mentioned, groups should make some decisions as to their mission or purpose before they begin. ADD adult support groups, in contrast, may start meeting with only a vague notion of what they hope to accomplish (Poast & Rembas, 1992). There is the desire to help, and to provide a vehicle for getting ADD adults together, but these ideas are not developed further at the outset. Since the mission statement is the essential underpinning of all group processes, ADD groups operating without one suffer from a significant handicap. As a result, other group structures are weakened.

Group rules and procedures are an aspect of group structure that may be inadequately addressed in an ADD adult support group. Sometimes the problem lies in the formulating of rules and at other times in neglecting to make the rules clear to the group.

The group leader with ADD may have difficulty seeing the need for specific rules until problems actually present themselves. Persons with ADD are known to have problems with understanding and complying with rules. Hallowell and Ratey (1993) report that ADD adults are also poor self-observers, and thus may tend to make inaccurate assumptions about their communications. The support group leader may think that everyone in the group knows the rules, when in fact they have not been clearly stated or stated often enough.

Boundary definition is clearly a problem for adults with ADD. Weiss (1992) describes the boundary diffusion typical of ADD adults. In an ADD support group this can play out in situations where members fail to appreciate when they have crossed an invisible line. A member may press others for their phone number or a ride home, not recognizing that the other person is not comfortable with the request. Groups without sufficient structure or experienced leadership fail to clarify the limits and boundaries. As a result, the group is experienced as chaotic and unsafe by members.

Current ADD adult support groups generally adhere to the self-help model and are led by ADD adults, both lay and professional. It is known that persons with ADD tend to have difficulty dealing with structure, both with creating it and in living within it. This particular disability may lead to the resistance to structure commonly observed in ADD adults. Persons with ADD have a love-hate relationship with structure, desperately needing it but at the same time resenting the constraints. This dynamic can surface in the ADD leader who resists setting boundaries and runs a group that is structured too loosely.

On the other hand, the ADD group leader may take the opposite approach, controlling and structuring the group too tightly. Many ADD adults cope with the chaos of ADD by attempting to exert powerful controls both on themselves and the world around them. It is likely that this particular coping style is common among ADD adults who have managed to function fairly successfully before treatment, as managing the symptoms of ADD without help requires an extraordinary effort of will.

From informal conversations and interviews with support group leaders as well as the proceedings of the adult conference, this writer has concluded that there is general resistance to the idea of running ADD adult support groups according to the 12-step model. One support group leader expressed dismay that a certain group had taken this direction, feeling that it was too rigid a model (Poast, 1993). Another commented that AA had some positive aspects and that ADD groups could do a better job sticking with guidelines, but that he had no desire to make the group like AA. He liked the spontaneity of a more freewheeling group (Poast, 1993).

Other group leaders seem to be crying out for more structure. At the adult conference support group leader discussion (Poast, 1993), a leader commented that he liked the AA dictum of keeping it simple. This leader expressed irritation at the tangents ADD groups take (Poast, 1993). Another leader expressed the opinion that groups needed to clarify their objectives (Poast, 1993). She stated that as an educator with a strong background in setting objectives, she did not consider the desire to have a meeting to be an objective.

Existing ADD adult support groups have struggled with the issue of criteria for attending or being a member of the group (Poast, 1993). This is symptomatic of a larger unresolved issue, that of defining the mission and boundaries of the groups. Some groups invite interested professionals or affected family members to join, while others close the groups to anyone but ADD adults. One support group leader reports that the larger organization that sponsors his group insists that all group members have a formal diagnosis (Poast, 1993). Several groups have launched other groups to address the needs of non-ADD spouses who are struggling with the problems of living with an ADD adult.

Group size was an issue that came up repeatedly in the forum for support group leaders at the first conference for ADD adults (Poast, 1993).

Some group leaders reported rapid growth, with one group leader sharing that her group had grown from 6 to 60 members in a few months. Other group leaders were asking for advice on keeping the membership up, having been embarrassed by poor attendance when a professional speaker was scheduled. The comment was made that support groups should focus on quality rather than quantity, and that the attendance was likely to fluctuate with the individual needs of members.

One support group has decided to follow the 12-step model, primarily because the group has become so large, with a membership of around 600. Melear (1993) reported that this decision was based on the need for additional structure in order to handle such a large group.

The final problem to be addressed in this exploration of the structural challenges involved in running an ADD adult support group is that of attempting to operate a group without adequate resources. ADD adults are often great improvisers, who cope with deficits in planning by dealing creatively with problems as they crop up. While the ability to use one's creativity to problem solve is a wonderful adaptation, this skill does not fully compensate for the lack of preplanning.

ADD adult group leaders have been known to found a group in a burst of enthusiasm, failing to ensure that adequate financial and manpower resources exist. In many cases, the groups manage to survive, but often do so at the expense of the leader who runs himself or herself ragged and who may use personal funds to cover group expenses (L. Poast, personal communication, August 22, 1993). Support group leaders from around the country complain of the difficulty with getting members to take on some of the responsibility. This problem might be lessened if a careful assessment of available and needed resources was made in the planning stages.

Communication

Dashiff (1982) states that "the efficiency of any group is directly related to the quality and clarity of its communication process" (p. 56). Jaffe (1991) reports that persons with ADD tend to have impaired communication skills related both to problems with receiving incoming messages and difficulty organizing thoughts into clear outgoing message. Associated memory problems also impinge on the process of communication.

As a result of these difficulties, ADD adults in a group setting experience problems with communication patterns in the group. The ADD leader may send distorted messages to group members as well as misinterpret statements made by participants. Member-to-member communication is similarly impaired. Further, the faulty memories of the ADD adults involved can contribute to the dissemination of inaccurate information in the group. A member may report scientific data inaccurately, for example.

Lay versus Professional Issues

ADD adult support groups have stronger linkages with professionals than do some other types of self-help groups. The Twelve Traditions of AA (AA, 1952) state that Alcoholics Anonymous should remain forever non-professional. There is no room in this model, or indeed in the general self-help model, for someone who takes on the role of expert or advice giver. Professionals in self-help groups attend meetings as observers unless they are full members suffering from the same problem as other members. Within self-help groups for persons with major mental illnesses, such as schizophrenia, there are fewer professional members than in ADD adult groups, largely because the more severely disabling illnesses prevent those affected from attaining that status.

ADD adult support groups, in contrast, have involved mental health professionals in several different roles. According to Poast (personal communication, August 20, 1993) about 25% of the existing support groups are led by mental health professionals, almost all of whom are also ADD adults. Psychologists, psychiatrists, psychiatric nurses, and social workers have either formed groups or been invited to colead a group with a lay leader. Some of these professionals function more in the role of clinical supervisor or consultant, while most actually run the groups themselves. Mental health professionals also join the groups as members, seeking help for their personal problems related to ADD.

ADD is a complicated disorder, causing disability that ranges from mild to severe. As a consequence, there are a number of ADD adults who have managed to attain professional status. These professional ADD adults can be an asset to the support groups, offering an infusion of accumulated experience and skills. On the other hand, the involvement of professionals can create difficulties, particularly if their role within a self-help group is not clarified.

As was previously mentioned, there is a history of mutual suspicion and turf battles between self-help groups and professionals. Grassroots organizers of these groups are often intimidated by "the experts," especially if they have obtained little status or education themselves. They fear that the professionals will take over and relegate them to a dependent, powerless position. This fear is not groundless, as many lay ADD activists report that their ideas and experiences have been discounted by mental health professionals. ADD adults are especially sensitized to this issue, as most have had multiple experiences of being misdiagnosed or given the wrong medicine by professionals who are not ADD-informed.

Mental health professionals, on the other hand, have some concerns about the conduct of ADD adult support groups they are associated with. They express concern about the dangers of running a group without structure, knowing the potential for psychological damage to individuals if the group is too chaotic. Mental health professionals also worry about the ability of a lay leader to handle a member who becomes suicidal, threatens harm to someone else, or admits to child abuse. They also have concerns about personal liability for problems occurring in the group.

Some professionals have expressed reservations about aspects of support groups for ADD adults. Lucius (1992) Asks "what is a support group anyway?" (p. 12) and expresses concern that a group can function without some type of screening mechanism. Thomasson (1991) is of the opinion that groups led by trained professionals may be preferable to those led by laypersons, since professionals are trained to handle crises such as a suicidal member, for example.

In spite of the potential problems, some ADD adult support groups have managed to incorporate both self-help principles and professional experience in their programs. Some groups were founded by professionals, who then trained laypersons to either colead, take over a group, or lead a new group that emerged from the original group. In some cases, the professional gradually backed out of the leadership role, but remained available to the lay leader as a supervisor or consultant.

In this writer's opinion, a combination of a lay and a professional coleader is ideal. The lay leader can get valuable on-the-job training and supervision, while the professional benefits from a close relationship with one who is often more sensitive to the needs of mental health consumers. Toro et al. (1988) found that peer-led groups for persons with mental health illness were more cohesive and expressive than similar groups led by professionals. A group may be more likely to enter a transference relationship with a professional leader, casting the professional in the role of Father, Mother, or Expert. Since that type of relationship is counterproductive in a self-help group, with the goal of helping members cope rather than change their personalities, a lay leader can provide needed balance.

Leadership Issues

ADD adult support groups generally lack mechanisms to train members for leadership roles. Currently, groups are facilitated both by mental health professionals and laypersons. Having a formally trained professional leader does not solve the leadership problem, however. Many professional group leaders have reported that they are burning out or that they would like to turn the group over to someone else, but that they are unable to find anyone to step in. Lay leaders state that they have to do all the tasks involved in running the group themselves.

This problem is not unique to ADD adult groups. In a needs assessment of a broad sampling of self-help groups, Meissen, Gleason, & Embree (1991) found that lack of member involvement and participation was a frequently reported problem. ADD adult support group leaders report that either no one volunteers or help is volunteered that never materializes. Although the disabilities of ADD members may contribute to this problem, in the writer's opinion the passivity of the members may be more a function of their lack of knowledge and experience about the tasks involved in running a group.

The leadership functions of an ADD adult support group are often unevenly addressed. Healthy groups have clearly defined leadership responsibilities and a designated person or persons in charge of keeping the group on track. Further, an optimally functioning group shares the leadership functions among the members. These two goals are not in conflict. Leadership functions include task and process concerns as well as housekeeping duties, such as collecting names for a mailing list or making coffee. It is very difficult for one person to attend to all of these matters. Certain tasks may be delegated while the designated leader retains overall responsibility for the functioning of the group.

Delegating tasks may be particularly difficult for group leaders with ADD, not because ADD adults have an excessive need for power, but because they often have deficits in communication and negotiation skills. Similar difficulties in communication may also interfere with the collaboration needed to form good working relationships between group coleaders.

Special Challenges

The great diversity in the population of persons with ADD is an ongoing and serious problem for persons offering ADD adult support groups. The functional capacity of individual ADD adults ranges from those with successful businesses to persons who are not far from homelessness (Jaffe, 1992). Within the support groups, higher functioning members often drop out, uncomfortable with identifying themselves as peers of very dysfunctional ADD adults. Some ADD adults try to distance themselves from their less fortunate peers, expressing the opinion that there must be something other than ADD causing such severe problems (Brians, 1992). This is a common dynamic found even among low-status groups, such as psychiatric inpatients (O'Mahony, 1982).

This reaction of higher functioning members is not just a function of the wish to deny the serious nature of ADD disabilities, however. Many of the eventual dropouts continue with the group for long periods of time, struggling with guilt over the wish to abandon their struggling peers.

When the higher functioning adults with ADD finally do leave the groups, the often confide in the leader that they feel bad about leaving, but that the group simply does not meet their own needs. These more successful adults have painful issues of their own that are not addressed in the group because the needier members' issues take precedence. Higher functioning adults with ADD frequently report that they fail to bring up their own issues because they seem trivial compared with problems of other members. This minimizing of their very real needs exacerbates and reflects a common problem experienced by adults with ADD.

The fact that ADD is a subtle disorder creates a situation whereby reasonably functional ADD adults can "pass" as normal, avoiding the stigma of having a disability, but falling into the trap of having to deny the real problems with which they struggle. Participating in a group that perpetuates the denial is counterproductive to the recovery of these ADD adults.

The less functional group members also experience problems with participating in a group that is highly diverse. Some struggling members of ADD adult support groups report that they are intimidated by others who are more socially skilled and successful. The presence of ADD adults who have been more successful is a continual reminder of their own failure to overcome the disorder. Another problem associated with mixed levels of functioning in ADD adult support groups is that members who have extreme difficulty processing information can be overwhelmed by the pace of speech of more verbally gifted members.

Level of functioning is not the only variable that contributes to the diversity in ADD adult support groups. Gender issues and the different ages and stages of group members are also factors that impinge on group functioning. In a group led by this writer, female members formed their own informal group which met for coffee after the meeting. The women expressed that they felt there were many issues they were not comfortable dealing with in a mixed-gender group. In addition, younger members of this group often had trouble relating to the issues of the middle-aged participants, and vice versa.

Comorbidity among ADD adults in support groups is a problem with which leaders of the groups frequently grapple (Poast, 1993). The leaders find it difficult to keep the group focused on ADD when so many of the members have additional diagnoses and complications. It becomes confusing for members who have little knowledge about ADD when other participants talk about problems actually related to Tourette's syndrome or Obsessive-Compulsive Disorder, for example. Group members frequently do not make the distinction between various problems when they share information about themselves. As a consequence, the leader often finds himself or herself in the position of needing to interrupt the flow of discussion to educate members about the different disorders.

This writer is not suggesting that all mixed adult ADD groups are dysfunctional. For example, mentoring relationships often develop between higher and lower functioning members, in which both benefit. The struggling member can gain a role model from whom he or she can learn valuable skills. The lower functioning ADD adult may begin to have some hope that he or she will be able to overcome the disability, too. The self-esteem of the successful ADD adult can be enhanced by being in the helping role. Gartner and Reissman (1982) stress that helpers influence themselves as well as those they are trying to help. The same dynamic can also occur between younger and older group members.

ADD symptoms also have an impact on the functioning of ADD adult support groups. Persons with ADD, particularly those who are impulsive and hyperactive, tend to be volatile, live from crisis to crisis, and challenge authority. These characteristics present a challenge to the leader, who is striving to maintain enough order to ensure that the group is a safe and helpful one. ADD adults often have a poor sense of boundaries and some impairment of social skills, both of which characteristics can impact negatively on group interactions. Impulsive group members may have difficulty complying with the rule of confidentiality.

Hypoactive persons with ADD are less obviously disruptive to a group, but their passive style can be a problem in the group as well. Yalom (1975) reports that silent group members contribute little to a group's process and also benefit less from being in the group. A poor sense of time and the tendency to wander mentally are ADD characteristics that can interfere with the task of keeping the group focused and on track.

The writer does not mean to imply that ADD adults are too impaired to form a successful group. It is important, however, to recognize the challenges presented by ADD adults in a group setting.

SOLUTIONS

The problems encountered in ADD adult support groups are certainly not unsolvable. Most current groups are managing fairly well, even with the obstacles they encounter. The positive aspects of ADD group members help to compensate for organizational deficits. Enthusiasm, curiosity, drive, intuition, and empathy are qualities that enhance both the formation of groups and the bonding that needs to occur within a group. If solutions to the organizational problems are found, the groups will emerge as an even more powerful force in the battle to help ADD adults successfully cope with their lives.

Planning

The first step to be taken involves the planning phase that should occur before a group is started. Even existing groups can benefit from going through this process. An existing group could form a committee, perhaps with the input of an experienced consultant, to study the current functioning of the group and also to plan its future direction.

It is strongly recommended that a group or prospective group utilize outside help during the planning phase. Consistent with the self-help model, the final authority for decisions should be retained by those who struggle with ADD. A consultant can offer advice, but should stay out of the decision-making process itself. The consultant's role is to offer the benefit of experience and to assist the group in learning how to plan for the group in an effective manner.

Clarifying the role of an expert or professional at the outset can help minimize some of the friction that can occur between professionals and laypersons in a self-help group. The consultant may be an experienced group leader or a person with some expertise in organizational issues. United Way is an excellent resource; for a reasonable fee, it offers training that is applicable to a variety of groups. Some of the training offered is in basic communication skills, while other programs teach participants how to set up an effective organization, including the rules and procedures involved.

The first order of business during the planning phase should be a formulation of a clear purpose or mission statement. ADD energy, enthusiasm, and individuality can become a force that drives a group in too many directions at once, dissipating resources and fostering confusion.

After the mission statement is articulated, a set of rules and procedures can be developed. Typical rules should address the issues of confidentiality, which subjects are allowed to be discussed, how order is to be maintained in the group, and how rule infractions will be dealt with. The rules should be stated at the beginning of every group and restated whenever there is an infraction. Having written information about group rules on hand is very helpful. One ADD adult support group leader has developed an orientation handout for group members that spells out the rules and boundaries of the group (Poast, 1993).

Criteria for membership should also be decided to eliminate confusion about who is allowed to attend the group. One possibility for dealing with the problem of how to include interested persons without ADD is to follow the AA model, offering two types of meetings: open meetings that include persons without ADD and closed meetings for ADD adults only.

A prospective group leader is ill advised to attempt setting up a group by himself or herself. The input and resources of others are needed if the potential pitfall of leader burnout is to be avoided. A sole individual is also not likely to possess all the skills that are needed. Dory and Reissman (1984) recommend that a person interested in starting a self-help group form a core group of interested parties early on in the planning process.

Attention needs to be paid to an assessment of resources during the planning phase. Issues such as finding an adequate place to meet, ensuring that there will be funds for the printing of needed written materials, and exploring the amount of time and labor needed to run the group should be addressed. The labor should be divided in an equitable way, satisfactory to all participants. In addition, some provision should be made for backup resources, such as an alternative place to meet if the current place becomes unavailable or a list of volunteers who can help fill in when a core group member is unable to perform his or her job.

A set of contingency plans should be developed for dealing with anticipated problems. The core group should decide how they will deal with rapid growth, dwindling membership, member crises and disruptive members, for example.

When the initial planning phase is complete, the core group should have in hand a mission statement, a set of rules and procedures for operating the group, and a set of contingency plans for anticipated problems.

Training

Before the support group starts meeting, it is recommended that the core planning group seek some form of leadership training. This does not have to involve a great deal of time or money. United Way offers a brief leadership course, as do many continuing education programs sponsored by colleges or community organizations. An experienced professional group leader can be hired or asked to donate time for a group leader training workshop. There are also written resources for group leaders on how to run a successful self-help group (Gartner & Reissman, 1980; Mallory, 1984).

In this writer's opinion, some of the problems reported with mobilizing group members to share leadership functions could be addressed if efforts were made to teach group members how to lead. The fact that ADD is a subtle disability often fools even those familiar with it into underestimating the gaps in knowledge that often coexist with above-average intelligence.

An adult with ADD may have little awareness of the details involved in organizing and running a group. He or she may not fully appreciate that a meeting should have an agenda, that a group needs a clearly spelled out purpose, and that the many tasks involved in running a group are too burdensome to be handled by one individual. Even if an ADD adult is aware of the tasks involved, he or she may need support and supervised practice to learn the necessary skills. Some time and effort should be devoted to the sharing of information learned about leadership skills with the general membership.

Communication problems can undermine the functioning of ADD adult support groups. It is recommended that both leaders and members receive some training in basic communication skills. This can be done by bringing in professionals skilled at both introducing the techniques and leading the group in structured practice of the skills. Assertiveness techniques, the use of "I" messages, and picking up nonverbal cues and clarifying messages should be included, for example. The information can also be reinforced with written handouts.

The core group of leaders may need additional help in identifying and addressing their own communication blocks. For example, they might benefit from help with less than optimal telephone skills, a typical ADD trait.

Jaffe (1993) suggests that since new members often make their first contact with a group over the phone, it is important that the person taking the calls is able to communicate clearly and make a good initial impression, in order to attract and retain new members. A seemingly simple task, such as that of giving directions to the meeting over the phone, is often difficult for the ADD adult group leader with both directional and communication problems. The prospective group member on the other end of the line may become so frustrated with the process that he or she decides to forgo joining the group. The prospective member may also spend the night of the meeting driving in circles because the directions were inadequate.

Ideally, the telephone contact person will be selected because he or she has good telephone skills. If all core group members are weak in this area, they might improve with some structured practice or the use of written scripts. The scripts could outline the information to be conveyed to new members and should include a clear set of directions to the meeting place.

ADD adult support group leaders may also be unfamiliar with simple communication devices used in groups and organizations. The use of phone trees, for example, could be explained as part of their general training. A group log is another communication tool that can be useful to group leaders, especially if individual leaders of a given group do not attend each session.

Implementation

Some of the solutions to problems encountered in ADD adult support groups will become apparent only when the group is fully operational. In spite of the commonalties, each group leader will encounter unique situations arising from the particular composition of his or her group.

While the mission or statement of purpose should be clear at the outset, it should not be written in stone, but be revised and updated as necessary. Group leaders may found a group with the express purpose of providing a forum for members to share experiences, but find that the members have a great need for general information about ADD. While it is ill advised for a group to deplete its resources by going in too many directions at once, it is possible to meet both of these needs as long as the boundaries are attended to. Since the behavior expected of members is different for educational and support formats, attempting to meet both needs in a single session may be confusing for ADD adults, who often have great difficulty when the rules change. Some ADD adult support groups have met both needs by offering two sessions per month, one educational and the other a more traditional sharing group.

At the support group leader session of the 1993 ADD adult conference, there was much discussion about the problems of interrupting and keeping the group on track (Poast, 1993). A support group leader stated that the interruptions are such a chronic problem in her group that she has resorted to using a "talking stick" to be held by the person who has the floor. She reported that the talking stick has not done much good, as group members continually reach across the table to grab the stick from each other.

Other support group leaders reported success with the technique of asking group members to write down their thoughts so they would be less likely to interrupt out of fear they would forget what they were going to say. Another suggestion was for the leader to make a rule that any group member could call a time-out if there was too much interruption. Still another idea was for the leader to remind participants to take their medicine before meetings.

The problem of group leaders themselves getting off track was mentioned. It was suggested that leaders avoid taking part in the discussion to alleviate this problem. In other words, the leader should stick to his or her role as conversational traffic controller.

Some discussion about how to deal with great diversity within the group should occur during the planning phase, but solutions to specific problems will need to wait until the needs of a particular group are clear. Current ADD adult support groups have been successful at spinning off other, more narrowly defined groups as the membership grows. Women's groups, spouse groups, and groups for professionals with ADD are some examples of groups that have been launched from a parent organization.

Some support groups deal with both the problem of size and diversity by breaking into smaller groups for part of a meeting. This is a viable option if adequate space and leadership are available. Still other groups meet the needs of a diverse membership in a less formal fashion, allowing for a period of socialization during which persons with similar interests can interact. Subgroups with similar interests also may meet socially outside of the group. It is possible to partly address the needs of subgroups with a careful choice of topics, which should be balanced to include issues of interest to both older and younger members, for example.

At least one ADD adult support group has a rule barring the sharing of specific information about diagnosis and treatment during the sharing group. The leaders have found that the group tends to avoid dealing with the impact of ADD on a personal level by becoming "experts" spouting the information they cull from books and journals. The defense of intellectualization may be a particularly comfortable one for persons with ADD, who are often very bright and who also have much trouble dealing with feelings. Many existing support groups have a "no talking about medications" rule (Poast, 1993), as the leaders find that the group gets too bogged down by this issue. In most cases, these groups allow general discussion of the impact of medicine on members' lives but discourage talking about specific medicines.

A leadership style characterized by clear limit setting combined with liberal doses of humor is particularly effective in ADD adult support groups. Persons with ADD tend to chafe at the structure and rules they so desperately need, but they also are very responsive to humor. This writer has found that phrasing comments on rule infractions in a humorous fashion avoids many of the power struggles that often emerge in groups of ADD adults. Veteran support group leader Jaffe (1993) recommends a leadership style that combines "flexibility and ruthlessness."

The use of the pronoun "we" when making comments on group behavior is also useful. A statement such as "it must be an ADD day, we are really getting off track here" avoids putting group members in a one-down position in relation to the group leader, and thus is more likely to be heard.

From an analysis of the types of structures that have worked well in support groups from different parts of the country, a distinct pattern emerges (Poast, 1993). Many of the group leaders have found that having professional speakers at the meetings is helpful and serves to attract members to the group. They have also found, however, that limiting the speaker to a short presentation, about 20 to 45 minutes, is optimal. The remainder of the meeting is devoted to group discussion and interaction.

Several support group leaders underlined the importance of allowing group members to share their stories with each other, especially success stories. Certainly, using successful role models to foster hope is a technique that other types of self-help groups have utilized (Kelly, Sautter, Tugrul, & Weaver, 1990). One support group leader found that group membership dropped from 25 to 6 members in a short period of time. He felt that the problem was due to overuse of speakers, with little time for group interaction.

Another common structure that seems to work well for existing support groups is the breaking of the meetings into segments. Frequent breaks allow for the difficulties ADD adults have with sitting and concentrating for long periods of time. The format of meetings is often mixed and varied, which increases the likelihood that members will be able to maintain interest in the group. A typical group may begin with a large group meeting, during which business is conducted and general announcements made.

The group may then break up into smaller discussion groups, break later for a period of socialization, and reconvene as one large group to summarize the smaller group discussions. This format is frequently altered to accommodate a speaker from time to time.

Dealing with extremely disruptive group members is the problem most frequently raised in discussions with ADD adult support group leaders (L. Poast, personal communication, August 20, 1993). Many group leaders report that the behavior of these members seriously undermines the group, chasing away other members. The leaders are in a quandary about how to deal with this situation, since they generally adhere to the belief that the groups should be open to all comers.

The inexperienced group leader may have difficulty separating the notion of accepting the individual from that of accepting the individual's behavior. Clear guidelines for expected behavior coupled with a plan for dealing with unacceptable behavior can help the leader deal with situations as they occur. The neophyte lay leader, however, may need support from an experienced group leader as he or she takes the difficult step of asking a member to leave the group, at least temporarily.

Evaluation

It is imperative that support group leaders find a way to periodically evaluate the functioning of their group. Even a robustly healthy group can weaken quickly, developing serious problems as the result of a change in leadership or extremely disruptive members.

Some type of backup assistance, similar to the clinical supervision given to professionals, is recommended for ADD adult support group leaders. A mental health professional or an experienced lay group leader could meet with the leader periodically to discuss problems encountered in the group. Phone consultation on an as-needed basis should also be available to leaders dealing with acute problems. If an experienced consultant is not available, group leaders can network with other leaders in order to discuss common problems. It is also recommended that the core group of leaders gather briefly after each meeting to review the session.

Group members should be surveyed periodically for their input on how the group is functioning. This could be accomplished by using a written questionnaire or facilitating a discussion among members about how the group is or is not meeting their needs.

RECOMMENDATIONS FOR PROFESSIONALS

While ADD adult support groups are confronted with a host of problems related to rapid growth and gaps in planning, they have met and continue to meet the needs of countless ADD adults trying to cope with a subtle handicap that has only recently been recognized, both by mental health professionals and the general public. These support groups have attempted to fill a large void. The void has been created because health professionals are unprepared to treat this newly discovered disorder (Lucius, Huessy, & Silver, 1991).

Existing ADD adult support group leaders are valiantly trying to close the gap by providing information, advocacy, and linkages to ADD-informed professionals, along with both practical and emotional support. Given the monumental nature of the task, support group leaders deserve recognition for all they have managed to accomplish to date.

Still, there is much work to be done to ensure the continued viability of ADD adult support groups. Mental health professionals can assume an important role in the process of developing the groups. Professionals can assist by providing places to meet, offering use of office equipment and secretarial services, and helping group leaders find sources of funding. In addition, they can offer their services as consultants and trainers of lay group leaders.

Mental health professionals with ADD can also function as group leaders, provided that they stay focused on the goals of self-help groups, resisting the impulse to professionalize the groups. Further, professional leaders should exercise sensitivity when dealing with issues of power and control in relation to lay leaders and members. Professionals should also bear in mind the finding of Meissen et al. (1991), that peer-led groups do not report more problems than those groups that are led by professionals.

Relationships between mental health professionals and ADD adult support groups can be mutually beneficial, as the groups can become an important adjunct in the treatment of the professional's ADD clients. It is therefore in the best interests of both ADD adults and professionals to work together in creating support networks for ADD adults. Krauss and Slavinsky (1982) discuss potential models for networking between self-help groups and professionals within the mental health service delivery system. While they acknowledge the communication difficulties involved in attempting to link two groups with very different philosophies, they stress that it is the key to successful community-based mental health care.

REFERENCES

AA. (1952). *Twelve steps and twelve traditions.* New York: AA World Services, The AA Grapevine.

Brians, R. H. (1992, Winter). [Letter to the editor]. *ADDult News*, pp. 5–6. (Available from Parents of Hyperactive/ADD Children, 2620 Ivy Place, Toledo, OH 43613).

Dashiff, C. (1982). Using group process skills in change. In J. Lancaster & W. Lancaster (Eds.), *The nurse as a change agent* (pp. 49–64). St. Louis: Mosby.

Dory, F. J., & Reissman, F. (1984). Training professionals in organizing self-help groups. In L. Mallory, *Leading self-help groups* (pp. 61–66). New York: Family Service America.

Gartner, A., & Reissman, F. (1977). *Self-help in the human services.* San Francisco: Jossey-Bass.

Gartner, A., & Reissman, F. (1980). *HELP: A working guide to self-help groups.* New York: New Viewpoints/Vision Books.

Gartner, A. J., & Reissman, F. (1982). Self-help and mental health. *Hospital and Community Psychiatry, 33*(8), 631–635.

Hallowell, N. M., & Ratey, J. J. (1993, Winter). Suggested diagnostic criteria for ADD in adults. *ADDult News,* pp. 1–2.(Available from Parents of Hyperactive/ADD Children, 2620 Ivy Place, Toledo, OH 43613).

Jaffe, P. (1991, Fall). Cognitive dimming. *ADDendum,* p. 10. (Available from ADDendum, 5041-A Backlick Road, Annandale, VA 22003).

Jaffe, P. (1992, Winter). Reflections on the break-up of the Manhattan ADD adult support group. *ADDendum,* p. 10. (Available from ADDendum, 5041-A Backlick Road, Annandale, VA 22003).

Jaffe, P. (Speaker). (1993). Starting or growing a support group in your town. (Cassette Recording No. 8). In *The changing world of adults with ADD.* (Available from Repeat Performance, 2911 Crabapple Lane, Hobart, IN 46342).

Kelly, K. M., Sautter, F., Tugrul, K., & Weaver, M. D. (1990). Fostering self-help on an inpatient unit. *Archives of Psychiatric Nursing, 4*(3), 161–165.

Krauss, J. B., & Slavinsky, A. T. (1982). *The chronically ill psychiatric patient and the community.* Boston: Blackwell.

Lucius, M. (1992, Spring). What is a support group anyway? [Letter to the editor]. *ADDendum,* p. 12. (Available from ADDendum, 5041-A Backlick Road, Annandale, VA 22003).

Lucius, M., Huessy, H., & Silver, D. (1991, Summer). [Letters to the editor]. *ADDendum,* pp. 10–14. (Available from ADDendum, 5041-A Backlick Road, Annandale, VA 22003).

Mallory, L. (1984). *Leading self-help groups: A guide for training facilitators.* New York: Family Service America.

Meissen, G. J., Gleason, D. F., & Embree, M. G. (1991). An assessment of the needs of mutual-help groups. *American Journal of Community Psychology, 19*(3), 427–442.

Melear, L. (Ed.). (1993, Mid-summer). Atlanta support group to test 12-step approach. *The ADDvisor,* p. 3. (Available from Attention Deficit Resource Center, PO Box 71223, Marietta, GA 30007-1223).

O'Mahony, P. D. (1982). Psychiatric patient denial of mental illness as a normal process. *British Journal of Medical Psychology, 55,* 109–118.

Poast, L. (Speaker). (1993). Panel of group leaders discuss, leaders network, sharing ideas & experiences. (Cassette Recording No. 17). In *The changing world of adults with ADD.* (Available from Repeat Performance, 2911 Crabapple Lane, Hobart, IN 46342).

Poast, L., & Rembas, P. (1992, Winter). Support group news. *ADDult News,* p. 7. (Available from Parents of Hyperactive/ADD Children, 2620 Ivy Place, Toledo, OH 43613).

Rioch, M. J. (1975). The work of Wilfred Bion on groups. In A. D. Coleman & W. H. Bexton (Eds.), *Group relations reader 1* (pp. 21–33). Washington, DC: A. K. Rice Institute.

Thomasson, M. (1991, September–October). ADD in adults. *Challenge,* p. 2. (Available from Challenge Inc., PO Box 488, W. Newbury, MA 01985).

Toro, P. A., Rieschl, T. M., Zimmerman, M. A., Rappoport, J., Seidman, E., Luke, D. A., & Roberts, L. J. (1988). Professionals in mutual help groups: Impact on social climate and member's behavior. *Journal of Consulting and Clinical Psychology, 56,* 631–632.

Turquet, P. M. (1985). Leadership: The individual and the group. In A. D. Coleman & M. H. Geller (Eds.), *Group relations reader 2* (pp. 71–87). Washington, DC: A. K. Rice Institute.

Weiss, L. (1992). *Attention deficit disorder: Help for sufferers and their spouses.* Dallas TX: Taylor.

Yalom, I. D. (1975). *The theory and practice of group psychotherapy* (2nd ed.). New York: Basic Books.

19

Future Directions in Research and Treatment of the ADD Adult

PAUL JAFFE

The needs of the ADD adult community run wide, and they run deep; the list of concerns is a long one. Everything that challenges non-ADD adults (education, jobs, housing, health care) is an issue for the adult with ADD, and each issue is probably magnified. At a recent meeting of ADD adults, dozens of suggestions—many of them excellent—were put forth. Unfortunately, at this point, resources are meager.

Priorities must be set, but here are a few possible directions for research, treatment, and advocacy.

1. By "ADD adults," what part of the population are we describing: 2%? 5%? 10%? In the popular press, a figure of 25% has recently been aired (Richardson, 1993). Reliable and accessible epidemiological data are lacking.

2. To establish an incidence rate or range, an agreed-upon set of diagnostic criteria will be needed. DSM-IV (APA, 1994) may help somewhat; see (25) and (26). But other lists, such as the Utah Criteria (Wood, 1986), the Hallowell-Ratey criteria (see Ratey, Hallowell, & Miller, chapter 12, this volume), and the Brown Attention-Activation Disorder Scale 2 (see Brown, chapter 6, this volume), will no doubt also continue to be used.

3. An adulthood ADD diagnosis implies a retrospective childhood ADD diagnosis—hence, the need for a structured interview aimed at confirming, or discounting, such a possibility. A rating scale designed for this purpose has recently appeared in print (Ward, Wender, & Reimherr, 1993), but it does not cover the entire ADD population.

4. Since 1989 several dozen ADD adult support groups have formed (see Kelly, chapter 18, this volume). Participants in these groups can express concerns, share experiences, gather information, socialize, and alleviate an often pervasive sense of isolation. Groups for spouses now meet in several cities as well.

These groups, however, need volunteer help, technical assistance, legal advice, leadership training, and fund-raising skills. Those who run the groups (especially those that are peer-led rather than led by a professional) are typically overworked and undercompensated.

5. Comparatively few physicians are both knowledgeable about ADD and available to treat adults. As adult ADD has been publicized, the caseloads of these clinicians have rapidly filled. Others may be sympathetic but inexperienced; such doctors may be reluctant to prescribe the full range of ADD medications, or to use the higher dosages that sometimes work best. Upgraded skills in the broader medical community are sorely needed.

6. The need for a nationwide data bank of physicians (and other professionals) has been periodically discussed. How might such a project be financed? Also, what can be done to teach consumers how to locate suitable clinicians, and how to present themselves should they find any?

7. Are physicians afraid to prescribe Schedule II medications such as methylphenidate, dextroamphetamine, and methamphetamine to adults? If so, is this because of fear of harassment by state medical boards or federal drug enforcement agents? Does the fact that the Food and Drug Administration authorizes doctors to use stimulants in ADD with children only (*Physicians' Desk Reference*, 1993) add to an existing climate of hesitation? If the answer to any of these questions is yes, can something be done to assist physicians who are willing to risk their practices in order to prescribe needed medications?

8. As word about ADD–including ADD in adults–has spread, demand for methylphenidate has at times outstripped supply. As a Schedule II drug, production (by its two manufacturers) is fixed each year by the federal government in accordance with the Comprehensive Drug Abuse Prevention and Control Act of 1970. In 1993 this contributed to a nationwide shortage (Leary, 1993). Some advocates have called for a rescheduling of methylphenidate from II to III, where its annual production would not be capped.

A second issue is whether the government, in effect, is assigning market shares to each company–thus undermining competition and some of the incentive for quality control. Could this have anything to do with the large volume of complaints about the reliability of one of the currently available forms of methylphenidate?

9. Little is known about the impact of stimulants on pregnancy (*Physicians' Desk Reference*, 1993). Scattered studies exist of methylphenidate (Diener,

1991) and dextroamphetamine (Shangraw, Seminer, & Zarr, 1985). As stimulants have historically been prescribed mainly for boys, this lack of data has never been an issue. Since these medications are now prescribed for women of childbearing age, should it be an issue?

10. Do preemployment drug scans pick up methylphenidate? Dextroamphetamine? Methamphetamine? Other medications? Have ADD adults not been hired because of this? Have others avoided applying for certain jobs because of fear of detection?

11. Can other medications alleviate ADD? A number of alternatives have been studied, primarily with adult test populations. (The concept of "informed consent" has limited meaning to children.) With varying degrees of success, investigators have tried the following:

- The tricyclic antidepressants desipramine and nortriptyline (Biederman, Baldessarini, Wright, Knee, & Harmatz, 1989; Ratey, Greenburg, Bemporad, & Lindem, 1992; Spencer, Biederman, Wilens, Steingard, & Geist, 1993)

- The dopamine reuptake blockers nomifensine and bupropion (Shekim, Masterson, Cantwell, Hanna, & McCracken, 1989; Wender & Reimherr, 1990)

- The (somewhat) selective inhibitors of Type B monoamine oxidase, pargyline and selegiline (Wender, Wood, Reimherr, & Ward, 1983; Wood, Reimherr & Wender, 1983)

- The amino acids dopa, tyrosine, phenylalanine, and methionine (Reimherr, Wender, Wood, & Ward, 1987; Reimherr, Wood, & Wender, 1980; Shekim, Antun, Hanna, McCracken, & Hess, 1990; Wood et al., 1982; Wood, Reimherr, & Wender, 1985)

- The NMDA (N-methyl-D-aspartate) receptor antagonist, MK-801 (Reimherr, Wood, & Wender, 1986)

Despite these studies, the primacy of stimulant treatment has not been seriously challenged.

12. Are certain medication *combinations* more than randomly useful in treating ADD? If so, which seem to be the best candidates? Would controlled studies involving more than one medication be worth the resources expended?

13. What can be done for ADD patients who have grown tolerant to the therapeutic effects of medications (Wender, 1971)? Is drug rotation (Eichlseder, 1985) a possibility?

14. How important is neuropsychological testing in making an ADD diagnosis? Are there data that link, or fail to link, testing or nontesting with

treatment outcomes? At it stands now, some physicians require these; others do not. Testing is not always affordable or covered by health plans. Do some doctors use testing as a hedge against the possibility of future legal challenges, as has been suspected of other branches of medicine?

15. How have adults seeking reimbursement for ADD-related expenses fared with medical insurers and health maintenance organizations? (Often, not well. By definition, adulthood ADD is a *preexisting* illness. By classification, it is a *psychiatric* illness. Neither is popular with insurers or HMOs.) What happens when a health plan says choose Dr. A, B, or C—and none is familiar with ADD? Must consumers accept limited expertise as a trade-off for affordability?

16. Do ADD treatment-seekers stand to gain, or lose, from the Clinton Administration's health care reform plan? Will the proposed expansion of managed care appeal to a community that is getting more than its share of resistance from existing HMOs?

17. Should ADD adults who have dropped out of school, or otherwise cut short their educations, be encouraged to pick up where they left off? What can be done to assist them? What can be done to assist those who will be teaching them? Is financial aid generally available?

18. Do state vocational rehabilitation agencies recognize ADD? If not all, then which ones do and do not? What services (e.g., testing, training, coaching) can they offer ADD adults?

19. How are ADD adults doing with their jobs? Can medication consistently cover an 8-hour shift? If someone is struggling still, can counseling help?

20. How can employers be made aware of ADD in such a way as to make them willing to accommodate ADD employees, at least to the "reasonable" extent mandated by the 1990 Americans with Disabilities Act (see Latham & Latham, chapter 17, this volume)?

21. Some percentage of ADD adults find themselves caught up in the criminal justice system. Do reliable statistics exist? How should such data be interpreted?

22. Of those who are imprisoned, how many are diagnosed? How many *might* be diagnosed?

23. Can inmates obtain appropriate medication? (Methylphenidate is not stocked by federal prison infirmaries, but can be special-ordered. Is this true of state prison systems as well?) Can inmates obtain counseling? What about access to published materials about ADD?

24. What is the medical and legal status of ADD adults in the armed forces? Should they need it, can enlisted men and women obtain access to medication and counseling?

25. Will the new psychiatric diagnostic manual (APA, 1994) promote professional acceptance of adulthood ADD? Like its predecessors, DSM-

IV will have a section on childhood disorders, or Disorders Usually First Diagnosed in Infancy, Childhood or Adolescence. (Among the classifications, most are lifelong conditions that first appear in childhood.) Did the placement of ADD and ADHD in similar chapters in earlier DSMs contribute to their neglect by adult psychiatry? Can the newest category, Attention Deficit/Hyperactivity Disorder (AD/HD)–which is comparably placed–expect a similar reception?

26. Adulthood ADD is represented in DSM-IV (APA, 1994), if rather quietly. There will *not* be a separate category along the lines of the old Attention Deficit Disorder, Residual Type (APA, 1980). However, the symptom list has been updated to describe adults too; it mentions "work" as well as "schoolwork" and "tools" as well as "toys." The text states that "a minority [of those with AD/HD] experience the full complement of symptoms of Attention-Deficit/Hyperactivity Disorder into mid-adulthood" (APA, 1994, p. 82).

Will these statements help adults get reimbursed for ADD-related treatment and counseling? Will they make it easier for ADD adults to use the Americans with Disabilities Act, or apply for federal disability assistance? Will they encourage the Food and Drug Administration to rewrite its stimulant-use guidelines so as to include adults? Finally, what else might DSM-IV affect?

27. For any advocate community, medical research represents an investment in the future. A bright future would be one in which advances in knowledge help create a progressively broader range of increasingly effective treatments. By that yardstick, ADD research has a long way to go. However, the following is a sample of work published in the last 4 years.

a. Psychiatrist Alan Zametkin has viewed the workings of the brains of adults with and without ADHD (Zametkin et al., 1990). Using positron-emission tomography (PET), Zametkin and his colleagues at the National Institute of Mental Health measured the rates at which specific brain regions made use of glucose, the brain's energy source. In regions associated with attention or motor inhibition, a pattern emerged: ADHD subjects displayed less activity than controls, suggesting a degree of neurological underfunctioning. These findings have been replicated–though not quite as sharply–in a sample of teenagers (Zametkin et al., 1993).

However, a comparison of off-drug and on-drug PET scans revealed little. Methylphenidate and dextroamphetamine did alter metabolic rates in certain brain regions, but their effects were neither sizable nor consistent (Matochik et al., 1993).

b. Psychiatrist Joseph Biederman and colleagues at Harvard Medical School have found patterns of ADD-related inheritance and comorbidity (depression, anxiety) within the families of ADD probands (Biederman,

Faraone, Keenan, Steingard, & Tsuang, 1991; Biederman, Faraone, Keenan, & Tsuang, 1991).

c. A seven-institution research team led by geneticist David Comings of California's City of Hope Medical Center has linked five disorders with a higher than expected incidence of a specific genetic abnormality (Comings, Comings, Muhleman, et al., 1991). The gene is said to govern the population density of the dopamine D_2 receptor, present in the brain and elsewhere. Comings thinks the abnormality may affect conduct: To an underlying disorder is added a behavioral element that is either "restless-hyperactive" or "impulsive-compulsive-addictive." In other words, there is a disruptiveness whose natural home seems to be the borderland between ADHD and conduct disorder.

The disorders that linked statistically with the presence of the D_2 abnormality were alcoholism, Tourette's syndrome, autism, ADHD, and conduct disorder. Those that did not so link were schizophrenia, Parkinsonism, obesity, depression, and panic disorder.

d. Psychiatrist-turned-geneticist Peter Hauser of the National Institutes of Health studied adults and children with an obscure condition known as generalized resistance to thyroid hormone (GRTH). Some 61% of those with GRTH met criteria for ADHD, versus 13% of a control group (Hauser et al., 1993). But while the incidence of ADHD among those with GRTH seems to be high, the incidence of GRTH among those with ADHD is not high—a maximum of 5%.

The hallmark of the disorder is the thyroid gland's relative inability to communicate with outlying organs such as the heart, liver, and pituitary. Would-be target cells lack the molecular receptors necessary to decode messages carried by the thyroid hormones triiodothyronine (T_3) and thyroxine (T_4), which, in an attempt to compensate, the thyroid secretes in large quantities. The thyroid hormone receptor has been linked to a specific gene, and GRTH has been linked to the presence of 1 of 15 mutations which cluster in the gene's protein segments.

Thyroid hormones influence neural development in the prenatal and neonatal periods. An excess of T_3 or T_4 might theoretically alter the expression of genes that control processes such as neuronal migration, differentiation, and myelination. Distortions in any of these could later affect attention or behavior. But in the present, according to Hauser, T_3 and T_4 might activate (or deactivate) neural circuits which use dopamine or norepinephrine as chemical messengers.

Hauser plans to study the incidence rate of GRTH in newborns, and the efficacy of replacement T_3 in children with both GRTH and ADHD. Both he and Comings are working a difficult and often treacherous terrain—one in which a cycle of sorts has emerged. With much fanfare, genetic researchers announce their findings; the findings are then challenged, and sometimes retracted; critics then catalogue these overstatements (Horgan, 1993) in *lieu* of documenting their own case—namely, that mental illness is social in origin.

e. In 1982, an experiment with a newly synthesized analog of meperidine brought the narcotics-abuse career of several young adults to an abrupt end. They succumbed to a severe form of Parkinsonism, with muscular rigidity to the point of paralysis. That outcome was traced to a chemical impurity known as 1-methyl-4-phenyl-1,2,3,6-tetrahydropyridine (MPTP), which in human dopamine cells is converted to an extremely potent neurotoxin.

This turn of events gave Parkinson researchers an "animal model"—a way of reproducing key aspects of a disorder for experimental purposes—of a quality they had not had before. In monkeys, MPTP administration has consistently generated symptoms of Parkinsonian rigidity and paralysis.

In a brilliant piece of work, researchers from Philadelphia's Hahnemann University altered the model. Substituting a series of smaller doses for one large dose, they were able to create cognitive rather than motor deficits (Schneider & Kovelowski, 1990). To an extent, these resembled Parkinsonian-type cognitive deficits. But, taken as a whole, the description of these monkeys—fidgety, restless, distractible, impersistent, irritable, easily frustrated—suggests ADHD (Roeltgen & Schneider, 1991).

The heaviest neural degeneration and chemical depletion took place among dopamine-bearing cells in the putamen and caudate nucleus (Schneider, 1990). These studies have thus revived the somewhat hackneyed "dopamine" interpretation of ADD, in which Parkinsonism and ADD have been viewed as neurological variants.

Indirectly, the Hahnemann research links up with recent advances in neurosurgery; work in which MPTP-damaged brains, both simian (Bakay et al., 1987) and human (Widner et al., 1992), have been repaired using transplants of dopamine-bearing fetal tissue.

f. Confirming an earlier study (Weiss & Hechtman, 1986), New York–based psychologists Rachel Klein and Salvatore Mannuzza have followed two groups of boys over a period of two decades (Mannuzza, Klein, Bessler, Malloy, & LaPadula, 1993). In that sample, 91 hyperactive boys, tracked alongside 95 nonhyperactive controls, displayed higher levels of persistent hyperactivity, antisocial behavior, and substance abuse. Statistically, the differences have been significant but not spectacular. As a group, the hyperactives had completed less schooling, held fewer professional jobs, and earned less. More than 3 times as many were self-employed.

Probands did not display the vulnerability to depression or anxiety presented by probands in studies (Biederman, Faraone, Keenan, Steingard, &

Tsuang, 1991; Biederman, Faraone, Keenan, & Tsuang, 1991; Shekim, Asarnow, Hess, Zaucha, & Wheeler, 1990) of more recent origin.

g. A Yale study of 298 treatment-seeking cocaine abusers (Carroll & Rounsaville, 1993) found that 35% could be retrospectively diagnosed as having had childhood ADHD. (In a sample of cocaine abusers who had *not* sought treatment, the figure was 23%.) Compared to non-ADHD abusers, those with ADHD described their abuse patterns in terms that suggested greater severity. They reported an earlier onset of cocaine use, more frequent use (with a preference for intranasal rather than intravenous or freebase delivery), and more concurrent alcohol use.

When the researchers analyzed family patterns, alcoholism seemed more like a *variant* of cocaine addiction than an *addition* to it. The proposed link between cocaine and alcohol recalls an earlier study (Wood, Wender, & Reimherr, 1983) in which a similar percentage (33%) of treatment-seeking adult alcoholics could be associated with ADD. Cocaine's attraction should be no mystery: Its pharmacological profile is similar in some respects to methylphenidate's. But what is the attraction of alcohol?

The researchers found that ADHD abusers had sought treatment earlier than those without ADHD, and more often, but with less success. A possible reason for this is that none had been treated *specifically* for ADHD.

If one out of every three treatment-seeking alcoholics has ADHD, and one of every three treatment-seeking cocaine addicts has ADHD, why are there no clinics geared specifically toward this subgroup of abusers? Has one factor been the opposition to the use of medication within the rehabilitation community?

28. A novel aspect of recent research is the degree to which some of it has been publicized. This phenomenon both reflects and contributes to a heightened public awareness of ADD. However, media coverage has created the impression that an abundance of ADD-oriented basic medical research (neurobiology, genetics, pharmacology) is now under way.

The reality is different. Figures are hard to come by, but on a per-patient basis, spending on ADD-oriented *medical* research must rank among the lowest for any recognized disorder. So low that ADD is not even mentioned in a recent survey (U.S. Congress, Office of Technology Assessment, 1992) of government-funded research into the putative biology of mental disorders.

29. This spending lag may have something to do with the relative lack of interest, within psychology, psychiatry, neurology, and neuroscience, in the phenomenon of mental concentration.

30. And some of it is bound up with the limited research orientation of child psychiatry (National Advisory Mental Health Council, 1990; Steinhauer, Bradley & Gauthier, 1992).

31. A third factor has been the lack of movement on the pharmacological front. Biological theorizations of depression or anxiety or psychosis derive from clinical experience: Medications work, but *why* do they work? The appearance of new drugs (with differing pharmacological profiles) provides fresh data for an ongoing process of theoretical consideration and empirical evaluation—if, of course, such drugs are being developed; and for much of psychiatry they are.

But not for ADD. The agents mentioned in point number 11 above are designed for other uses, with ADD representing at best a secondary application. There is no evidence that any pharmaceutical house is developing a product targeted *specifically* at ADD.

Since even the lowest estimates suggest that ADD adults might form a sizable market, what would explain this reluctance to research and develop?

32. A number of advocate communities now make a two-pronged effort to promote biomedical research. They lobby for federal money; and they develop private sources of funding and disbursement (whether through large grants to established scientists or small grants designed to encourage younger investigators to commit to particular areas of research). On both fronts, the ADD community is lagging.

33. Why? For those with ADD, the pressure of present needs is at times overwhelming. What is true of individuals is true also of the ADD community: Day-to-day issues, particularly in the area of education, seem to absorb the available energy.

34. Lay support for ADD science is also held back by another factor: low expectations among those who might benefit from its expansion. Findings are hailed because they imply that ADD is rooted in physiology, rather than parenting or personal laziness. Quite rightly, this makes people feel better about themselves. However, is guilt reduction *all* the ADD community wants from its investigators? Because if it wants more, it will have to invest more.

35. If new medical treatments are not being developed, what does this bode for the future? Does it mean that 20, 50, and 100 years from now, ADD children and adults will be treated with essentially the same remedies available now? Does the ADD community find that prospect acceptable?

36. Within the ADD community, there is tremendous pressure to look at the bright side, to put on a happy face, to sugarcoat the disorder. Some suggest that ADD is really an asset, or could be, if those who had it knew what to do with it. In part, this seems to be an attempt to ease the burden of ADD through rhetorical manipulation. But any such relief has come at a price: a degradation of language and discourse.

When deaf activists insist that deafness is not a disability but a culture (Solomon, 1994), an element of rationalization is easy to detect. But comparable statements by ADD activists have been taken at face value (Reiff, Gerber, & Ginsberg, 1993; Wallis, 1994). In other words, the ADD

community's feel-good rhetoric, when raised to the level of public procla-
mation, can also trivialize and misinform; and thus hinder efforts to promote ADD awareness, research, and treatment.

REFERENCES

American Psychiatric Association. (1980). *Diagnostic and statistical manual of mental disorders* (3rd ed.). Washington, DC: Author.

American Psychiatric Association. (1994). *Diagnostic and statistical manual of mental disorders* (4th ed.). Washington, DC: Author.

Bakay, R. A. E., Barrow, D. L., Fiandaca, M. S., Iuvone, P. M., Schiff, A., & Collins, D. C. (1987). Biochemical and behavioral correction of MPTP Parkinson-like syndrome by fetal cell transplantation. *Annals of the New York Academy of Sciences, 495,* 623–640.

Biederman, J., Baldessarini, R., Wright, V., Knee, D., & Harmatz, J. (1989). A double-blind placebo-controlled study of desipramine in the treatment of attention deficit disorder: I. Efficacy. *Journal of the American Academy of Child and Adolescent Psychiatry, 28,* 777–784.

Biederman, J., Faraone, S. V., Keenan, K., & Tsuang, M. T. (1991). Evidence of familial association between attention deficit disorder and major affective disorders. *Archives of General Psychiatry, 48,* 633–642.

Biederman, J., Faraone, S. V., Keenan, K., Steingard, R., & Tsuang, M. T. (1991). Familial association between attention deficit disorder and anxiety disorders. *American Journal of Psychiatry, 148,* 251–256.

Carroll, K. M., & Rounsaville, B. J. (1993). History and significance of childhood attention deficit disorder in treatment-seeking cocaine abusers. *Comprehensive Psychiatry, 34,* 75–82.

Comings, D. E., Comings, B. G., Muhleman, D., Dietz, G., Shahbahrami, B., Tast, P., et al. (1991). The dopamine D_2 receptor locus as a modifying gene in neuropsychiatric disorders. *Journal of the American Medical Association, 266,* 1793–1800.

Diener, R. M. (1991). Toxicology of Ritalin. In L. L. Greenhill & B. B. Osman (Eds.), *Ritalin: Theory and patient management* (pp. 35–43). New York: Mary Ann Liebert.

Eichlseder, W. (1985). Ten years of experience with 1,000 hyperactive children in a private practice. *Pediatrics, 76,* 176–184.

Hauser, P., Zametkin, A. J., Martinez, P., Vitello, B., Matochik, J. A., Mixson, A. J., & Weintraub, B. J. (1993). Attention-deficit hyperactivity disorder in people with generalized resistance to thyroid hormone. *New England Journal of Medicine, 328,* 997–1001.

Horgan, J. (1993, June). Eugenics revisited. *Scientific American,* pp. 122–128, 130–131.

Leary, W. E. (1993, November 14). Blunder limits supply of crucial drug. *New York Times,* p. 20.

Mannuzza, S., Klein, R. G., Bessler, A., Malloy, P., & LaPadula, M. (1993). Adult outcome of hyperactive boys: Educational achievement, occupational rank, and psychiatric status. *Archives of General Psychiatry, 50,* 565–576.

Matochik, J. A., Nordahl, T. E., Gross, M., Semple, W. E., King, A. C., Cohen, R. M., & Zametkin, A. J. (1993). Effects of acute stimulant medication on cerebral metabolism in adults with hyperactivity. *Neuropsychopharmacology, 8,* 377–386.

National Advisory Mental Health Council. (1990). *National plan for research on child and adolescent mental disorders.* Rockville, MD: U.S. Department of Health and Human Services.

Physicians' Desk Reference (47th ed.). (1993). Oradell, NJ: Medical Economics Data.

Ratey, J. J., Greenburg, M. S., Bemporad, J. R., & Lindem, K. J. (1992). Unrecognized attention-deficit hyperactivity disorder in adults presenting for outpatient psychotherapy. *Journal of Child and Adolescent Psychopharmacology, 2,* 267–276.

Reiff, H. B., Gerber, P. J., & Ginsberg, R. (1993). Definitions of learning disabilities from adults with learning disabilities: The insiders' perspectives. *Learning Disabilities Quarterly, 16,* 114–125.

Reimherr, F. W., Wender, P. H., Wood, D. R., & Ward, M. (1987). An open trial of L-tyrosine in the treatment of attention deficit disorder, residual type. *American Journal of Psychiatry, 144,* 1071–1073.

Reimherr, F. W., Wood, D. R., & Wender, P. H. (1980). An open clinical trial of L-dopa and carbidopa in adults with minimal brain dysfunction. *American Journal of Psychiatry, 137,* 73–75.

Reimherr, F. W., Wood, D. R., & Wender, P. H. (1986). The use of MK-801, a novel sympathomimetic, in adults with attention deficit disorder, residual type. *Psychopharmacology Bulletin, 22,* 237–242.

Richardson, D. (1993, August 20-26). A scientific explanation for a crazy-quilt career. *National Business Employment Weekly,* pp. 5–7.

Roeltgen, D. P., & Schneider, J. S. (1991). Chronic low-dose MPTP in non-human primates: A possible model for attention deficit disorder. *Journal of Child Neurology, 6,* (Suppl.), S82–S89.

Schneider, J. S. (1990). Chronic exposure to low doses of MPTP. II. Neurochemical and pathological consequences in cognitively-impaired, motor asymptomatic monkeys. *Brain Research, 534,* 25–36.

Schneider, J. S., & Kovelowski, C. J. (1990). Chronic exposure to low doses of MPTP. I. Cognitive deficits in motor asymptomatic monkeys. *Brain Research, 519,* 122–128.

Shangraw, R. E., Seminer, S. J., & Zarr, M. L. (1985). Attention deficit disorder, amphetamine, and pregnancy. *Biological Psychiatry, 20,* 926–927.

Shekim, W. O., Antun, F., Hanna, G. L., McCracken, J. T., & Hess, E. B. (1990). S-adenosyl-L-methionine (SAM) in adults with ADHD, RS: Preliminary results from an open trial. *Psychopharmacology Bulletin, 26,* 249–253.

Shekim, W. O., Asarnow, R. F., Hess, E., Zaucha, K., & Wheeler, N. (1990). A clinical and demographic profile of a sample of adults with attention deficit hyperactivity disorder, residual state. *Comprehensive Psychiatry, 31,* 416–425.

Shekim, W. O., Masterson, A., Cantwell, D. P., Hanna, G. L., & McCracken, J. T. (1989). Nomifensine maleate in adult attention deficit disorder. *Journal of Nervous and Mental Disease, 177,* 296–299.

Solomon, A. (1994, August 28). Defiantly deaf. *New York Times Magazine,* pp. 38–45, 62, 65–68.

Spencer, T., Biederman, J., Wilens, T., Steingard, R., & Geist, D. (1993). Nortriptyline treatment of children with attention-deficit hyperactivity disorder and tic disorder or Tourette's Syndrome. *Journal of the American Academy of Child and Adolescent Psychiatry, 32,* 205–210.

Steinhauer, P. D., Bradley, S. J., & Gauthier, Y. (1992). Child and adult psychiatry: Comparison and contrast. *Canadian Journal of Psychiatry, 37,* 440–447.

U.S. Congress, Office of Technology Assessment. (1992). *The biology of mental disorders: New developments in neuroscience.* Washington, DC: U.S. Government Printing Office.

Wallis, C. (1994, July 18). Life in overdrive. *Time,* pp. 42–50.

Ward, M. F., Wender, P. H., & Reimherr, F. W. (1993). The Wender Utah rating scale: An aid in the retrospective diagnosis of childhood attention deficit hyperactivity disorder. *American Journal of Psychiatry, 150,* 885–890.

Weiss, G., & Hechtman, L. T. (1986). *Hyperactive children grown up.* New York: Guilford Press.

Wender, P. H. (1971). *Minimal brain dysfunction in children.* New York: Wiley.

Wender, P. H., & Reimherr, F. W. (1990). Bupropion treatment of attention-deficit hyperactivity disorder in adults. *American Journal of Psychiatry, 147,* 1018–1020.

Wender, P. H., Wood, D. R., Reimherr, F. W., & Ward, M. (1983). An open trial of pargyline in the treatment of attention deficit disorder, residual type. *Psychiatry Research, 9,* 329–336.

Widner, H., Tetrud, J., Rehncrona, S., Show, B., Brundin, M., & Gustavin, B. (1992). Bilateral fetal mesencephalic grafting in two patients with parkinsonism induced by 1-methyl-4-phenyl-1,2,3,6-tetrahydropyridine (MPTP). *New England Journal of Medicine, 327,* 1556–1563.

Wood, D. R. (1986). The diagnosis and treatment of attention deficit disorder, residual type. *Psychiatric Annals, 16,* 23–24, 26–28.

Wood, D. R., Reimherr, F. W., & Wender, P. H. (1982). Effects of levodopa on attention deficit disorder, residual type. *Psychiatry Research, 6,* 13–20.

Wood, D. R., Reimherr, F. W., & Wender, P. H. (1983). The use of L-deprenyl in the treatment of attention deficit disorder, residual type (ADD,RT). *Psychopharmacology Bulletin, 19,* 627–629.

Wood, D. R., Reimherr, F. W., & Wender, P. H. (1985). Treatment of attention deficit disorder with DL-phenylalanine. *Psychiatry Research, 16,* 21–26.

Wood, D. R., Wender, P. H., & Reimherr, F. W. (1983). The prevalence of attention deficit disorder, residual type, or minimal brain dysfunction, in a population of male alcoholic patients. *American Journal of Psychiatry, 140,* 95–98.

Zametkin, A. J., Liebenauer, L. L., Fitzgerald, G. A., King, A. C., Minkunas, D. V., Herscovitch, P., Yamada, E. M., & Cohen, R. M. (1993). Brain metabolism in teenagers with attention-deficit hyperactivity disorder. *Archives of General Psychiatry, 50,* 333–340.

Zametkin, A. J., Nordahl, T. E., Gross, M., King, A. C., Semple, W. E., Rumsey, J., Hamburger, S., & Cohen, R. M. (1990). Cerebral glucose metabolism in adults with hyperactivity of childhood onset. *New England Journal of Medicine, 323,* 1361–1366.

Resource List

Only a short time ago, resource lists for Adult ADD issues were disappointingly brief. Now, in late 1994, I struggle to pare this list down to a reasonable length! Such is the explosion of interest in adult ADD. The following list is not comprehensive, but is a good starting point for accessing the flood of infomation on adult ADD. References to other resource lists are included.

BOOKS

A User-Friendly Guide to Understanding Adult ADD. By Kathleen G. Nadeau, Ph.D. New York: Brunner/Mazel (in press).

A companion guide to *A Comprehensive Guide to ADD in Adults,* written as an introduction to adult ADD. It offers brief, up-to-date, accurate answers to FAQs (frequently asked questions) including checklists, practical tips, and questionnaires. This "ADD-friendly" format is designed especially for adults with ADD.

Driven to Distraction: Recognizing and Coping with Attention Deficit Disorder from Childhood through Adulthood. By Edward M. Hallowell, M.D., and John Ratey, M.D. New York: Pantheon Books, 1994.

Enormously popular, and one of the recent forces leading to greatly increased awareness of ADD in adults. The style is engaging, anecdotal, and highly readable.

You Mean I'm Not Lazy, Stupid, or Crazy?! A Self-Help Book for Adults with Attention Deficit Disorder. By Kate Kelly and Peggy Ramundo. New York: Scribner's, 1995.

Written by two women with ADD who have much experience both from a personal and professional point of view. It is full of information and practical tips.

The Hyperactive Child, Adolescent, and Adult: Attention Deficit Disorder through the Lifespan. By Paul Wender, M.D. New York: Oxford University Press, 1987.

Only one chapter of this book deals exclusively with adult issues. However, it is an excellent reference book on ADD, however, and provides a good overview of ADD across the lifespan.

Attention Deficit Disorder: Practical Help for Sufferers and their Spouses. By Dr. Lynn Weiss. Dallas: Taylor Publishing Company, 1992.

The first book published that exlusively deals with adult ADD issues. It is a great reference, and it contains useful resource lists and guidelines for diagnosis. Recently Lynn Weiss has published a companion workbook.

Succeeding in the Workplace - Attention Deficit Disorder and Learning Disabilities in the Workplace: A Guide for Success. By Peter S. Latham, J.D., and Patricia H. Latham, J.D., 1994. (Available through JKL Communications, PO Box 40157, Washington, D.C. 20016.)

Addresses workplace concerns for adults with ADD. It provides clear, complete information regarding the Americans with Disabilities Act as it pertains to ADD in the workplace, and it also provides lists of reasonable accommodations and coping strategies for the adult with ADD in the workplace.

Attention Deficit Disorder and the Law: A Guide for Advocates. By Peter S. Latham, J.D., and Patricia H. Latham, J.D. 1992. (Available through JKL Communications, PO Box 40157, Washington, D.C. 20016.)

A comprehensive guide to the legal issues pertaining to ADD. A very useful reference for adult ADD clients who are facing legal proceedings involving ADD issues.

ADD and the College Student. Edited by Patricia Quinn, M.D. New York: Brunner/Mazel, 1993.

The first book devoted entirely to ADD college issues. It is comprehensive and highly readable, written as an introduction to ADD and as a guide to college success for students with ADD.

College Survival Guide for Students with ADD or LD. By Kathleen G. Nadeau, Ph.D. New York: Brunner/Mazel, 1994.

Written as a companion to *ADD and the College Student*, the *Survival Guide* is a very practical, hands-on book full of direct advice about choosing a college, about what services to ask for to accommodate ADD, and about success strategies that students need to employ in college.

ADULT ADD RESOURCE LISTS

For those who want a more complete listing of all books, articles, videos, and tapes, there are a number of reference and resource lists available.

Resources for People with Attention Deficit Disorder (ADD) and related Learning Disabilities (LD). By Marcia L. Connor, Director of Employee Development Wave Technologies International, Inc. FAX: 404-947-0303, Vmail: 800-994-5767, Ext. 5040. Internet: p00350@psilink.com.

A very extensive, and frequently updated resource list. Although it is copywritten, the author allows it to be copied and distributed free of charge, provided credit is given and it is not reproduced for commercial purposes.

Adulthood ADD Lay Bibliography. Compiled by Paul Jaffe.

Available from ADDendum, 5041-A Backlick Rd., Annandale, VA 22003

Adulthood ADD Professional Bibliography. Compiled by Paul Jaffe.

Available from ADDendum, 5041-A Backlick Rd., Annandale, VA 22003. Both of these lists are updated regularly, and provide a very good overview of articles available on adult ADD.

Good resource lists can also be found in both Driven to Distraction *and* You Mean I'm Not Lazy, Stupid or Crazy?!

ORGANIZATIONS CONCERNED WITH ADULT ADD

CH.A.D.D. (Children and Adults with Attention Deficit Disorder)
499 NW 70th Avenue
Plantation, FL 33317
305-587-3700

CH.A.D.D. is the largest national organization concerned with ADD issues. It's scope has become international. In 1994 CH.A.D.D. held the first international conference on ADD in New York City. CH.A.D.D. has historically been concerned with ADD and children, but has become very active regarding adult issues beginning in 1993. CH.A.D.D. is now encouraging the development of adult support groups, in conjunction with their parent support groups.

The National Attention Deficit Disorder Association (ADDA)
PO Box 972
Mentor, OH 44063

ADDA is an ADD organization which has been very active in addressing adult ADD issues. ADDA sponsors an annual conference devoted exclusively to adult ADD issues, the only one of its kind in the country. You can write to the president, Mary Jane Johnson, who is also the editor of *ADDult News*.

Adult ADD Association
1225 E. Sunset Drive, Suite 640
Bellingham, Washington 98226

This organization has been very active in disseminating resource lists on adult ADD, and in collecting and maintaining lists of existing adult ADD support groups across the country.

NEWSLETTERS

ADDendum

A quarterly newsletter available by annual subscription by writing: ADDendum, c/o Beverly Horn, 5041-A Backlick Road, Annandale, VA 22003

Attention!

Covers child, adolescent and adult ADD issues, and is the main CH.A.D.D. publication. It is available by joining CH.A.D.D. Address is listed under "ADD Organizations."

ADDult News

Published and edited by Mary Jane Johnson, President of ADDA. It includes articles by professionals as well as personal accounts by adults with ADD. *ADDult News* also actively promotes the development and maintenance of adult ADD support groups, and offers information packets on starting support groups. Address is: 2620 Ivy Place, Toledo, OH 43613.

ON-LINE SERVICES

For an extensive listing of on-line ADD services, the reader should refer to the resource list: Resources for People with ADD and LD, *by Marcia Connor, referenced earlier.*

America On-line: There is an adult ADD support room where adults with ADD share support and information. For more information send email to ERICNJB@AOL.COM.

CompuServe: Look up GO ADD. For more information send mail to 70006.101@compuserve.com.

Prodigy: Has adult ADD support groups listed under Support Groups Medical

Listservs: has numerous internet discussion lists on various topics pertaining to ADD

TAPES AND VIDEOS

Many adults with ADD may prefer to listen to tapes or videos rather than the printed page.

Videos on adult ADD have been produced by several, including Authur Robbins, Ph.D. and Russell Barkley, Ph.D. Information on ordering copies of these can be obtained through the ADD Warehouse. Call 1-800-233-9273 to request a free catalog.

Tapes have been made of many adult ADD lectures that have been presented both at the national CH.A.D.D. conference, and at the Adult ADD conferences.

Adult ADD Conference (Ann Arbor, 1993 & 1994) tapes may be ordered through: Take Two Recording and Duplicating Services, 1155 Rosewood, Suite A, Ann Arbor, MI 41804.

Tapes from the National CH.A.D.D. Convention may be ordered through: Cassette Associates, 3927 Old Lee Highway, Fairfax, VA 22050, 800-545-5583.

Name Index

Subject Index

Abuse: physical, 36; potential for, 245; sexual, 36; substance, xiv, 36, 43–46, 58, 82, 99, 136, 137, 138, 169, 170

Accommodation: in educational institutions, 284–305; and self-identification, 285, 286, 297; workplace, 193, 327–328

Acetylcholine, 19

ADDult Support Network, 10

Adult ADHD Questionnaire, 112

Advocacy, 349–350

Affirmative action, 337

Alexithymia, 224

Americans with Disabilities Act, 10, 337–338, 339, 341, 346–347

Amino acids, 181

Amphetamines, 4, 5, 20

Anticonvulsants, 79, 80

Antidepressants, 7, 20, 24, 26, 37, 41, 83, 99, 177–180, 227, 377

Antihistamines, 80, 177

Antihypertensives, 180

Anxiety, xiv, 7, 19, 27, 36, 40–43, 45, 86, 99, 125, 136, 137, 146, 168, 169, 177, 225, 237; generalized, 41–42; social, 42

Anxiolytics, 41–42

Association for Higher Education and Disabilities, 287

Attention: and sensory overload, 198–199; training, 196–199; types, 196

Attentional Capacity Test, 120

Attention Deficit Disorder: acquired, 76, 198; assessing impairment, 97–100; associaton with learning disabilities, 4; cognitive styles, 223; in college students, 284–305; communicating diagnosis, 138–141; comorbid conditions in, 21, 35–53, 99, 170; consequences of, 136–138; "crossovers," 99–100; defining, 4; delayed diagnosis, 287–288; diagnosis, 35–53, 74–89, 93–106, 109–128; disclosure in workplace, 323–325; distinguishing from other disorders, 110–111; emotional function in, 224–226; and employment, 308–331; empowerment of adult with, 135–144, 193; family issues in, 236–257; future directions in, 375–384; as genetically based neurobiological disorder, 26–28; genetic transmission, 9, 74, 379–380; in girls, 3; historical perspective, 3–11; identification in college students, 288–291; impact on families, 236–257; legal issues, 337–350; management of, 157–164; moderating factors, 237–238; neurobiology of, 18–28, 76, 263–266; neurodevelopmental variation in, 58–71; neuroendocrine considerations, 263–266; neurological comorbidity in, 74–89; neuropsychological considerations, 263–266; and parenting issues, 243–251; positive traits, 310–311; psychosis, 50, 125; recognition in adults, xiv; and sexuality, 222, 256; silent symptoms, 98; situational variability, 98; strengths in, 66; subtypes, 8, 18, 26, 94–95, 262; support groups for, 9, 10, 193, 352–373; symptoms, 8, 26, 35, 74; without hyperactivity, 35, 75, 93–106, 111, 262; in women, 260–280; in workplaces, 308–331